Social Practices of Rule-Making in World Politics

Social Practices of Rule-Making in World Politics

MARK RAYMOND

OXFORD
UNIVERSITY PRESS

OXFORD
UNIVERSITY PRESS

Oxford University Press is a department of the University of Oxford. It furthers
the University's objective of excellence in research, scholarship, and education
by publishing worldwide. Oxford is a registered trade mark of Oxford University
Press in the UK and certain other countries.

Published in the United States of America by Oxford University Press
198 Madison Avenue, New York, NY 10016, United States of America.

© Oxford University Press 2019

CIP data is on file at the Library of Congress
ISBN 978–0–19–091311–3

CONTENTS

ACKNOWLEDGMENTS

This book would not have been possible without the support, encouragement, and assistance of a great many people. I am extremely grateful for the opportunity to say a few words of thanks to them here.

First, I want to thank the members of my doctoral committee at the University of Toronto, where this project began. David Welch, Emanuel Adler, and Steven Bernstein were kind enough to read and comment on the draft chapters in their earliest forms and to help them take shape. Matthew Hoffmann served as the internal reader and played a valuable role in improving the final dissertation. Richard Price went well beyond his role as the external examiner and provided extensive constructive comments. In addition to his role as my doctoral adviser, David Welch has provided invaluable advice, constant encouragement, and lasting friendship.

Next, I owe my thanks to the reviewers for Oxford University Press, and especially to Nick Onuf, who was kind enough to reach out and offer his assistance with revising the manuscript. As a result of the reviewers' careful comments, the book is substantially improved. That improvement was ultimately made possible by my editor, Angela Chnapko. I would like to thank her for choosing such constructive reviewers for the manuscript, and also for her belief in the project and her patience as the revisions unfolded.

I would like to thank the Department of International and Area Studies at the University of Oklahoma for its support as I revised the book manuscript. Suzette Grillot and Mitchell Smith helped me secure essential assistance in the form of course releases and summer research fellowships that facilitated the addition of the fourth case study, as well as other revisions to the manuscript. Keith Gaddie and the staff of Headington College at the University of Oklahoma provided a congenial atmosphere in which to finalize the revisions, for which I am very grateful.

During the process of writing the book I have benefited from the assistance of many of my friends and colleagues, some of whom have read part or all of the manuscript at various points in its development, and all of whom have provided valuable advice and encouragement. The following list is in alphabetical order: Samantha Bradshaw, Aaron Brantly, Benjamin de Carvalho, Derrick Cogburn, Ron Deibert, Laura DeNardis, Amy Eckert, Martha Finnemore, Bill Flanik, Harry Gould, Tim Gravelle, Fen Osler Hampson, Erin Hannah, Jarrod Hayes, Eric Heinze, Wendy Hicks, Aaron Hoffman, Terilyn Johnston Huntington, Jill Irvine, Patrick Thaddeus Jackson, Patrick James, Ron Krebs, Alanna Krolikowski, Charlotte Ku, Halvard Leira, Daniel Levine, Joseph MacKay, James Manicom, David McCourt, Chris McIntosh, Lilly Muller, Michelle Murray, Iver Neumann, Daniel Nexon, Joseph S. Nye, John Owen, Roland Paris, Darren Purcell, Maria Rost Rublee, Niels Nagelhus Schia, Rebecca Sanders, Ole Jacob Sending, Jason Sharman, Erika Simpson, Charmaine Stanley, Brent Steele, Michael Struett, Jelena Subotic, and Jessica West. I am deeply grateful to all of you for your time, and even more for your friendship.

I would also like to thank my graduate students at the University of Oklahoma. While I have immensely enjoyed working with all of you, particular thanks are due to Stefanie Neumeier for reading the entirety of the revised manuscript, and to Nela Mrchkovska and Josie Smith for their assistance with the launch of the Cyber Governance and Policy Center.

It should go without saying that I apologize to anyone inadvertently omitted from this list, and that any remaining errors in the manuscript are my own.

Finally, I would like to thank my family. My parents, Alan and Elva Raymond, have provided unconditional love and support, without which I would never have had the chance to write this book. I also want to thank them for encouraging my interest in the wider world. I want to thank my in-laws, Ray and Irene Raatzs, for welcoming me into their family. Most of all, I want to thank my wife Kate for believing in me, for talking through the argument with me as it evolved, for reading draft chapters and offering her wisdom, and for her love and friendship. Thank you for sharing this journey with me.

Introduction

It is commonplace to assert that we live in a rule-based global order, though assessments of the vitality and future trajectory of that order vary widely. This book takes the existence of such an order as its starting point, and seeks to contribute greater understanding of its nature and dynamics. Perhaps the most crucial question about this order is how its substantive contents (i.e., the rules) are determined and changed. That is the fundamental question that this book seeks to answer.

The constructivist literature identifies a number of mechanisms and processes—such as norm creation, social learning, strategic social construction, socialization, persuasion, contestation, and others—by which actors accomplish both the continuous reproduction and transformation of the rules, institutions, and regimes that constitute their worlds. However, it is less clear how these mechanisms *relate* to each other. Are they synonyms? Alternative explanations? Is it a matter of scope conditions, in which some mechanisms predominate in some circumstances while different ones are at work in others? In order to maximize the comparability of existing and future constructivist empirical research, and to avoid conceptual duplication, it is important that these questions be resolved. However, this proliferation of mechanisms also raises two deeper questions for which the field thus far lacks clear answers: (1) how do actors know *how* to engage in all the various processes available to them for changing or reproducing norms and rules, and (2) how do they know *when* to utilize one mechanism rather than another?

The answer, I argue, is that participants in world politics are also simultaneously engaged in an ongoing social practice of rule-making, interpretation, and application. This social practice of rule-making is itself governed by procedural rules. These rules about rule-making are analogues to what the legal philosopher H. L. A. Hart referred to as secondary rules (Hart 1994). They provide an instruction manual that enables actors to engage in contextually appropriate modalities for making and interpreting rules, and for applying rules to novel cases.

1

The procedural rules that constitute practices of rule-making in specific social settings do more than help actors understand how to engage in various processes for making and interpreting rules. They also play a vital role in determining the success or failure of individual proposals about rules, because actors will typically evaluate others' proposals according to the requirements of the relevant procedural rules as they understand them. Thus, proposals advanced in a manner consistent with relevant procedural rules are (all things equal) more likely to be accepted than those advanced in a manner inconsistent with these rules.

By identifying a crucial overlooked social practice in the international system, the book contributes to describing the international system and its operation. It also contributes to explaining the form, process, and timing of changes in rules and institutions at the global level, as well as to explaining the success or failure of particular attempts to change those rules and institutions. In doing so, it makes four significant contributions to International Relations (IR) theory. First, it shows how actors know how and when to use various means to change rules and institutions, as well as how they know how to respond to such efforts by other actors. Second, the book shows how attention to procedural rules enhances the ability of practice-turn constructivist approaches to specify the content and account for the existence of particular practices. It also extends the range of applications of practice-turn constructivism to rule-making itself—a highly consequential practice endemic to virtually all social settings, but one that has largely escaped study in the context of the international system. Third, the book shows that this practice of making, interpreting, and applying rules is vital to understanding the causal mechanisms and processes associated with both the reproduction and transformation of social institutions. Choice between substantively similar proposals turned on procedural grounds. Practices of rule-making led to unanticipated outcomes. Actors continued to utilize accepted practices of rule-making even when they proved inconvenient or counterproductive. They commonly portrayed these practices as closely connected to their understandings of basic values and of the proper goals and purposes of political community. The cases also show that social practices of rule-making are vital to explaining several outcomes across the cases that are at odds with the expectations of prevailing theories. Finally, the book connects the literature on global governance to the literature on the international system. It shows that practices of global governance are centrally concerned with making, interpreting, and applying rules, and argues for placing global governance at the heart of the study of the international system and its dynamics. In doing so, it also builds on the emerging literature on hierarchy in the international system by foregrounding the authoritative nature of legitimate rules and the ways that rules can authorize actors to make certain decisions—including decisions about making, interpreting, and applying rules. The presence of these kinds of authoritative rules suggests that despite the important advances contained in recent work in authority and hierarchy in the international system, increased attention to procedural rules for rule-making and the social practices of rule-making they constitute and govern offers important benefits.

Plan of the Book

The first chapter contains the conceptual and theoretical arguments, while the final four chapters present cases that demonstrate the existence and operation of a social practice of rule-making, and show that the procedural rules constituting and regulating this practice simultaneously enable and constrain actors both in making and evaluating attempts to change rules and institutions in the international system. As I have already presented the theoretical argument in brief, I will not elaborate further here on chapter 1.

I examine four cases: (1) the social construction of great power management in the aftermath of the Napoleonic Wars; (2) the creation of a rule against the use of force, except in cases of self-defense and collective security, as enshrined first in the Kellogg-Briand Pact; (3) contestation of the international system by al-Qaeda in the period immediately following the 9/11 attacks; and (4) efforts to establish norms for state conduct in the cyber domain conducted in the First Committee of the United Nations General Assembly.

These cases each consist of multiple attempts to alter social rules and institutions—some of which failed and some of which succeeded. Overall, the cases support my argument's core claims: proposals for change in rules were typically presented and evaluated according to relevant secondary rules; properly presented proposals were more likely to be accepted than improperly presented ones; deviations from accepted practices of rule-making and rule interpretation were consistently met with an expected range of discursive responses including denial, justification, and criticism; and, especially in the al-Qaeda case, disagreement over secondary rules resulted in acrimony and an inability to conduct a joint process of rule-making.

The deliberate selection of both difficult and important cases enhances confidence in these findings. All the cases examined touch centrally on issues of international security. The expectation of mainstream IR theories is that such cases are least amenable to the influence of ideational factors. In the realm of "high politics," at least in cases where the strategic context is seen as threatening, considerations of material power and interest are generally believed to predominate. Contra these expectations, the evidence clearly shows rule-guided behavior as well as concern on the part of key actors with the standards of appropriateness for conduct in rule-making and rule interpretation established by relevant procedural rules. Actors knowingly engaged in practices of rule-making, and this social practice clearly shaped the ultimate outcome in each of the cases examined.

The cases stand out for their importance even among the universe of possible cases involving contestation of rules and institutions related to international security. The construction of practices of great power management marked a critical step toward the modern system of active, multilateral collaboration in the day-to-day governance of the international system; the world's oldest inter-governmental organization (the Central Commission for the Navigation of the Rhine, or CCNR) was established by the Final Act of the Congress of Vienna. Likewise, the Kellogg-Briand Pact's rule against the use of force except in cases of self-defense or collective security was preserved in the Charter of the United Nations, and marked a clear diminution of the sovereign prerogatives of modern states. The 9/11 attacks are part of a sustained challenge to the basic practices of the international system. Al-Qaeda and its supporters prompted controversial responses by the United States—some of which constituted further proposals to change key international rules and institutions. In addition, al-Qaeda's actions directly inspired the Islamic State, which has taken up a similar cause. The contentious, fractured dialogue between Islamic fundamentalists and officials embedded in the international system highlights the risk of a possible break-down in the legitimacy of contemporary international practices of rule-making and interpretation. Finally, agreement among states on making, interpreting, and applying rules of international law appears to have facilitated the emergence of agreement on basic norms for state conduct in the cyber domain despite the persistence of contention and conflict over a variety of cyber issues. If practices of rule-making, interpretation, and application shape the outcome of such cru-cial cases in International Relations, it seems reasonable to conclude that the practice is operative in less contentious cases, with the important proviso that this may change if the legitimacy of current practices deteriorates.

Chapter 2 examines the social construction of the Concert system in the aftermath of the Napoleonic Wars. Statesmen employed secondary rules constituting a clear practice for making and interpreting social rules in order to moderate the conflict potential of the international system. They accomplished this task by establishing new practices of active collective conflict management that accorded special rights and responsibilities to great powers. Such institu-tional devices survived the formal Concert system, and continue to inform state practice. While other accounts have noted the institutional innovations of 1815, none have identified the role of a rule-governed practice of rule-making in ac-counting for the outcome. The case also clearly demonstrates the potential gains from relatively greater social competence in practices of rule-making and rule interpretation. Metternich and, to a lesser extent, Castlereagh proved able to leverage social competence both to achieve their own goals and to defeat undesirable proposals made by other actors. While historians and biographers have highlighted the key roles of both men, and while political scientists have noted the importance of skill as a power resource, the book advances knowledge by identifying a *particular* skill of critical importance—skill at performing social practices of rule-making and interpretation.

Chapter 3 revisits the standard interpretation of the interwar period as a momentous failure of statecraft resulting from liberal or "utopian" policies. The Kellogg-Briand Pact fundamentally altered the international system by rendering war illegal except in cases of self-defense and collective security; this new rule survived the Second World War and is enshrined in clearly recognizable form in the Charter of the United Nations. Notably, this outcome was not the initial intention of either of the two men whose names the agreement bears, nor of their governments. Instead, it is attributable in large part to tactical efforts by both the French and American governments to force the other to abandon the issue or accept a disadvantageous bargain by manipulating and tactically employing procedural rules. Thus, the case shows that these rules do not simply constrain actor behavior; in at least some circumstances, they can play key roles in generating initially unintended outcomes. Further, the treaty prompted consistent responses from a broad array of states. Not only did the treaty gain near-universal acceptance, states routinely identified the same political concerns with the text and, most notable, reached similar evaluative conclusions on issues of concern by employing similar procedures and lines of reasoning. The treaty also prompted socially competent replies from two relative newcomers to the international system (Japan and the Soviet Union). This pattern suggests broad familiarity with, and general acceptance of, applicable procedural rules.

Chapter 4 examines the attempt by al-Qaeda to refashion the international system via a coordinated strategy of terror attacks and public messages, and the corresponding response of the American government. The case covers the period from al-Qaeda's 1996 "Declaration of Jihad" to the American intervention in Iraq in March 2003. This delimitation of the case allows the evaluation of several discrete proposals for alterations in the rules and institutions governing the international system. It also examines the case prior to the effect of the Iraq War, which shifted attention toward the legitimacy of the American intervention. My central finding in this case is that the practice of rule-making, interpretation, and application was substantially inhibited by a "Tower of Babel" effect; each side relied almost exclusively on its own culturally prescribed secondary rules, rendering meaningful engagement exceedingly difficult. This highlights the robustness of the generic practice of rule-making, which exists across cultural divides and which is highly resistant to compromise. The case is notable for the unusual emotional valence surrounding the participants' positions. Both sides connected procedural legitimacy to notions of "the good life," and thus to fundamental questions about justice that have been largely overlooked in IR scholarship (Welch 2014). These findings shed light on efforts by the Islamic State to articulate a critique of the international system, and have implications for efforts to undermine its attractiveness as a political project. They also illustrate the danger in an increasingly culturally heterogeneous international system if greater consensus on procedural rules for rule-making cannot be forged.

Finally, chapter 5 investigates efforts to create norms for state conduct in the use of information and communications technologies (ICTs), focusing on efforts in the First Committee of the United Nations General Assembly. While the First Committee has been engaged in work on these questions since 1998, a 2013 report by the Group of Governmental Experts on Developments in the Field of Information and Telecommunications in the Context of International Security (GGE) contained an important advance in state thinking about these issues. It asserted that "international law, and in particular the Charter of the United Nations, is applicable and is essential to maintaining peace and stability and promoting an open, secure, peaceful and accessible ICT environment." Beyond the UN Charter, it specifically enumerated state sovereignty, human rights, and the law of state responsibility as among the applicable bodies of international law governing state use of ICTs (UNGA 2013a, 8).

Remarkably, this rapid progress on norms for state conduct in the cyber domain came amid two trends not conducive to norm development: (1) a precipitous decline in diplomatic relations between Russia and most advanced industrial democracies; and (2) increased contention over Internet governance and cybersecurity issues at the global level. Despite these obstacles, state representatives to the GGE engaged in a rule-governed social practice of applying old rules to new cases. They drew on existing rules of diplomacy and international law to advance their positions on the most desirable and appropriate rules to govern state use of ICTs. These rules simultaneously empowered and constrained state representatives in advancing their positions and in evaluating proposals made by their counterparts. The rejection of a Russian proposal for a new international treaty in favor of an alternate approach based on applying existing rules of international law demonstrates the robustness of existing rule-making practices in the international system. This is especially true given that this position was endorsed by a diverse group of countries with different values, interests, and capabilities in the cyber domain—and that it occurred during a period in which cyber issues have become increasingly contentious. This agreement represents only a beginning in this crucial frontier for the rule-based global order, and it is likely that these rules will still be violated quite frequently by some actors. However, the public declaration that international law is applicable in the cyber domain places processes of rule-making and interpretation on a much more stable foundation by establishing agreement on the applicable secondary rules. This enables violations to be identified and criticized more easily and effectively.

The book concludes by consolidating its contributions to IR theory. It makes the case that the book improves upon existing specifications of the international system by identifying an overlooked class of social practices pertaining to rule-making, interpretation, and application. It shows that the book provides insight about ways to deal with the problem of comparing and perhaps consolidating the large number of mechanisms identified in the constructivist literature for creating and altering intersubjective knowledge such as rules. It argues that attention to procedural rules about rule-making and the social practices they constitute and govern can improve upon existing constructivist tools for explaining change in the rules and institutions that structure international systems, both in explaining the form, process, and timing of change, and also in explaining the success or failure of specific attempts. And, finally, it links social practices of rule-making with processes and institutions of global governance. In doing so, it demonstrates the importance of global governance to the study of the international system; and by foregrounding the importance of authoritative rules in the international system, it suggests the potential that additional focus on secondary rules and social practices of rule-making can expand upon existing understandings of authority in the international system, and thereby enhance the emerging literature on hierarchy and authority in International Relations.

CHAPTER 1

Social Practices of Rule-Making

The everyday conduct of International Relations involves a great deal of ongoing effort to make, interpret, and apply social rules. This effort can be collectively understood as a social practice. Like all social practices, this practice of making, interpreting, and applying rules is itself governed by a set of procedural rules. These procedural rules have changed over time and, like all rules, continue to exist only as they are instantiated in practice by actors. These rules both empower and constrain actors in making, interpreting, and applying social rules. And, finally, these procedural rules differentially empower and constrain different actors.

This practice of rule-making, interpretation, and application is vital to understanding the causal mechanisms and processes associated with both the reproduction and transformation of institutions, and thus to explaining the form and timing of an important subset of change in the international system. The procedural rules constituting this practice provide an instruction manual that enables authorized actors to engage in contextually appropriate ways of making and interpreting rules, and for applying rules to particular cases. Accordingly, they play a vital role in determining the success or failure of specific proposals for change in the rules of the game in the international system, because actors typically evaluate such proposals according to their understanding of the relevant procedural rules. Proposals for social change advanced in a manner consistent with relevant procedural rules are (all things equal) more likely to be accepted than those advanced in a manner inconsistent with these rules.

If I am correct, we should see particular kinds of evidence. First, actors should present and evaluate proposed rules or interpretations of rules in a manner consistent with relevant procedural rules. That is, they should engage in both critical and justificatory behavior that makes reference to such procedural rules. Second, to the extent that procedural rules are causally effective, more procedurally competent proposals and interpretations should be more likely to generate agreement than less procedurally competent proposals and interpretations.

This argument does not require that actors engage in this practice perfectly sincerely. Actors can comply with rules for a variety of reasons, and often do so with mixed motives. What matters is that the rules shape behavior—simultaneously empowering and constraining actors as they pursue both their values and their interests.

In this chapter, I briefly deal with definitions of some key concepts in my argument, review relevant constructivist literature and identify the central research questions that motivate the book, and develop an account of this social practice of rule-making and its significance for IR theory. The chapter concludes with a brief overview of the methods and evidence employed in the four empirical case studies that comprise the remainder of the book.

Rules

The starting point of this book is that rules are fundamental to human social life, and that this is no less true of the international system than it is of domestic politics or any other kind of social context. As Nicholas Onuf has written, "many, perhaps most, deeds are responses to rules" (1994, 18). Accordingly, the book belongs in the diverse constructivist body of IR scholarship. The breadth of this community complicates efforts to make concise theoretical statements, and resolving debates within constructivism is beyond the scope of my purpose in this book. Broadly, I situate my work at the intersection of rule-oriented and practice-turn constructivisms. I treat rules as both formal and informal, and as simultaneously regulative and constitutive. Further, I argue that social practices are constituted and governed by procedural rules. However, actors live in social settings structured by multiple rule sets and in which actors have overlapping but not identical understandings about the content of these rules and how to apply them in particular cases. Accordingly, societies have additional practices of rule-making, interpretation, and application governed by rules about rules. These interpretive rules and practices are context-dependent, varying across cultures and across time. I begin by briefly elaborating the understandings of rules and other relevant social theoretic concepts that inform my efforts to demonstrate how procedural rules shape international outcomes.

Put simply, "rules are statements that tell people *what* we *should* do." In so doing, they provide "a standard for people's conduct in situations that we can identify as being alike and can expect to encounter" (Onuf 2013, 4). They "describe some class of actions and indicate whether these actions constitute warranted conduct on the part of those to whom these rules are addressed" (Onuf 1994, 10). In this respect, then, rules are very similar to norms—typically defined in constructivist research as a "standard of appropriate behavior for actors with a given identity" (Finnemore and Sikkink 1998, 891). Indeed, Onuf argues that the components of Stephen Krasner's classic definition of an international regime—"principles, norms, rules and decision-making procedures" (Krasner 1982, 185)—"are all categories of rules" (Onuf 2013, 14). Throughout the book, I adopt this expansive understanding of norms as a subset of rules.

I also follow Onuf in maintaining that "all rules are always constitutive *and* regulative at the same time." Onuf explains that "by definition, rules regulate the conduct of agents because rules are normative—they tell agents what they should do." They are necessarily also constitutive because "the regulation of conduct constitutes the world within which such conduct takes place, whether agents intend this consequence or not" (Onuf 2013, 12). However, this dual character of rules is tempered by the reality that "some degree of functional specialization among rules is not only possible but likely." Insofar as this is the case, "a few rules are disproportionately weighty in constitutive effect" (Onuf 1994, 7).

Rules leave particular identifiable traces in the world. The most obvious are written rules of various kinds, including formal legal rules and more informal texts. However, whether or not rules are recorded in written form, "dealing with rules prompts people to talk about them, and involves them in the many arguments to which rules relate." Further, "by virtue of such talk, rules do exist—not just as inferences, but as things, however protean or transitory" (Onuf 1994, 6).

Since I take the position that rules are elementary to social life, it is necessary to be somewhat more specific about the scope of the book. I am particularly concerned with rules in two ways. First, I am concerned with the subset of procedural rules that pertains to procedures for making, interpreting, and applying rules—that is, with rules for rule-making. Such rules constitute and regulate what I argue are contextually specific social practices for rule-making. Though I believe such practices to be endemic to social life at all levels of analysis, the empirical scope of this book is what International Relations scholars traditionally refer to as the international system, which I understand expansively to include what scholars of the English School refer to as international society.[1] Second, I am concerned with the way these procedural rules and their associated practices of rule-making shape the ways that actors present and evaluate proposals for changes in other rules, and thus help explain the success or

---

[1] Systemic theorizing has a long history in International Relations, and crosses virtually every paradigmatic divide (see, among many others: Bull 2002; Waltz 1979; Gilpin 1981; Keohane 1984; Wendt 1999; Holsti 2004). That said, I do not claim that this system is hermetically sealed, or that international rules are completely divorced from the domestic level (Ruggie 1982; Putnam 1988; Milner 1991).

failure of particular attempts to change them. In particular, rule-governed social practices of rule-making offer the potential to build upon existing approaches to explaining the form, process, and timing of changes in the rules of the game for international relations.

Rules are closely related to several other important concepts in IR theory. Here, I deal briefly with the relationship of rules to language, institutions, identities, and practices. Language and speech are central to rule-oriented constructivism. Indeed, such variants of constructivism start from the premises that "language is action" and that "speech acts (promising, declaring, apologizing, etc.) are both plentiful and central to social life" (Duffy and Frederking 2009, 328). Onuf argues that "rules always and necessarily derive from performative speech—utterances through which people accomplish social ends directly." Three forms of speech acts correspond to three types of rules: assertive speech acts to instruction rules; directive speech acts to directive rules; and commissive speech acts to commitment rules (Onuf 1994, 10–11). Instruction rules "inform agents about the world—the way things are, the way it works—and inform them what consequences are likely to follow if they disregard this information." In contrast, "directive speech acts are recognizable as imperatives." Finally, "commissive speech acts involve promises" and "give form to rules when hearers, as speakers, respond with promises of their own." Such rules create "the *rights* and *duties* that agents know they possess with respect to other agents" (Onuf 2013, 11–12).

Procedural rules for rule-making and interpretation, the primary focus of this book, can take any of these three forms. Sets of procedural rules will almost certainly include rules of all three types. For example, instruction rules might establish the existence of a category of actor, such as states or international organizations, and specify criteria for identifying members of that class. Directive rules and commitment rules addressed to particular kinds of actors enumerate the various rights and responsibilities of different agents in making, interpreting, and applying rules. Additional instruction rules may provide relevant details about appropriate modalities for exercising and fulfilling these rights and responsibilities. Accordingly, this typology of rules is for the most part orthogonal to the argument I am making. As a result, I distinguish among instruction, directive, and commitment rules only where my argument specifically requires it.[2]

Christian Reus-Smit defines institutions as "stable sets of norms, rules, and principles that serve two functions in shaping social relations: they constitute actors as knowledgeable social agents, and they regulate behavior" (1999, 12–13). Onuf likewise regards rules as integral components of institutions, but

---

[2] On the relationship between these three types of rules and H. L. A. Hart's notion of secondary rules, see Onuf (1994, 14).

he adopts a slightly broader definition that treats institutions as "recognizable patterns of rules and related practices" (Onuf 2013, 5). This broader definition takes into account the existence of divergence between nominal rules and actual practices, as well as the difficulty posed by the inevitable development of informal, unwritten rules that "spring up in the margins of any rule set, no matter how assiduously the appropriate agents promulgate new legal rules" (Onuf 1994, 13). Determining whether an apparent inconsistency is the result of a difference between nominal rules and actual practices, or is instead the result of an additional (perhaps unwritten) rule, poses a difficult problem not only for the analyst but also for agents themselves. This is especially true when agents have differing understandings of the answer to this question or even the appropriate way to go about answering it. Ultimately, however, this problem is an empirical one that needs to be sorted out with reference to the actual rules that agents believe to be operative in a particular context.

Further, Onuf acknowledges that rules and practices "are almost impossible to separate in practice, because every time agents respond to rules, whether by making choices or observing the choices that other agents make, they have an effect on those rules and their place in families of rules" (Onuf 2013, 13). This acknowledgment raises two key points. The first is that rules (and therefore institutions) are continually in flux, rather than fixed objects that change periodically in response to exogenous shocks that upend stable equilibria.[3] Instead, "institutions are continuously subject to unintended development and periodically subjected to alteration by design" (Onuf 2013, 169).[4] The second is that institutions are typically understood as containing sets of rules.[5] Onuf argues that while "it is possible to think of a single rule as an institution," in practice "we never find a single rule standing by itself" (Onuf 2013, 17). Further, the rule sets that comprise individual institutions or regimes are linked by additional rules. Indeed, Onuf argues that "international regimes are hard to see because the rules connecting the institutions that make them up tend to be informal" and taken for granted by agents (2013, 14). These connective rules have attracted recent attention in the literature on regime complexes.[6]

The relationship between rules and practices is particularly complex; a full treatment of this topic is more properly the province of social theory and thus

---

[3] As, for example, in the rationalist literature on institutions. See, among many others, Keohane (1984); Koremenos, Lipson, and Snidal (2001).

[4] This view of institutions is common among constructivists and other scholars with more sociological leanings. See, for example, March and Olsen (1998); Wendt (2001).

[5] Hart (1994), Sandholtz (2008), and O'Mahoney (2014) also emphasize the importance of sets of rules.

[6] See, for example: Raustiala and Victor (2004); Keohane and Victor (2011); and Orsini, Morin, and Young (2013).

beyond the scope of this book. Adler and Pouliot define practices as "socially meaningful patterns of action which, in being performed more or less competently, simultaneously embody, act out and possibly reify background knowledge and discourse in and on the material world" (2011, 4). They further suggest that "practice rests on background knowledge, which it embodies, enacts, and reifies all at once" (2011, 9). This definition of practice clearly benefits from engagement with the closely related concepts of rules and institutions. Most directly, rules and institutions are essential to any satisfactory account of what comprises background knowledge. In order to competently perform any social practice, agents must know what they should do in that context; that is, they must know the rules applicable to the practice they are attempting to enact. As Harald Müller has shown, actors determine when to engage in strategic behavior such as bargaining according to rules that tell them whether it is appropriate to do so; and even in cases where bargaining is permissible, actors tend to perform this practice in different ways in different contexts (2004).

However, it is equally true that practice cannot be reduced to rule-following. This is because practice "entails making use of knowledge and skills but on the basis of the particular circumstances of a case," and doing so requires actors to use judgment in choosing among potential ways of proceeding (Kratochwil 2011, 41). Like the rule sets that govern them, practices are rarely if ever determinative. Further, an important class of practices (very much including the practices of rule-making that are the primary concern of this book) involves joint action. Such cases resemble the performance of musical duets, in that "simply working by the rules, or following the score irrespective of what the other(s) is (are) doing, is likely to derail the project" (Kratochwil 2011, 42).

Like rules and institutions, practices are not found in isolation. Accordingly, "complexities arise . . . from the complex interdependence of various simultaneous games," creating conditions in which actors and analysts alike have to contend with "the existence of several practices and their combination" (Kratochwil 2011, 54). Complicating matters further, Onuf notes that "all of the ways in which people deal with rules—whether we follow the rules or break them, whether we make the rules, change them or get rid of them—may be called practices" (Onuf 2013, 4). Following this observation, I argue that international actors are always and necessarily engaged in a distinctive, rule-governed practice of making, interpreting, and applying the rules of international politics. In many cases, especially in the contemporary international system, this practice is explicit; actors engage in it knowingly and deliberately, in order to advance both their interests and their values. However, in important respects the practice is ubiquitous and may often be implicit. Any case of criticizing another actor's behavior as inappropriate implies the existence of an (asserted) standard of appropriate behavior (i.e., a rule) against which the conduct is being evaluated.

Such an action necessarily entails both interpretation and application of the rule. Similarly, any instance of justifying behavior (even preemptively) requires that the actor engaging in justification is aware that others may regard that behavior as inappropriate with reference to a rule. In order to evaluate or justify behavior with respect to rules in a manner that will be intelligible to others, and thus capable in principle of eliciting the desired response, actors must know *how* to evaluate and justify behavior in that particular social context. The ubiquity of at least minimal rules about rules is what makes this crucial class of actions possible.

The relationships between various practices (as with the relationships between particular rules and institutions) are ultimately empirical questions about rule-making, since relationships among practices are part of background knowledge expressible in the form of rules, or standards of appropriate behavior. Specifically, "investigating how different practices are nested, bundled, or subordinated" requires investigating "the sites of *political struggles* where these assemblies occur" (Kratochwil 2011, 37–38). In other words, practices of making, interpreting, and applying rules—including rules about the relationships between various rules and practices—are profoundly political. The fundamental wager of this book is that increased attention to these sites of political struggles, in Kratochwil's evocative language, offers significant payoffs for understanding the dynamics of international rules and institutions.

Rules have most often been associated in IR theory with the structure of the international system (e.g., Donnelly 2012) and particularly with institutions. However, rules are also relevant to understanding agents (Banerjee 2015, 275). This is in large part because rules are constitutive of agents' identities. Onuf goes so far as to argue that "to any observer, including ourselves, identities are summary statements of the rules constituting us as agents (persons, institutions)" (Onuf 2016, 13). These sets of rules establish the conditions of possibility for individuals to enjoy agency. Onuf concludes that "people are agents, but only to the extent that society, through its rules, makes it possible for us to participate in the many situations for which there are rules." Further, individuals are not equally empowered by such rules, and the same individual will not be equally empowered in all contexts: "no one is an agent for all situations" (Onuf 2013, 3). Identity rules not only inform individuals' choices about their behavior, but also shape others' assessments of and responses to those choices. For example, even if an agent claims a certain identity or status, that claim will not be socially efficacious if the relevant audience rejects the claim and refuses to treat the claimant in accordance with the asserted identity. Nevertheless, identities understood as sets of rules can never be sufficient causes of agents' behavior since "people may choose not to follow the relevant rules" (Onuf 2016, 13), even if doing so may sometimes entail significant costs.

This latter point is common to a loose family of constructivist approaches that emphasize process-oriented treatments of rules and of social construction more broadly (among others, see Crawford 2002; Wiener 2004; Sandholtz 2008; Hayes 2013; O'Mahoney 2014). Such approaches have significantly advanced our understanding of the dynamics of social arrangements.[7] A focus on the procedural rules that constitute and regulate practices of rule-making, interpretation, and application can build on existing process approaches by accounting for the *existence* of these various processes, for the *forms* they take, and (at least in important part) for the success or failure of specific attempts at rule-making and interpretation. The next section of this chapter situates the book and its central research questions within this constructivist literature.

Accounting for Patterned Practices of Global Rule-Making

Constructivists have done a great deal of work attempting to explain the emergence, diffusion, and dynamics of international norms. This literature contains a large number of proposed theoretical mechanisms, including strategic social construction (Finnemore and Sikkink 1998; Keck and Sikkink 1998), norm cascades (Finnemore and Sikkink 1998), persuasion (Risse 2000; Payne 2001), learning (Checkel 2001), socialization (Johnston 2001), argumentation (Crawford 2002), norm creation (Klotz 2002), contestation (Wiener 2004), norm localization (Acharya 2004), and norm change (Sandholtz 2008). Each of these mechanisms is concerned with the way that intersubjectively shared knowledge is created, spread, reproduced, and/or transformed. However, it is not yet clear whether these mechanisms are competing or complementary. What are the scope conditions? When will actors employ socialization versus persuasion versus strategic social construction? Are each of these even truly distinct mechanisms, or should some of them be understood as effectively synonymous? Do actors engage in a mixture of these behaviors simultaneously, or are they at least to some degree mutually exclusive choices?

Further, the constructivist literature has not yet engaged three more basic questions. First, how do actors know how to engage in each of these different kinds of mechanisms for creating or altering intersubjective knowledge? Second, how do they know how to do so in a particular social context? After all, what counts as persuasive in one context (a courtroom, for example) may differ from what counts as persuasive in another context (such as a romantic relationship).

---

[7] On this term, see Onuf (2013, 7).

Third, how do actors know which contexts call for particular forms of social construction? The existence of patterned practices of global rule-making suggests a gap in the constructivist literature. Actors have ideas about how to appropriately engage in making, interpreting, and applying rules in international politics. Further, as the cases in the book make clear, actors care deeply about these procedural matters; actors with more skill using them tend to exert more influence over outcomes, and procedural rules can also play important roles in generating outcomes that the participating actors did not originally intend.

Answering these more basic questions by focusing on the role of procedural rules about rule-making can contribute to consolidating and integrating the gains made from constructivist research on social dynamics in International Relations. Drawing on both rule-oriented and practice-turn constructivism, I argue that actors' choices about how to present and respond to proposals about making, interpreting, and applying rules are shaped in important part by preexisting procedural rules for making, interpreting, and applying rules. This book therefore fills an important gap in the constructivist literature by providing evidence about how actors know how and when to engage in particular forms of social construction. As such, it also provides a way forward in addressing conceptual fragmentation in the constructivist literature. Specifically, it suggests that mechanisms for creating and changing intersubjective knowledge should be classified empirically according to the (formal and informal) rules that structure them.

Despite the aforementioned gaps, the constructivist literature offers a solid if incomplete foundation for understanding the dynamics of intersubjectively shared rules and norms, and thus the politics of global rule-making. The common denominator in this literature is recognition that the success of efforts to create intersubjective agreement about a rule's content, meaning, or proper interpretation depends upon both the ideas' content and the tactics adopted by the agents advocating them. While both factors clearly matter, the literature has thus far largely overlooked a third vital factor: the relevant procedural rules. These rules are critical because they provide an explanation of how actors are able to competently perform social practices of rule-making. In the remainder of this section, I demonstrate the need to expand the constructivist literature to include procedural rules.

The primary constructivist hypothesis relating to the content of ideas to their chance of acceptance is that "fit" matters. Ideas compatible with preexisting ideas will be accepted; incompatible ones will be rejected. Existing literature correctly regards this as an insufficient explanation. First, it cannot account for selection between two ideas that have a similar degree of "fit" with prior ideas. This is a particular problem in complex cultures that may often contain internally incompatible ideas (Bukovansky 2002, 43–44). Against which standard will "fit" be established? Second, the "fit" hypothesis renders anomalous cases in which actors *do* accept new ideas that have a low degree of compatibility with dominant ideas. Recourse might be made in such cases to the notion of an exogenous shock that leaves decision makers cognitively motivated to search for new ideas. But *which* new ideas? What criteria are employed in selecting new ones? Third, through the related notions of framing, strategic social construction, and localization, constructivists have repeatedly highlighted the socially constructed nature of "fit" between new and existing ideas.[8]

Examining the means employed by actors in promoting ideas has improved on the "fit" hypothesis. If two ideas evince a similar degree of "fit," advantage may go to the idea presented more effectively by its advocates. Similarly, exogenous shocks may create windows of opportunity for actors to successfully inject previously marginalized ideas into the mainstream (for example, the rise of neoconservative ideas about foreign policy within the Bush administration after 11 September 2001). However, the case-oriented nature of the existing literature has resulted in significant time spent reinventing the theoretical wheel. Thus, we are left with virtually as many theoretical accounts as case studies, and little obvious basis for comparison or theoretical progress. Constructivists have established important differences between the various processes and mechanisms they have described; however, we currently lack agreement on (and systematic discussion of) how they are related. Work on persuasion and strategic social construction can be employed to illustrate the utility of such knowledge in furthering the development of the constructivist research agenda in IR.

Persuasion and strategic social construction are distinct social activities. The Habermasian literature identifies stringent preconditions for persuasion: genuine argumentation requires actors that share a common lifeworld to engage in "truth-seeking" behavior. Both sides must remain open to persuasion and proceed in a non-hierarchical fashion. In contrast, work on strategic social construction explicitly allows for the use of leverage and power by purposive "norm entrepreneurs" or activists, who are marked by strong commitment rather than an openness to persuasion. On this view, then, the relationship between the two processes seems best characterized in terms of scope conditions— identifying circumstances under which actors will either persuade or proselytize.[9] Argumentation and strategic social construction present perhaps the simplest contrast between processes in the constructivist literature. Arranging relationships and specifying scope conditions becomes significantly more difficult when the list is expanded to include additional theoretical accounts.

---

[8] See, among others, Finnemore and Sikkink (1998); Keck and Sikkink (1998); and Acharya (2004).

[9] This approach is taken in Risse (2000) and in Johnston (2001).

In addition to the difficulty of specifying scope conditions for various mechanisms, it is not at all clear that all instances of each process will be identical, or even strongly similar. Habermasian accounts come closest to specifying a particular social practice—engaging in reasoned debate in which all parties are open to persuasion. Even here, though, it is not clear either that a compelling argument in one context will remain persuasive in another, or even that the *procedure* for making a convincing argument will remain the same. Rules for determining what counts as relevant evidence are one important example. The Habermasian account contains no criteria for determining what counts as a good argument.[10] It seems likely that this is precisely because such criteria are determined by the actors themselves, and thus variable. How actors engage in persuasion is thus a function of additional, procedural rules.[11]

The same is true of strategic social construction. Keck and Sikkink conclude that ideas framed in terms of preventing harm to the vulnerable and providing equality of opportunity are most likely to prove persuasive, but these are offered as inductively generated conclusions rather than theoretically derived propositions (1998, 27). Even if correct in a given social context, they are not necessarily generally applicable. Further, they deal as much with "fit" as tactics; these ideas are powerful because they are consistent with deeply held normative beliefs. More generally, Keck and Sikkink identify four tactics employed by transnational advocacy networks: information politics, symbolic politics, leverage politics, and accountability politics. This broad typology provides considerable scope for varying means and combinations, and thus serves to highlight my point. Asserting that actors engage in strategic social construction raises significant further questions about *how* they do so—questions that may well prove to have significant bearing on whether or not the effort is successful in a particular case.[12]

Even if processes of persuasion and strategic social construction consistently unfolded in the same manner, constructivists would have need of procedural rules in understanding the creation of shared knowledge. This is because we would still need to show how actors know *how* to engage in persuasion, strategic social construction, or any of the other mechanisms described in the literature. Without a notion of procedural rules, the very existence of patterned, consistent means of producing shared knowledge about rules and how to interpret and apply them constitutes a puzzle. While examining the content of ideas and the

---

[10] Checkel (2001, 580); Johnston (2001, 493).

[11] Müller (2004) argues that the same is true for strategic modes of interaction such as bargaining.

[12] This gap also exists in a related model of the "norm lifecycle" identified in Finnemore and Sikkink (1998). In that model, norm entrepreneuers shepherd norms through three stages: norm diffusion, norm cascade, and norm internalization. How norms reach the "tipping point" that creates the "cascade" remains unclear, as does the mechanism by which they are subsequently internalized.

means employed to promote them are necessary and important parts of the constructivist research agenda, attention must also be paid to the role of procedural rules. In essence, they provide actors with an instruction manual, informing them how to legitimately make, interpret, and apply rules—and how to legitimately respond to others' attempts to do these same things. Indeed, among other functions, such procedural rules shape both the processes by which "fit" is socially constructed and the choices actors make about the tactics they employ.

Social Practices of Rule-Making

In establishing when and how particular actors (and not others) are authorized to engage in making, interpreting, and applying rules in a given social context, procedural rules constitute a practice of rule-making. Recent work has demonstrated the utility of analyzing international politics through the conceptual lens of social practices (Neumann 2002; Adler 2005; Adler and Pouliot 2011; Navari 2011; Kustermans 2016). Adler and Pouliot define practices as "socially meaningful patterns of action which, in being performed more or less competently, simultaneously embody, act out and possibly reify background knowledge and discourse in and on the material world" (Adler and Pouliot 2011, 4). Drawing on the work of Pierre Bourdieu, Adler and Pouliot understand background knowledge as "practical" in nature; they argue that "it is oriented toward action and, as such, it often resembles skill much more than the type of knowledge that can be brandished or represented, such as norms or ideas" (Adler and Pouliot 2011, 7). This conception is closely tied to their understanding of practices as performances of varying competence. Following Goffman, they argue that "the structured dimension of practice stems not only from repetition but also, and in fact primarily, from the fact that groups of individuals tend to interpret its performance along similar standards." It follows from this that "social recognition is thus a fundamental aspect of practice; its (in)competence is never inherent but attributed in and through social relations" (Adler and Pouliot 2011, 6).

This approach to practices is an important advance in IR theory; however, I argue that its conception of background knowledge is overly expansive, and that it would provide a superior guide for empirical research if it were specified more narrowly in terms of procedural rules. Procedural rules are a subset of rules that deal with establishing legitimate processes for taking certain actions. They therefore fulfill Adler and Pouliot's understanding of background knowledge as oriented toward action. Procedural rules also fulfill their criterion of being similar to skill, for the simple reason that it is possible to say that two different actors have performed a set of procedures with varying degrees of skill. Indeed, Adler and Pouliot make a similar suggestion when they acknowledge that audience evaluation of performance according to shared standards is crucial to accounting for the structuring effect that practices exert on the social world. Their notion of shared standards, or in other words procedural rules, is doing more work than their definition makes clear. These procedural rules in fact constitute particular social practices.

Many such procedural rules are informal or even unwritten.[13] This is another reason why such knowledge seems similar to skill, which carries connotations of being an actor property; it is easier to attribute adept utilization of informal, unwritten rules to actor skill (Onuf 2013, 135). Jorg Kustermans writes that "in international negotiations, practical knowledge means that one exercises power by drawing up 'crafty compromises,' by 'skillfully framing' events," and "by 'making creative use of procedures.'" He concludes that "practical knowledge hovers somewhere between tactical and strategic skill" (2016, 12). Recognizing the importance of skill does not mean denying that practices are rule-governed. Adler and Pouliot are correct to note that the competent performance of practice leaves room for agency and creativity (2011, 6), but this space is not infinite and is most effectively exploited with deep understanding of the form in question. In this way it is similar to jazz improvisation, which is itself a form of creative practice.[14]

Focusing more closely on the role of procedural rules in constituting practices foregrounds the fact that the practice-turn constructivist literature has thus far focused on a small number of practices distinctive to International Relations. The largest group of such studies examines practices of diplomacy (Neumann 2002; Adler-Nissen 2009; Bjola and Kornprobst 2013; Adler-Nissen and Pouliot 2014; Pouliot and Cornut 2015; Pouliot 2016). Another group examines practices pertaining to international security, either in general terms (Pouliot 2010) or in terms of more specific security practices like deterrence (Morgan 2011), balancing (Adler and Greve 2009; Ripsman 2011), and security community (Adler and Greve 2009). A third group examines international legal practices (Brunnée and Toope 2011; Raymond 2013). A consequence of this focus on practices specific to the international system is the neglect of equally important practices that are more generic in nature.

The practice of making, interpreting, and applying rules is an example of such a generic practice. It is a socially meaningful pattern of action that can be performed more or less competently. In order for rule-making conduct to be

---

[13] On the ubiquity of informal rules, see Onuf (1994, 13).

[14] Jazz saxophonist Charlie Parker is quoted as having advised musicians to "learn the [chord] changes, then forget them." This possibly apocryphal quotation captures the sense of what I mean here, in that it points out that skillful improvisation requires deep knowledge of the form and idiom in which the improvisation is couched. Absent such knowledge, improvisation is likely to be judged as amateurish and incompetent by the relevant insider audience.

mutually intelligible to the actors involved, they must share crucial background knowledge about who is entitled to make what kinds of rules and what the appropriate modalities are for doing so. That is, they must agree (at least to a certain extent) on the relevant procedural rules for rule-making. This generic practice of rule-making occurs in parallel to any other social practice, even when no explicit proposal to change the rules has been made. This is because social arrangements are always at least potentially in flux. As Onuf notes, "a ruled environment resists change on any scale," while "every act in response to a rule entails a change in that rule, in the environment of rules and in the agent as a product of that environment" (1994, 18–19). However, one hallmark of the contemporary international system is that practices of rule-making have become more highly institutionalized and more formalized (Ikenberry 2001; Weiss and Wilkinson 2014). Accordingly, the case studies in this book focus largely on situations explicitly understood by the actors involved as instances of global rule-making, with the potential exception of the case examining interactions between the United States and al-Qaeda. Doing so facilitates illustration of the existence of such practices, but future research should also examine the ways that practices of rule-making, application, and interpretation unfold in less formalized cases, in part to investigate the extent to which formalization leads to systematically different outcomes.

One possible objection to the study of a generic practice of global rule-making is that these functions, at least in the contemporary international system, are accomplished by the contextually specific practices of diplomacy and international law that have been studied within the existing practice-turn literature. At one level, this is obviously true. Both diplomacy and international law are clearly practices for making, interpreting, and applying rules. Two distinct literatures help to illuminate the written and unwritten procedural rules for rule-making, interpretation, and application in contemporary international politics.

The first examines the dynamics of the international legal system. Rational-choice scholarship on legalization in world politics provided important advances in understanding the interplay between international law and international politics. Scholars distinguished between forms of legalization according to their degrees of obligation, precision, and delegation (Abbott, Keohane, et al. 2000), and emphasized the importance of soft law (Abbott and Snidal 2000). However, these approaches were also criticized by constructivists for their truncated understanding of international law. Martha Finnemore and Stephen J. Toope argued that international law must be understood as "more than the formal, treaty-based law" emphasized by rationalists and that "law is a broad social phenomenon deeply embedded in the practices, beliefs, and traditions of societies, and shaped by interaction among societies" (Finnemore and Toope 2001, 743). Finnemore employed such an understanding of international law in arguing that disputes over the Bush administration's interpretations of international law pertaining to the use of force "look less like a fight between unilateralism and multilateralism than a fight over what exactly multilateralism means and what the shared rules that govern use of force are (or should be)" (Finnemore 2005, 187). This formulation foregrounds the importance of rule-governed interpretation and application of general rules to particular cases. Jutta Brunnée and Stephen J. Toope have pointed out correctly that these processes take place over extended periods of time and require the work of large numbers of experts trained in social practices of international legality, or what they aptly call "the hard work of international law" (2010). Paul F. Diehl and Charlotte Ku, drawing on Hart's work, point out that such practices of interpreting and applying rules draw on a procedural "operating system" as well as a substantive "normative system" of international law (2010).

The second literature of interest in assembling an inventory of contemporary procedural rules for global practices of rule-making examines international diplomatic practices. Rebecca Adler-Nissen examines what she calls "late sovereign diplomacy" in the European Union, arguing that processes of European integration have fundamentally changed member states' understandings of their national interests (2009). Adler-Nissen and Pouliot argue that differences in diplomats' competence or skill in performing within the broad context set by the rules of the game help to explain the outcome of multilateral diplomacy in the case of international intervention in Libya (2014). Pouliot has expanded on this argument about how differences in players' abilities to creative improvise using accepted rules of the game help to explain outcomes in world politics. He argues that "a key consequence of the multilateralization of international security" has been "the production, reproduction, and contestation of local diplomatic hierarchies that practitioners often call 'international pecking orders.'" In his view, "the multilateral diplomatic process *does* something to the politics of international security: it generates a distinctive set of endogenous opportunities and constraints in the making and remaking of international hierarchies" (2016, 6). But these opportunities and constraints are, at least in large part, the product of written and unwritten rules that constitute the specific game of multilateral diplomacy. These rules, especially the more formal ones, are well known in the literature on multilateralism.[15] Pouliot adds important social texture to understandings of multilateralism, which have typically been understood as having a benevolent and leveling effect in the international system, by showing that multilateralism sometimes instantiates hierarchy. His account also notes the importance of "local codes and rules, which competent diplomats know how to use." Development of these local codes is fostered by high social density and

---

[15] See, among many others: Keohane (1990); Ruggie (1992); Reus-Smit (1999).

iterated interaction in institutional contexts such as the United Nations Security Council (Pouliot 2016, 17).

Each of these literatures adds a great deal to identifying the procedural rules relevant to understanding contemporary practices for making, interpreting, and applying rules in the international system, but neither is sufficient on its own. This is the case, if for no other reason, because diplomacy and international law are tightly intertwined; both are essential to a more generic rule-governed social practice of rule-making, interpretation, and application. However, there are two other reasons why I believe a study of a practice of rule-making contributes to the practice-turn literature specifically and to IR theory more broadly. First, the objection that rule-making is accomplished via diplomacy *and* international law already suggests the need for the kind of approach I adopt in this book. This is because the functions of making, interpreting, and applying rules in the international system are distributed among at least these two specific international practices (I would add the practice of global governance as a third contender). Existing empirical studies thus risk creating the false impression of distinct practices, when reality is significantly more complex. This is not to say that the study of diplomacy or of international law or global governance or any other specific practice should be abandoned. Rather, it simply shows the value of the kind of cross-cutting analysis pursued in this book, which can assist with Kratochwil's important observations about the value of studying the ways that "different practices are nested, bundled, or subordinated" (2011, 37–38). Second, studying the generic practice of rule-making in International Relations facilitates further comparative analysis of this important social activity in other empirical domains, including historical analogues to the contemporary international system along the lines of the approach taken by Reus-Smit (1999) and other historically inclined scholars of International Relations, as well as analogues at the domestic and small group levels of analysis.

PROCEDURAL RULES FOR RULE-MAKING

Given my claim that practices are constituted in significant part by their procedural rules, a study of the generic practice of rule-making, interpretation, and application in international politics begins with an effort to say something about the relevant subset of procedural rules. In doing so, I draw heavily on the work of H. L. A. Hart. Hart famously utilized the concept of secondary rules, in contrast to primary rules. When a primary rule exists, "human beings are required to do or abstain from certain actions, whether they wish to or not." Secondary rules "provide that human beings may by doing or saying certain things introduce new rules of the primary type, extinguish or modify old ones, or in various ways determine their incidence or control their operations" (Hart 1994, 81). Effectively, secondary rules are a subset of procedural rules that differentially empower certain actors to make, change, interpret, and apply other rules. Since I am interested in this book specifically in the social practice of rule-making constituted by this special subset of procedural rules, other than when I discuss Hart's work directly, I simply use the terminology of procedural rules.

For Hart, the presence of secondary rules sets complex social structures apart from simple ones. The paradigmatic example of a simple social structure is "a small community closely knit by ties of kinship, common sentiment, and belief, and placed in a stable environment" (Hart 1994, 92). Such a society's exclusive reliance on primary rules creates three significant problems. The first is uncertainty as to the exact content of its primary rules and their criteria of validity (Hart 1994, 92). Second, primary rules cannot provide means for their own alteration. Third, simple social systems encounter enforcement problems stemming from "disputes as to whether an admitted rule has or has not been violated" (Hart 1994, 93).

Hart argues that each of these three problems can be ameliorated by a specific type of secondary rule. The remedy for uncertainty about the content of rules is found in a "rule of recognition" that "specifies criteria for identifying rules" (Hart 1994, 94). Stasis in primary rules is addressed by "rules of change"; this subset of secondary rules "empowers an individual or body of persons to introduce new primary rules for the conduct of the life of the group, or of some class within it, and to eliminate old rules" (Hart 1994, 95). Finally, difficulty in efficiently determining rule violations is addressed via "rules of adjudication" that authorize certain agents to perform these tasks according to certain procedures (Hart 1994, 96–97).

Hart leverages his distinction between primary and secondary rules in order to differentiate legal rules from other social rules; the mechanics of their operation are tangential to his project and are thus left underdeveloped. He relies on a distinction between *systems* of rules united by secondary rules, and *sets* of rules that lack this degree of coherence (Hart 1994, 234). For Hart, both etiquette and international law are sets of rules because they lack a rule of recognition; rules of change and rules of adjudication largely drop out of his analysis. Given my interest in studying practices of rule-making and interpretation in the international system, these latter two categories are of considerable interest.

In addition to his relative neglect of rules of change and adjudication, there are difficulties with Hart's position that both etiquette and international law are examples of sets of rules—rather than of rule systems with secondary rules. In fact, such secondary rules are virtually ubiquitous features of social life and exist wherever actors participate in mutually intelligible practices of rule-making and interpretation. On Hart's view, secondary rules are not just specific to complex societies; even within such social contexts, secondary rules are confined to legal systems. He states explicitly that there is no possibility of a rule of recognition governing the rule that men remove their hats upon entering a church (Hart 1994, 109–10). More generally, Hart asserts that the entire category of rules of etiquette lacks a rule of recognition (1994, 234). The situation is similar with respect to international law. Its lack of the centralized lawmaking authority characteristic of a modern domestic legal system underpins Hart's conclusion that international law also lacks secondary rules (Hart 1994, 236).

The functions performed by secondary rules are generic. There is little reason to expect, a priori, that these functions are performed only in modern domestic legal systems. Hart sets the bar too high by defining secondary rules in terms of a limiting case. This limiting case, the domestic legal system, is distinct from other social institutions (both within and between groups) in its specificity, formality, and centralization. Domestic legal systems also generally emerge and flourish only within groups that already enjoy a relatively high degree of cohesion; it seems likely that social systems with less cohesion evolve secondary rules that are less specific, less formal, and less centralized. The effect of Hart's argument is to render secondary rules in these contexts invisible. Therefore, I reject Hart's view that the presence of secondary rules differentiates law from other kinds of rules. Rather, I suggest that legal systems are best understood as highly specific, formal, and centralized instantiations of a much more general phenomenon.[16]

Hart's work has not received significant attention within the constructivist IR literature, with one important exception. Paul F. Diehl, Charlotte Ku, and Daniel Zamora employ his distinction between primary and secondary rules as the basis for their own distinction between the normative and operating systems of international law (2003, 43–44). While the normative system amounts to specific rules for behavior, "the operating system provides the framework within which international law is created and implemented and defines the roles of different actors as well as providing mechanisms for the settlement of disputes" (Diehl et al. 2003, 50). Diehl, Ku, and Zamora thus part ways with Hart, as I do, over his assertion that international law lacks secondary rules.[17] However, they are silent as to whether or not secondary rules can exist outside of a legal system. Their claim that international law "provides the framework for political discourse" in world politics suggests that, like Hart, they view secondary rules as a property of legal systems (Diehl et al. 2003, 43). Even if this is currently true, however, such a state of affairs would be a product of contingent, context-specific secondary rules that grant international law this function. Reus-Smit's work comparing

---

[16] This point is similar to the treatment of international legalization as varying continuously along dimensions of obligation, precision, and delegation in Abbott et al. (2000).

[17] On this point, see also Kratochwil (1989, 191).

anarchies, some of which predate modern international law, clearly shows that other forms of secondary rules have governed inter-group relations.[18]

Also, as with Hart, the argument presented by Diehl, Ku, and Zamora does not fully develop all functions of secondary rules. In enumerating the components of the "operating system," the authors include rules governing the sources of international law and the nature of actors, as well as jurisdictional rules and the rules establishing courts. Absent is an explicit account of the procedures by which rules are changed and interpreted on an ongoing basis, or what Brunnée and Toope have called "the hard work of international law" (2010). Within the realm of contemporary international law, candidates include rules on the formation of customary international law; the procedural parts of the law of treaties; the law of state responsibility; and the various international legal instruments constituting and specifying procedures for the International Court of Justice, the International Criminal Court, and other judicial or quasi-judicial bodies.

Finally, and most important, the causal relationship between primary and secondary rules is reversed. Diehl, Ku, and Zamora investigate "the conditions under which operating system changes occur in response to normative ones" (2003, 44). Such an analysis serves as an important reminder of the recursive relationship between primary and secondary rules, but it is not directly helpful in determining whether, or how, secondary rules matter in explaining the success or failure of particular attempts to change rules. Though the authors note the possibility of examining "how the operating system conditions the adoption of new norms" and suggest that "some new norms may be more rapidly adopted if they 'fit' within current operational rules," they defer consideration of these possibilities (Diehl et al. 2003, 72).

In a book expanding on the original article, Diehl and Ku devote a chapter to the possibility that the operating system of international law may affect the content of the normative system; however, they "anticipate that most of the influence from the operating system on the normative system will be indirect" and relatively weak. They further report that their review of the existing literature reveals that "previous research has not addressed the question of how the operating system conditions the normative system" (Diehl and Ku 2010, 130). Diehl and Ku provide a list of six potential effects of the operating system on the normative system of international law, but they do not specify causal mechanisms. Further, the entire enterprise remains restricted to the domain of international law rather than attempting to more broadly leverage the relevance of Hart's secondary rules to explain the success or failure of efforts to make, interpret, or apply rules. While their work is instructive, and a valuable addition to understanding

---

[18] See, especially, the chapters on the Greek system of city-states and on the city-states of Renaissance Italy in Reus-Smit (1999).

the operation of both primary and secondary rules in the modern international system, it is not a substitute for the project undertaken here.

The procedural rules for rule-making in the international system include rules of recognition, instructing actors on who may make legitimate rules and how. They also include rules of change that indicate how existing rules may be altered, and rules of adjudication indicating who may interpret rules and apply them to cases, as well as the appropriate modalities for doing so. As discussed above, contemporary versions of these rules are drawn largely from rule sets for diplomacy and international law. These rules instruct actors both on how to present and evaluate proposals for change in the rules of the game. Such proposals and evaluations may occur in relatively formal terms, for example in an explicit negotiation about rules. But they may also occur in more informal ways, to the extent that procedural rules are understood by the relevant actors to provide such avenues of expression. One general example is that inaction or lack of comment in response to an action or utterance is understood differently across social settings—in some cases being taken as consent, in other cases as indicating a clear refusal, and in still other cases as ambiguous. An example from international politics is the use of naval maneuvers to communicate views about the application of rules for the freedom of navigation in particular bodies of water. Another more general example is the rule of international law that regards patterns of consistent state practice as a criterion for the determination of rules of customary international law. This rule imbues nonverbal acts with significance for rule-making.

Such procedural rules differentially empower various actors and classes of actors with respect to participation in global rule-making. The use of standards of civilization to deny standing and agency to non-European political communities is a powerful example (Gong 1984; Keene 2007), but the category of great power status has also played an important role in unequally allocating rights and responsibilities pertaining to global rule-making even in an era of nominal sovereign equality (Keene 2013; Mitzen 2013, 87–90).

While procedures for rule-making and interpretation in contemporary international politics do vest some centralized authority to make and interpret rules in particular organs like the United Nations Security Council, the International Court of Justice,[19] and the dispute settlement mechanism of the World Trade Organization, there is no inherent requirement that practices of rule-making be highly centralized. And the absence of centralized authorities to perform these functions is therefore not evidence that there are no relevant procedural rules for rule-making. A body of customary international law known as the law of state responsibility provides an important example. This body of law enumerates

[19] At least in cases where the parties have agreed to compulsory jurisdiction.

modalities for determining and responding to breaches of international legal obligations, or what are termed internationally wrongful acts (Crawford 2002). While the provisions of this body of law afford states wide latitude in making such determinations, it is clear that meaningful limits on auto-interpretation and self-help do exist. These rules vindicate Onuf's claim about the ubiquity of rules and rule (1989) and Wendt's observation that anarchy is what states make of it (1992).

Like all rules, procedural rules for rule-making inform but do not determine agents' actions. In addition to the possibility of clear rule violations, procedural rules provide opportunities for agency in the ways that they can be combined (both with other procedural rules for rule-making and with other rules) and applied to particular situations or sets of circumstances. Procedural rules for rule-making do not exist in isolation, but rather as part of larger systems or sets of rules.

Wayne Sandholtz has developed a particularly valuable model for explaining what he refers to as "norm change" in the international system. Sandholtz is especially sophisticated in his treatment of rules as existing in systems, and in his recognition that the relationships among such connected rules create endogenous sources of change in rules over time. He starts from the premise that "disputes about acts are at the heart of a process that continuously modifies social rules" (Sandholtz 2008, 101). In particular, "two important features of rule systems guarantee a constant stream of disputes: incompleteness and internal contradictions." Rule systems are necessarily incomplete because "rules cannot spell out the behavioral requirements for every situation, nor can they foresee all possible circumstances or disagreements."[20] As a result, for a significant range of situations, uncertainty will exist as to whether a particular action violates applicable rules (Sandholtz 2008, 105). Further, "because there are multiple rule structures in any given society, tensions and contradictions between different rules are commonplace." The resulting internal contradictions in the society's overall system of rules mean that "some actions can therefore evoke different rules, entailing divergent requirements" (Sandholtz 2008, 106). Joseph O'Mahoney has further developed Sandholtz's concept of rule tensions, "by formally specifying precise types of tension: ambiguity, inconsistency and inadequacy" (O'Mahoney 2014, 835). Rule ambiguity exists when "an existing rule covers a set of acts or situations and does not distinguish between subsets of those acts or situations." Rule inconsistency exists "when the rules conflict with each other," such as a situation in which "an act may be allowed under one set of rules but forbidden under another." Finally, rule inadequacy "concerns the

---

[20] This feature is described in the rationalist literature on international law as a problem of incomplete contracting. See Abbott and Snidal (2000).

ineffectiveness of sanctions, which may include the absence of a sanction" as well as cases in which rules are "ambiguous over which acts are covered or the steps to be taken in the event of a violation" (O'Mahoney 2014, 841–42).

Sandholtz argues that norm change takes place within particular rule-structured environments in a cyclical fashion; "the cycle begins with the constellation of existing norms, which provide the structure within which actors choose what to do, decide how to justify their acts, and evaluate the behavior of others." Once inevitable disputes arise due to the incomplete and internally contradictory nature of rule sets, "actors argue about which norms apply, and what the norms require or permit." Crucially, "the outcomes of such arguments is always to modify the norms under dispute, making them stronger or weaker, more specific (or less), broader or narrower" (Sandholtz 2008, 103–4).

Once in a dispute about the meaning and application of rules and norms, an actor "must persuade other relevant actors that her conduct complies with the group's rules, and therefore should not be sanctioned. She must offer the most convincing arguments possible that her position in the current dispute best fits what the rules require, and best conforms to the ways in which previous disputes were resolved (precedents)" (Sandholtz 2008, 105). Sandholtz argues that "the actor that can offer several pertinent precedents consistent with her interpretation of the current dispute will generally be more persuasive than the actor who cannot cite relevant precedents." He makes clear that the argument is probabilistic in nature, and that exceptions can occur when there are "other persuasive reasons" such as "powerful ethical values" (Sandholtz 2008, 107).

A notable strength of this argument is that it remains agnostic about the underlying logic of action and allows for the existence of mixed motives. While pressing the constructivist argument that norms and rules are often genuinely internalized even in international politics,[21] Sandholtz notes that even "strategic, insincere actors are constrained in their actions and arguments by social norms" (2008, 104).[22] In order to make rational calculations about the consequences of actions, an actor "must understand not only the society's rules abut also the community's current standards for interpreting and applying the rules." This

---

[21] On this point, see Onuf (1989); Wendt (1992); Hurd (1999); Reus-Smit (1999); Wendt (1999). The point also features prominently in the most important review articles on constructivism: Adler (1997); Ruggie (1998); Hopf (1998); Finnemore and Sikkink (2001).

[22] Hurd notes, similarly, that rule compliance can stem from motives aside from genuine internalization (1999). Johnston shows that socialization can stem from social status rewards and punishments that likewise do not depend for their efficacy, at least fully, on genuine internalization (2001).

argument shares a great deal with Müller's claim that even the most apparently rational forms of human action are in fact constituted by rules (2004).[23]

A further strength of Sandholtz's argument, evident in the passage above, is its explicit focus not simply on the act of *proposing* a rule change, but also on the evaluative acts necessary to the acceptance required to yield change in intersubjective agreements about the existence, content, and relation of applicable rules. As Sandholtz correctly notes, "the notion of persuasiveness implies an audience that weighs the arguments and reaches conclusions" (2008, 107).[24] These kinds of social processes are composed of speech acts and related performances; ultimately, "whether speech acts accomplish anything depends on whether others respond to what they hear" (Onuf 2013, 10).

A final strength of Sandholtz's argument is its treatment of the indeterminate relationship between rule-breaking and rule change. He notes that "escaping punishment for violations of international rules is not necessarily the same as making or changing the rules." Rather, "the effect of a violation depends crucially on the justifications offered by the violator and the reactions of other states." On the one hand, rule-breaking conduct does not necessarily weaken a rule; when a rule violator "justifies its conduct as a permissible exception to a general rule, the effect is generally to strengthen the norm." Similarly, even cases involving clear violation of a rule by a great power are capable of strengthening a norm "if most other states condemn the great power's conduct." On the other hand, "if an apparent violation provokes only mild or *pro forma* condemnation" or if it "is followed in subsequent years by similar behavior on the part of other states," the strength and even the continued existence of the rule is more questionable (Sandholtz 2008, 108–9).[25] Processes of rule-making are rarely concluded quickly and are rarely concluded beyond the possibility of reconsideration at a future point in time.[26]

Taken together, these features of Sandholtz's argument suggest the existence and causal importance of procedural rules for making, interpreting, and applying rules that shape the ways actors propose and evaluate potential rule changes in

---

[23] Some constructivists go so far as to conclude that motives are a red herring and that scholars should "examine instead what actors say, in what contexts, and to what audiences" (Krebs and Jackson 2007, 36).

[24] Mitzen argues that many forums in international society are relatively closed and thus do not include an audience in the sense of observers who are not otherwise participants (2013, 50). However, she argues that actors in such settings can nonetheless engage in public reason, arising from "public discussion about common problems" (Mitzen 2013, 10). Mutual undertakings in such settings can generate intersubjective agreements as well as pressure for compliance with rules even apart from reputational pressure arising from audience effects understood in a more narrow sense (Mitzen 2013, 50).

[25] On the question of norm disappearance, see also Panke and Petersohn (2012).

[26] On the various outcomes of a potential rule violation, see also Onuf (2013, 17–18).

the international system.[27] Without such rules, actors would have no mutually intelligible way to resolve disputes about the proper meaning and interpretation of general rules in particular cases. However, such rules and the practices they constitute are not explicitly identified in the model. Rather, the argument relies implicitly on assumptions about their nature and content, and leaves underdeveloped the mechanisms of their operation. Specifically, Sandholtz's argument assumes the existence of sovereign states interacting within a fairly conventional version of the contemporary international legal system (2014, 102, 106–7). Given his immediate empirical concern (the development of norms against wartime plunder), this is clearly sensible; nor is it problematic for a broad range of other important cases. But this approach also has costs.

Most important, it acts as an implicit scope condition that limits the applicability of the findings in both temporal and potentially also in geographic ways. A large and important literature has documented the evolution of the international system over time (examples include Bull 2002; Watson 1992; Spruyt 1994; Reus-Smit 1999; Bukovansky 2002; Holsti 2004; Keene 2007; Nexon 2009; Suzuki 2009; Owen 2010; Phillips 2011; Keene 2013; Buzan and Lawson 2015; Phillips and Sharman 2015). Crucially, this literature demonstrates the diversity and variation across instances of organized inter-group relations. Some such variation pertains precisely to the kinds of rules for making, interpreting, and applying rules that are performing key work in Sandholtz's argument and that are a more explicit focus in this book. Reus-Smit shows, for example, how a range of cases differ in their notions of what he calls the "moral purpose of the state." These differences have implications, inter alia, for related notions of pure procedural justice. Greek city-states employed practices of arbitration instead of the more judicialized notions of contemporary international law evident in Sandholtz's analysis. City-states in Renaissance Italy employed highly stylized practices of oratorical diplomacy to resolve disputes about rules. Absolutist monarchs employed practices of diplomacy rooted in sovereign inequality, and also employed an explicitly religious conception of naturalist international law (Reus-Smit 1999). In each of these cases, as well as in others outside the Western tradition (Suzuki 2009) and in hybrids that emerged in the process of colonization (Keene 2007; Phillips and Sharman 2015), there is no reason to expect that processes for interpreting and applying rules will operate in a manner highly similar to that found in the contemporary international system.

Further, scholarship on practices of private governance (Büthe and Mattli 2011; Abbott, Green, and Keohane 2016) and multistakeholder governance

---

[27] In a similar vein, O'Mahoney explicitly acknowledges that rule tensions are causes of change in norms and rules only in the important but limited sense that "they *allow* actors to dispute the collective interpretation of action"; accordingly, "they are a permissive condition" (2014, 840).

(Raymond and DeNardis 2015) suggests that there may also be limits to the utility of assuming even that contemporary practices for making, interpreting, and applying rules in the international system are structured entirely by conventional understandings of positive international law. Likewise, international organizations exercise independent agency in setting international agendas and performing other tasks connected to making, interpreting, and applying international rules (Barnett and Finnemore 1999; Barnett and Finnemore 2004; Johnson 2014; Abbott, Genschel, Snidal, and Zangl, eds. 2015). This agency extends significantly beyond the earlier rationalist view of international organizations as the delegated agents of states (Abbott et al. 2000; Hawkins, Lake, Nielsen, and Tierney, eds. 2006). To the extent that various kinds of nonstate actors participate in rule-making alongside (or even apart from) states in relatively consistent, patterned ways, this suggests the existence of additional procedural rules authorizing such actions.

Accordingly, Sandholtz's claim that the probability an attempt to change international rules will succeed rises with the ability of its proponent to secure support from multiple powerful states, demonstrate compatibility with existing rules, and draw on a larger number of recent precedents than proponents of alternate interpretations (2008, 109) is valuable, but still ultimately limited by its truncated treatment of procedural rules for rule-making. For these reasons, while I build on the argument developed by Sandholtz, the approach I take in this book explicitly allows for variation in the relevant procedural rules that constitute social practices of rule-making, and treats them as contingent and context-specific factors to be empirically identified rather than as things assumed ex ante.

This inductive approach to procedural rules limits what can be said about them beyond the general discussion of rules (including secondary rules and the relation of rules to practices) contained in this chapter and in the case-specific discussions contained in the empirical chapters that follow. In the remainder of this section, I provide a concise statement of my main argument and discuss its significance for IR theory.

Actors know how to propose new or changed rules, and how to interpret and apply rules, because (and to the extent that) they have knowledge about context-specific procedural rules for making, interpreting, and applying rules. These procedural rules also provided the shared social resources that actors use in evaluating and responding to other actors' attempts to make, interpret, and apply rules. Like all rules, these procedural rules for rule-making and interpretation do not fully determine behavior. Rather, they constitute a mutually intelligible social practice that actors perform more or less competently. These rules and related practices are endemic to social life, including to international relations. They explain how actors know how to engage in particular means of social construction such as norm localization, persuasion, socialization, argumentation, bargaining, and strategic social construction. Variation in these rules and practices over time and space, and between different social contexts (e.g., familial, national, international), further explain why such modalities for social construction vary in form. Because procedural rules for rule-making shape outcomes, my argument expects that attempts to promote new or altered rules or interpretations of rules will be more successful to the extent that they are made in ways consistent with relevant procedural rules. They are a cause (though not the sole cause) of listeners' reactions—whatever these may be— to proposals for social change. Finally, in the absence of mutually agreed-upon rules and practices of rule-making, actors will find it extremely difficult both to resolve conflicts over rules peacefully and therefore to sustain cooperation.

SIGNIFICANCE AND CONTRIBUTIONS

The book identifies an important yet overlooked social practice in the international system, building on the recent "practice turn" in IR theory. As such, this study is a descriptive advance in understanding the international system and its operation. Further, it demonstrates empirically the importance of procedural rules for rule-making in explaining the success or failure of particular attempts to change social rules and institutions. In doing so, it builds upon existing work by constructivists as well as by others that investigates the dynamics and morphology of the international system. Beyond these more empirically oriented contributions, the book makes four main contributions to IR theory.

First, the existing constructivist literature identifies a number of mechanisms and processes (enumerated above) that are all essentially instances of the creation or alteration of intersubjective knowledge, and of rules in particular. My account of the generic social practice of rule-making, interpretation, and application provides an account of how actors know *how* and *when* to engage in these various different forms of social construction. This knowledge is derived by actors from contextually specific formal and informal procedural rules. Such an account is valuable in consolidating the existing constructivist literature by clarifying the relationships between the various mechanisms identified within it. These relationships are ultimately dependent on the nature of the procedural rules adopted by actors themselves. This suggests that the question of how to distinguish among the various processes and mechanisms identified by constructivists should be treated as an empirical problem to be resolved by determining what categories and concepts are meaningful and salient to actors themselves.

Second, my argument demonstrates the potential gains from pairing practice-turn and rule-oriented constructivist approaches. The book foregrounds the importance of procedural rules in comprising what practice-turn constructivists call background knowledge, thereby enhancing the ability of such approaches to properly specify the content, and account for the existence, of particular practices. Further, the book extends the range of applications of practice-turn constructivism to rule-making itself—a highly consequential practice endemic to virtually all social situations, but one that had largely escaped study as such in the context of the international system. Treating the politics of global rule-making as a distinct field of inquiry facilitates comparative analysis that examines temporal variation in such practices as well as variation in practices of rule-making at different social scales.

Third, the book shows that this practice of making, interpreting, and applying rules is vital to understanding the causal mechanisms and processes associated with both the reproduction and transformation of rules and institutions. In this regard, I seek to help counter the unfortunate and inaccurate perception that constructivism is either better or only able to explain social continuity—that it unavoidably privileges structure over agency.[28] I also advance an account of international system dynamics that breaks with rationalist scholarship that relies on punctuated equilibrium models driven by exogenous shocks (Keohane 1984; Ikenberry 2001). Instead, I build on constructivist accounts that allow for multiple behavioral logics (March and Olsen 1998; Müller 2004; Hopf 2010; Adler and Pouliot 2011) and that take seriously the endogenous dynamics of complex rule sets (Onuf 1989; Onuf 1994; Sandholtz 2008).

Finally, the book contributes to IR theory by providing a way to connect the literature on global governance more closely with the literature on the international system. One recent stock-taking effort in IR theory concluded (wrongly, in my view) that the discipline has effectively entered a period of "normal science," in which the parameters of the field can be largely taken for granted (Dunne, Hansen, and Wight 2013, 406). While there is certainly a great deal of such work being done, to substantial benefit, this is an incomplete characterization that leaves a dynamic literature on global governance to one side and misses its implications for many of the field's foundational assumptions—such as the existence of an anarchic world dominated by rational, sovereign states.

Global governance scholars have tended to focus on applying tools and concepts from IR theory to the study of global governance in an array of issue areas including climate (Keohane and Victor 2011; Abbott, Green, and

---

[28] The notion that constructivism privileges structure over agency, and is thus at least potentially limited in its ability to explain social change, was noted as a challenge for constructivism in early constructivist work. See, for example, Finnemore and Sikkink (1998) and Checkel (2001). David M. McCourt argues that practice-turn constructivism and scholarship employing relational approaches should be understood as part of the constructivist approach to IR precisely because they help to avoid this kind of "structuralist bias" (2016).

Keohane 2016; Bernstein 2011), trade and finance (Wilkinson 2006; Helleiner and Pagliari 2011; Helleiner 2014), migration and refugees (Betts 2010), and the cyber domain (DeNardis 2014; Nye 2014; Carr 2015). While such work is of tremendous value, the implications of global governance for the field's understanding of the international system and its dynamics remain relatively unexamined. The global governance literature is therefore a case of a more general turn away from the study of macro-level phenomena.[29] Recent efforts to evaluate the state of the art in global governance (Weiss and Wilkinson 2014; Murphy 2014; Finnemore 2014; Pegram and Acuto 2015; Paris 2015) have sought to push the frontiers of knowledge *about* global governance, but have not dealt in depth with the ways that this literature can inform study of the international system and of international relations more generally.

While the field lacks a consensus definition of global governance comparable to the iconic (though flawed) definition of an international regime (Krasner 1982, 186), any reasonable candidate for such status would need to accord a prime place to the social practices for making, interpreting, and applying rules that are the primary subject of this study. Thus, the book places global governance at the heart of the study of the international system and its dynamics. In doing so, it makes the case that this system cannot be either described or understood without recourse to the theoretical and conceptual tools that have been developed by scholars of global governance, and that concerns about lack of innovation in IR theory (e.g., Mearsheimer and Walt 2013) stem in significant part from a failure to recognize scholarship on global governance as a vital, theoretically progressive site within the discipline.[30]

Recognizing the extensive literature on global governance as relevant to the dynamics and morphology of the international system reinvigorates what had risked becoming seen as a moribund part of the academic field of IR. However, it also places an onus on scholars investigating the various constellations of international institutions and regimes that comprise contemporary global governance to take a more generalized and historically contextualized view of global governance instead of the common view that treats it as a product of late modernity.[31] It also highlights the need to consolidate findings across issue-specific domains and to produce research that explicitly connects various practices of global governance with the operation, reproduction, and transformation of the international system. My hope is that by demonstrating the importance of

[29] On this point, see Onuf (2016).

[30] My point here in some ways resembles the claim made by Levine and Barder (2014): that the ontological and epistemological commitments held by Mearsheimer and Walt, among others, preclude recognition and valuation of this kind of global governance research, along with other bodies of IR scholarship more closely indebted to critical theory.

[31] For a critique of this view, see Weiss and Wilkinson (2014).

procedural rules for rule-making in explaining international political outcomes, this book will make a contribution in this regard.

Methods and Evidence

In this section, I discuss several issues pertaining to the methods and evidence I employ in the book to empirically investigate my theoretical claims. The first key point in this regard is that the book makes both constitutive and causal claims; following Wendt, I take both kinds of claims to be explanatory in nature (Wendt 1998). The book argues that procedural rules constitute practices for making, applying, and interpreting rules in particular social contexts. These claims are constitutive in nature; they explain how *particular* kinds of rule-making practices exist, and how agents know when and how to engage in them. For example, they explain that states are accorded dominant roles in rule-making and interpreting rules in the contemporary international system because the system's procedural rules for these activities endow them with that role and prescribe certain methods of accomplishing it.

The book also advances a causal argument about why some attempts to change rules governing the international system succeed while others do not. Put simply, the argument is that attempts to create social change are more likely to succeed if they are pursued in a manner consistent with existing procedural rules. These rules provide instruction manuals, informing actors about how to present and evaluate proposals for change. Procedural rules are not deterministic; actors clearly may break them in performing both acts of presentation and evaluation. However, even in such cases, procedural rules are not irrelevant. In addition to guiding actors in their choices about how to perform social acts, they also guide other actors in selecting *responses* to those acts. This latter choice is crucial for the purpose of studying rule dynamics. The most important question is not what makes actors decide to initiate attempts to change rules and institutions—it is what makes their audience either accept or reject the attempt. This argument is both *probabilistic* (reflecting the importance of causal factors other than procedural rules, as well as the possibility that conflicting proposals may be presented in procedurally legitimate ways) and *process-oriented* (in that it specifies a particular causal mechanism).

Both the constitutive and causal arguments advanced here are empirical in nature. Accordingly, it should be possible to say something about the kinds of evidence that support my argument.[32] Broadly, if I am correct, it will be possible to identify a social practice for the creation and alteration of rules. This entails,

[32] In positivist language, I am referring here to the expected observable implications of my argument. Constructivists vary in their comfort with such language, for a variety of important metatheoretical reasons. I share many of these misgivings; however, I am convinced that

first, the possibility of identifying the procedural rules that constitute this practice in a given social context. Second, actors should generally present proposals for social change according to such rules. Where inconsistencies exist between rules and tactics, these should be explained, excused, minimized, denied, or criticized. Similarly, these same procedural rules should guide the evaluation of proposals for social change. Further, deviations from accepted evaluative procedures should prompt the same range of discursive responses generated by improper presentations. Finally, disagreement on relevant procedural rules should compromise attempts to engage in collective rule-making and rule interpretation. In such cases, actors should typically criticize other participants for failing to adhere to legitimate practices for making and interpreting rules.

Since the constitutive and causal arguments are centrally concerned with social kinds, the book requires methods capable of discerning intersubjective agreements (especially rules) and of tracing particular attempts to change these social facts. Fortunately, these requirements are not very exotic. They can be satisfied by standard qualitative case studies.[33] Accordingly, I turn next to issues of case selection and finally to a discussion of my approach to the cases.

The cases chosen are both difficult and important for my argument. They are difficult because they deal centrally with issues of international security, which is typically regarded in IR theory as the realm in which considerations of material power are most likely to predominate. While I do not argue that either material factors or, especially, issues of interest more broadly conceived are absent from the cases, I show that procedural rules constrained and enabled actors engaged in processes of collective rule-making and interpretation, and also that these rules generated unintended consequences in at least some circumstances. Further, actors complied with procedural rules in cases where doing so was costly. These results are inconsistent with realist theories; while they are broadly consistent with existing constructivist work, the attention to procedural rules

---

constructivists are still engaged in an enterprise (however provisional our conclusions) of gaining knowledge about the world, and that we can meaningfully distinguish between the quality of alternative claims, at least in relative terms. Further, similar positions have been taken both by prominent "conventional" and "postpositivist" or "critical" constructivists. Alexander Wendt has argued that although "all observation is theory-laden, and this means we can never test our theories against the world, but only indirectly via other, competing theories ... for both kinds of theory the 'scientific' solution to the problem is the same, namely to rely on publicly available, albeit always theory-laden, evidence from the world, which critics of our theoretical claims can assess for relevance, accuracy, and so on" (Wendt 1998, 106). Audie Klotz and Cecilia Lynch have asserted that "constructivists of all epistemological stripes agree on basic standards of scholarship" that are similar to those articulated by Wendt. Most notably, they maintain that "researchers strive to gather a variety of source materials in order to check against one another ('triangulate')" and that "empirical inconsistencies undermine the persuasiveness of interpretations" (Klotz and Lynch 2007, 20–22).

[33] On case studies in social science, see George and Bennett (2005).

and demonstration of the existence of structured practices of rule-making, interpretation, and application are novel contributions. The selection of cases dealing with international security contributes, as well, to the importance of the cases; procedural rules and the resulting practices of rule-making and interpretation are employed by agents in dealing with problems of the greatest consequence for their political communities. Further, the cases stand out even among the universe of international security cases because they involve leading states in the international system in each period investigated; and also because they deal with proposed changes to critical system-level rules and institutions (respectively: great power privileges and responsibilities, the legitimacy of the use of force, the basic nature of international order, and the implications of disruptive technology for international law).

I conclude this chapter by addressing the design and execution of the case studies. The most rudimentary question that can be asked about the cases I examine is whether or not there were changes in the prevailing rules. In the first two cases—the aftermath of the Napoleonic Wars, and the interwar period—I believe that there were. The creation of the Concert of Europe established new practices of collaborative, active management of the international system by the great powers;[34] such practices are institutional ancestors of modern summitry and of the UN Security Council's permanent membership. This case also clearly demonstrates that relatively greater social competence (on the part of Metternich and, to a lesser degree, Castlereagh) in social practices of rule-making is a significant power resource that can explain outcomes at odds with those predicted by the distribution of material power resources.

A series of events in the decade following the Treaty of Versailles culminated in the Kellogg-Briand Pact, which created a rule severely circumscribing the sovereign prerogative to make war. While this rule was often violated over the early part of its lifespan, these violations were routinely criticized and the rule was reaffirmed following the Second World War in the UN Charter. In addition, the Pact itself was a vital legal foundation for war crimes trials. The interwar case is of interest for two further reasons. First, the treaty negotiations reveal competent social performances by two relative novices—Japan and the Soviet Union. The fact that states with, respectively, non-Western cultural traditions and revolutionary aims could participate in this instance of rule-making suggests an influential and widely understood social practice. Second, the creation of the Kellogg-Briand Pact is noteworthy because it occurred despite the fact that neither of its principals (nor their governments) deliberately sought to create a rule generally limiting the sovereign prerogative to declare war. The case thus highlights the productive power of social practices of rule-making,

[34] See also Mitzen (2013).

interpretation, and application, as well as the importance of path dependency in world politics. Procedural rules do more than constrain actor behavior or enable pursuit of predetermined goals; in at least some conditions they can have independent effects.

In contrast, I am much more circumspect about concluding that significant rule change took place as a result of the exchanges between the American government and the al-Qaeda leadership examined in the third case. Overall, this instance of rule-making and interpretation was marked by what I call a Tower of Babel effect. The primary parties operated with such different sets of procedural rules that they were unable to participate meaningfully in a single practice of rule-making. This negative finding has two important implications for my argument. If rule change is a product of a social practice of rule-making, interpretation, and application, then failure to agree on the rules of that practice should mean that consensus on rules and how to interpret them cannot be reached. If actors with fundamentally different sets of procedural rules were able to arrive at stable and mutually legitimate intersubjective agreements about applicable social rules, this would cast doubt on my argument. This case is one where my argument should expect failed attempts at rule-making and interpretation. Second, and more interesting, despite deep disagreement about the specific *content* of procedural rules, the post-9/11 case clearly establishes that both sides continued to play according to their respective understandings of how to make, interpret, and apply rules. This finding supports my claim that practices of rule-making are robust and generic across different cultures. Even when actors disagree on *how* to play, they do not disagree on *whether* to play; nor do they stop playing when another party breaks the rules.

Assessment of rule change in the fourth case, which examines rule-making efforts on cybersecurity issues in the United Nations, is complicated by the fact that these deliberations are ongoing. However, as the case study demonstrates, there are clear signs of a puzzling shift toward broad acceptance of claims advanced by the United States and its allies that state conduct in the cyber domain is subject to the existing rules of international law. This shift is puzzling because it includes states who remain opposed to Western policy preferences on specific rules for state conduct in the cyber domain, and because the shift has taken place despite increased global contention over cybersecurity issues. The evidence suggests that the arguments and interpretations advanced by the United States and its allies have been hard for other states to oppose because they have skillfully shown that existing rules of international law, such as the law of armed conflict, international humanitarian law, and the law of state responsibility can be applied in the cyber domain. Further, these interpretations have been advanced in a procedurally competent manner, and existing procedural rules for international law have likewise shaped the evaluations of these proposals by other states. However, the evidence also shows that Russia, China, Iran, and other states skeptical of American positions remain confident in their own ability to employ the existing rules of international law (particularly those pertaining to sovereignty and sovereign equality) to advance their own preferences for rules governing cybersecurity and the Internet more broadly, despite any constraints created by accepting the claim that state conduct in the cyber domain is subject to the existing rules of international law.

These observations serve to foreshadow the cases, but they also emphasize that simply asking whether change occurs in a particular case is insufficient to understand when, and why, rule change occurs. Instead, the book engages three distinct questions. First, is it possible to identify procedural rules and to speak of a structured social practice of rule-making, interpretation, and application? Second, does this social practice influence and shape actor decisions at the point of creating and altering rules? Third, are rule changes subsequently adhered to and do they therefore represent widespread and lasting changes in the international system? Collectively, I believe that the cases comprising the remainder of the book warrant clear affirmative answers to the first two questions. More caution is required with respect to the third question. On one level, this is simply a function of scope. Demonstrating the existence and importance of social practices of rule-making across these cases entailed a major effort and an extended argument. Beyond the difficulty of the task, however, I believe there are sound reasons to accept that a more modest demonstration of subsequent compliance is not a fatal shortcoming in this study. First, as all norms and rules are constantly subject to potential revision and are dependent on continuing instantiation for their existence, any finding on the existence of a norm or rule must remain provisional. It is impossible to show that a norm has been definitively "created" because this is simply not how social facts behave. Thus, to evaluate norm existence in terms of subsequent compliance is insufficient. Put another way, rule creation is logically independent of subsequent adherence, even if the continued existence of the rule is not. Finally, future compliance and the continuing existence of a rule reflect subsequent iterations of practices of rule-making as actors respond to their own rule-following and rule-breaking and that of others, and attempt to apply general rules to particular cases. Even when rules are well accepted, practices of rule-making, interpretation, and application continue.

The cases share a common format. First, the primary rules at stake are identified. This is essential to assessing which rules, if any, have changed. Second, the relevant secondary or procedural rules constituting the practice (or practices) of rule-making operative in that social context are elaborated. The specification of procedural rules addresses the constitutive questions posed by the book, in that such rules are necessary to the existence of the social practice of rule-making that I posit. Identification of procedural rules is also critical to evaluating the book's causal claims about the rule dynamics—namely, that actors will often present and evaluate proposals for rule change in light of relevant procedural rules, that improper social acts will prompt critical and/or justificatory responses, and that attempts to pursue or resist rule change are more likely to succeed if they are pursued in a procedurally legitimate manner. The third section of each case investigates the operation of social practices of rule-making and interpretation, and attempts to make determinations about the role of such practices in explaining actor behavior and accounting for the outcomes in that case.

The book examines successful and unsuccessful attempts to create change both within and across the cases. Each case contains multiple distinct proposals for change in rules or rule interpretations. This feature of the cases serves to greatly increase the number of observations, thereby increasing confidence in the findings. Disaggregation of the cases allows comparative evaluation of individual proposals—facilitating analytical leverage on the differential success of distinct proposals. One concrete example of just such a comparison is the rejection of the Holy Alliance in favor of the Quadruple Alliance; these substantively similar proposals generated different audience evaluations primarily because of divergence in their forms. Consistent with my argument, the procedurally illegitimate proposals were rejected. Most important, this disaggregation of the cases is not merely a methodologically driven move. Disaggregation is substantively consistent with my argument since it corresponds to the sequencing of proposals for rule change and discursive responses to such proposals; that is, it reflects the fact that the social practice of collective rule-making and rule interpretation is an iterative social practice.

Finally, I turn to evidentiary issues relating to both my constitutive and causal arguments. Investigating both arguments requires a means of identifying rules. Essentially, evidence of the existence of rules must be drawn from the statements and practices of actors. This is the most basic insight behind what Hart called the "internal aspect of rules" (1994, 56–57)—what constructivists today know as intersubjective understandings. In particular, the identification of rules relies heavily on what actors say about their understandings of applicable rules, as well as on examination of the reasons given by actors both for compliance and for noncompliance (Hurd 1999, 391). In the following I discuss three problems that arise in identifying rules: (1) how to determine what actors truly believe about rules, as opposed to how they may portray them for strategic reasons; (2) how to aggregate individual subjective understandings to arrive at intersubjective rules; and (3) how to resolve variance between nominal rules and actual social practice.

With respect to the first problem, Hart provides useful guidance. He writes that the best evidence that action is rule-guided "is that if our behavior is challenged we are disposed to justify it by reference to the rule"; further, "the genuineness of our acceptance of the rule may be manifested not only in our past and subsequent general acknowledgements and conformity to it, but in our criticism of our own and other's deviation from it" (1994, 140). The idea is to check actors' declarations about the rule against their behavior with respect to it. While this is hardly a perfect research practice, especially given the often limited information available to scholars of International Relations, it presents a starting point and in many cases a best available practice.

The easiest solution to the second problem, the problem of aggregation, is often provided by actors themselves. Multiple subjective understandings can be reconciled via discussion, negotiation, or any of a number of other forms of communication, and the outcome expressed in a formal manner such as a treaty, agreement, or other document. Indeed, the undesirability of uncertainty about rules is part of the rationale for secondary rules (or procedural rules about rule-making), and the negotiation of shared agreement is central to practices of rule-making. The difficulty here is that few social contexts display the degree of formalization found in a domestic legal system; further, the fact of codification is not free from considerations of power. If relevant procedural rules for rule-making are not codified, or if codification does not reflect genuine agreement among the relevant actors, the task is more difficult; the task of the analyst in such cases is inductive—to assemble the best possible account both of commonalities and nodes of disagreement among actors' individual subjective understandings of the applicable procedural rules for rule-making, application, and interpretation.

A similar strategy is indicated in addressing the third problem. In the face of contradictory evidence about the content of rules, whether in the form of actors' declarations, social practices that diverge from apparent rules, or conflicting social practices, the appropriate response is to be explicit about such tensions and to reach a most likely conclusion. Vincent Pouliot has made a similar argument, calling on researchers to employ methods of triangulation, in order to put "experience-near concepts . . . under the light of experience-distant contextualization" (2007, 370). Jeffrey Checkel has made a similar argument stressing the importance of multiple sources of evidence for increasing confidence in conclusions about intersubjective meanings (2001, 565–66).

Beyond identifying rules, the causal argument requires demonstrating that proposals are made and evaluated in light of secondary rules—that improper proposals and evaluative acts are minimized, denied, justified, or explained by their makers, and criticized on procedural grounds by observers; and, finally, that properly presented proposals are more likely to be accepted. This entails showing specific discursive sequences culminating in either accept-ance or rejection of proposals and evaluations. These sequences will typ-ically (though not necessarily exclusively) take the form of official written and verbal declarations. Non-linguistic communication should generally take forms clearly recognizable to actors in a particular social context—for example, walking out of a speech at the United Nations, voting against a res-olution in an international organization, refusing to become party to a treaty, or publicly violating an asserted rule of customary international law. Each of these acts has an intelligible meaning in the contemporary international system.

Ideally, the argument should also include evidence that actors were motiv-ated at least in part by concerns about procedural legitimacy. Notably, however, this is not the same as requiring actors to have fully internalized and accepted applicable procedural rules. Compliance with rules can be motivated by self-interest and even by coercion, in addition to genuine internalization of the norm as an appropriate standard of conduct (Hurd 1999). Actors may make, inter-pret, and apply rules according to applicable procedural rules because they be-lieve these rules to be appropriate, because they calculate that doing so enhances their chances of securing desired rules or rule interpretations, or even because they fear coercion in the event they do not comply. Actors may also have mixed motives.

In conducting the case studies, I have drawn on an array of primary and secondary sources. These include treaty texts, news reports, public speeches, documents and memos prepared by government officials, private letters by state officials, and the work of professional historians who have consulted these and other sources. While it would always be better to have more infor-mation from a wider variety of sources, the reality of research on the social world is that all conclusions remain provisional. I have endeavored to be rel-atively conservative in drawing conclusions from the available evidence, and to point out places of lingering uncertainty. Even on the basis of this careful approach to the evidence, the book makes important empirical and theoret-ical contributions.

CHAPTER 2

The Social Construction of Great Power Management, 1815–1822

The transition from the eighteenth to the nineteenth century was accomplished at the Congress of Vienna. More than a conclusion to the Napoleonic War, the congress and its associated diplomacy fundamentally changed the "rules of the game" for International Relations in the European state system. The competitive balance of power characteristic of the eighteenth century was replaced with a new system of collaborative great power conflict management. This outcome represents an unsolved puzzle for International Relations theory.

Neorealist theories clearly predict competitive balancing—not collaboration or condominium.[1] Neither was the congress a clear example of hegemonic influence. As Paul Schroeder has argued, the post-1815 system was marked by a duopoly rather than a hegemony—among the great powers, Britain and Russia stood clearly above the so-called Continental powers (France, Prussia, and Austria).[2] Claims of British hegemony in the period also overlook the fact that the Austrian foreign minister, Metternich, was as influential as his British counterpart in shaping the settlement.[3] If institutions were truly epiphenomenal reflections of hegemonic power, then Metternich's remarkable influence would constitute an important anomaly.

Robert Jervis has suggested an additional explanation for the development of concert systems. He argues that concerts are temporary deviations from the behavioral norm represented by the balance of power. Concerts are possible "after, and only after, a large war with a potential hegemon" because such an episode presents alliance handicaps and renders statesmen abnormally reluctant

---

[1] The classic statement is provided in Waltz (1979).

[2] Schroeder (1994, 591).

[3] For an argument defining the post-1815 system as a British hegemony, see Ikenberry (2001, ch. 4). Metternich's influence is consistently acknowledged in historical accounts of the period. See, for example, Kissinger (2000); Rene Albrecht-Carrié (1968); Nicolson (1946).

to resort to war in the pursuit of national interest (Jervis 1985, 60–61). The operation of the balance of power is thus temporarily impaired by incentives that unfortunately prove all too fleeting. But incentives may not be recognized and, even if they are, there is no guarantee actors will reach agreement on the particular institutional form for a solution to their common problem. Even if an agreement is reached, a theory predicting behavior on the basis of incentives has limited ability to explain particular institutional forms or to describe the social processes involved in their creation. Further, in 1815, the statesmen had no existing concept or model of "concert" behavior that they could apply. For all of these reasons, Jervis's theory cannot adequately explain the emergence of the concert system in 1815 and after.

In this chapter, I argue that this shift in the primary rules governing state behavior was the result of a rule-governed social practice of making, interpreting, and applying rules. Accordingly, the argument advanced here draws on and contributes to a constructivist literature on the post-1815 international order.[4] Jennifer Mitzen has shown that the concert system laid important foundations for practices of contemporary global governance (Mitzen 2013). My analysis supports these claims, but my main purpose is to show how social practices of rule-making and interpretation were crucial to the emergence and development of concert practices in the first place.

The statesmen at the Congress of Vienna agreed on a system of collaborative great power conflict management that broke significantly from their prior balance of power practices in part because of, and in ways significantly shaped by, the procedural rules governing this practice of rule-making. The record shows that actors were generally aware of themselves as participants in a mutually intelligible practice of rule-making and interpretation. They generally presented proposals in a manner consistent with their understandings of how to legitimately do so, and both criticized and justified proposals on procedural grounds. Further, procedural rules shaped (but did not typically determine) outcomes. They constrained the proposals that actors were willing to make, and provided reasons to support or oppose particular plans. Accordingly, the evidence highlights that skill with procedural rules can function as an important power resource in international politics. The argument proceeds in two parts. The first describes the relevant primary and secondary rules. The second demonstrates the role of secondary rules and associated practices of rule-making in accounting for key events and outcomes.

---

[4] See Reus-Smit (1999), Bukovansky (2002), and Mitzen (2013).

Rules of the Game

In this section, I outline the rules relevant to the shift from the eighteenth-century European balance of power to the nineteenth-century concert system. First, I discuss the central primary rules of the European state system before and after the creation of a practice of collective great power management. Second, I discuss the secondary rules that governed the social practices of rule-making and interpretation that were fundamental to this historic change in primary rules. In the next section, I leverage this analysis to provide an explanation for the system of collaborative great power management created in the aftermath of the Napoleonic War.

PRIMARY RULES: FROM BALANCE TO CONCERT

European international relations in 1815 had been fundamentally unsettled by the French Revolution and then by Napoleon's empire-building project. Both had important long-term effects on the international system, particularly on the development of nationalism, but these effects would not be fully realized until the mid-nineteenth century (Bukovansky 2002). The relevant prior rule-system is the eighteenth-century balance of power that preceded the outbreak of the French Revolution. In contrast to the spare, mechanical vision of the balance of power popularized by neorealist theories, this balance system was deeply social and highly complex.

While the Peace of Westphalia has come to serve as a kind of shorthand for the modern state system, this system in fact emerged over a much longer period and in a highly contingent manner (Spruyt 1994; Holsti 2004; Nexon 2009). Rules and practices constituting the balance of power emerged, in particular, over the decades following Westphalia. The balance of power was first codified in the Utrecht peace settlements, which marked the end of Louis XIV's drive for hegemony in the War of the Spanish Succession. This timing was no coincidence; after 1713, "the balance of power became a means of maintaining state independence and preventing hegemony" (Holsti 1991, 63). Despite this desire to utilize the notion of a balance of power to restrain bids for hegemony, the Utrecht settlement did not contemplate a lasting international organization or any other limitation on the use of warfare as an instrument of foreign policy (Holsti 1991, 80–81). In the century between Utrecht and the Congress of Vienna, warfare was common—especially among the emerging great powers. Major wars in this period included the War of the Polish Succession (1733–1735) and the Seven Years' War (1756–1763). Moreover, as the eighteenth century wore on, "competition among great powers became subject to fewer legal and dynastic constraints" (Bukovansky 2002, 95). Thus, the initial European balance of power must be seen as a practice enabling competition among states, as well as a restraining factor that mitigated the effects of anarchy.

The purpose of the balance of power was well understood, and there was general agreement on its major rules.[5] Schroeder eloquently enumerates the rules of the game: "compensations; indemnities; alliances as instruments for accruing power and capability; *raison d'état*; honour and prestige; Europe as a family of states; and finally, the principle or goal of balance of power itself" (1994, 6). The military aspects of the balance are most familiar. Simply put, the notion was that gains made by another state—both allies and adversaries—must be matched. Both gains and potential compensations were broadly understood, going beyond territory acquired in armed conflict to encompass "gains acquired legally (e.g. by dynastic inheritance or marriage) or from natural growth and development" as well as "gains in honour, prestige, and standing in the international system." Similarly, "one would try to exact the costs of war from the enemy whenever possible, but states also expected their allies to indemnify them for aid they supplied" (Schroeder 1994, 6–7). Despite the free resort to force as "a regular and accepted means of achieving and defending certain objectives" (Bukovansky 2002, 64), eighteenth-century wars were marked by significant tactical restraint. Elaborate rules limiting the conduct of war were augmented by ritualized social forms for the initiation and termination of hostilities, for surrender, and for prisoner exchange (Holsti 1991, 104). Such rules "were fairly effective" in limiting the impact of war on civilian populations, especially in comparison to the religious conflicts of the seventeenth century, despite the lack of a centralized enforcement mechanism (Craig and George 1995, 19).

Just as possible gains and losses were broadly defined, interstate competition extended beyond the battlefield. Concern with honor and prestige were central to International Relations in eighteenth-century Europe.[6] One important manifestation of this concern was preoccupation with rules of precedence and diplomatic etiquette. As Reus-Smit has argued, "even when hierarchy was not the core issue animating interstate negotiations, it structured the process by which those negotiations were conducted" (1999, 109). This concern stemmed from identification of the state's moral purpose with enhancing the personal glory of the monarch. Beyond the issue of relative standing in diplomatic ceremonies, the pursuit of dynastic glory was conducted through "dynastic marriages, competing legal claims, alliance politics, and spying" (Bukovansky 2002, 72).

---

[5] This point is widely agreed upon, even by authors who differ in their precise descriptions of the balance system. See Albrecht-Carrié (1973, 5–6); Craig and George (1995, 19); Schroeder (1994, 5).

[6] On the role of honor in International Relations, see Lebow (2008).

The pursuit of prestige was not merely a matter of rational utility maximization. Instead, particular rivalries were regarded as historic and natural; Anglo-French and Franco-Austrian enmities are important examples of such "culturally constituted" relationships (Bukovansky 2002, 76). While this depiction of the European state system as hierarchical is at odds with the discipline's foundational assumption of anarchy (Waltz 1979; Keohane 1984; Wendt 1992), the IR literature increasingly questions this starting point (Donnelly 2006; Sharman 2013; Bially Mattern and Zarakol 2016).

The eighteenth-century balance of power was a subtle, rule-governed social system that opened multiple avenues to Europe's royal houses in their pursuit of prestige. And yet, it did not completely define their international relations; "despite the wars that pitted European states against each other, there was a general assumption that they were members of a comity of states that were bound together by common ties of family relationship, religion, and historical tradition" (Craig and George 1995, 19). However, this thin European identity did not lead to robust cooperation among states in pursuit of common aims. Instead, the belief was that "the play of forces arising from each power's pursuing its own interest would ensure the preservation of an overall balance and thereby prevent empire" (Schroeder 1994, 9). Thus, while the balance was rule-governed, it was also highly decentralized in its operation.

The Congress of Vienna did not represent a complete rupture from the eighteenth-century system. States ruled primarily by monarchs remained the dominant actors in International Relations;[7] they conducted their relations at least largely in terms of pursuing interest, through both diplomacy and armed force; common pan-European identity provided an important foundation for notions of collaborative crisis management, and concern with prestige was compatible with the emerging notion of special rights and responsibilities for the great powers.[8] Beyond the practical innovation of periodic great power conferences, this also marked a shift away from purely incidental diplomacy focused on solving the problem at hand, in favor of designing enduring systems for explicitly managing conflict.[9] Reus-Smit argues that the modern system of contractual international law and multilateral diplomacy emerged later in the nineteenth century. He sees the Vienna settlement as "archaic" because it reasserted monarchical rule and did not establish a deliberative assembly with wide membership (Reus-Smit 1999, 139). Both of these things are true; however, such changes

---

[7] It is worth noting that most of these actors were, by this point, not simply states but rather the centers of extensive overseas colonial empires (Hobson and Sharman 2005) engaged in extensive relations with non-European powers in various other regional subsystems (Keene 2007; Suzuki 2009; Phillips and Sharman 2015).

[8] On the latter point, see Keene (2013).

[9] The incidental nature of eighteenth-century diplomacy is noted in Reus-Smit (1999, 107).

would have required significant alteration of secondary rules.[10] Thus, my argument is able to explain not only the *accomplishments* of the Vienna settlement in changing the rules of the game, but also its *failure* to go further than it did.

The years after 1815 were marked by a series of conferences. Aix-la-Chapelle (1818), Carlsbad (1819), Troppau (1820), Laibach (1821), and Verona (1822) put into practice the essential ideas—first articulated in the Treaty of Chaumont (1814)—that informed the treaties of 1815: the Quadruple Alliance, the Final Act of the Congress of Vienna, and the Holy Alliance. Despite the importance of the 1815 treaties, the settlement was neither fully articulated in 1815 nor static in the years following. Over this period, the focus of great power collaboration shifted—the initial concern with preventing a great power war (in the form of either a renewed French threat or a war between the Eastern Powers over the Polish-Saxon question) giving way to a concern with the maintenance of order against revolutionary movements in the German states, Naples, Piedmont, Spain, and Greece. Thus, explaining the shift from the balance to the concert requires examination of more than simply the treaties of 1815.

The settlement of 1815 and its evolution in the period from 1815 to 1822 are the focus of the second major section of this chapter. Before addressing the crucial causal question about the outcomes in this case, I sketch the secondary rules that governed the relevant process of rule-making, interpretation, and application.

SECONDARY RULES: DIPLOMACY AND INTERNATIONAL LAW

The secondary rules relevant to the construction of the concert system were located within three social institutions: sovereignty, international law, and diplomacy.[11] Sovereignty identified state officials, including monarchs, as the sole actors competent to engage in rule-making and interpretation at the international level. On its own, however, this says little about the legitimate means for creating or altering rules. International law and diplomacy thus serve to fill the gaps in the system of secondary rules.

The eighteenth century saw a fundamental shift in the foundations of international law. The legitimacy of rules, and in particular rules of international law, shifted from a basis in natural law to the emerging doctrine of positive or contractual law. Mlada Bukovansky attributes this shift to "the religious divisions

---

[10] I argue below that the movement from natural to contractual international law was more advanced in this period than its domestic counterpart, the shift from monarchical or dynastic to constitutional legitimation of state authority.

[11] This is not to suggest these institutions are concerned only with rule-making and interpretation.

and strife of the previous century, and the precipitous decline of the pope's influence in temporal matters" (2002, 71). Though "traditional religious symbolism and sanction" were still invoked, domestic legitimacy was increasingly seen in constitutional terms (Bukovansky 2002, 70); the corollary in international law was to cast the legitimacy of agreements in the consent of states and their legitimate rulers. One important manifestation of this transition was a decline in "the rigid adherence to family inheritances and rights deriving from ancient conquests and marriages" in favor of the view that territory could be "an exchangeable commodity" (Holsti 1991, 56). The shift in this basic rule led to a discernible shift in state practice; "dynastic rights were systematically violated in the numerous territorial exchanges of the period" (Holsti 1991, 90). The increasing commoditization of territory was part and parcel of a general lessening of constraints on balance of power practices in the latter part of the eighteenth century (Bukovansky 2002, 95). While the French and American revolutions were indicative of the growing strain on the traditional basis of domestic legitimacy, the situation in international law was further advanced. By the time of Napoleon's first defeat, the legitimacy of a proposed rule for international relations was primarily dependent on the consent of states, as embodied either in duly authorized treaties or in less formal diplomatic arrangements.

The rules for reaching such arrangements, which partially constitute social practices of rule-making, are a subset of the rules of diplomacy. Perhaps more than any other institution in the international system, diplomacy has fulfilled a double role. On the one hand, it provides the means for states to pursue their interests within the existing framework of rules and institutions—for instance, by concluding trade agreements or defensive alliances. On the other, it has provided the social grammar and vocabulary that have enabled sweeping changes in the state practice, and that have blocked other such attempts. It is this latter function of diplomacy with which I am concerned here.

Reus-Smit has characterized early European diplomacy as incidental, bilateral, secretive, and hierarchical (1999, ch. 5). As with the justificatory foundations for sovereignty and for international law, the Congress of Vienna sat astride a transition in secondary rules. Where previous peace settlements, for example at Westphalia and Utrecht, took the form of a collection of bilateral treaties, the concert system marks the first tentative steps toward modern multilateralism. But this is more an outcome of the concert system than a secondary rule operating at the time of its creation. A great deal of the diplomacy in the period from 1815 to 1822 remained bilateral in nature. Though the great powers negotiated together and issued joint declarations, there were also shifting alliances among them more consistent with bilateral diplomacy. Above all, even though multilateral diplomatic processes were conceivable, there was as yet no consensus that they were particularly appropriate as a form of diplomatic practice—either in general terms or for the more limited purpose of creating, interpreting, and applying rules.

A similar situation existed with respect to the incidental characteristic of diplomacy, or the notion that diplomacy was intended to address issues as they occurred rather than to enact rules that would foresee future eventualities. As noted above, the introduction of an enduring set of rules for conflict management and global governance is one of the lasting legacies of the Vienna settlement (Mitzen 2013). This is a contrast to the more modest settlements created in 1648 and 1713. The important point for the purposes of my argument is that the shift away from incidental diplomacy was limited to the domain of primary rules. The great powers were largely satisfied with the settlement, and none of them sought to leverage concert diplomacy as part of an attempt to contest secondary rules. Indeed, if anything, the settlement envisaged a conservative or even a reactionary system designed precisely to delay or halt the development of more democratic trends in secondary rules. As a result, it is hardly surprising that the conference failed to revolutionize the secondary rules governing global rule-making. The Congress of Vienna was seen as an extraordinary event; insofar as it addressed secondary rules, it tended to make incremental changes or to reinforce existing rules.

The conservative bias of the Congress serves to highlight the two characteristics of traditional European diplomacy most consistently adhered to in the rule-making processes surrounding the concert system: secrecy and hierarchy. The diplomacy leading to the 1815 settlement is replete with examples of secret agreements, the most important of which was the agreement of 3 January 1815 between Britain, France, and Austria for the purpose of forcing Prussia to yield its expansive claims on Saxon territory. The three governments each pledged 150,000 troops in order to compel Prussia to accept a compromise brokered by the other alliance members (Schroeder 1994, 535–36). Despite this considerable reversal of fortune, Prussia accepted the compromise and remained active within the concert system. Less consequential, but still an important indication of attitudes toward secrecy in diplomatic procedure, the Congress of Vienna was the scene for a substantial amount of political espionage—especially by the Austrian hosts (Nicolson 1946, 203–6). Other governments took some countermeasures, and it is doubtful how much espionage influenced the outcome of the Congress; the important point, however, is that such activity never threatened to derail diplomatic progress. Instead, it was accepted as relatively routine, and certainly not as an outrage or betrayal.

While the pursuit of prestige had been an integral part of the eighteenth-century balance of power, and one often pursued via diplomacy, the statesmen at the Congress of Vienna adopted the rule that diplomatic precedence would be accorded on the basis of seniority. By the time of the first great power conference at Aix-la-Chapelle (1818), agreement had also been reached to sign treaties alphabetically, in order of states' formal names in the French language. These rules lasted for the next century (Nicolson 1946, 219). Even by themselves, these are developments of significant importance. At the negotiations to end the Thirty Years' War, separate sessions were held at Münster and Osnabruck because Protestant princes refused as a matter of principle to participate in negotiations including the pope (Holsti 1991, 32). Settling major issues of diplomatic protocol did not result, however, in a general social leveling among European rulers. A committee report prepared during the Congress explicitly proposed a three-tiered categorization of states (Nicolson 1946, 219). Further, the Final Act of the Congress included the first use of the term "great power" in a treaty—thus consolidating and codifying terminology that had developed over the previous half-century (Craig and George 1995, 3). Hierarchy among states remained a central characteristic of European diplomacy, shaping both primary rules governing behavior and secondary rules governing social practices of rule-making. The increased formalization of the great powers as a collective club thus represented an elaboration of an existing theme, rather than a revolutionary development.

The shift in primary rules entailed by the concert system thus occurred against the backdrop of relatively stable and generally well-understood rules of sovereignty, international law, and diplomacy that decisively shaped actors' understandings about how to advocate and evaluate proposed changes in social rules and institutions. Where such procedures were in doubt, or were slightly altered to facilitate the task of preventing systemic war, these changes were often explicitly codified in the terms of treaties and joint great power declarations.

The Congress of Vienna and the Concert System, 1815–1822

The creation of a collective system for great power management of international relations was not accomplished in a grand moment of institutional design.[12] Rather, it was the product of a more extended process of rule-making, interpretation, and application. This process was contingent and path-dependent (March and Olsen 1998; Wendt 2001). It depended on the interaction of multiple simultaneously valid rule sets (Sandholtz 2008) that crucially included procedural rules for rule-making, as well as on the ongoing interpretive practice of particularly positioned agents endowed by these rules with the authority to

---

[12] Examples of this approach include Ikenberry (2001) and Koremenos, Lipson, and Snidal (2001).

perform that work (Brunnée and Toope 2010). In this section, I demonstrate how procedural rules about rule-making and the social practices of rule-making they constitute shaped outcomes over the first seven years of the great power concert.

THE VIENNA SETTLEMENT: THE CREATION OF GREAT POWER MANAGEMENT

The roots of the Vienna settlement can be located in the coalition diplomacy of 1814, conducted as the four allied powers (Britain, Prussia, Austria, and Russia) pressed their campaign to defeat Napoleon. Despite this significant common danger, maintaining the unity of the alliance challenged the parties. Aside from the problem of negotiating common war aims, Napoleon's intransigent refusal to accept moderate peace terms generated concern that France would remain a threat after the war. On 1 March 1814, the allies concluded the Treaty of Chaumont. In most ways, it was typical of contemporary alliance treaties; it "bound the allies to continue the war" while going at least some distance toward articulating common war aims, "provided new subsidy arrangements for another year's campaign if necessary, and most important, united them for twenty years in jointly maintaining peace" (Schroeder 1994, 501). This was significant because of its "assumption that France would continue to be a threat even after Napoleon's defeat" (Kissinger 2000, 131). The treaty thus had clear and limited objectives, a specific (if atypically long) duration, and was not regarded as a model for future state practice. It did, however, articulate a feeling among allied statesmen that preserving unity constituted a vital goal.

By the spring of 1814, Napoleon had been forced to abdicate his throne; the restored Bourbon monarchy under Louis XVIII had been compelled to accept both a domestic constitution and a treaty with the allied powers. As at Chaumont, much of this treaty was conventional in form: the heart of the treaty reduced France's frontiers to their pre-1790 extent, save some slight concessions (Kissinger 2000, 142). The innovation in the Treaty of Paris did not concern the perpetuation of the alliance. Instead, Article 32—a secret article—provided for a plenary meeting of "all the Powers engaged on either side of the present War" (The Treaty of Paris, as quoted in Albrecht-Carrié 1968, 30). In addition to the familiar diplomatic form of a secret article in the treaty, the notion of a general diplomatic conference to end a major war was also consistent with past practice at Westphalia and at Utrecht.

The purpose of the congress expressed in the treaty is similarly familiar, at least on the surface. It declared that "the relations from whence a system of real and permanent balance of power is to be derived shall be regulated at the

Congress upon principles determined by the Allied Powers amongst themselves" (The Treaty of Paris, as quoted in Nicolson 1946, 100). The invocation of balance of power language here is misleading, however, unless it is considered in terms of the prevailing social context. The notion of a *permanent* balance founded on rules represents a departure from the supposedly self-regulating and constantly shifting balance of power that would have served as the shared referent for these actors. Further, the notion of general rules created by a group of powerful states, acting collaboratively to secure lasting peace rather than competitively to increase their power and prestige, directly contradicted prevailing notions (to borrow Reus-Smit's terminology) about the moral purpose of the state and the norm of procedural justice. Notions of the state as a means for enhancing dynastic glory and the propriety of diplomatic focus on incidental agreements were becoming increasingly unstable.

These instabilities undoubtedly provided a window of opportunity for change in primary rules; however, the eventual outcomes were shaped by a relative island of intersubjective stability—the notion of a prestige hierarchy. In addition to the four allied powers, the Treaty of Paris was signed by France, Sweden, Portugal, and Spain—all of which had, at one point, played leading roles in European politics. While the treaty accorded invitations to the Congress to all states involved in the war, it also codified the determination of the allied powers to exercise sole discretion in designing the first general European settlement that would seek to consciously solve the problem of large-scale war. Thus, the notion of a designed and directed remedy for hegemonic war was wedded to the traditional notion of interstate hierarchy—which itself was given a twist with the emerging idea of a great power "club."

While the Congress of Vienna would ultimately be dominated by the great powers, it was attended by the entire range of European states. In addition to the signatories of the Treaty of Paris, it included delegations from thirty-two minor German states, two delegations from Naples, a papal delegation, a representative of the Ottoman Sultan, and at least three non-state groups: a Jewish delegation from Frankfurt, a group of German Catholics, and representatives of the publishing trade (Nicolson 1946, 128–32). These groups all arrived "under the impression that they would be granted the opportunity to establish their respective claims or at least to contribute their influence and opinions to the new European order" (Nicolson 1946, 135). In an interesting lapse, "none of the Big Four seems to have realized in advance to what an extent the problem of organization and procedure would create opportunities for dissension and intrigue" (Nicolson 1946, 36). If the Congress of Vienna would rewrite the rules of the game for international relations, it did so in a manner governed by procedural rules.

Initial negotiation among the four allied powers centered around the respective roles of the so-called Big Four and the plenary congress. On 20 September

1814, the allies "agreed that decisions would be taken by the 'Big Four,' but that they would be submitted to France and Spain for their approval and to the Congress for their ratification" (Kissinger 2000, 148). In a testament to the degree of consensus on the necessity of great power unity, the possibility of disagreement among them "was not even considered" (Kissinger 2000, 150). This procedural arrangement was efficiently destroyed by Talleyrand's masterly exploitation of the very secondary rules the allies relied upon to craft it. This outcome bears further emphasis: the chief negotiator for the defeated power, lacking the military means to press his claims, was able to score a major diplomatic victory. Without minimizing the degree of intellect and skill required for such a feat, Talleyrand's accomplishment was not to conjure agreement from a vacuum; rather, he adroitly deployed his audience's own rules against them. He began by insisting that the initial procedural agreement was objectionable in that it made reference to "the Allies," when the Treaty of Paris had ended the alliance (Nicolson 1946, 142). Further, the "Big Four" lacked legitimacy as a decision-making body because their own treaty had called for a congress between all parties to the war. On this view, the proper directing body for the congress could only be the eight signatories to the Treaty of Paris or the entire plenary body. He began to organize secondary states in order to press the allies on this issue (Kissinger 2000, 151–52). As Nicolson reports, "the Big Four could find no reply to this argument." Entrapped by Talleyrand's maneuver, they "agreed to tear up the protocol which they had signed" and to allow the French diplomat to participate in drafting a replacement (Nicolson 1946, 142).

Talleyrand's motives were clearly strategic. After securing his goal of French participation in procedural negotiations on an equal footing with the allied powers, "he rapidly abandoned all of his small allies" (Nicolson 1946, 143; see also Schroeder 1994, 530). Procedural rules constituted this interest, just as they had provided Talleyrand his opening with his counterparts. In the first place, rules of diplomatic prestige provided the incentive: achieving equal states would allow France a claim to participation in future deliberations. Recognition as a great power could guarantee restoration of France's diplomatic relevance. This claim to great power standing was enabled, as Kissinger has noted, by the fact that the Bourbon restoration removed the crucial justification for denying France the diplomatic status it traditionally enjoyed (Kissinger 2000, 148).

In the immediate term, though, Talleyrand achieved only marginal gains. The four allied powers continued informal discussions of the crucial remaining territorial issues surrounding Poland and Saxony, the German Committee started work under the joint leadership of Prussia and Austria, and the group of eight signatories to the Treaty of Paris appointed committees to deal with international rivers and diplomatic precedence, as well as an informal body to study abolition of the slave trade (Nicolson 1946, 144–45). France would not gain full access to Congress deliberations until January 1815, and then largely in return for assistance in securing a settlement of the Polish-Saxon question.[13]

The root of this dispute was the Convention of Kalisch, an agreement between Prussia and Russia signed on 28 February 1813, during the aftermath of Napoleon's disastrous Russian campaign. The treaty was a classic example of territorial compensation consistent with the rules of the eighteenth-century balance of power. Prussia agreed to forfeit the majority of its Polish possessions to Russia to facilitate Tsar Alexander's plan for a Polish state reconstituted as a Russian satellite; in return, Alexander pledged to support Prussian claims to Saxony as compensation (Nicolson 1946, 167). For various reasons, Britain, Austria, and France opposed this outcome; the essence of their opposition related to its impact on political equilibrium, in that it would clearly strengthen both Russia and Prussia. Schroeder makes a convincing case that, rather than a reversion to the balance of power, this crucial episode instead represented the first instance of great power condominium in operation. By December 1814, Russia had essentially consolidated its gains in Poland; "balance-of-power tactics were tried and failed" (Schroeder 1994, 537). As a result, the focus shifted to preventing similar Prussian consolidation in Saxony. Prussian threats of war were defused by a secret alliance between Britain, Austria, and France, and because Russia "controlled its junior partner and joined the others in imposing the chief costs of the settlement on it" (Schroeder 1994, 537). Russia played essentially the role that the United States would later play in the Suez Crisis with respect to its erstwhile allies (Bially Mattern 2004). Schroeder attributes Russian moderation to sincere belief in the notion of a European system for peace that the Tsar had first suggested to William Pitt in 1804 (Schroeder 1994, 559).

Several other minor institutional innovations achieved at Vienna would later prove their worth in buttressing the general principle of great power management. First, the Statistical Committee was created to facilitate territorial settlements by developing accurate estimates of populations in various contested regions (Nicolson 1946, 146). The committee was appointed on 24 December 1814 and finished its mandate by 19 January 1815, simultaneously serving as the first test of France's reintegration into the ranks of the great powers, a demonstration of the application of scientific study to managing international conflict, and an important example of diplomatic efficiency. Second, the committee for the management of international rivers served as proof of the potential for transnational regulation. Third, the informal "conference" on the abolition of the slave trade created "a Conference of Ambassadors charged with the duty of watching the execution of the several agreements come to" (Nicolson 1946, 215). While

---

[13] The first instance of France working with the other four great powers was provided by the Statistical Committee, which began work in December 1814 (Nicolson 1946, 146).

it was not particularly effective, it "was at the time a startling innovation and provided a useful precedent for the future" (Nicolson 1946, 216). Finally, "in a move of major symbolic and practical importance, all the various treaties were tied together into one great package, so that while there was no formal guarantee of the whole settlement, the violation of any treaty implicitly threatened them all" (Schroeder 1994, 573).

Napoleon's escape from Elba and subsequent final defeat at Waterloo resulted in another restoration of the Bourbon dynasty in France, as well as the Second Treaty of Paris. The treaty imposed more punitive, though not ruinous, conditions on France: primarily a 700 million franc indemnity, and a requirement to financially support 150,000 occupation troops for a period of five years (Nicolson 1946, 240–41). On the same day the peace treaty was signed, 20 November 1815, the four allies renewed the Quadruple Alliance first codified in the Treaty of Chaumont. Article Six of the renewed alliance "provided for future European reunions to promote repose, prosperity, and peace, and thus became the basis for the post-war European Concert and its conferences" (Schroeder 1994, 557). The article marks a broadening of the ambit for great power management beyond preventing hegemony. Over the next seven years, this shift would find expression in state practice.

THE CONCERT SYSTEM: THE EVOLUTION OF GREAT POWER MANAGEMENT

The shift from preventing hegemony to more robust great power management occurred more gradually than the initial creation of a great power alliance. While the idea of continued cooperation was relatively uncontroversial, at least for the limited purpose of avoiding another general war, both the particular purposes that would be served by joint action and the means by which it would be accomplished were worked out over a longer period. This period begins with the Holy Alliance of September 1815, and encompasses the initial set of great power conferences—starting at Aix-la-Chapelle in 1818 and ending at Verona in 1822. Throughout these crucial seven years, as at Vienna, statesmen were explicitly concerned with relevant secondary rules in advancing and evaluating proposals for social change.

The Holy Alliance and the Quadruple Alliance

The first crucial junction in the transition from the more modest agreements at Vienna to a more robust practice of collectively managing international crises took place in the fall of 1815, with the creation of the Holy Alliance and the renewal of the wartime Quadruple Alliance. These agreements were largely redundant; both expressed a shared sentiment that the great powers would collectively direct international relations among the European states. Why would essentially the same parties conclude two substantively similar agreements within a span of three months? I will argue that this outcome can best be explained by procedural rules for rule-making and interpretation. The renewal of the Quadruple Alliance, as well as significant alterations to the draft of the Holy Alliance, were intended and understood as attempts to found a new European political order in a manner consistent with existing secondary rules.

The Holy Alliance was signed by the monarchs of the three eastern powers, largely at the behest of the Russian Tsar. Article One of the agreement (crucially, it did not take the form of a treaty) bound its signatories to "remain united by the bonds of a true and indissoluble fraternity" (quoted in Albrecht-Carrié 1968, 33). Article Two couched this union in terms of Christianity; it committed the parties "to consider themselves all as members of one and the same Christian nation" (quoted in Albrecht-Carrié 1968, 34). However, the final draft of the agreement had been significantly altered from the Tsar's original proposal. Overall, the tenor of the changes was conservative: the revised document "called, not for a fraternal union between monarchs and their peoples, but for a paternal alliance of monarchs over their peoples" (Schroeder 1994, 559). These alterations were made at the behest of Austrian foreign minister Klemens von Metternich. Metternich also secured the removal of language calling for constitutional reforms in domestic politics, as well as criticism of the eighteenth-century balance of power (Kissinger 2000, 189). According to Nicolson, the result was achieved by Metternich's strategy of "playing adroitly upon the Tsar's increasing repudiation of his former liberal sentiments" (Nicolson 1946, 253). Nicolson's account is consistent with Metternich's attempts to constrain the Tsar, as well as other actors, throughout the period under examination. His interventions in the debates that forged great power cooperation employed two predominant analogies: criminality and disease. The success of both depended heavily on secondary rules, and will be dealt with in more detail below. The point, for now, is that the diplomacy surrounding the creation of the Holy Alliance demonstrates that social change occurs through the practice of rule-making and interpretation by rule-regarding actors.

In its altered form, the content of the Holy Alliance was consistent with the renewed Quadruple Alliance that would be signed in November 1815, and with the great power practices that would emerge in the following years. Further, the agreement was eventually acceded to by every sovereign in the system—save the British, the Ottoman Empire (for obvious religious reasons), and the Vatican. The British abstention was primarily driven by domestic political and constitutional constraints; in lieu of British accession, Castlereagh "urged the Prince Regent to subscribe to it personally, though without involving the British government" (Schroeder 1994, 559). As late as 28 September 1815, Castlereagh had written to Lord Liverpool about a "Project of Declaration" he proposed for the Congress of Vienna, "in which the sovereigns were solemnly to pledge themselves in the face of the world to preserve to their people the peace they had conquered, and to treat as a common enemy whatever Power should violate it" (quoted in Derry 1976, 187). Like his counterparts, Castlereagh remained consistently supportive of continued great power cooperation.

Despite widespread agreement on the basic substance of the Holy Alliance, it was superseded less than three months later by the renewal of the Quadruple Alliance. Further, the Holy Alliance was denigrated both by Castlereagh, who called it "a piece of sublime mysticism and nonsense" (quoted in Hinde 1981, 233) and by Metternich, who wrote that it "had no more sense or value than that of a philosophical aspiration disguised beneath the cloak of religion" (quoted in de Bertier de Sauvigny 1962, 131). These criticisms were rooted in what Nicolson called the Tsar's "fatal error of concluding the Holy Alliance in the name of the Sovereigns personally, and not in the name of their governments or peoples" (Nicolson 1946, 251). Castlereagh had proposed a declaration appended to the Final Act of the Congress of Vienna, consistent with contemporary diplomatic procedure. In the same letter to Lord Liverpool referred to above, Castlereagh reported that the Tsar rejected this idea, indicating that the agreement "ought to assume a more formal shape, and one directly personal to the sovereigns" (quoted in Derry 1976, 187). As a result, the Holy Alliance did not take the form of a treaty; it was not presented in a manner consistent with relevant secondary rules, and this seriously compromised its importance in the international system.

Not only was it superseded by the renewed Quadruple Alliance, but attempts to invoke the Holy Alliance as a legitimate basis for great power action were rare and consistently rejected. For example, in preparing instructions for Austrian representatives to a meeting on 8 October 1824 with France, Prussia, and Russia regarding domestic political difficulties in Spain, Metternich explicitly rejected a proposal to justify action in terms of the Holy Alliance. To do so, he wrote, "would be like giving sanction to a defection from, or a schism in, the grand alliance" (quoted in de Bertier de Sauvigny 1962, 132). Metternich's reasoning stressed the non-legal nature of the Holy Alliance. He asserted that "it was agreed between the monarchs and it belongs to their Cabinets neither in its origin nor in its drafting; thus not once has it been quoted by the Cabinets in any of their diplomatic exchanges (quoted in de Bertier de Sauvigny 1962, 133). The Quadruple Alliance, in its expanded form to include France after the 1818 conference at Aix-la-Chapelle, was the operative legal instrument for managing great power cooperation. This difference in the status and importance accorded to the two agreements was explicitly attributed by participants to their differing forms. While the Quadruple Alliance took a form accepted under prevailing secondary rules, the Holy Alliance did not.

In contrast to the Holy Alliance, the Quadruple Alliance was quintessentially a document of international law. It provided for the renewal of what had been a familiar alliance treaty, while at the same time introducing a significant innovation in its sixth article. The article declared that "the High Contracting Parties have agreed to renew their meetings at fixed periods . . . for the purpose of consulting upon their common interests, and for the consideration of the measures which at each of these periods shall be considered most salutary for the repose and prosperity of Nations, and for the maintenance of the peace of Europe" (quoted in Albrecht-Carrié 1968, 32). Thus, the lasting institutionalization of great power cooperation took the form of a binding treaty rather than a hortatory declaration of the type exemplified by the Holy Alliance. This development was the result of rule-governed interaction that guided agents in evaluating available proposals for change. Two substantively similar proposals were evaluated; one was accepted, and the other was not. The crucial factor in this outcome was that the form of the Holy Alliance was incompatible with secondary rules as the major players understood them.

The Conference of Aix-la-Chapelle

The various agreements of 1814–1815 served merely to set the stage for the latter phases of rule-making and interpretation surrounding the creation of the great power concern. Despite agreement that the great powers would assume responsibility for the operation of the European state system, "the issues which would be considered proper topics for international discussion were still undefined" (Kissinger 2000, 215). This issue was resolved over the course of five great power conferences held between 1818 and 1822. The first, held at Aix-la-Chapelle in the fall of 1818, was largely concerned with reintegrating France into the great power club. The "Protocol of Conference," issued on 15 November 1818, made this objective—and the rationale underlying it—clear: "assuring to France the place that belongs to her in the European system, will bind her more closely to the pacific and benevolent views in which all the Sovereigns participate, and will thus consolidate the general tranquility" (quoted in Albrecht-Carrié 1968, 44). By the conclusion of the conference, these objectives had been met. In fact, the other great powers had agreed prior to the conference to end their occupation of France, in response to the restored Bourbon government's authorization of reparation payments stipulated by the Second Treaty of Paris. However, the outcomes of the Aix-la-Chapelle conference were not achieved without substantial efforts at rule-making, interpretation, and application.

These efforts began in advance of the meeting. In June 1817, Metternich wrote to his subordinate Baron Vincent expressing a desire to significantly expand upon the institutional innovation of regular great power conferences achieved in Article Six of the Quadruple Alliance. His proposal was to dramatically heighten the profile of the permanent conference of ambassadors that had been established in Paris to provide coordination of monitoring for the implementation of peace terms. His aspiration was for it to "become the centre of a system of surveillance over those revolutionary intrigues both at home and in other countries, a surveillance which would be instructed to consider and put forward repressive measures to be adopted against them" (quoted in de Bertier de Sauvigny 1962, 137).

Castlereagh responded to this plan by arguing that "such a mode should not be a habitual occurrence and especially ought not to proceed from the ministers in conference at Paris" (quoted in Kissinger 2000, 219). The predominant interpretation of British relations with its conference partners is one of gradual estrangement forced on Castlereagh by a Cabinet and Parliament that saw the system of great power cooperation as anti-democratic and as antithetical to British policy of isolation from the political affairs of the Continent.[14] The strength of this argument is its recognition that rule-making and interpretation are multilevel social activities that governments engage in simultaneously at the international and domestic levels.[15] It is certainly true that as the threat posed by Napoleon receded, Castlereagh found himself increasingly limited by domestic constraints. Available evidence suggests a more complex picture, however.

Castlereagh wrote glowingly of the conference system on numerous occasions. Writing during the meeting at Aix-la-Chapelle, he expressed the belief that "past habits, common glory, and these occasional meetings, displays, and repledges, are among the best securities Europe now has for a durable peace" (quoted in Bartlett 1966, 201–2). He thus clearly recognized that the system required periodic practice and affirmation in order to maintain and reproduce it, consistent with the expectation of practice-turn constructivism. He was also clear about the causal mechanism linking conferences with peace. The value of the conferences was that they were capable of "giving the counsels of the Great Powers the efficiency and almost the simplicity of a single State" (Bartlett 1966, 202). Why, then, had Castlereagh objected to Metternich's proposal to strengthen precisely the features of the conference system that Castlereagh held responsible for maintaining peace, especially since strong and effective domestic opposition to Castlereagh's policy had not yet developed?[16]

---

[14] This account can be found in Kissinger (2000), as well as in Nicolson (1946).

[15] On simultaneous, multilevel state action, see Putnam (1988).

[16] Existing accounts are consistent in portraying domestic constraints as slow to develop, and as increasing in strength during the period under consideration. Early in the period, Castlereagh enjoyed considerable latitude in directing British policy.

The answer, I argue, can be found in a memorandum interpreting the treaties of 1814–1815 submitted to the conference at Aix by the British delegation. In this memo, the British argued that the First Treaty of Paris, the Final Act of the Congress of Vienna, and the Second Treaty of Paris "contain in no case engagements which have been pushed beyond the immediate objects which are made matter of regulation in the treaties themselves" (quoted in Albrecht-Carrié 1968, 37). Further, though the great powers may choose to oppose breaches of the peace, it was the British position that "the treaties do not impose, by express stipulation, the doing so as a matter of positive obligation" (quoted in Albrecht-Carrié 1968, 37). Rather, the Quadruple Alliance represented a great power agreement "to interpose their good offices for the settlement of differences subsisting between the States, to take the initiative in watching over the peace of Europe, and finally in securing the execution of its treaties in the mode most consonant to the convenience of all the parties" (quoted in Albrecht-Carrié 1968, 41–42).

The British position favored a more politically flexible system that frankly acknowledged the necessity of applying general principles only in context of particular cases. In contrast, Metternich had sought to effectively "lock in" cooperation by delegating its application in particular cases to lower-level diplomats. For my purposes, however, this substantive disagreement about institutional design is of lesser importance than the manner in which the British replied to Metternich's proposal. They did so in terms of international law, by parsing treaty obligations and showing the plan to be beyond the scope of existing treaties. The British argument was essentially an assertion of the notion that a sovereign state can be bound only by the treaties it has consented to.

Despite his genuine skepticism with regard to binding *ex ante* commitments to intervention, Castlereagh nevertheless believed in the conference system embodied in Article Six of the Quadruple Alliance, and supported convening the conference on this basis. However, in the face of resistance from the British Cabinet and, surprisingly, from Metternich, the meeting was eventually held on the much more limited basis of Article Five of the Treaty of Paris, which "provided for a review of the Allied relations with France at the end of three years" (Kissinger 2000, 221). As noted above, British resistance to Castlereagh's policy stemming both from liberal values and from considerations of national interest have been well documented. The more interesting feature of this episode is Metternich's argument for a limited mandate at Aix-la-Chapelle.

In addition to the difference between British and Austrian positions on the nature of the new international order, there was an equally significant gulf between Metternich's position and that of the more liberally inclined advisors to the Tsar, chief among whom was the Count Capo d'Istria. In preparation for the meeting at Aix, Capo d'Istria had pressed for the inclusion of lesser European states, on the grounds that restricting invitations would "only excite the jealousy of the Powers not admitted . . . and injure both monarchs and Cabinets by the want of results" (Metternich 1970, 163). As at the time of the Holy Alliance, Metternich believed the Tsar's tendency—encouraged by Capo d'Istria—to play both to liberals and to smaller states "revives by its expressions the hopes of innovators and sectaries of every kind" (Metternich 1970, 164). Indeed, the attempt to recreate the broad attendance of the Congress of Vienna was consistent with a range of Russian proposals. For example, Kissinger notes that, in the spring of 1816, Alexander had sought British support for a multilateral plan for general disarmament (Kissinger 2000, 219).

Again, the crucial issue is Metternich's method for opposing the Russian proposal to convene a broad conference at Aix in 1818. Despite his preference for a generalized system of great power intervention, Metternich was willing to adopt a more limited basis for the meeting in order to defeat a proposal he saw as likely to undermine legitimate monarchical and great power authority, and to disproportionately advance Russian power. In response to Capo d'Istria, he argued that any potential objection by secondary states to a great power conference was without proper legal basis. To support this contention, he noted that "the Five Courts which are assembled at Aix are not only invited there, but by the treaty of November 20, 1815 [the Second Treaty of Paris], they are bound to come. All the European Courts have by their consent" in the Final Act of the Congress of Vienna "acknowledged and confirmed this treaty and all its stipulations" (Metternich 1970, 164). Metternich went on to argue that the text of the treaty not only restricted participation to the members of the Quadruple Alliance plus France, but that it also demanded that the parties limit their agenda to a review of matters pertaining to the execution of the terms of peace with France (Metternich 1970, 164). Metternich was not completely successful in this regard. The conference also saw at least informal discussion of German issues, the slave trade, the Barbary pirates, and the status of Spain's rebellious colonies; nevertheless, he did achieve his goal of removing the most objectional Russian proposals from the table (Hinde 1981, 248).

Convening the Aix conference on the basis of the Second Treaty of Paris rather than the renewed Quadruple Alliance was an attempt on Metternich's part to invoke secondary rules in order to defeat Russia's efforts to convene the conference on grounds amenable both to broader participation and a more ambitious agenda. Both sides sought to leverage secondary rules to advance their goals, and also to evaluate and respond to alternative proposals. Metternich's actions in this instance serve to highlight an important feature of my argument. Social practices of rule-making and interpretation do not require, and indeed perhaps rarely involve, purely altruistic or principled actors. Participants are free to advance self-interested proposals, as well as to make arguments that could potentially be seen as inconsistent with their own past positions. The crucial characteristic of these practices of rule-making is that agents evaluate proposals on the basis of a relatively stable set of mutually accepted rules for doing so—even if they sometimes do so on the basis of mixed, or even completely cynical, motives. Metternich's conduct in this episode also highlights the importance actors placed on a seemingly esoteric procedural point—whether the Aix conference would be convened on the basis of the Second Treaty of Paris or the Quadruple Alliance. In contrast to rationalist theories and existing constructivist work, a constructivist account of the kind I advance offers theoretically grounded reasons for the attention paid by actors to such matters and for the ways these procedural issues shaped outcomes.

The third important instance of rule-making and interpretation surrounding the great power conference at Aix-la-Chapelle pertains to the final compromise whereby France was reinstated as a great power in good standing. Once again, issues of form and procedure play an important role in shaping the outcome. The parties concluded a secret renewal of the Quadruple Alliance, as well as a public protocol that extended to France an invitation to future meetings called for by Article Six (Kissinger 2000, 223). In Castlereagh's words, the idea was "to give France her concert, but to keep our security" (quoted in Hinde 1981, 248). The first noteworthy feature of the agreement was that it returned to Article Six of the Quadruple Alliance as the basis for future great power conferences—highlighting the anomalous nature of the meeting at Aix, which had been convened on the basis of the Treaty of Paris. However, unlike the regular meetings that had been envisioned in 1815, emerging doubts in the British Cabinet required Castlereagh to secure an agreement that meetings "shall be special, namely that they shall arise out of the occasion and be agreed upon by the Courts at the time" (quoted in Bartlett 1966, 211). While the foreign policy debate in Britain represents a potential site of analysis for social practices of rule-making at the domestic level, the relevant structure of secondary rules would clearly have been more complex and somewhat divergent from its international analogue. For this reason, I will merely note here the potential for the future study of social practices of rule-making in varying social contexts. Questions of potential interaction effects between processes of rule-making at various levels of analysis also offer fertile ground for further inquiry.

In this case, however, the interaction appears reasonably straightforward. Rather than reflecting weakness in the consensus regarding great power management by conference, the accommodation of Castlereagh's domestic political constraints more accurately reflects a robust intersubjective common denominator among relevant actors at the international level. This conclusion is suggested by the fact that the continental powers, especially Metternich's Austria, consistently sought British participation in the conference system, despite the broadening of domestic opposition. Castlereagh and his counterparts were sufficiently confident in their mutual commitment to settling disputes via conference that they felt able to forego the reassurance of a specific legal commitment to regular meetings. The successful reintegration of France and the general lack of serious disagreement at Aix-la-Chapelle likely heightened this confidence. While this conclusion is circumstantial, the interpretation it is based on has the advantage of consistency with the parties' subsequent practice.

Beyond the abandonment of periodic meetings, the other significant difference between the Quadruple Alliance and the agreement at Aix-la-Chapelle was that the latter did not take the form of a treaty. The parties explicitly rejected the notion of expanding the Quadruple Alliance to include France. Metternich, in a diplomatic report describing the proceedings, notes that expanding the alliance was impossible because "there is no possibility of establishing a *casus foederis* between the five Courts" (Metternich 1970, 186). That is, there was no external party against which the five great powers could form a defensive alliance that would be triggered under specified conditions. An alliance treaty, as understood by these actors, was therefore inappropriate to the circumstances they faced in 1818. Rather than altering the shared understanding with regard to the possible purposes of an alliance treaty (which would have required alteration of secondary rules of diplomacy and international law), the response was to pursue an agreement that was consistent with legal and diplomatic rules. Metternich described this as "a diplomatic agreement (other than a treaty) between the five Courts, having for its one definite end the maintenance of the general peace" (Metternich 1970, 186). Thus, rules of international law acted to restrict the potential forms of cooperation available to the great powers.

Though the great powers claimed for themselves broad authority to direct the political affairs of the European state system, these powers were not without limit, and were not established without attempts to acknowledge the legitimate rights and prerogatives of Europe's secondary and minor powers—or without efforts to secure their acquiescence, if not their consent. Metternich himself noted that the diplomatic agreement reached at Aix-la-Chapelle was potentially troubling to minor states concerned for their sovereignty. In response, he detailed several measures designed to "deprive it of any tendency to disturb the other Courts of Europe" (Metternich 1970, 186). These proposals are reflected in the diplomatic protocol issued at the conclusion of the conference. Its second article establishes that the union of great powers "can have no other object than the maintenance of peace founded on sacred respect for the engagements set out in the treaties" (quoted in de Bertier de Sauvigny 1962, 140). Beyond this expression of support for the fundamental principle of *pacta sunt servanda*, the protocol established more concrete commitments intended to reassure other states. In particular, the protocol's fourth article pledged "that in the event of these meetings having as their object matters specially bound up with the interests of the other European States, they shall only be held in response to a formal invitation on the part of such states as are concerned in the aforesaid matters and on the express condition that such states be allowed to participate in them either directly or through their plenipotentiaries" (quoted in de Bertier de Sauvigny 1962, 140). As will become evident in the analysis of later conferences at Troppau and Laibach, this concession did not amount to a dramatic restriction of great power autonomy. Instead, it was manipulated to further great power agendas—but this is immaterial to my argument here that the great powers were constrained by procedural rules of diplomacy, international law, and sovereignty that accorded standing to the secondary powers, thereby legitimizing at least to some extent their participation in establishing the rules of the international system.

Attempts to assuage minor states extended beyond the text of the protocol. Austrian diplomat Friedrich Gentz, Metternich's confidant, wrote an extended memo to a minor nobleman, Prince Souzo, in which he sought to present the actions of the great powers in a positive light. He argued that, if not for the system of great power cooperation, its members "would enter into new political combinations" that "would bring us to a general war" (Metternich 1970, 191). In addition to the specter of systemic war, Gentz invoked what was to become one of Metternich's favored rhetorical devices—the likening of revolution to illness or disease. Gentz asserted that "all European countries, without exception, are tormented by a burning fever" and that without determined efforts to oppose revolutionaries, "we should all be carried away in a very few years" (Metternich 1970, 194). In military terms, it is unlikely that any combination of secondary powers could have forced the great powers to abandon their plans. The fact that they devoted diplomatic resources to securing the consent of secondary states is therefore indicative of rule-oriented social activity.

Finally, in addition to their impact on the diplomatic agreements reached at Aix-la-Chapelle and on the efforts of great powers to secure the acquiescence of small states, secondary rules also exercised an influence on the agreements that were not reached. Two such proposals will be considered here. The first is an ambitious Russian proposal, which Tsar Alexander described as "a common league guaranteeing to each other the existing order of things in thrones as well as in territories, all being bound to march, if requisite, against the first power that offended either by her ambitions or by her revolutionary transgressions" (quoted in Bartlett 1966, 209). The proposal was officially made to the conference in an 8 October 1818 memo (Kissinger 2000, 23). The essence of the proposal was not only a collective security system, but also a compact committing the great powers to oppose revolution in any European state.

Kissinger notes that Castlereagh "rejected the principle on which the Russian memorandum was based as impractical and as a violation of the doctrine of non-interference" (Kissinger 2000, 226). Castlereagh's objection, as with Metternich's earlier plan to empower the Paris Conference of Ministers, was not to intervention but rather to a legally binding *ex ante* commitment. His preference was for a system of diplomatic consultation in which intervention would be considered on a case-by-case basis (Kissinger 2000, 227). This distinction is evident in Castlereagh's contrast of the aspirational Holy Alliance, which he likened to the Tsar's proposed Treaty of Guarantee, with binding treaties. While he could accept a declaration of the kind the Tsar supported as a description of state policy, at least under some circumstances, casting the same policy as a legal commitment seemed both imprudent and counter to the doctrine of nonintervention derived from the institution of sovereignty. Despite his general support of the Tsar's principle, Metternich replied to the proposal in a manner very like Castlereagh. His response had two components. First, he argued that a new document would run the risk of undermining the Holy Alliance, Alexander's prized creation. While the appeal here was at least partially directed to the Tsar's vanity, the fact that he was sufficiently committed to the Holy Alliance that such an appeal seemed to Metternich likely to work suggests that such arguments were regarded as meaningful. Second, Kissinger notes that Metternich argued that "the Treaty of Chaumont still existed in full force because the lapsing of clauses contingent on the war with France could not affect the permanent provisions" that committed the great powers to defend each other (Kissinger 2000, 226). As a result, the proposal for a treaty of guarantee was redundant.

The most significant aspect of this episode is that despite different interests—Castlereagh's in avoiding a legal commitment to reactionary intervention, and Metternich's in restraining Russian freedom of action—the Tsar's chief counterparts reacted in virtually the same manner. Further, this response was expressed not in terms of the balance of power or of deterrence, but rather in the language of international law. Actors engaged in evaluating a proposal in terms of preexisting rules that provided guidance in making just this sort of evaluation. The end result in this case was that the Tsar withdrew his proposal.

The second failed proposal considered here is a more limited treaty of guarantee advanced by Prussia in the closing days of the conference. While it contained territorial guarantees not only for the great powers but also for the Netherlands and the German Confederation, it omitted the troublesome notion of a commitment to reactionary intervention. This alteration addressed both British domestic concerns about the anti-democratic nature of great power cooperation and Austrian fears of Russian aggrandizement. Nevertheless, the proposal failed. While Metternich lent it his support, he was unable to find a compromise that allowed Britain to "express its moral approval without undertaking the obligatory commitments of the treaty" (Kissinger 2000, 230). The case of the Prussian guarantee thus provides another instance in which attempts to guarantee peace were limited by the procedural rules that governed the great powers' practices of rule-making and interpretation. Britain had sought to strengthen both the Netherlands and the German states as essential components in its plan to constrain any potential French drive for hegemony, and had displayed no disposition toward making or supporting territorial claims at the expense of its fellow great powers. Despite the congruence between basic British security interests and the substance of the Prussian proposal, considerations of form rendered it unpalatable.

Failure to reach agreement for reasons of form and procedure, despite broad agreement on the proper policy, is emblematic of the meeting at Aix-la-Chapelle. While rehabilitating France proved unproblematic, attempts at institutional innovation—beyond support for further conferences—were less successful. This result is consistent with my argument. The most important disagreements were not over whether joint great power management of the international system were appropriate; they were not even over whether such management included the right to intervene jointly in other states' domestic affairs. Rather, agreement foundered over considerations of form, as well as over the circumstances in which intervention was justifiable. These issues—what constitutes the form of a legitimate rule for behavior, who is entitled to make such rules, and the proper procedure for determining whether or not case X falls under the scope of rule Y—are precisely the kinds of problems that secondary rules are designed to solve. The fact that they were regarded as important issues by relevant actors engaging in evaluating proposals for institutional change lends crucial empirical support to my theoretical argument.

The Conferences of Troppau and Laibach

The first joint intervention was conducted by the great powers almost two years after their gathering at Aix-la-Chapelle, in response to the outbreak of revolution in Naples. Because the prior conference had been inconclusive with respect to a policy on intervention, the response to the Neapolitan revolt was vigorously contested; the two conferences held on this matter, at Troppau in late 1820 and at Laibach in early 1821, were clear cases of actors engaging in practices of rule-making, interpretation, and application.

The Neapolitan revolt broke out on 2 July 1820. After achieving initial success, the rebels obligated King Ferdinand to accept a constitution closely modeled on the extremely liberal document imposed on the Spanish king in March 1820 (Schroeder 1994, 608). This apparent revolutionary contagion, coupled with the existence of a treaty barring Naples from instituting such domestic changes without consulting Austria (Kissinger 2000, 251), helps to account for the fact of intervention in Naples and not in Spain.

There was no serious disagreement among the great powers over the notion of suppressing the rebellion. As in 1815 and 1818, the crucial issues surrounded the justificatory basis for intervention. Castlereagh, conversing with a Russian diplomat, argued that "the revolution should be treated as a special rather than a general question, as an Italian question rather than as an European, and consequently in the sphere of Austria rather than of the Alliance" (quoted in Kissinger 2000, 251). The existence of the Neapolitan treaty obligation to consult Austria before instituting domestic constitutional reforms allowed Castlereagh to cast the situation in more limited terms, in an attempt to forestall a renewed attempt on the part of the Continental powers to establish a binding general commitment to intervention. On 16 September 1820, Castlereagh disclosed his reasoning in a letter to his half-brother, Sir Charles Stuart. He acknowledged that "if the existing danger arose from any obvious infractions of our treaties, an extraordinary reunion of sovereigns and their cabinets would be a matter of obvious policy" (quoted in Derry 1976, 203). Absent such a condition, there was no basis for a general conference.

As a result, the Troppau conference began on 20 October 1820, with Britain and France present only as observers (Kissinger 2000, 259). Further, the Prussian king would not arrive until 7 November, a decision indicative of his general disengagement from the conference (Kissinger 2000, 268). Of the five great powers, only Austria and Russia participated enthusiastically in the meeting. Moreover, existing historical accounts agree that Metternich was a dominant figure throughout the Troppau and Laibach conferences, effectively controlling both the agenda and the results.[17] The outcomes depended, in important part, on his ability to skillfully deploy arguments that drew upon relevant secondary rules.

The chief obstacle in Metternich's path, once again, was Capo d'Istria. By 2 November 1820, an agreement had begun to take shape. A Russian memo submitted on this date "laid down three principles which justified the intervention of the Alliance: that a revolution automatically excluded the affected power from the Alliance; that the Alliance had a right to take the requisite measures to prevent the epidemic from spreading and to restore the affected nations to the bosom of the Alliance; but that these measures could not affect the territorial arrangements of the treaties of 1814–15" (Kissinger 2000, 261). Note the broad nature of this draft—it explicitly contemplated intervention in another great power, and it repudiated the eighteenth-century practice of territorial adjustments as a means of preserving the balance of power. The problem for Metternich was Capo d'Istria's interpretation of how this policy required the great powers to act with respect to the Neapolitan revolt. He argued that

---

[17] See Kissinger (2000), de Bertier de Sauvigny (1962), and Schroeder (1994).

intervention was justifiable only after the failure of moral suasion and after the great powers had designed institutions for Naples that had an essentially liberal-internationalist character (Kissinger 2000, 262).

Metternich dismissed this interpretation by appeal to the fundamental rule of sovereignty and the 1818 Aix-la-Chapelle Protocol, which required both the invitation and participation of affected secondary states. By 6 November 1820, Metternich was able to provide his emperor with a text declaring support for his position, entitled "Principles of the Policy of Intervention." Rather than a set-tlement negotiated with revolutionaries, this document made clear that "what the King in his wisdom considers satisfactory for the interests of the kingdom, and consequently satisfactory to the sound part of the nation, will be taken as the legal basis of the order to be established in the King of Naples" (Metternich 1970, 444). The rationale here rests on an assessment of the competence of the king as an actor entitled to create rules for Naples and in the international system, capacities not shared by the revolutionaries. The issue of fitness to de-cide is explicitly invoked via the reference to "the sound part of the nation" and in the reference to a proper legal basis for a new domestic order.

The Troppau conference produced a common diplomatic circular agreed on by the governments of Austria, Russia, and Prussia. The text of this document, dated 8 December 1820, closely echoes the Russian draft of 2 November, in that it asserts a joint right of intervention. This right is justified in terms of dangers posed by revolutionaries that "endeavor to spread to neighbouring countries the misfortunes which they had brought upon themselves" (Metternich 1970, 445). The circular continues by asserting that revolutions "are an evident viola-tion of contract" in that their spread denies legitimate governments the rightful enjoyment of their authority (Metternich 1970, 445). As at Aix-la-Chapelle, the language employed in the document clearly reflects an attempt to persuade a broader audience of relevant opinion, at least among the rulers of Europe's sec-ondary states. In this light, the circular notes the invitation of King Ferdinand to a follow-up conference at Laibach, casting it as "a step which would free the will of his Majesty from every outward constraint, and put the King in the posi-tion of a mediator between his deluded and erring subjects and the States whose peace was threatened by them" (Metternich 1970, 446). Once again, we see the discourse of incapacity stemming from illness (in this case, delusion). Finally, it casts the Troppau agreement as "in perfect harmony with the agreements for-merly concluded," namely at Vienna and at Aix-la-Chapelle.

These public arguments are consistent with those Metternich made privately in a memo to Tsar Alexander on 15 December 1820. In attempting to impress upon the Tsar the nature of the revolutionary threat, he referred to "one of the most active and at the same time most dangerous instruments used by the revolutionists of all countries . . . the secret societies, a real power, all the more dangerous as it works in the dark, undermining all parts of the social body, and depositing everywhere the seeds of a moral gangrene" (Metternich 1970, 464). Not only were the aims of the revolutionaries wrong and dangerous, Metternich again returned to the theme of proper authority. He insisted that "even real good should be done only by those who unite to the right of authority the means of enforcing it" (Metternich 1970, 471). Accordingly, it was imperative not to acknowledge any actor other than a legitimate government as a rightful participant in political affairs. Intervention could thus be justified as necessary to ensure the proper, legitimate operation of a political system with operative rules for rulemaking and interpretation. To allow the destruction of legitimate governments would be to undermine existing mechanisms for political change.

The interpretation embodied in the Troppau agreement remained sharply at odds with that of the British government. Castlereagh was particularly concerned with the assertion the Troppau agreement was consistent with the agreements reached at Vienna and Aix. This concern was sufficient to prompt him to take the public step of issuing his own diplomatic circular, dated 19 January 1821. In this document, Castlereagh broke openly with his erstwhile alliance partners. He denounced the agreement as "in direct repugnance to the fundamental Laws of this Country," as well as in violation of international law (quoted in Albrecht-Carrié 1968, 49). Particularly, he maintained his position that intervention was justifiable only "where a state's immediate security, or essential interests, are seriously endangered by the internal transactions of another state" (quoted in Derry 1976, 208). Further, he noted a problem of moral hazard. A consistent doctrine of intervention may induce leaders not to "accommodate themselves with good faith and before it is too late by some prudent change of system to the exigencies of their particular position" (quoted in Bartlett 1966, 220). Castlereagh's reply focused on the criteria for deciding whether a given revolution posed a genuine threat to other states and on whether a doctrine of intervention was an effective means of addressing such a threat.

These arguments failed to persuade the continental powers. I argue that this is unsurprising, for the reason that they hinged on determinations of fact. Such issues are vital to rule interpretation and application, and are thus governed by the secondary rules that constitute practices of rule-making in particular contexts. But under international law (then as now), the ultimate authority to make factual determinations of threat is vested with individual states in a relatively unconstrained manner.[18] Unfortunately for Castlereagh, the great power

---

[18] In the modern system, this right is somewhat modified by the Charter of the United Nations, which authorizes the Security Council to determine the existence of threats to international peace and security; nevertheless, this capacity limits but does not extinguish state capacity provided by the customary international law of self-defense and the customary law of state responsibility.

settlement had not established either common criteria or procedures for determining when a revolution posed a general European danger. Left without rules
he could appeal to, Castlereagh had no option other than to refuse British participation in a joint intervention in this particular case.

Encouraged by promises of great power support, King Ferdinand repudiated
the liberal constitution of 1820 immediately after departing for the conference
at Laibach (Schroeder 1994, 611–12). This act provided the necessary pretext
to make a great power intervention consistent with the restraints adopted at Aix-
la-Chapelle as a fig leaf acknowledging the sovereign rights of secondary states.
King Ferdinand, however, would not prove completely pliable. Freed from immediate danger, he reverted to a rigidly reactionary stance that demonstrated the
wisdom of Castlereagh's concerns about moral hazard. Interestingly, Metternich
preferred to establish "the principle of a qualified monarchy, thus excluding both
despotism and the representative system" (Metternich 1970, 516). Though King
Ferdinand's preferences differed, he was ultimately dependent on Austrian military support for the restoration of his throne and had no choice but to acquiesce to Metternich's wishes. The significance of this episode is that it suggests
an important degree of nuance in Metternich's thinking. While he was not completely opposed to domestic reforms, he regarded it as vital that such reforms
be established with the consent of legitimate governments, who were the only
actors entitled to approve such changes. This suggests a rule-regarding actor,
rather than a blindly reactionary ideologue, and thus lends further support to
my theoretical argument.

As at Troppau, Metternich employed a diplomatic dispatch in order to press
his case in the various European capitals. In this document, dated 12 May 1821,
he casts the great powers as supporting actors that "content themselves with
seconding by their most ardent wishes the measures adopted by this sovereign
for the reconstruction of his Government, and the securing, by good laws and
wise institutions, the real interests of his subjects and the constant prosperity of
his kingdom" (Metternich 1970, 544). His argument returns again to the notion
of proper legal standing and the issue of determining capacity to participate in
practices of rule-making and interpretation, at both the domestic and the international levels. The circular asserts that "useful or necessary changes in the
legislation and administration of States should emanate from the free will, the
thoughtful and enlightened conviction of those to whom God has given the responsibility of power" (Metternich 1970, 545). This secondary rule is the basis
on which the great powers "regard as legally void and unauthorized according to
the principles which constitute the public law of Europe all pretended reforms
effected by revolt and open force" (Metternich 1970, 546).

The Laibach circular thus makes explicit a second crucial dimension to the
practices of rule-making and interpretation associated with the creation of great

power management. In addition to an attempt to persuade his fellow statesmen, Metternich understood his actions as a defense of existing secondary rules, especially at the domestic level, against an attempt by revolutionaries to gain standing in (and thus influence over) processes of rule-making. Understanding the role of secondary rules is therefore critical not only to understanding how Metternich attempted to persuade his counterparts to engage in the suppression of revolutions, but also to understanding the *source* of his anti-revolutionary stance. Failure to oppose revolution elsewhere ran the risk of giving the appearance of weakness in the face of domestic revolt—the constant specter of which hung over an ethnically polyglot Austrian Empire.

The Conference of Verona

Initially the conference at Verona in the autumn of 1822 was intended to review the results of the allied operation, initiated at Laibach, to suppress the Neapolitan and Piedmontese rebellions. However, these plans were altered by the success of the Italian interventions, as well as by crises in Greece and Spain. Whereas the conferences at Troppau and Laibach resulted in interventions by the allied powers, the diplomacy associated with the Verona conference did not. Despite the differing result, the conference at Verona furnishes proof that new practices of great power management had become stabilized.

Perhaps the most striking aspect of the resolution to the Greek crisis was that Metternich, Castlereagh, and Alexander all essentially "played by the rules," despite factors that suggest any of them may well have acted differently. The precedent set at Troppau and Laibach made great power intervention in other states a real option—and one that Metternich, in this case, wanted very much to avoid. Rather than denying the importance of the new great power practices, or seeking to abolish them, Metternich instead relied centrally on them by engaging in an argument that asserted essentially that Russia was playing the new game improperly. Castlereagh found, in the Greek revolt, an opportunity to return to the conference system that he had repudiated publicly for its interventions in Italy. The mere fact that he sought to oppose Russian intervention in the new language of great power management, rather than in the prior language of balance of power, is indicative of a relatively stabilized social practice. Deepening domestic opposition to the conference system, and his own objections to a more legally binding form of great power management, were insufficient to prevent Castlereagh from responding to the Greek crisis in terms of what the agreed-upon principles of great power management did (and did not) legitimate. Further, Alexander had strong reasons to back an intervention. Leaving aside any potential gains from a successful war, Russia possessed valid treaty claims against the Ottoman Empire stemming from its response to the revolt. Nevertheless, Alexander consistently acknowledged the need for an allied endorsement of his position and ultimately accepted a diplomatic solution that fell short of his initial demands. Finally, the Greek revolt presented an interesting case in that one of the main players—the Ottoman Empire—was not a part of, or at least an equal member in, the European state system.[19] Accordingly, it was at least possible for the great powers to decide either that: (1) the practice of great power management was inapplicable in this case, allowing Russia to proceed as it wished; or (2) the principles of the Holy Alliance required the Christian powers to collectively defend the Christian Greeks. Instead, they opted to extend the European system and to apply their existing social practice to a new situation.

The Greek revolt was not a trivial case; the great powers had strong differences, and the stakes were high—a war between Russia and the Ottoman Empire was regarded by the players as a major threat. Yet the crisis did not cause the breakdown of the new practice of great power management. This suggests that it was broadly regarded as legitimate—even by Russia, whose claims were partially rejected by its peers, and by Britain, which had previously rejected an outcome of essentially the same practice. In the following, I detail major episodes of rule-making and interpretation in the resolution of the Greek crisis, paying particular attention to the role of secondary rules in guiding actors' decisions. For the most part, the actors were engaged in a dispute over whether this particular case was one that warranted joint intervention. In Hart's terms, the problem was not one of recognizing a valid rule or of changing an existing rule—rather, the Greek revolt presented, and was treated as, a problem of adjudication.

March 1821 saw the initial outbreak of political violence in the Ottoman province of Moldavia. The great powers, still gathered at Laibach, acted swiftly and unanimously; "Alexander promptly and publicly condemned the rebels and gave his consent to a Turkish occupation of the Principalities as required by the Treaty of Bucharest" (Schroeder 1994, 616). This was reassuring, since the revolt was led by Ypsilanti (a former aide to the Tsar) (Hinde 1981, 248), and because a faction within the Russian government led by Capo d'Istria favored the establishment of a Greek state. Ottoman troops ended the Moldavian insurrection relatively easily; however, "Turkish troops remained in occupation of the Principalities, while the Sultan refused to nominate new hospodars to replace the old ones compromised in the revolt—violating Russian treaty rights in both instances" (Schroeder 1994, 617). The outbreak of a second revolt in Greece escalated tensions further. The Greek revolt was more successful than

[19] Edward Keene argues, persuasively, that the treatment of Muslim states (including the Ottoman Empire) declined in the early nineteenth century; such states were increasingly relegated to unequal status in the international system, in large part due to an emerging discourse that differentiated between states and populations on the basis of their conformity or nonconformity with "civilized"—or, rather, European—norms and standards. See Keene (2007) and Gong (1984).

the Moldavian one, and thus generated more intense reprisals; these included attacks on Orthodox churches and culminated with a massacre of Greeks in Constantinople on Easter Sunday, 1821 (Kissinger, 290). The result was a diplomatic stalemate, with Russia demanding a withdrawal of Ottoman troops from Moldavia, as well as further concessions on the protection of Christians under Turkish rule, and the Ottoman government asserting its sovereignty.

Metternich's initial reaction, just as with the Troppau conference, was to write a memo to the Tsar. The aim of the Laibach memo was to buy time, and to delay any possible unilateral Russian intervention by invoking Russian commitment to the conference system itself. His primary argument was that "the transactions at Laybach should be regarded by the two Courts as an unchangeable basis until the meeting of the Cabinets in 1822" (Metternich 1970, 539). The principle *pacta sunt servanda* thus provided Metternich a way of establishing a presumption against unilateral action. He also sought to commit the Tsar to a common process of consultation; to "judge any fortuitous case according to the principles which were applied at Laybach in similar cases" and "to put off any explanations with other Courts until after an exchange of communications . . . rather than run the risk of differing in their explanations or their conduct" (Metternich 1970, 539). The obvious contrast is the failure of Castlereagh's argument that intervention in Naples was factually unwarranted; rather than leave such a determination with respect to the Ottoman case in the hands of the Tsar, Metternich sought to establish common rules and processes of adjudication for determining whether any further events warranted great power intervention. Having achieved a more general statement of the principle at Troppau and Laibach, Metternich sought now to create a framework to codify its application in future cases. Such a strategy had been unavailable to Castlereagh precisely because he opposed a general principle of intervention. Despite their significance as an attempt to increase the formalization of great power management by more explicitly codifying relevant secondary rules, Metternich's efforts were not a sufficient resolution to the crisis.

The true challenge for the allies, pursued in coordination by Metternich and Castlereagh, was twofold. First, the plan was to firmly commit the Tsar to a policy that would foreswear the pursuit of an independent Greek state. Second, the two statesmen sought to resolve the crisis within the institutional framework of the alliance and without a war that could both risk the internal cohesion of the Ottoman Empire and significantly strengthen Russia's position in the Balkans and eastern Mediterranean. Both goals entailed deflecting Russian requests for allied endorsement of intervention, in the event that the Ottoman Empire continued to refuse strong Russian demands.

Three primary arguments were used to achieve these aims. The first denied the existence of a fundamental similarity between the Italian and Greek cases, by pointing out that the Italian case involved intervention in defense of a legitimate government. In contrast, Russia was proposing to back a revolution against a le-gitimate government. According to Derry, "Castlereagh advised that the Powers would be well advised to support the Turks as the rightful government, while extending their protection to the Greeks once order had been restored" (Derry 1976, 213).

While Castlereagh framed his appeals to the Tsar largely in terms of the le-gitimate claims of the Ottoman government, Metternich relied principally on a related argument about the dangers of appearing to endorse a revolution. These complementary lines of argumentation were not accidental; they were coordinated at a meeting between Metternich and Castlereagh in Hanover, in October 1821 (Bartlett 1966, 226). In a letter to Lebzeltern dated 22 January 1822, his representative in St. Petersburg, Metternich provided a clear indica-tion of his views to be communicated as the Austrian position. He first argued that "the revolt of the Greeks, however different might be its long-standing and permanent causes from the revolutions which the Grand Alliance was called upon to combat, nevertheless directly originated in the plots of the disorgan-ized faction which menaces all thrones and all institutions" (Metternich 1970, 601). Metternich then cast doubt on the continued existence of the alliance in the event of a unilateral Russian war, and made the further claim that even if the alliance went to war with Russia it "would cease to be formidable in the eyes of the revolutionists when the forces of several of the Powers were employed in the East" (Metternich 1970, 603).

Notably, both types of argument resisted the Russian position by making use of secondary rules, particularly with respect to the relative standing or le-gitimacy of the Greek rebels as compared with the Ottoman government. This broader social rule about the nature of actors entitled to govern, and to partic-ipate in the international system, was crucial in guiding the responses of actors called upon to determine whether or not this particular case fit the criteria for joint intervention.

The same letter to Lebzeltern also contains the crucial distinction that pro-vided both Metternich and Alexander, as well as the Ottomans, with an accept-able escape from the crisis. Metternich acknowledged that, while "the Greeks, as rebels, had no title to the favor of the Emperor of Russia," it was true that "these same Greeks, as persecuted Christians, placed in certain relations with Russia by virtue of existing treaties, were in some sort justified in invoking the support of that monarch" (Metternich 1970, 605–6). The *basis* of the Greek appeal to Russia was of vital importance in this formulation, and it determined the extent of the claims that were warranted. While Metternich would not support an independent Greek state or the imposition of new Russian rights in protecting Christian subjects of the Ottoman Empire, he was prepared to back more modest Russian demands pertaining to the enforcement of existing treaties.

By March 1822, Alexander had dispatched a diplomat, Tatistscheff, to Vienna for the purpose of achieving an agreement with Metternich. On 8 March, Tatistscheff wrote to Metternich to confirm the details of a settlement based closely on the compromise laid out in the letter to Lebzeltern. The agreement called on the Ottomans to begin by "evacuating entirely and without delay the principalities of Wallachia and Moldavia," the occupation of which violated de-militarization provisions of the Treaty of Bucharest, and by nominating new hospodars, or local vassals (Metternich 1970, 609). Tatistscheff, writing again on 14 March, agreed that the goal for the negotiation was to end the violence in the provinces and "to secure their tranquil possession to the Ottoman Porte" (Metternich 1970, 610). This acknowledgment amounted to abandonment of a Greek state as a Russian policy objective, as well as a retreat from the threat of war.

On 19 April 1822, Metternich again wrote to the Tsar, providing a review of the negotiations as well as arguments about how to proceed. The memo upholds the requirement that treaties be observed, conceding that "Russia has the undoubted right of requiring the strict fulfilment of all the stipulations contained in her different treaties and conventions with the Porte" (Metternich 1970, 612). The document also provides information about the Ottoman response. Metternich reminds the Tsar that the Ottoman government "invariably recognized the duty of executing existing treaties and conventions, and has openly declared its wish to conform to them; but it has added to these declarations restrictions founded on pretended difficulties either temporary or local—restrictions which have up to this time made all reconciliation impossible" (Metternich 1970, 612). He then expressed the allied position in more general terms: "the respect due to treaties is the basis of public right in Europe, and the Porte, unless it wishes to renounce the position it has hitherto occupied among the European Powers, cannot hesitate for a moment to recognize this principle" (Metternich 1970, 614).

The Ottoman Empire's claims for special consideration were not sufficient to absolve it of its treaty obligations, but neither was this an absolute endorsement of Russia's prior strong demands. Metternich distinguished between "strict rights" and questions of "general interest." Demands for new rights to supervise treatment of Christians fell into the latter category; on this score, Metternich made clear that a strong position was impermissible. He insisted that "any ideas which the Cabinets may bring forward concerning the future condition of the Greeks, must be restricted to subjects of legislation and administration, and not touch on the fundamental relations between the Turkish Government and its Christian subjects" (Metternich 1970, 614). He recommended, particularly, that the powers make such recommendations only on the explicit basis of the parties' mutual interest in "a solid and permanent peace" (Metternich 1970, 615). For this to be achieved, Metternich argued, "it is above all indispensable that the Ottoman Government should proceed to an act of real amnesty, and that it should cause it to be observed and executed in its full extent. It is equally indispensable that the insurgents should submit to this act" (Metternich 1970, 615). By 30 May 1822, Metternich was able to report to Emperor Francis that "the evacuation of the Principalities has made such an impression . . . that his Majesty [Tsar Alexander] is ready to re-establish diplomatic relations with the Divan immediately" (Metternich 1970, 626).

After this point, the dispute between the great powers was essentially re-solved, leaving only negotiation with the Ottoman Empire over implementation of the agreement. Schroeder argues that credit for the peaceful resolution of the Greek crisis belongs to Alexander, because "he insisted on getting a European mandate for action like Austria's in Naples" (Schroeder 1994, 620). To an extent this is true; however, Alexander's decision was not made in a vacuum. As I have shown, the Greek crisis was resolved in the context of an increasingly stabilized social practice of great power management. A potential crisis between the great powers was resolved by resort to arguments that sought to interpret and apply relevant rules on the basis of agreed-upon procedures for doing so. The outcome was regarded as sufficiently legitimate that Alexander was convinced to forgo both a potential opportunity to advance key Russian interests in the Balkans and the Mediterranean, and a chance to act as a champion for Greek Christians. This decision is best explained by a practice-based theory that understands it in its social context, and that also explains the behavior of the other actors involved.

Just as a peaceful resolution to the Greek crisis was being worked out, in April 1822, a simmering situation in Spain acquired new urgency when King Ferdinand VII requested great power assistance. After being restored to the Spanish throne by the allies as part of the campaign against Napoleon, Ferdinand had insisted on waging military campaigns to maintain Spain's colonies in the Americas. These unpopular adventures eventually led to a military coup in January 1820. By March 1820, the rebels had gained control of the government and forced Ferdinand to accept the radical constitution of 1812, which "gave real power to a unicameral, broadly elected Cortes" (Schroeder 1994, 607–8).

In response, royalists established an alternate government in the north, near the French border. This faction then "appealed to France and the other powers for money, arms, and intervention" (Schroeder 1994, 624). Alexander responded eagerly, agreeing to intervene with the proviso that the intervention would be conducted by a European army composed of contingents from all five great powers. Though the French delegation to Verona was itself divided, the

French government was generally prepared to consider an intervention, both to enhance French prestige and to restore Bourbon rule in Spain. Metternich harbored reservations, especially about a multilateral intervention that would entail deployment of Russian troops in Western Europe, but he was not opposed in principle to the notion of suppressing liberal revolutions. Only Britain was fundamentally opposed to intervention—both because of its sympathy for liberal causes and because it worried about a resurgent France reestablishing its influence over Spain. This opposition hardened with George Canning's appointment as foreign minister just before the conference at Verona, following Castlereagh's suicide. Canning's policy placed far greater emphasis on supporting democracies, and rejected the conference system as reactionary in nature.

The compromise produced by the conference of Verona was a fragile one that serves as an important reminder that the new social practice of great power management was not the sole such practice in international politics, even among the great powers. On 19 November 1822, a joint protocol was released by Austria, France, Prussia, and Russia. Article One of the protocol defined three circumstances under which the four parties agreed that intervention would be necessary. These were: (1) "an armed attack on the part of Spain against the French territory, or of an official act of the Spanish Government provoking directly to rebellion the subjects of one or other of the Powers"; (2) a declaration that the king had forfeited his throne or an attempt to harm him; and (3) "a formal act of the Spanish Government infringing the rights of the legitimate succession of the Royal family" (Metternich 1970, 651). All these conditions relate to the locus and source of state authority. The great powers made clear that attempts by the rebels to seize state authority in Spain or to incite similar rebellions in other states would constitute cause for war to overthrow the liberal Spanish government.

The protocol's second article went further, providing that in the event of a similar case not explicitly covered by Article One, "the ministers of the allied Courts accredited to his Most Christian Majesty should unite with the Cabinet of France to examine and determine if the case in question should be considered as belonging to the class of the *casus foederis* foreseen and defined" (Metternich 1970, 652). This language represents a further development of the strategy Metternich employed in his memo to Tsar Alexander after the Laibach conference. It commits the great powers to engaging in a process of adjudication—determining whether case X is covered by rule Y—one of the three categories of secondary rules crucial to the smooth operation of social practices of rule-making. The fact of this agreement is, in itself, significant evidence that these actors understood themselves to be engaged in an ongoing collective practice of the kind I posit in this book.

However, I do not claim that secondary rules are determinative of behavior. Rules are often susceptible to multiple interpretations, and actors find themselves simultaneously subject to multiple valid rulesets; as Metternich's second article indicates, rules cannot explicitly cover every conceivable situation; and, finally, actors sometimes break the rules. The handling of the situation in Spain presents such a situation. After the publication of the protocol, Britain broke with the allies, largely on the basis of Wellington's sense of betrayal (Schroeder 1994, 625). Metternich had assured him "that there shall be no general Protocol on the negotiations and conference relative to the Spanish affair" and "that the despatches exchanged between the ministers or presented to the Conferences shall be regarded as simple communications from Cabinet to Cabinet" (Metternich 1970, 653). Given the low probability that Britain, under Canning's leadership, would participate in joint action, this promise makes little sense. More serious was the collapse of a plan for the four remaining powers to issue joint instructions recalling their ambassadors from Spain in order to exert diplomatic pressure on the rebels.

Ultimately, the French government balked at having its freedom of maneuver restricted by its fellow great powers. The initial French proposal, to delay the recall of the ambassadors past the conclusion of the Verona conference, was rejected by Metternich and Alexander. As a result, a diplomatic circular was issued by the three eastern powers in December 1822 without French participation. The circular touched briefly on the Italian and Greek situations before addressing Spain. It did so by posing a rhetorical question on behalf of the monarchs, asserting that they "must ask themselves whether it can be longer permitted to remain quiet spectators of calamities which daily threaten to become more dangerous and more horrible, or even by the presence of their representatives give the false appearance of a final consent to the measures of a faction ready to do anything to maintain and support their pernicious power" (Metternich 1970, 653). The circular went on to answer this question in the negative, and to declare publicly that the three powers had recalled their ambassadors.

Separated from the other great powers, French policy was driven by a vigorous internal debate among liberals, moderate royalists, and ultra-royalists. This contest was decided in favor of the ultras by late January 1823. Over the next two months, France independently broke relations with Spain and declared war (Schroeder 1994, 626). This intervention, according to Schroeder, "was a political and military success, overcoming just enough Spanish resistance to give the army and regime some glory and to raise French morale" (Schroeder 1994, 627). The Spanish case clearly saw the French break the rules of great power management to act unilaterally. That said, the significance of this outcome should not be overstated. Even though cooperative management of the international system was not established as an ironclad practice, neither did France behave in a manner consistent with the relatively unconstrained balance of power practices typical of the late eighteenth century. As Schroeder notes, "France, having occupied all of Spain, withdrew with nothing permanent to show for it" (Schroeder 1994, 627). If, at the end of the Verona conference, the new institution of great power management was not all that Metternich had hoped, neither was the international system the same as it was before Napoleon—or, for that matter, immediately after his defeat.

Conclusion

The argument in this chapter has been that changes to the structure of the international system after 1815 were socially constructed by actors engaging in a mutually intelligible social practice of rule-making, interpretation, and application. This social practice was constituted by secondary rules drawn from the contemporary institutions of sovereignty, diplomacy, and international law. These rules shaped, but did not fully determine, the manner in which actors presented their positions and evaluated those of their counterparts. Actors consistently framed their responses to proposals in terms of these secondary rules; such rules also proved persuasive to actors, even in the face of contrary interests. By the time of the conference of Verona, when the new social practice of great power management was relatively stabilized, evidence shows actors attempting to apply the new rules, and to codify the applicable rules for doing so. Finally, the evidence suggests that states able to marshal skill and creativity in deploying these rules exerted disproportionate influence on outcomes. Austria and France under Metternich and Talleyrand routinely outperformed Russia and Prussia in this regard, suggesting that this particular kind of knowledge is an often-overlooked source of power.

Overall, available evidence provides a relatively good fit for the expectations of the theoretical argument advanced in the book. The two potentially problematic outcomes are the eventual split between Britain and the continental powers, and the failure of great power coordination to constrain France in the case of its intervention in Spain. As I have argued, the split between Britain and the continental powers was, at least until the time of Castlereagh's suicide, primarily a difference of interpretation as to how the new rules of great power cooperation should be institutionalized. This difference was rooted in Castlereagh's insistence that great power cooperation take a diplomatic, rather than a legal, form. Britain was committed to the overall endeavor of great power conflict management, as well as to practices of collective rule-making and interpretation, but ultimately could not accept the manner in which these goals were to be achieved. With respect to France, the key point is that despite its unilateral intervention, it did not take advantage of the opportunity to aggrandize itself, as would have been expected under prevailing norms of international politics in the late eighteenth century. The rules of the game had changed; even where they were not obeyed completely, they exercised a moderating and restraining influence on actors' behavior. These changes were the outcome of a mutually intelligible social practice of rule-making and rule interpretation engaged in by leading statesmen of the great powers.

CHAPTER 3

Banning War

SOCIAL PRACTICES OF RULE-MAKING IN THE INTERWAR PERIOD

The First World War and its aftermath have played a central narrative role in both the theory and practice of International Relations.[1] The most familiar interpretation of the interwar period is that of a momentous failure of statecraft resulting from liberal, or on some accounts utopian, policies aimed at recasting the international system. Efforts to eliminate war as a means of conflict resolution and replace it with an expanded system of international law were, on this view, inevitably consigned to failure. Such assertions have been central to the development of realist IR theory as a purported antidote to the flawed assumptions and policy prescriptions proffered by liberal theories.

The Kellogg-Briand Pact stands out as a symbol of failure among a number of international agreements intended to avoid another general war. My purpose in this chapter is to ask why and how such allegedly naïve and disastrous agreements were signed, and how they attracted widespread official adherence. In contrast to the realist view, evidence shows the creation of a rule banning resort to war except in cases of self-defense or collective security. Crucially, this norm was the unintended outcome of a clearly identifiable practice of rule-making and interpretation. Creating a rule banning war was not the initial intent of either of the treaty's chief architects, American secretary of state Frank Kellogg and French politician (then foreign minister) Aristide Briand. Secondary rules did not simply constrain actor choice among preexisting preferences; in this case, they fundamentally shaped the outcome by leading to the generation and ultimate adoption of a new alternative.

---

[1] On narrative in IR theory, particularly in the American context, see Krebs (2015).

The case also contains two other key findings. On one hand, actors were often frustrated in reaching procedural agreements, even when they agreed in substance. Slight differences in interpretations of legitimate practices for making and interpreting rules mattered to the participants, sometimes independently of whether those differences had substantive implications. On the other hand, the case also features socially competent performances in the practice of global rule-making by a range of interesting actors—most notably the British Dominions, Japan, and the Soviet Union. These actors were either new participants in global rule-making, non-Western in their political and philosophical traditions, avowedly hostile to the institutions and practices of the international system, or some combination of the three. The fact that they nevertheless participated as knowledgeable social actors is remarkable. Collectively, these two findings indicate a broad level of awareness and acceptance of international practices for making and interpreting rules.

The chapter leaves aside the Treaty of Versailles to focus on the Locarno agreements of 1925 and the Kellogg-Briand Pact of 1928. With respect to the prevention of future wars, and thus to the particular change in the international system of interest here, the Treaty of Versailles was very much an unfinished document. Aside from the fact that the United States ultimately failed to ratify the treaty, even ratifying states regarded the peace as incomplete. The flurry of diplomatic activity related to international security and the prevention of war during the 1920s is a clear reflection of the prevailing sentiment that more work remained to be done. The Locarno agreements and the Kellogg-Briand Pact represent the zenith of interwar efforts to replace war as a means of conflict resolution. In addition, both were conceived, negotiated, and created after the end of the Wilson presidency. Unlike the Treaty of Versailles, these agreements cannot be attributed to Wilson's public popularity or intellectual force of will. Indeed, the impetus for both came from European leaders, with the United States playing a limited, unofficial role at Locarno and an initially reluctant role in the case of the Kellogg-Briand Pact. The question is why, and how, these particular agreements were signed at those particular moments.

Explanations can be grouped in two broad categories. The first attributes antiwar agreements to psychological aversion to the destruction caused by the world's first large-scale industrial war. Such explanations sometimes supplement psychological explanations at the elite level with arguments about the importance of mass communication and democracy in subjecting foreign policy to increased popular pressure. The second explanation for 1920s diplomacy dismisses the agreements as "cheap talk," noting the intensification of great power rivalries in the 1930s and the eventual outbreak of the Second World War.

Both of these explanations deal with the motives of relevant actors. However, in any interesting social situation involving multiple parties, it is likely that motives are mixed. In such cases, the relevant question is how mixed motives, interests, values, and ideas are translated into intersubjectively agreed-upon outcomes. Neither the aversion hypothesis nor the "cheap talk" hypothesis accounts for the particular form or timing of the Locarno agreements or the Kellogg-Briand Pact. In this chapter, I show that interwar agreements restricting the use of war as a legitimate means of conflict resolution were the product of a defined social practice accepted as the legitimate means for altering the rules of the game in international politics. This social practice was constituted and governed by secondary rules.

The events of the 1930s culminating in the Second World War tempt the observer to conclude that Locarno and Kellogg-Briand were failures, and potentially even that no change in the rules of the international system took place.[2] While it is certainly true that these agreements did not end the use of military force by states, this view lacks nuance. The norm restricting states' use of warfare to cases of self-defense and collective security clearly informed subsequent state practice despite being imperfectly adhered to. The Kellogg-Briand Pact was explicitly invoked in response to Japanese aggression in Manchuria, not only by the League of Nations but also by the United States in the form of the Stimson Doctrine (O'Mahoney 2014). While efforts at enforcement were unsuccessful, the norm violator was criticized for its actions and the puppet state of Manchukuo was ultimately dismantled after 1945 and its territory returned to Chinese control. In addition, the Kellogg-Briand Pact was pressed into service as the legal basis for charges of aggression at Nuremberg (Stimson 1947); this move casts the Second World War itself as an instance of norm enforcement. While the motives and causes of the war were surely more complex than this, it would also be wrong to completely dismiss the treaty's causal role. In any event, utilizing the pact to legitimate war crimes trials indicates at least that the Allied governments believed the norm existed and that it could be socially useful. Finally, the pact also formed the basis for United Nations rules on the use of force, which adopted the Kellogg-Briand formulation restricting the use of war to cases of self-defense and collective security. These events suggest that while Locarno and Kellogg-Briand were less than a complete success, they were also more than "cheap talk"—and that they played a largely underappreciated role in the development of the international system.

The chapter is divided in three parts. The first discusses primary rules related to the use of warfare as a means of conflict resolution, both before and after the conclusion of the Locarno and Kellogg-Briand treaties. The second identifies relevant secondary rules governing contemporary practices of rule-making,

---

[2] For example, John Mearsheimer refers to the Kellogg-Briand Pact in passing as "an attempt" to "foster international cooperation and eliminate war as a tool of statecraft" (Mearsheimer 2001, 189).

interpretation, and application. Finally, the third part demonstrates the role of secondary rules and practices of rule-making in shaping the creation of these treaties.

Primary Rules: Delegitimizing War as a Means of Conflict Resolution

Prior to the First World War, the rules of the game governing warfare were primarily the product of the Concert of Europe.[3] War was seen as a normal, functional, and legitimate part of international politics, instrumental to maintaining the balance of power and preventing hegemony. In cases where hegemony was not at stake, war was regarded as a permissible form of self-help when state rights were infringed or when conceptions of national self-interest suggested a potential benefit. The latter half of the nineteenth century was characterized by two apparently contradictory trends with respect to the rules of war. On the one hand, mass nationalism and rising militarism made warfare more acceptable, rather than less. Late nineteenth-century militarism posited war as "a desirable and constructive social activity." The accompanying expectation that war entailed "short, decisive battles between armies" enabled "increased jingoism of the press" (Holsti 1991, 159–161). On the other hand, the closing decades of the 1800s also saw increasingly influential humanitarian and pacifist movements that sought to restrain, if not eliminate, war. The most significant of these antiwar achievements came at the Hague peace conferences of 1899 and 1907. Notably, these steps toward curtailing states' rights to employ military force relied crucially on the creation of legal obligations to use alternate rule-based dispute resolution processes. Thickening existing practices for making, interpreting, and applying rules was therefore an essential part of the movement away from warfare as a normal and appropriate part of world politics.

At the First Hague Peace Conference, twenty-seven states "formulated a new body of codified laws governing the conduct of war and the nature and use of armaments, and they established the Permanent Court of Arbitration to interpret and adjudicate these and other international laws" (Reus-Smit 1999, 142). In fact, the practice of arbitration as a means of interstate dispute resolution had become reasonably robust by the eve of the First World War. The Permanent Court of Arbitration (PCA) completed fourteen arbitrations by 1914, and approximately fifty more international arbitrations took place outside of its ambit (Boyle 1999, 35).

---

[3] For more details on the creation of the concert system, see the previous chapter.

The enthusiasm for arbitration, moreover, was widespread even among the great powers. The 1899 peace conference had been proposed by the Russian foreign minister in a circular note dated 30 December 1898. The United States accepted on condition that the agenda exclude the ongoing Spanish-American War; however, the Republican administration of President McKinley was prepared to play a constructive role in advancing the cause of arbitration. Secretary of State John Hay instructed the American delegation to propose a court Francis Boyle describes as "a permanent international tribunal organized along the lines of the U.S. Supreme Court." While the British were supportive of the principle of arbitration, they preferred an ad hoc panel created for each dispute. The only major opposition to the principle of arbitration came from the German government, which opposed it out of concern that the delay entailed by the process would nullify the substantial advantage in mobilization speed Germany enjoyed over its neighbors (Boyle 1999, 27–28). The practice of concluding bilateral arbitration treaties according to Article 19 of the 1899 Convention on the Pacific Settlement of International Disputes proved popular; "between the First Hague Peace Conference in 1899 and 1908 some seventy-seven arbitration treaties were concluded by the various countries of the world, and all but twelve provided for some sort of reference to the Permanent Court of Arbitration." The first such treaty, between France and the United States, was concluded on 14 October 1903. The United States signed eleven bilateral treaties modeled on the Anglo-French treaty between November 1904 and February 1905 (Boyle 1999, 30).[4]

While the PCA constituted an important advance in efforts to institutionalize peaceful conflict resolution, it did not attempt to ban war—only to reduce the incidence of wars caused by disputes over the interpretation and application of treaties. Even the most ardent supporters of arbitration embraced it only for a narrowly circumscribed set of issues; questions relating to political independence and territorial integrity were explicitly excluded. In addition, "the U.S. government insisted on omitting from a Russian list of proposed subjects deemed suitable for obligatory arbitration international conventions relating to rivers, interoceanic canals, and monetary matters" (Boyle 1999, 28). Restriction of arbitration and international courts to so-called justiciable questions relating to the interpretation and application of existing treaties continued in the Covenant of the League of Nations (Reus-Smit 1999, 147). Arbitration was not employed

---

[4] These so-called Hay arbitration treaties were undermined by the insistence of the US Senate that submission of any dispute to arbitration required its assent, in the form of a two-thirds affirmative vote. President Theodore Roosevelt rejected the treaties, so amended, as ineffective and withdrew his support (Boyle 1999, 30). The obstructionist tendency of the Senate, although rooted in its constitutional prerogatives, foreshadowed the fate of the Treaty of Versailles.

to evaluate more basic disputes about the fundamental rules of the game in the international system. Therefore, even though arbitration is a rule-governed practice of interpreting and applying general rules to particular cases, I do not treat it with the secondary rules relevant to the more general practices of global rule-making that are my main focus in this book.

Delegates to the Second Hague Peace Conference sought to build on and strengthen the machinery for arbitration of international disputes. The United States remained ready to make PCA arbitration obligatory in cases that fell into the court's jurisdiction. Even Germany "had dropped its objection to the principle of obligatory intervention, but now insisted that the proper approach should be the negotiation of a series of bilateral arbitration treaties" rather than a multilateral agreement (Boyle 1999, 31). This shift in justification highlights the growth in the legitimacy of arbitration as a practice for the resolution of international disputes. Ultimately, the creation of a more robust successor to the PCA foundered not on differences of principle, but over the selection of judges—a procedural matter. Secondary states, especially Brazil, objected to being represented only on a rotational basis, in contrast to the permanent representation accorded to the great powers (Boyle 1999, 44). These objections, framed in the language of sovereign equality, limited the 1907 conference to recommending adoption of the Draft Convention Relative to the Institution of a Court of Arbitral Justice "as soon as an agreement shall have been reached upon the selection of judges and the constitution of the court" (Boyle 1999, 44). Selection of judges to proposed permanent international courts remained a contentious issue until the League of Nations adopted a proposal by Elihu Root of the United States; Root argued that judges should be selected by concurrent vote of the League's two major bodies, the Assembly and the Council (Rappard 1940, 142–43).

In 1919, peacemakers confronted a world in which the rules of the game for international relations did not ban war. This remained true, albeit with additional restrictions, after the conclusion of the Paris peace conference and the creation of the League of Nations. Article 10 of the Covenant declared that "the Members of the League undertake to respect and preserve as against external aggression the territorial integrity and existing political independence of all Members of the League." This famous collective security provision was supplemented by an Article 12 undertaking between League members to submit their disputes with other League members "either to arbitration or judicial settlement or to enquiry by the Council" before resorting to war, as well as by Article 16, which declared that failure to do so constituted an act of war against all other League members and empowered the Council to specify military contributions from member states intended to coerce the recalcitrant state. In the event of a dispute between a League member and a nonmember, Article 17 provided for the nonmember to resolve the dispute according to League rules; its refusal to do so would authorize activation of the collective enforcement provisions of Article 16.[5]

The overall effect of the League Covenant on the status of war in international relations amounted to the provision of increasingly detailed alternate dispute resolution procedures—and corresponding obligations on the part of states to avail themselves of these mechanisms—on the one hand, alongside the creation of legal machinery that provided for the authorization of collective use of military force. That the League did not outlaw war was understood at the time. A widely published state paper authored by South African foreign minister Jan Smuts declared that "as long as members of the league submit their disputes for inquiry and report or recommendation or decision by some outside authority, their obligation to the league will be satisfied, and thereafter they will be free to take any action they like, and even to go to war" (quoted in Rappard 1940, 115). Smuts's analysis was taken seriously both among the British Cabinet and by President Wilson (MacMillan 2003, 89–90).

The collective enforcement provisions of the covenant were similarly incomplete. The early League of Nations Assembly meetings were occupied, in part, by a Canadian effort to establish a heavily circumscribed interpretation of Article 10; this effort culminated at the Fourth Assembly in the fall of 1923, where an interpretive resolution was adopted stating that it was the sovereign prerogative of each individual state to decide whether or not to contribute troops to particular League enforcement actions, and that members were bound by the Covenant only to consider League of Nations decisions in good faith (Rappard 1940, 209–18). The failure of the United States to join the League, as well as the initial exclusion of Weimar Germany and the Soviet Union, further illustrate the incomplete and uncertain status of the rules regarding the legitimacy of warfare in the immediate aftermath of Versailles.

The Locarno agreements, signed 16 October 1925, were the first significant achievement in efforts to end war as a means of international conflict resolution. Bilateral arbitration treaties between Germany and its neighbors were subsumed under the multilateral Treaty of Mutual Guarantee. This umbrella document constituted the heart of the Locarno agreements. In addition to guaranteeing Germany's western frontier, the parties agreed "that they will in no case attack or invade each other or resort to war against each other." This broad, clear language contained in the treaty's second article was qualified by only two exceptions: self-defense, either in the event of violation of the treaty's border guarantee or of the demilitarization provisions of the Treaty of Versailles (Articles 42–43), and League of Nations enforcement action under Articles 15 and 16 of the Covenant. In addition to the negative commitment contained in

---

[5] Covenant of the League of Nations (1919).

Article 2, the treaty's third article contained a positive obligation "to settle by peaceful means and in the manner laid down herein all questions of any kind which may arise between them and which it may not be possible to settle by the normal methods of diplomacy." After specifying measures for dispute resolution, the treaty established a second positive obligation for the parties severally to "come immediately to the assistance of the Power against whom the act complained of is directed" in the event that the treaty was breached.[6]

These obligations represented a significant departure from a system in which war was seen as a legitimate and sometimes even positive aspect of international politics. They did not, however, represent a system-wide change. Locarno took the form of an international treaty and, as such, bound only the signatories in their mutual relations. While Germany, France, Great Britain, Italy, and Belgium were core members of the international system, that system was considerably more pluralistic than it had been in 1815; further, the ranks of the great powers now clearly included the United States, and arguably also Japan and the Soviet Union.

The significance of the Locarno agreements was twofold. First, they were a major step in the diplomatic rehabilitation of Weimar Germany; in voluntarily recognizing the legitimacy of its western frontier as established at Versailles and pledging to pursue alteration of its eastern border solely by peaceful means, the German government achieved a victory in its policy of reclaiming Germany's status as a great power. In the months following Locarno, for instance, allied occupation and military control over the Rhineland began to ease. By September 1926, Germany had joined the League of Nations, fulfilling a condition of the Locarno negotiations (Cohrs 2006, 266–68; Jacobson 1972, 60–68). More broadly, the Locarno agreements revitalized, even if temporarily, many of the diplomatic practices associated with the concert period after the Napoleonic Wars. Regular meetings of the Locarno principals took place, and diplomatic rhetoric publicly noted the existence of a "spirit of Locarno" entailing a commitment to cooperation and peaceful dispute resolution (Cohrs 2006, 257–58; Jacobson 1972, 68–70). Second, Locarno would act as a crucial precedent for the 1928 Kellogg-Briand Pact, which generalized rules against resort to warfare by securing the adherence of virtually every member of the international system.

The Kellogg-Briand Pact originated as a French proposal for a bilateral agreement between France and the United States (Miller 1928, 7). By the time it was signed in Paris on 27 August 1928, it had become a multilateral pact for the renunciation of war. Upon its entry into force on 24 July 1929, it had already acquired the adherence of thirty-two states in addition to the original signatories; eight more states would eventually adhere, bringing the total number of parties

---

[6] Treaty of Mutual Guarantee (1925).

to fifty-five, encompassing virtually the entire international community. The treaty contained three brief operative articles following a short preamble. The first article declared that the parties "condemn recourse to war for the solution of international controversies, and renounce it, as an instrument of national policy in their relations with one another." The second article contained an equally broad undertaking "that the settlement or solution of all disputes or conflicts of whatever nature or of whatever origin they may be, which may arise among them, shall never be sought except by pacific means." The only exception to these obligations was found in the preamble, which noted that "any signatory Power which shall hereafter seek to promote its national interests by resort to war should be denied the benefits furnished by this Treaty." The third article specified provisions for ratification and entry into force.[7]

The pact is notable both for its strong renunciation of war, and for its near universality. Contemporary enthusiasm is reflected in J. W. Wheeler-Bennett's conclusion that "the Great Powers are taking a step towards the prevention of war and the maintenance of permanent peace essentially different from any they have previously attempted" (Wheeler-Bennett 1928, 9). Though the agreement lacked specific sanctions and did not specify mechanisms for pacific dispute resolution, these were not necessarily fatal flaws. Wheeler-Bennett, for instance, saw the agreement as a starting point, to be expanded upon in future diplomatic talks (Wheeler-Bennett 1928, 10). American international lawyer (and later State Department official) David Hunter Miller went further, arguing that it was a mistake to evaluate the Kellogg-Briand agreement out of context of the League of Nations; he concluded that "in the matter of sanctions the Treaty is to a large extent implemented in advance by the Covenant." The same held true with regard to mechanisms for dispute resolution (Miller 1928, 137).[8] On this view, the Kellogg-Briand Pact supplemented the League of Nations and closed a vital loophole in the Covenant.

In a span of ten years after the Treaty of Versailles, the leading states in the international system championed efforts to relegate war from its historical place as a means of national glory and aggrandizement, as well as the ultimate arbiter of disputes, to a new status as either a duty of authorized collective effort to preserve peace or—barring such authorization—an act of aggression contrary to international law. They further created detailed and plausible alternate means of dispute resolution marked by a consistent reliance on arbitration and positive international law as supplements to diplomacy and negotiation. In the remaining sections of this chapter, I show that this outcome (in terms of form, process, and

---

[7] Kellogg-Briand Pact (1928).

[8] The importance of contextualizing the Kellogg-Briand Pact has been asserted more recently in Cohrs (2006, 419–20).

timing) was the result of a rule-governed practice of rule-making, interpretation, and application.

Secondary Rules: Increasing Institutionalization and Rule System Complexity

In the previous chapter, I argued that the construction of the Concert of Europe was accomplished according to socially accepted rules of international law and diplomacy. Particularly, actors relied on procedural rules for reaching, institutionalizing, interpreting, and applying agreements among sovereign states. These secondary rules constitute context-specific practices for rule-making, interpretation, and application. They instruct actors both on how to present and how to evaluate proposals for change in primary rules governing behavior.

In this section I review the secondary rules relevant to state officials in the 1920s. The most important point in this regard is the fundamental continuity in secondary rules from the post-Napoleonic period to the interwar period. Although the formal locus of sovereignty had shifted from the person of the sovereign to various conceptions of popular or constitutional sovereignty, the state remained uniquely empowered to create, interpret, and alter the rules of international politics. Nationalism and democratization subjected state officials to greater scrutiny and increasingly compelled justificatory defenses of major policies for domestic audiences; these shifts represent an important thickening of the social practice of rule-making in International Relations, but they had not—at least by the 1920s—undermined the central role of the state as the dominant actor in this process.[9]

The most striking characteristics of practices of global rule-making in the interwar period were a thoroughgoing commitment to legal positivism and an emerging norm of multilateralism. Reus-Smit argues that multilateralism stemmed from "the precept that social rules should be authored by those subject to them," while the expansion of international law reflected "the precept that rules should be equally applicable to all subjects, in all like cases" (Reus-Smit 1999, 133). Both multilateralism and especially international law represent elaboration and development of trends evident in the aftermath of the Napoleonic Wars. Diplomacy surrounding both Locarno

---

[9] On the impact of early nationalism in International Relations, see Bukovansky (2002). For more on the role of public opinion as a constraint on state action, see Carr (2001). Finally, on the role of transnational advocacy networks in advancing antiwar efforts, see Ferrell (1952).

and the Kellogg-Briand Pact was suffused with the language of international law. States couched their proposals in legal forms and language, evaluated proposals in terms of their compatibility with existing rules of international law, and accorded prominent roles at decisive moments to their in-house legal experts (Boyle 1999; Reus-Smit 1999; Cohrs 2006). States engaged in a patterned and mutually intelligible social practice in order to arrive at a legitimate decision regarding proposals for change to the primary rules governing the use of warfare in the international system.

Despite the essential continuity and thickening of secondary rules in the "long nineteenth century," two primary fault lines are relevant to understanding the politics of rule-making and interpretation surrounding Locarno and Kellogg-Briand. The first dealt with the tension between great power responsibility—the cornerstone of the concert system—and the legal principle of sovereign equality. Eastern European and Latin American states resisted attempts by the United States and the European great powers to assert special authority in processes of global rule-making. The second, and ultimately more important, fault line divided American and European notions regarding the proper roles of government and private society—including, but not limited to, the role of the market. While the American government remained an ardent supporter of international law throughout the 1920s, it refused to join the League of Nations and generally ruled out even official diplomatic participation in major efforts aimed at strengthening the rule of law at the expense of war. Rather than simply disengagement, disinterest, or disagreement with the goals of these efforts, the American stance also reflected principled disagreements regarding the role of government and the proper rules for diplomacy that handicapped efforts to build and sustain new rules limiting the use of warfare in international relations.

Overall, this system of secondary rules had become both more institutionalized and more complex. Its institutionalization entailed its spread to newly independent states that practiced global rule-making in ways similar to their largely European counterparts, as well as the formalization of various diplomatic and legal procedures in the League of Nations and other emerging intergovernmental organizations. Increased complexity is evident in this expansion of the corpus of procedural rules about rule-making, as well as in the fault lines arising from differing interpretations of how to reconcile different parts of a larger rule set. The result was a system of procedural rules that constrained all states in the system—including the great powers—but that also simultaneously empowered states to advance creative interpretive arguments.

An Unexpected Outcome: The Path to the Kellogg-Briand Pact

Locarno and Kellogg-Briand each amounted to major steps in restricting the legitimate role of warfare in international politics. In the remainder of this chapter, I show that these agreements were the product of a social practice of rule-making and interpretation. In concrete terms, this means that actors presented and evaluated proposals for social change according to secondary rules, and that deviations—both in presentation and evaluation—generally prompted justification and criticism. Procedural considerations were important to the ultimate outcomes; indeed, the final substance of the Kellogg-Briand Pact was not initially intended by either of its principal architects and cannot be adequately explained without accounting for the role of secondary rules.

As noted earlier, the crucial agreements of the latter 1920s were not sui generis. Efforts to employ arbitration and other quasi-judicial means of dispute resolution gathered strength in the early twentieth century. The creation of the Permanent Court of Arbitration at the First Hague Peace Conference both reflected and encouraged the further development of this trend. The provision of alternate means of dispute resolution is clearly relevant to the later success of attempts to delegitimize warfare, the traditional last resort for settling international disputes. However, nothing in the Hague Conferences nor in the Treaty of Versailles made the pursuit—much less the conclusion—of a ban on warfare inevitable. Any attempt to understand the form, process, and timing of this outcome must be centrally concerned with the diplomacy surrounding the agreements in question.

PRECURSORS TO LOCARNO

The Locarno agreements can be usefully contrasted with two similar but unsuccessful efforts pursued over the course of 1924—the Cecil-Requin Draft Treaty of Mutual Assistance and the proposed Geneva Protocol of 1924. What would become the Cecil-Requin draft had its origin at the Third League of Nations Assembly in the fall of 1923. A call for an agreement explicitly linking disarmament and collective security led to the referral of the matter to the Temporary Mixed Commission; the draft treaty was submitted a year later to the Fourth Assembly for member comment and review (Rappard 1940, 243–44, 48–49). The draft had four key features. Its first article read, in part, that "the High Contracting Parties solemnly declare that aggressive war is an international crime and severally undertake that no one of them will be guilty of its commission" (quoted in Rappard 1940, 250). The treaty called for members to assist victims of aggression generally, while allowing for regional defensive treaties as additional insurance. Third, "the draft treaty endowed the [League of Nations] Council with executive powers extending far beyond those of the Covenant." Collective security decision-making would thus be centralized above the level of the state. Finally, it made such collective security assistance "contingent on fulfilment of specified disarmament duties." States that maintained excessive levels of military preparedness would be left to fend for themselves. Twenty-eight League members replied to the draft, and "about half accepted the draft in principle, while suggesting various amendments." Rappard attributes this response to a strong desire for disarmament, while noting that states ultimately "did nothing more than discuss these proposals, which were in reality stillborn" (Rappard 1940, 250–52).

The crucial decisions regarding the Cecil-Requin treaty were taken by the United Kingdom's first Labour government, led by Ramsay MacDonald. The MacDonald government sought both to overcome the Ruhr crisis, precipitated by French occupation of the Ruhr valley in late 1923, and to generally strengthen the League of Nations and its fledgling collective security system. Initially, MacDonald was faced with a choice between the Cecil-Requin treaty and a proposal championed by Foreign Office stalwart Eyre Crowe and the Viscount D'Abernon (British ambassador to Berlin) for a regional nonaggression pact that would include Germany as an equal signatory. The latter proposal was an expansion of an idea proposed by German foreign minister Gustav Stresemann on 11 February 1924. Ultimately, MacDonald chose a third option—to develop his own proposal. On 26 February 1924, MacDonald wrote Stresemann that he had rejected the notion of a regional pact as too closely resembling the system of alliances that had contributed to European devastation in the First World War (Cohrs 2006, 97–89). Instead, he pursued a solution rooted in the League of Nations.

The resulting document was the proposed Geneva Protocol of 1924. This document reflected the influence of Ramsay MacDonald as well as of Edouard Beneš, the prime minister of Czechoslovakia. It sought, like the Cecil-Requin treaty, to modify the League of Nations Covenant. First, "the prohibition to resort to aggressive war was made unconditional and absolute." Second, "the jurisdiction of the Permanent Court of International Justice was rendered compulsory in all legal disputes." In disputes not relating to the interpretation of treaties, "the procedure before the Council, under Article 15 of the Covenant, was so defined as necessarily to lead to a peaceful settlement" (Rappard 1940, 157–58). Finally, parties would pledge to "carry out in full good faith any judicial sentence or arbitral award that may be rendered" or to "comply . . . with the solution recommended by the Council" (quoted in Rappard 1940, 158). Thus, the primary difference between the Cecil-Requin treaty and the draft Geneva

Protocol was the latter's increased specificity with regard to alternate dispute resolution mechanisms short of war. Both documents aimed to eliminate war as the policy prerogative of sovereign states, except in cases of self-defense or of collective security action against an aggressor. These exceptions were, further, to be codified in international law and thus made subject to scrutiny by the international community.

The crucial point is that MacDonald clearly sought to advance proposals for substantial change in practices of international politics by employing channels of international law and diplomacy, and in the clearly recognizable form of a draft treaty. The abandonment of the Cecil-Requin draft in favor of a draft Geneva Protocol distinguished by expanded, and highly legalistic, alternate dispute resolution mechanisms indicates the presence of a norm favoring legal responses to problems of international governance. The high response rate to the abandoned Cecil-Requin draft further indicates that other governments accepted the legitimacy of this procedural approach, even if they were unwilling, as yet, to accept such substantive proposals.

The Geneva Protocol met, at best, a mixed response. Debate revolved centrally around the nature and extent of the commitments to collective action. Beneš's statement to the League's Fifth Assembly (1924) acknowledged that compliance must be judged according to whether a state met expectations "to an extent consistent with its geographical position and its particular situation as regards armaments." While he maintained that states could not deny the existence of their obligations, he allowed that "each state is judge of the manner in which it shall carry out its obligations" (quoted in Rappard 1940, 256–57). Rather than indicating the lack of secondary rules, Beneš's position indicates the operation of a decentralized, polycentric (Ostrom 2010) set of arrangements for making, interpreting, and applying rules. These rules authorized states—and not other types of actors—to participate in processes of global rule-making. Further, they imposed constraints on the ways in which states were authorized to judge their own conduct. Most notably, as Beneš's statement reveals, he understood states to be entitled to consider their levels of armaments and geographic positions as mitigating factors in determining how to meet their collective security obligations. While these criteria certainly presented states with opportunities for good-faith differences of opinion as well as bad-faith excuses for shirking obligations, such opportunities were circumscribed by the likelihood that these public speech acts would be criticized by other actors in the international system. This kind of arrangement is consistent with older and more general practices for determining and responding to breaches of international obligations, generally grouped under the heading of the customary law of state responsibility.[10] Beneš

---

[10] On the modern history of international legal doctrines of state responsibility, see Nissel (2016).

sought to deflect criticism that the draft protocol was overly expansive, that it would circumscribe sovereign authority with respect to commitments of military resources, and that it failed to recognize crucial prudential exceptions to the requirement for participation in collective action. In each respect, he publicly accepted the conventional position consistent with established international practice, thereby limiting the protocol's legal force. Although the Assembly voted in favor of the draft protocol 48–0, the resolution stopped short of adopting the protocol; instead, the Assembly merely recommended its adoption to individual member states (Rappard 1940, 259).

Ultimately, the draft Geneva Protocol was derailed by the collapse of MacDonald's government in October 1924, after the publication of the so-called Zinoviev letter, which alleged Soviet efforts to fulminate revolution in Britain. The MacDonald government had supported re-establishing relations with the Soviet Union and, eventually, bringing it into the League of Nations (Cohrs 2006, 202). Though the Conservative Baldwin government withdrew its support for the Geneva Protocol, it felt compelled to offer justification. On 8 September 1925, almost a year after the protocol had been abandoned, Austen Chamberlain (Baldwin's foreign secretary) justified his government's stance to the League Council by arguing that the text had suggested "that the vital business of the League is not so much to promote friendly co-operation and reasoned harmony in the management of international affairs as to preserve peace by organizing war, and it may be war upon the largest scale" (quoted in Rappard 1940, 259–60).

In substance, this justification made little sense; if taken seriously, it would preclude any measures to guarantee peace, on the basis that these might involve (non-pacifist) enforcement measures. Further, it was inconsistent with the Conservative party's traditional support of the military, the empire, and the balance of power system. This cynical attempt to justify a decision taken on grounds of prudence (avoiding overcommitment) in terms of antiwar principle demonstrates the constraining power of social expectations. The Baldwin government opted to express a false basis for its decision to avoid the charge that it was less than fully committed to the goal of European peace and the avoidance of war, or that it had abdicated its systemic responsibility as a great power for self-interested reasons.

The United States remained outside the League and assiduously refrained from involvement in diplomacy relating to the Cecil-Requin draft treaty and to MacDonald's proposed Geneva Protocol. This was undoubtedly due to the Coolidge administration's desire to avoid entanglement with Wilson's creation, as well as a desire to avoid antagonizing isolationists in the Senate. It would be a mistake to conclude, however, that the administration was hostile to the goal of promoting peace or to the means provided by international law. Rather,

Republican foreign policy in the 1920s reflects a distinct view emphasizing the virtues of limited government activity and the dangers of traditional European diplomacy. This view had important implications for legitimate means of making, interpreting, and applying global rules. Efforts on both sides of the Atlantic succeeded only in achieving partial reconciliation of the European and American perspectives on secondary rules. The partially divergent American conception provides explanatory leverage on key inadequacies in attempts to restrict the resort to warfare. Within these parameters, the Coolidge administration sought to play a positive, if tragically limited, role in fostering peace and stabilization.

In a speech to the Canadian Bar Association on 4 September 1923, US secretary of state Charles Evans Hughes stressed informal efforts to pursue peace rather than diplomatic agreements. He argued that the crucial factor in success would be "the constant effort to diminish among people the disposition to resort to force" (quoted in Cohrs 2006, 86). The "cure" for war was to be found, in more familiar IR terms, at the individual level of analysis. Just as crucially, Cohrs notes that "Hughes consistently emphasized that not only the war-debt issue but also strategic questions, especially possible security commitments in Europe, fell outside the 'province of the executive' in Washington" (Cohrs 2006, 88). This view of the American constitution is starkly different from more modern interpretations and affords Congress a far more decisive voice in issues of foreign policy. Both under Coolidge and his successor, Herbert Hoover, American foreign policy "was driven by a pronounced faith in the blessings of minimal governmental interference and a staunch belief in the self-invigorating dynamism of peaceful change via the economic sphere" (Cohrs 2006, 191). These views were supplemented by a strong commitment to international law.

How, then, did this distinct viewpoint inform American diplomacy during 1924? While the US government did not take part in European efforts through the League to ban warfare, it was a vital participant in simultaneous efforts to settle the Ruhr crisis and the underlying dispute over German reparations and the continuing Allied occupation. The basis for American policy on reparations can be traced to a speech by Hughes in New Haven, Connecticut, on 29 December 1922. The heart of his plan called for the creation of two expert committees to deal, respectively, with Germany's capacity to pay reparations and with the timing and mechanisms for payment. The underlying concept was to "depoliticize" the loaded question of sanctions, and to set clear rules and guidelines for an ultimate solution. States would delegate the key functions of secondary rules—especially rule determination and rule adjudication. On the one hand, this approach evinces a sophisticated understanding of the difficulty of adjudication in international politics—of determining the facts of a particular case and identifying applicable rules. The Republican approach, then, was to treat the sanctions question as one about the proper application of legal rules; this method presupposes a basic agreement among actors on how to appropriately undertake such adjudication. On the other hand, the United States repeatedly refused to become an "official" participant in negotiations aimed at resolving the sanctions issue and the Ruhr crisis. Much of the actual negotiation was carried out through the auspices of Thomas W. Lamont, a partner of American financier J. P. Morgan. Indeed, the American loan to Germany—the so-called Dawes loan crucial to ensuring Germany's financial stability and capacity to pay reparations—was provided by Morgan and his partners rather than the American government; further, the loan was not guaranteed by any of the governments involved.[11]

While the negotiation leading to the eventual Dawes plan did not directly address efforts to ban warfare, two further aspects of these talks deserve mention. First, one of the key stumbling blocks among the Allied powers was directly related to secondary rules. The French, and to a lesser degree the British, government was vitally concerned with specifying procedures to be employed in the event of German default on its reparation obligations. The central issue was determining which body would be endowed with the authority to declare a default and subsequently apply sanctions. Whereas France preferred a strong role for the League's Reparations Commission, the United States preferred that this authority be incorporated within the ambit of the new expert committees. This issue was the subject of intense bargaining in late July and early August 1924. The first potential compromise "proposed a new sanction mechanism whereby in the case of 'flagrant default' the decision would still be made by the Reparations Commission, yet only with the participation of a US representative and after hearing the newly-appointed agent-general for reparations." The American desire to avoid even unofficial involvement with the League led President Coolidge to propose on 29 July that the chief justice of the United States be given the authority to determine if Germany was in default. This proposal would have amounted to an unprecedented extension of the authority of a national court to the international level, and it led Ramsay MacDonald to counter by supporting a plan enabling the Permanent Court of International Justice (PCIJ) to fulfill the crucial adjudicative task. The clear difference was that the PCIJ proposal would preserve the nominal sovereign equality of the parties, with the additional (ultimately unacceptable) effect of bringing the United States into a relationship with a body closely connected to the League. By 2 August, the allied powers had agreed to a proposal vesting the authority to declare default with the Transfer

---

[11] A detailed account of the negotiations leading to the Dawes agreement of 16 August 1924 is provided by Cohrs (2006, see especially ch. 9–11).

Committee, the second of the two expert bodies at the heart of the Dawes process (Cohrs 2006, 165–68).

That the United States prevailed despite its partially divergent conception of secondary rules demonstrates that procedural rules do not determine outcomes, and that other sources of power also matter. However, the American view of procedural rules was only *partially* divergent. While the administration held idiosyncratic, unhelpful views on the virtues of minimal government action, it was deeply committed to the basic rules and norms of contemporary international law. As a result, it was able to contribute to a solution of the reparations problem that was consistent with these rules in most key respects. Further, regardless of the outcome, it is significant that issues related directly to the smooth operation of rule-governed practices for rule-making were crucial to the resolution of a major dispute that touched directly on the national security of the world's great powers.

The Dawes negotiations are also noteworthy as the first instance of direct negotiation between France and Germany in the aftermath of the First World War. This outcome was not a certainty until late in the initial phase of inter-allied negotiation, which lasted from 15 July to 2 August. MacDonald had written to Edouard Herriot, the Radical Socialist French premier, on 8 July expressing the rationale for direct negotiation with Germany rather than the French preference for communication via the exchange of diplomatic notes: a directly negotiated agreement would have "greater moral value than the acceptance of the Treaty of Versailles" (quoted in Cohrs 2006, 170). This "moral value" stemmed directly from the resolution of the untenable second-class diplomatic status to which Germany had been relegated at Versailles.

The German delegation was invited on 2 August and arrived three days later, after an unofficial visit to Berlin by Charles Evans Hughes, reinforcing that Germany would be expected to accept inter-allied compromises and to trust Britain and the United States to jointly ensure its interests against French pressure. In fact, Stresemann exceeded these limitations to engage directly in negotiations with Herriot. His strategy was to use financial concessions as a lever to gain an end to French occupation of the Ruhr and, eventually, an end to allied control of the Rhineland; however, he also placed great importance on restoring Germany to an equal sovereign footing with the other parties. A deal was reached on this basis, calling for evacuation of the Ruhr by 16 August 1925, one year after the signing of the Dawes plan. The resumption of direct diplomatic contact between Germany and the allied powers was a prerequisite to the proper operation of global practices of rule-making, and therefore crucial to future efforts to ban warfare. This result was achieved by the deployment of interest-based arguments, but these interests were themselves constituted by the secondary rule according sovereign states a nominally equal status under international law, and by the secondary rules assigning special systemic governance responsibilities to great powers. Further, France's attempts to change her relations with Germany met opposition from an otherwise sympathetic ally in Austen Chamberlain, in large part because of their nonconformity with secondary rules.

THE LOCARNO AGREEMENTS

The Locarno agreements comprise five treaties signed on 16 October 1925. The first four are bilateral arbitration treaties between Germany and France, Belgium, Poland, and Czechoslovakia (Jacobson 1972, 3). The crucial fifth treaty is known as the "Treaty of Mutual Guarantee between Germany, Belgium, France, Great Britain and Italy." As noted earlier, this treaty contained numerous advances in the attempt to displace war as a means of conflict resolution, including a pledge between the parties not to resort to war,[12] a positive pledge to resolve all conflicts by peaceful means, and a pledge to assist any party subject to a breach committed by any other. In this section, I demonstrate that this outcome was achieved by the operation of the social practice of rule-making and interpretation instantiated in this period.

The initial proposal was made by the German government in a note delivered to London on 20 January 1925 and to Paris on 9 February (Jacobson 1972, 4). The conditions surrounding the proposal illustrate the complex politics of rule-making at Locarno. The proposal was a clearly self-interested one, made in hopes of furthering Stresemann's policy of regaining Germany's sovereignty and great power status via negotiation with the Allied powers. In particular, Stresemann's note was intended to prevent an Anglo-French security alliance and to avoid a potential delay in evacuation of allied troops from the Cologne occupation zone.[13] He also sought to secure the withdrawal of the Inter-Allied Military Control Commission (IMCC) and to prevent a French plan to create permanent international commissions to verify German disarmament (Jacobson 1972, 6).

Germany had proposed an international guarantee for the Franco-German border as early as 1922 (Carr 2001, 99), and this proposal was made in renewed form to the British government in 1924 (Cohrs 2006, 259). The diplomatic push in early 1925 was driven by two factors. The first was the December 1924 note

---

[12] Article 2 specifically enumerated two exceptions to this pledge: cases of self-defense, and cases of collective security actions pursuant to either Article 15 or Article 16 of the League Covenant.

[13] The Treaty of Versailles called for the evacuation of one of three occupation zones (Cologne, Koblenz, and Mainz) every five years beginning in 1925, provided that Germany fulfilled its treaty obligations. Spurred by the French, the Inter-Allied Military Control Commission (IMCC) issued findings in December 1924 to the effect that German compliance was inadequate. Germany was informed on 5 January 1925 that, on this basis, the evacuation of Cologne would be indefinitely delayed (Jacobson 1972, 7–8).

from the IMCC and the looming delay in the evacuation of Cologne. German ambassadors in allied capitals had been instructed, even before Germany had been officially notified of the delay, "to argue that an Allied refusal to negotiate a Cologne settlement would have an extremely adverse impact on the German public" (Jacobson 1972, 11). In fact, Stresemann declared that "it would mean the complete bankruptcy" of his cooperative foreign policy (quoted in Jacobson 1972, 12). The failure of this argument emphasizing domestic constraints prompted a new strategy: "to break the link between occupation and treaty enforcement, Stresemann proposed an alternative form of military security—a pact of nonaggression and a treaty of guarantee" (Jacobson 1972, 9). Stresemann thus pursued German interests—most immediately the end of occupation—by making a proposal for new rules binding Germany and its neighbors. He did so in a mutually intelligible form according to what the actors understood as legitimate processes for making rules.

Unfortunately for Stresemann, issues of process would significantly complicate British reception of his proposal. The second factor driving the timing and form of the German proposal was a visit from the British ambassador to Berlin. On 29 December 1924, D'Abernon warned Carl von Schubert, Stresemann's state secretary, that France sought a military alliance with a receptive Chamberlain. Though D'Abernon had proposed schemes similar to Locarno, both to the German government and to his own, since 1923, Germany mistakenly believed his approach to have been officially authorized. In fact, it was not. Proceeding under this misconception, "by January 14 Stresemann and Schubert had decided to subordinate D'Abernon's suggestion for a multilateral nonaggression pact to a scheme prepared by Friedrich Gaus, the legal expert at the Wilhelmstrasse—an international guarantee of Rhineland demilitarization and the *status quo* in Western Europe." The key role for a legal expert in crafting the proposal illustrates awareness of social rules regarding proper form and procedure, and the existence of patterned practice in this regard. This view is further buttressed by the method chosen to communicate the proposal. Because the suggestion had come unofficially from the British ambassador, the reply was made in the same fashion. However, the proposal was made only to London at first, because German policymakers "feared that leaks to the Paris press would result in quick rejection of the proposal" (Jacobson 1972, 9–13).

Because D'Abernon's approach had not been made under instructions from the Foreign Office, Austen Chamberlain instead saw the German proposal as an unsolicited "attempt to initiate secret Anglo-German negotiations" designed to create a rift between Paris and London. This interpretation led to awkward attempts to deflect the proposal. "Eyre Crowe, the Permanent Under-secretary, first tried to postpone the official delivery of the proposal to London, and when Chamberlain did see the German ambassador, Friedrich Sthamer, on January

30, he all but rejected it." In fact, he "even declined to let Sthamer report to Berlin that he favored the German proposal in principle" (Jacobson 1972, 13–14). Given this hostile initial reception, it is remarkable that the German proposal eventually resulted in the Locarno agreements. However, both Britain's eventual reversal and the French reaction were both shaped in important ways by the influence of secondary rules.

The British reversal was decided within the Conservative Baldwin cabinet—particularly the Committee of Imperial Defence (CID). British public opinion had, since the end of the war, become more sympathetic to German claims of unequal treatment and of French excesses in occupation, particularly with respect to the Ruhr. By 19 March 1925, Chamberlain informed the French ambassador, Aimé de Fleuriau, that he was convinced public opinion would not support a security pact between France and Britain that excluded Germany (Cohrs 2006, 210). The combination of press scrutiny with the postwar adoption of universal male suffrage presented a novel constraint; domestic democratic processes of rule-making were at least potentially more relevant to international rule-making than they had ever been. This amounted to a thickening of practices of global rule-making among states, in that it involved new actors (political parties, interest groups, voters, etc.) and presented new opportunities for comparison of rule-making processes in different social contexts.

While democratization represents a novel and important influence on global rule-making in the 1920s, the British reconsideration of Germany's pact proposal ultimately took place in the CID. When the German proposal reached London, the CID remained actively engaged in crafting a further justification of its rejection of the MacDonald government's Geneva Protocol, to be delivered at the League Council meeting in March. The basic problem was that, while "all agreed that a simple statement of rejection would expose the government to the charge that Britain was an obstacle to the resolution of the security problem and to the pacification of Europe . . . they disagreed among themselves as to what alternative constructive suggestion should be proposed" (Jacobson 1972, 15). The matter had been assigned on 16 December 1924 to a subcommittee chaired by Maurice Hankey, which recommended on 13 February 1925 that the government propose a new protocol that would amend the League Covenant to bolster collective security. At this same meeting, Chamberlain mentioned Stresemann's proposal as potential evidence of German moderation, and Lord Curzon "asked him to prepare drafts of an agreement for a four-power security pact which would include Germany along with Britain, France, and Belgium." Thus, British acceptance of the German proposal was driven at least in part by a desire to avoid criticism that Britain was blocking attempts to bolster European security. The Baldwin government's withdrawal of the MacDonald government's Geneva

Protocol created this vulnerability because it allowed critics to point out the reversal in policy and to demand an explanation.

At the 19 February CID meeting, Chamberlain refused to produce the draft Curzon had requested and instead proposed a draft Anglo-French alliance treaty. At decisive meetings on 2 and 4 March, the CID rejected both the new protocol and Chamberlain's proposed alliance. Instead, Chamberlain was instructed "to tell Herriot that a quadrilateral pact including Germany 'might be of great assurance to the peace of Europe.'" Notably, his initial instructions "rigidly precluded him from committing the British government to any specific formula for participation in the Rhineland Pact." They allowed him merely to promise the Baldwin government would "do its best to make possible such a mutual agreement" (Jacobson 1972, 17–20). Dissatisfied with such weak assurances for France, Chamberlain ultimately threatened to resign, prompting Baldwin to personally support Chamberlain's request for a more definitive British stance. The cabinet thus formally committed Britain to negotiation of a multilateral security pact on 20 March, and Chamberlain announced the policy in Parliament four days later (Jacobson 1972, 21).

Chamberlain ultimately accepted the outcome of cabinet deliberations according to established British political practice, though only after exhausting his alternatives. Interestingly, Chamberlain came to embrace the notion of the Locarno agreements, seeing them not as anathema to British interests but rather as consistent with the traditions of British foreign policy. According to Cohrs, by March 1925 Chamberlain "now espoused a policy of reviving the 'concert of Europe'" (Cohrs 2006, 209). Indicative of his change of heart, on 14 March Chamberlain wrote: "Britain's part is now the same as in 1815 and *mutatis mutandis* Castlereagh's policy is the right one today" (quoted in Cohrs 2006, 217). This was a striking change from a man who initially advocated a pure balance of power security alliance with France to contain a rising Germany.

Counterintuitively, French policymakers accepted the German proposal more readily than did Chamberlain, despite the fact that public pressure in France was strongly against concessions to Germany—the opposite situation to that confronted by Britain. To some extent, the French response was driven by financial necessity: subject to an American loan embargo pending resolution of war-debts, Paris was under acute pressure for much of the 1920s. Within the French government, the victorious point of view belonged to Jacques Seydoux, a reparations expert and the sub-division director for economic affairs in the French Foreign Ministry. In his estimation, Cohrs reports, rejecting the offer would lead to France being "accused of 'bad faith' by Anglo-American politicians who could eventually 'oblige' Paris to abandon its hold on Germany 'without any compensations.'" Thus, the French *expected* to be criticized and to incur substantial consequences for breaching secondary rules requiring negotiation in good faith, not only by the Germans but also by their own alliance partners.

Faced with this possibility, the better strategy was to, at minimum, "play along." Indeed, "French policymakers came to see the pact as an opening for more substantial British guarantees" (Cohrs 2006, 212). Accordingly, France began from a maximalist bargaining position; "Herriot demanded that Germany first recognize all French occupation rights in the Rhineland and sign treaties with Poland and Czechoslovakia guaranteeing their territorial *status quo*," but "the *Quai d'Orsay* knew that these were unacceptable demands" (Cohrs 2006, 211). Regardless, to reach its aims, the French government consciously accepted the German proposal as the basis for further negotiation and thus committed itself to engage in a process of rule-making and interpretation with the German government as a legitimate participant.

The influence of secondary rules did not end with the initial acceptance of the German proposal as the basis for negotiation of a multilateral security pact. The next phase in the creation of the Locarno agreements was an extended pre-conference negotiation over several key issues—most notably the conditions under which Germany would join the League of Nations, the question of security guarantees for France's eastern alliance partners (Poland and Czechoslovakia), and the precise circumstances under which the guarantee of military assistance among the parties would be triggered. This negotiation displays the characteristics associated with social practices of rule-making: actors generally made proposals in forms consistent with secondary rules, and denied or justified inconsistencies; also, other actors generally responded to such proposals according to the guidance provided by secondary rules, and denied or justified inconsistencies.

Although Britain and France had accepted the notion of a multilateral security pact by the end of March 1925, the official allied response would not come for another two months. Even before this initial response, contained in a French diplomatic note dated 16 June, the parties had to grapple with the problem of French maximalism, expressed in terms of disarmament demands via the IMCC. Another IMCC report released on 4 June contained mixed findings. While it found considerable compliance, it raised concerns that the Reichswehr was subverting police forces in an attempt to create de facto militias. The note was controversial mainly because its "tone was that of an allied decree commanding the execution of the Treaty of Versailles and threatening sanctions in the case of non-compliance." It was an attempt by Aristide Briand, who had become foreign minister in April 1925, to "establish the principle that ending disarmament inspections and, crucially, an early termination of the Rhineland occupation were contingent on enhanced assurances of security." Despite sympathy for the French position, "Chamberlain insisted that the exchanges over

German disarmament should quickly be eliminated as an irritant in the pact negotiations." He recognized the French attempt to wring concessions from Germany and undermined it with a narrow, process-based argument to separate the thorny problem of disarmament from the German proposal, which was designed in large part to render the disarmament-occupation problem more tractable by providing alternate security reassurances. The German government ably supported Chamberlain's position by declaring that it was willing to discuss any "justified" concerns over its disarmament at some unspecified future time. Though the twin issues of disarmament and occupation would figure prominently in the eventual Locarno conference, Stresemann and Chamberlain succeeded in using process-based arguments to effectively table these issues in order to allow progress on other fronts (Cohrs 2006, 244–45).

The basic French strategy of making onerous demands for participation in security pact negotiations remained intact in Briand's diplomatic note of 16 June. In lieu of more complete German disarmament or extension of deadlines for withdrawal from the Rhineland, France now sought satisfaction on two other fronts: the conditions for German entry into the League of Nations, and security guarantees for Poland and Czechoslovakia—states France had enlisted to balance or contain Germany. Under the initial proposal, Germany would join the League and receive a permanent Council seat, in accordance with its great power status; this was uncontroversial. The Germans insisted, due to Germany's disarmament and its central position in Europe, that it be explicitly exempted from participation in Article 16 collective security actions. The French note, in contrast, sought Germany's entry without any such exemption. Briand also sought to strengthen the eastern arbitration agreements in two ways. First, he proposed that they be made an essential part of the security pact rather than an officially unrelated gesture of German good faith. Second, he demanded that Britain (and, after Chamberlain refused, France) be given the right to guarantee—if necessary by force—that the parties abided by any arbitral award (Cohrs 2006, 245–46).

The German reply, a diplomatic note of 20 July, refused each of these requests. With respect to Article 16, it reiterated the familiar arguments relating to Germany's position and disarmed status. Despite the official defense of its initial position, the note did contain attempts to advance the negotiation; it called for "an extension of the 'system of arbitration treaties' developed by Schubert with the assistance of the Foreign Office's legal expert Friedrich Gaus. In essence, Germany offered to enshrine in the pact the renunciation of war as a means of territorial revision—and to give Warsaw an informal assurance that a modification of Germany's eastern border was not 'acute.' Further, to placate Paris, an explicit linkage of the pact and the Rhineland occupation was avoided." The German note also proposed that further negotiation take place in person, rather than through diplomatic note (Cohrs 2006, 251–52).

Though this initial exchange of diplomatic notes did not lead to any con-crete agreement, it is evident that the French and German governments both engaged in a political process of rule-making and interpretation, and that each regarded this process as legitimate. Proposals were framed in legal language, and drafted with the assistance of legal experts; additionally, the notes contained justifications for positions that were developed at least with reference to, if not in conformity with, shared standards of appropriate state behavior for in-ternational rule-making. Equally striking is that, while France sought to delay the evacuation of the first Rhineland occupation zone around Cologne, it did not seek to delay completion of the Ruhr withdrawal, which was completed in July 1925—ahead of the schedule laid out in the Dawes agreement of 1924 (Cohrs 2006, 245). Such a move would almost certainly have generated oppo-sition not only from Germany, but also from Britain, on the basis that France was disregarding her earlier commitments. Finally, the German note contained one important substantive amendment to the initial proposal: the treaties with Poland and Czechoslovakia would not merely require arbitration *before* resort to war; they would instead contain a pledge not to settle territorial disputes by force in any circumstance. Thus, this process of rule-making led to compromise in the pursuit of agreement.

The core of the Locarno bargain was between France and Germany; how-ever, Britain's essential guarantor role sparked crucial inter-allied discussion in advance of the final conference. This debate concerned the precise nature of the guarantee afforded by the proposed pact. In London, "Locarno was taken to mean that Britain was to come to the immediate assistance of the French only in the event of an actual German attack on France, or if German troops entered the Rhineland with the obvious purpose of immediately marching across the border and invading French territory" (Jacobson 1972, 30). The case of actual or imminent invasion was a clear one, however; the key question was whether the guarantee would be triggered by provocations that fell short of this standard. Britain, largely motivated by considerations of self-interest, sought to mini-mize its commitment. Chamberlain valued an outcome that preserved max-imum freedom of action. The important point is the method by which Britain sought to gain French and Belgian acquiescence. The key figure in this effort was Foreign Office legal adviser Cecil Hurst, who expressed the British view that smaller provocations should be referred to the League of Nations Council and that the Council should only act "if it were convinced that Germany intended war" (quoted in Jacobson 1972, 30). Thus, Britain attempted to employ ex-isting international law and established institutional mechanisms to minimize its Locarno commitment.

The French and Belgian governments, led by Briand and by French Foreign Ministry legal expert Henri Fromageot, responded in kind, arguing that such a procedure would defeat the object of the agreement: by providing Germany with ample mobilization time, the British proposal would diminish the practical value of the Locarno guarantee. Chamberlain, assisted by new Permanent Under-secretary William Tyrell, replied that any mobilization would be preceded by a period of political tension similar to the "July Crisis" of 1914 and that the League could capitalize on this obvious tension to act with sufficient alacrity. The inter-allied debate was ultimately settled at a meeting between Briand and Chamberlain in London on 11–12 August. "As a compromise, the distinction between flagrant and non-flagrant violations of the demilitarized zone was adopted. The two men agreed that British military assistance was to be immediate, and take place without League deliberation, only if Germany resorted to force and committed an unprovoked act of aggression, or if immediate action were necessary because armed forces had been assembled in the demilitarized zone." Chamberlain explained the Anglo-French understanding explicitly in terms of international law. He informed Stresemann that Britain interpreted Locarno as modifying the Treaty of Versailles. Articles 42–44 of Versailles authorized Britain to regard German violations of the demilitarized zone as hostile acts; Locarno applied only to a *class* of such violations, but made military assistance mandatory in response to acts falling within that class (Jacobson 1972, 31–33).

The London meeting also produced an Anglo-French draft treaty that served as the basis for the final phase of negotiations prior to the actual Locarno conference: a meeting of British, French, and German legal experts that took place during early September in London. The very fact of this meeting was a reversal for Briand, who "had long sought to insist on completing the negotiations by way of diplomatic notes, intent on maintaining the appearance of two *entente* powers pursuing a concerted policy vis-à-vis Germany" (Cohrs 2006, 255). Ultimately, the precedent of the 1924 Dawes agreement and the secondary rules according states the right to act as their own legislators could not be overcome, especially given Chamberlain's interest in reviving concert diplomacy. The experts' preparatory meeting largely continued the overall trajectory of negotiations. The most significant development was a clarification of the German position with regard to the eastern treaties. Chamberlain would report to D'Abernon that "Gaus had in fact explained that his government could not sign a document explicitly renouncing war with respect to the eastern frontiers because Berlin regarded this as tantamount to recognizing them. But he had also stressed that the Germans 'were willing to tie themselves up with such conditions that recourse to war would in fact be impossible'" (quoted in Cohrs 2006, 256). Germany's paramount concern with form reflects awareness of the applicable rules of international law, and the way that agreement to one rule could interact with other valid rules. Stresemann was careful to avoid even the appearance of accepting the legitimacy of Germany's territorial status quo with Poland and Czechoslovakia because he realized this would negatively affect Berlin's hope of eventual peaceful territorial gains that could be pursued by means of diplomatic argument. This stance makes sense only if he was aware of the standards by which arguments would be evaluated, and if he believed other actors were likely to place importance on them.

The Locarno conference opened on 5 October 1925, and was attended by British, French, German, Belgian, and Italian delegations. Poland and Czechoslovakia were present only to deal with the eastern arbitration treaties. This difference in status reflected the status hierarchy in the European state system and the way that it was believed to affect standing to participate in rule-making efforts. The proceedings, which lasted until 16 October, were marked by a "remarkably constructive atmosphere" that reflected the substantial legitimacy of the process as well as the actors' relatively consistent commitment to operating according to relevant secondary rules (Cohrs 2006, 259–61). The result was a series of compromises on Germany's League of Nations membership, on security guarantees for Poland and Czechoslovakia, and on the difficult problems of disarmament and Rhineland evacuation.

The first major issue resolved at Locarno was the form of the eastern treaties. On the second day of the conference, Briand reiterated his problematic demand for the inclusion of a French right to guarantee the accords; this was followed promptly by a renewed German refusal justified in terms of domestic opposition. In addition, Germany objected to the inclusion of the agreements in the security pact, for the reasons articulated by Gaus at the meeting of legal experts the previous month. The impasse was broken by a British proposal under which France concluded separate guarantee treaties with Poland and Czechoslovakia on the same day as Locarno was signed. In addition, "article 2 of the Locarno accords stated that France had the right to intervene against Germany under article 16 of the League Covenant—if its Council had declared Germany the aggressor in a conflict with its eastern neighbours" (Cohrs 2006, 262–63). This compromise is an example of the creative use of international law to resolve a deadlock. The French desire to guarantee the security of its eastern alliance partners was preserved, at least in instances where Germany acted as the aggressor according to a mutually agreeable standard of determination, and this was accomplished without the formal appearance of creating a super-sovereign status for France.

The key exchanges on Germany's Article 16 obligations in the League took place in sessions on 7 and 8 October. Chamberlain, despite his empathy for the French position, accepted German arguments; "he deemed it natural that Stresemann had to take into consideration Germany's geo-political position." Ironically, Chamberlain's support for a compromise that would enable the

Locarno agreement was also driven, in part, by his conclusions that the League was weak. On this view, "what mattered more than obligations under article 16, which would always be subject to different interpretations, was the clear commitment of all pact signatories in one specific area: on the Rhine." Chamberlain's view was at once an acknowledgment of the important *limitations* on international practices of rule-making in the 1920s and a pragmatic attempt to overcome these limits in order to improve security. Supplement F explicitly recognized the special circumstances created by Germany's geographic location and disarmament, and acknowledged that this reality limited German ability to take part in collective security measures (Cohrs 2006, 263–64).

In the spring of 1925, Stresemann and Chamberlain had resisted French attempts to extort Germany into making concessions on disarmament and Rhineland occupation as a price for French participation in what would become the Locarno negotiations. By the fall, the tables had been turned. In a series of meetings from 12 to 15 October, Stresemann sought to employ this leverage strategy, seeking to obtain a firm date for the evacuation of the Cologne occupation zone, as well as further concessions on French disarmament and inspection demands (Jacobson 1972, 60). The initial reaction was outrage—Chamberlain went so far as to call them an "attempt at blackmail" (quoted in Cohrs 2006, 266). Despite this strong emotional reaction and the analogy to criminal behavior, both Chamberlain and Briand remained willing to proceed according to applicable secondary rules. They initially sought to dispense with German demands by arguing that "Stresemann had raised issues too numerous and too difficult to be resolved during the conference." Stresemann stood his ground. In response, the allies relied again on a process-based argument. They argued that it was impossible to bypass the Conference of Ambassadors, which oversaw occupation and disarmament, but that the successful conclusion of the Locarno treaties would enable progress on these issues (Jacobson 1972, 62; Cohrs 2006, 267). Similar to the compromise on the arbitration treaties, the strategy was to formally disaggregate elements of the overall political agreement in order to allow the denial of unpalatable quid pro quo arrangements. In this case, this was achieved by a narrow reading of existing rules about which bodies were authorized to make specific kinds of factual determinations. Thus, "it was agreed at Locarno that after their return to Berlin, the Germans would address a note to the Conference of Ambassadors indicating that they had made a serious beginning on disarmament and promising to carry out the most important remaining points. The Allies would then respond, promising to evacuate Cologne by a specified date without waiting for the completion of German disarmament" (Jacobson 1972, 62).

The German note was sent on 23 October; it reported completion of some tasks, progress on others, and also refused to provide any assurance of compliance on five specific issues. This mixed response prompted France's Marshal Foch to insist on a lengthy verification process that would delay evacuation; however, he was jointly opposed in this argument at the late October Conference of Ambassadors meeting by Quai d'Orsay official Jules LaRoche and the Marquess of Crewe (Britain's ambassador to France), who "insisted on a speedy reply in the spirit of Locarno." By 16 November, Briand, in his capacity as chairman of the Conference of Ambassadors, notified the German ambassador in Paris that the evacuation of Cologne would begin on 1 December 1925 and be completed by 26 January 1926. In addition, a diplomatic note dated 14 November promised that troop reduction in the second and third occupation zones (Koblenz and Mainz) would be forthcoming, along with a reduction in the size of the IMCC (Jacobson 1972, 62–64). Stresemann had achieved the most crucial of his objectives, helping him to sell the Locarno treaties to a skeptical domestic public; however, he was obliged to achieve these results by employing the procedures and mechanisms of the Conference of Ambassadors, thereby implicitly legitimizing this creation of the Treaty of Versailles.

Beyond the evidence that secondary rules account for key facets of the process leading to Locarno, the text of the agreement itself supports the conclusion that actors took collective practices of rule-making and interpretation seriously. The treaty of guarantee contained extensive provisions intended to facilitate its interpretation. These provisions amount to the codification of applicable rules of international law analogous to Hart's rules of adjudication. Article 3 of the Locarno treaty commits the parties specifically to submitting disputes relating to the interpretation of treaties to "judicial decision," and all other disputes to a "conciliation commission" or—as a last resort—to the League Council. The fourth article specifies that any allegation of breach must be brought to the Council, which was endowed with the authority to determine if a breach had occurred, and that parties would immediately assist any other party against whom a breach was directed. The sole exception to this procedure was the case of a so-called flagrant violation of the treaty, in which case the other parties were required to immediately assist the victim without waiting for the League Council to act. Article 5 provides that failure to submit disputes for settlement as required by Article 3 triggers the provisions of Article 4. The sixth and seventh articles state the collective interpretation of the parties that the Locarno treaty did not prejudice either their respective rights under the Treaty of Versailles or the authority of the League of Nations to "safeguard the peace of the world." Finally, Article 8 provided for the official deposit of the treaty with the League of Nations and specified that the treaty would remain in force until one year after a two-thirds majority of the League Council "decides that the League of Nations ensures sufficient protection to the High Contracting Parties." Instructions for interpreting and applying the treaty, and for resolving disputes between the parties, make up the bulk of the treaty's text. The care taken in providing such clarification demonstrates that actors were aware of the importance of secondary rules and that they were able to achieve substantial agreement on their precise modalities. The clear legal form of these provisions, combined with the fact that such rules were not a topic of contestation among the Locarno principals, indicates that the treaty's final provisions were not regarded as extremely controversial or as inconsistent with accepted practice.[14]

The Locarno agreements were adopted easily in the French Chamber of Deputies; the October 1925 vote yielded a 413–71 margin in favor, albeit with 60 abstentions. Briand's initial fears of nationalist opposition were largely unrealized. Though the army remained reluctant, even nationalist stalwart Raymond Poincaré came to back Briand's general policy, though largely because of the lack of a viable alternative. Stresemann's domestic situation was more challenging. As in France, the army remained opposed to the accord; in addition, the primary German nationalist party (the DNVP) refused to accept the agreement and resigned from the coalition government on 23 October, focusing its criticism on the continued occupation of Koblenz and Mainz. The agreements would not be approved by the Reichstag until 27 November, when they passed by a slim margin (Cohrs 2006, 76–78; Jacobson 1972, 66).

Internationally, Locarno was received with considerably more enthusiasm. The Seventh Assembly of the League of Nations (fall 1926) declared that "the general ideas embodied in the Treaties of Locarno . . . may well be accepted among the fundamental rules which should govern the foreign policy of every civilized nation" and requested that the Council "recommend the States Members of the League of Nations to put into practice the above-mentioned principles and to offer, if necessary, its good offices for the conclusion of suitable agreements likely to establish confidence and security" (quoted in Rappard 1940, 266). The Eighth Assembly attempted to further the Locarno principles of territorial guarantee, war renunciation, and peaceful dispute resolution by creating a special committee on arbitration and security. It would ultimately report to the Ninth Assembly in the fall of 1929 with three model treaties, one of which was a mutual assistance accord similar to the Rhine guarantee (Rappard 1940, 266–68). These steps were ultimately surpassed by other events, including the 1928 Kellogg-Briand Pact; however, they are indicative of considerable support for legal measures to replace war as a means of conflict resolution.

Germany's entry into the League, however, became a fiasco. After Germany's initial application for membership, including a permanent Council seat as agreed to at Locarno, Poland, Spain, and Brazil also demanded permanent Council seats. Each claim had a slightly different rationale—Spain on the basis

---

[14] "Treaty of Mutual Guarantee between Germany, France, Great Britain, and Italy."

of historical, if faded, great power status; Poland and Brazil on grounds of in-cipient power. Regardless, all the claims were enabled by the nominal equality of sovereign states under international law and by demanding League decision rules. The eventual solution was to offer each of the three "semi-permanent" places on the Council; "Poland accepted this, while Spain threatened to with-draw from the League and Brazil actually did so." The fact of concessions cannot be explained by the material power of the claimants. Instead, their arguments demanded (and received) attention because of the secondary rules of interna-tional politics—especially the tension between sovereign equality and great power responsibility.

The process by which the League Council debacle was resolved highlights the underlying strength of the practice of global rule-making and interpreta-tion: "on four occasions during the League Council meeting (March 7–17), the Locarnites [Briand, Stresemann, and Chamberlain, plus Emile Vandervelde of Belgium and Benito Mussolini] met in Chamberlain's hotel room to discuss, without complete success, the competing claims of the four powers to council seats." Locarno thus led to the revival of concert diplomacy Chamberlain had sought since March 1925; "for the next three and one-half years there persisted a pattern of negotiation by means of meetings of the representatives of the Locarno powers, usually meetings of the Locarno Big Three—Stresemann, Briand and Chamberlain." The meetings dealt with disarmament, the Rhineland and reparations; the leaders "also arbitrated the affairs of the rest of Europe and coordinated their policies in matters considered by the League Council." This informal system of management "came to surpass negotiations through normal diplomatic channels, which were utilized largely to handle low-level or routine matters or, at best, to prepare for future foreign ministers' meetings and to follow up on those previously held" (Jacobson 1972, 69–70). The fate of these diplomatic efforts is outside the scope of my argument here; the im-portant point is that leaders continued to engage in the kinds of social commu-nication entailed by practices of rule-making and interpretation: discussing, justifying, and criticizing proposals and policies on the basis of shared rules and standards. Further, this social practice was not only a tool of the weak, intended to level the playing field of international politics; rather, it was the domain of the great powers and a central mechanism for the management of the international system.

The primary limitation of the Locarno agreements was their regional char-acter. As treaties between a limited set of countries, they had not effected change at the systemic level and had no legal force to bind non-parties. Similarly, the declarations of the League Assembly were hortatory in nature, even if they carried a degree of moral authority. This regional character was not accidental. When approached in the spring of 1925, the new American secretary of state

Frank Kellogg had expressed strong support for the substance of the agreement yet flatly refused to involve the United States as a party to the negotiations (Cohrs 2006, 222). Likewise, Britain had staunchly opposed the French desire to expand the pact's guarantee to encompass Germany's eastern border.

THE KELLOGG-BRIAND PACT

The conclusion of the Kellogg-Briand Pact was hailed as a major progressive step in international politics. Briand's speech at the signing ceremony, held at the Quai d'Orsay on 27 August 1928, allegedly moved the American secretary of state to tears (Miller 1928, 219). The initial list of fifteen signatories comprised the great powers—save the Soviet Union—plus the remaining Locarno signatories, the British Dominions, and India (Miller 1928, 3). By the time of its entry into force, triggered by the Japanese ratification on 24 July 1929, thirty-one more states had ratified the treaty, and another seventeen would ratify it after it became operative, bringing the total number of ratifications to sixty-three by 10 May 1934 (Ferrell 1952, 258). The treaty, which contained a strong legal ban on the use of warfare to settle disputes, had become essentially universal.

The fascinating truth is that this remarkable outcome was completely unintended. The Kellogg-Briand Pact, in its multilateral form, was a product of the social practice of rule-making that neither of the two men whose name it bore had sought to create. Briand made the initial proposal on 6 April 1927, the tenth anniversary of American entry into the First World War. He did so in the unorthodox form of a direct statement to the American people via the Associated Press, a fact that would cause significant confusion and delay. In his statement, Briand offered that France would "subscribe publicly with the United States to any mutual engagement to outlaw war, to use an American expression, as between these two countries" (Rappard 1940, 168). He famously called for "the renunciation of war as an instrument of national policy," in language that would survive the negotiations (ironically because of American insistence) and appear in the final treaty (Cohrs 2006, 448). Crucially, the French proposal was for a *bilateral* treaty.

Briand's proposal was driven by an interest in improving relations with the United States, and in achieving assurances of American neutrality—if not assistance—in the event of a European war. Franco-American relations suffered under two primary sources of strain at the time of Briand's proposal: differences in disarmament talks, and the question of French war debts owed to the United States. The disarmament issue was reflected in Kellogg's testimony to the House of Representatives Foreign Affairs Committee on 11 January 1927. He informed the committee that France insisted on the conclusion of security guarantees before disarmament, on international inspection to verify the fulfilment of disarmament obligations, that agreements should be universal in scope, and that accords must take into account each state's military-industrial potential in addition to its current level of armament. These concerns were directed at maintaining the French position of strategic superiority vis-à-vis Germany. In contrast, the United States sought to conclude disarmament agreements without incurring obligations to provide military assistance, in keeping with its policy of minimizing its diplomatic activity. Further, Kellogg opposed verification on the grounds that such mechanisms would merely "create new elements of suspicion" between states, and sought to restrict talks to dealing with actual armament levels, on the grounds that assessing a state's military capacity was too difficult (Cohrs 2006, 427–30). In addition to differences over disarmament, France and the United States had not yet resolved repayment of French war debts. France sought to reduce its obligations, while the American government insisted on complete repayment.[15] Finally, the proposed treaty was consistent with ongoing French efforts to secure guarantees of military assistance against possible German irredentism. The language of the pact, calling for a ban on war between the parties, was intended to preclude the United States from entering a war on the opposite side from France. Moreover, this language was consistent with French diplomatic practice in its alliance treaties with states in Eastern Europe—particularly its 1926 alliances with Romania and Yugoslavia, which contained language banning war between the parties (Ferrell 1952, 64, 67).

Clear French interests in proposing the pact do not, however, fully explain its form. Beyond the consistency with the 1926 alliances, there is compelling evidence that Briand sought to frame his proposal such that it would resonate with the American public. On 22 March 1927, Briand met in Paris with Professor James T. Shotwell of the Carnegie Endowment for International Peace, one of the leading American antiwar organizations. Briand convinced Shotwell that it was he who persuaded Briand to make the proposal, despite the apparent incongruity of a bilateral agreement approximating what were clearly French alliance treaties having been written by an American advocate of world peace. Beyond the initial proposal, Briand would continue to encourage and even orchestrate the efforts of the American peace movement, in an attempt to exert pressure on the Coolidge administration to reach an agreement (Ferrell 1952, 68–72). This strategy displays a sophisticated awareness of the evolving role of citizens and non-governmental organizations (NGOs) in processes of global rule-making.

---

[15] The question of war debt was eventually resolved by the Mellon-Bérenger agreement, which was signed in 1926 but not ratified by the French Chambre until 1928. See Ferrell (1952, 69). For additional background, an excellent general history is provided in Cohrs (2006).

Despite Briand's innovative best efforts, the initial results were lackluster. His message to the American public attracted little popular attention; it appeared on page 5 of the *New York Times*, page 4 of the *Washington Post*, and page 12 of the *Chicago Herald-Tribune*, while it was not carried at all by the *Chicago Daily Tribune* or the *Los Angeles Times* (Ferrell 1952, 74). The proposal failed to generate a response from the State Department as well; "since there was no communication to the Department . . . those in authority in Washington appeared to consider the Briand message simply as an expression of friendship" (Miller 1928, 6). Briand's message was, perhaps, too innovative in form. By departing from accepted procedures for international practices of rule-making, he had undermined the efficacy of his proposal.

At this juncture, however, Briand's courtship of the American peace movement proved useful. A letter to the editor written by Dr. Nicholas Murray Butler appeared in the *New York Times* on 25 April 1927. Butler was the head of the Carnegie Endowment, the president of Columbia University, an unsuccessful candidate for the Republican presidential nomination in 1920 and 1928, and a prominent public intellectual who would eventually share the 1931 Nobel Peace Prize. In the weeks following the publication of Butler's letter praising Briand's proposal, at least three draft treaties were released to the press by American peace groups (Miller 1928, 7–8), and the general atmosphere was one of a "rush for the bandwagon, hitherto so empty" (Ferrell 1952, 74). Amidst the public pressure, Kellogg nevertheless insisted that the State Department refrain from comment, on the grounds that the proposal had not been properly transmitted through diplomatic channels. Privately, he met with George Barton French, a mutual friend to Kellogg and to Butler, in order to express strong displeasure with Butler's actions, which Kellogg saw as diplomatically embarrassing to the administration (Ferrell 1952, 78, 82).

Seeking to capitalize on the shift in American public opinion, Briand made an informal inquiry through US ambassador Myron T. Herrick as to whether the administration would enter negotiations on a bilateral treaty for the renunciation of war (Ferrell 1952, 89). Kellogg's basis for ignoring the French overture had vanished. Accordingly, he directed Herrick to reply that "the United States will be pleased to engage in diplomatic conversations on the subject of a possible agreement along the lines indicated by M. Briand's statement to the press on April sixth last" (quoted in Miller 1928, 9). Diplomatic niceties aside, Kellogg was certainly not pleased. As a delay tactic, he instructed Herrick to suggest the opening of negotiations through the French ambassador to the United States, Paul Claudel, who was currently in France. This attempt to delay by manipulating diplomatic process backfired badly; "Philippe Berthelot, Secretary-General of the French Ministry of Foreign Affairs, sent for Sheldon Whitehouse, the American *chargé d'affaires* in Paris, on the evening of June 21. He informed Whitehouse that Secretary Kellogg's suggestions as to conversations on the proposed pact were very pleasing to his chief, Aristide Briand. But as the French Ambassador to the United States would not reach Washington until the end of August, Briand thought that was too long a time to delay doing anything about the proposed pact. Briand had, therefore, drafted a suggested text" (Ferrell 1952, 94–96). The French draft consisted of a preamble, standard procedural clauses dealing with ratification and entry into force, and two operative articles consisting of one sentence each. In a departure from standard practice, it was not accompanied by a diplomatic note (Miller 1928, 10). Article 1 declared that "the high contracting Powers solemnly declare, in the name of the French people and the people of the United States of America, that they condemn recourse to war, and renounce it respectively as an instrument of their national policy towards each other." Article 2 provided that "the settlement or the solution of all disputes or conflicts, of whatever nature or of whatever origins they may be, which may arise between France and the United States of America, shall never be sought by either side except by pacific means" (quoted in Wheeler-Bennett 1928, 72–73). Briand had turned Kellogg's attempt to delay against him, and effectively presented the Coolidge administration with a fait accompli rather than a three-month delay in the start of negotiations over a potential text.

The United States did not reply to the French draft of 20 June 1927 for a full six months. The intervening period was marked by extensive internal discussion of how to respond. State Department officials were conscious both of the French attempt to use the language of war renunciation to bolster their strategic freedom of action and of strong American public support for outlawing war. J. T. Marriner, chief of the State Department's Division of Western European Affairs, wrote in a 24 June memo that the French proposal amounted to "a kind of perpetual alliance between the United States and France, which would seriously disturb the other great European Powers—England, Germany and Italy" (Cohrs 2006, 450). Despite this unwanted outcome, Marriner treated future negotiations as inevitable; he wrote that:

> *when* the time comes to actually negotiate, it would seem that the only answer to the French proposition would be that, as far as our relations with France were concerned, adequate guarantees were contained in the Bryan Treaty, and that if any step further than this were required, it should be in the form of a universal undertaking not to resort to war, to which the United States would at any time be most happy to become a party. Before such a time, treaties of the nature which France suggests become practically negative military alliances.[16]

---

[16] Ferrell (1952, 107). The Bryan Treaty referred to was one of a series of identical arbitration treaties concluded by the United States under Secretary of State William Jennings Bryan; the treaty with France was up for renewal at the time of initial negotiations on Briand's new proposal.

Marriner's belief that the United States would ultimately need to engage in negotiations over the French proposal was shared by senior State Department official William R. Castle Jr., who wrote in his diary on 6 May 1927 that there was "too much pacifist feeling in this country to permit a refusal" (quoted in Cohrs 2006, 451). In addition to its assumption that the French proposal would require a response even if its substance ran counter to American interests, Marriner's memo is noteworthy in that it is the first appearance of the eventual American move to counter the French proposal. Both the secretary of state and his political mentor, the isolationist Idaho Republican senator William Borah, would later claim the idea as their own, but Marriner's memo appears to predate either man's articulation of such a concept. In fact, Kellogg and Coolidge would exchange letters in late June indicating their mutual acceptance of Marriner's analysis (Ferrell 1952, 107).

The French proposal had been the subject of informal diplomatic discussions among the great powers throughout the spring of 1927. By 30 June, the United States made more formal assurances to the Japanese ambassador, Tsuneo Matsudaira, that it would not conclude a bilateral accord with France. On 6 July, Kellogg went further, assuring British ambassador Sir Esme Howard that the United States would conclude no agreement with France that it would not be willing to sign with any other state (Ferrell 1952, 107–8). These assurances reflect the conclusion in Marriner's memo and foreshadow the eventual American reply.

State Department officials spent much of the remainder of summer 1927 focused on disarmament talks in Geneva that adjourned in failure on 4 August. Geneva, however, would remain the site of important diplomatic discussions related to Briand's proposed pact. At the Eighth League of Nations Assembly in September, smaller states sought to insert themselves in the dialogue regarding war renunciation. The Dutch foreign minister noted international sentiment favoring the outlawry of war and, on this basis, proposed a resolution on 6 September calling on the League Assembly to reconsider the "general principles" embodied in the stillborn Geneva Protocol of 1924. Three days later, the Polish delegate proposed a different resolution designating war of aggression "an international crime." The Polish resolution contained three substantive clauses: "(1) That all wars of aggression are, and always shall be, prohibited; (2) That every pacific means must be employed to settle disputes, of every description, which may arise between States; (3) The Assembly declares that the States Members of the League are under an obligation to conform to these principles" (quoted in Cohrs 2006, 121).

In substance, the resolutions—especially the Polish one—were similar to the text under consideration between France and the United States. The crucial difference was the involvement of the League and the resulting provision for sanctions. Austen Chamberlain objected on the grounds that he could not commit Britain to guaranteeing every border in the same fashion as it had agreed to do at Locarno; however, he would not raise similar objections in the multilateral negotiations that followed between the great powers. Ultimately, both the Dutch and Polish resolutions were referred to the Assembly's Third Committee, which dealt with the body's agenda. An attempt to combine the two was stymied by Chamberlain because it relied on the former Labour government's Geneva Protocol (Ferrell 1952, 122–23). This exchange highlights the importance placed by actors on the institutional context in which proposed rules were located. While Chamberlain was willing to negotiate a ban on war on an ad hoc basis, he ruled out a similar proposal advanced by smaller powers via the machinery of the League. This difference displays the tension between conflicting secondary rules providing for sovereign equality and for great power responsibility in managing the international system, and the crucial role for power in practices of rule-making. However, it is noteworthy that Britain opposed the Dutch and Polish resolutions in the first instance by referring them to committee for further discussion—effectively removing them from the spotlight before decisively opposing them.

The United States was not involved in the League Assembly deliberations; instead, American officials concentrated on the domestic politics related to the war renunciation treaty—primarily the problem of reconciling strong public support for the plan with the perceived likelihood of strong opposition in the Senate. The Senate had consistently blocked efforts by various administrations to conclude international arbitration treaties, on the grounds that referring an individual dispute to arbitration required the advice and consent of the Senate.[17] It was expected that the Senate would object to a war renunciation treaty on similar grounds. On 25 November, President Coolidge referred to the problem at a press conference, where he said: "I have given some thought to the outlawry of war. Any treaties made on that subject are somewhat difficult under our Constitution." It is unclear whether this declaration was intended as a justification to legitimize rejection of the French proposal in the eyes of public opinion or a genuine attempt to ascertain the Senate's likely reaction. In any event, Senator Borah, chairman of the Senate Foreign Relations Committee, declared the following day that, in his view, such a treaty would not trespass Congressional authority but rather make the exercise of that authority (in the form of a declaration of war) unnecessary. Given the close relationship between Borah and Kellogg, it is difficult to rule out a coordinated political strategy either to facilitate or impede a treaty. The president remained sufficiently concerned about the constitutionality of a potential treaty that he addressed the matter in his State of

---

[17] The history of American arbitration treaties is covered comprehensively in Boyle (1999).

the Union address on 6 December. He sought to minimize the importance of treaties for preventing war, arguing that "the heart of the Nation is more important," while allowing that the United States should "promote peace . . . by such international covenants against war as we are permitted under our Constitution to make" (Ferrell 1952, 117–18, 131).

The constitutionality of the treaty was not a major obstacle either to the negotiations or the eventual ratification of the treaty by the Senate, rendering this set of exchanges something of a mystery. There seem to be at least two broad possibilities, both of which are consistent with my argument that procedural rules shape international political outcomes. The first is that Coolidge sought a legitimate "out," both for domestic and international audiences, in the event that negotiations created an outcome deemed unacceptable. The reiteration of his concern in the State of the Union address indicated a repudiation of Borah's opinion that the treaty was constitutional, and the lack of constitutional complication merely indicates that the administration was satisfied with the resulting treaty. On this view, Coolidge utilized secondary rules with an eye to preserving his freedom to reject an eventual treaty.

The second possibility is that Coolidge sought to ascertain the Senate's reaction, and that both his initial acknowledgment of potential constitutional issues and Borah's optimistic interpretation were trial balloons. On this account, the State of the Union reference simply indicates the possibility that Borah's interpretation would not be accepted, particularly if the treaty contained strong sanctions provisions that could definitively commit the United States to collective security actions—thus effectively warning European governments against inclusion of the kinds of measures contemplated by resolutions introduced at the League Assembly. That Kellogg did not raise the constitutional issue in negotiations would then suggest either that the message was received or that the European great powers did not press for strong sanctions for other reasons, or both. The greater puzzle in this scenario is why the Senate accepted Borah's interpretation. Given that treaties are incorporated into American domestic law, the approval of a complete antiwar treaty would have created a situation whereby the Congress would violate international and American law in exercising one of its explicit constitutional prerogatives. It thus seems likely that either the Senate was generally convinced the text contained loopholes sufficient to avoid this untenable situation, that they regarded the Borah interpretation as effective political "cover" allowing them to support a popular but constitutionally suspect treaty, or both. The crucial point is that, under any of these scenarios, actors regarded rules about legitimate rule-making procedures as both real and effective. Secondary rules about the role of Congress in foreign policy shaped the administration's actions in the fall of 1927, creating and foreclosing options and demanding that the president engage in particular kinds of speech acts in pursuit of his policy goals.

Four days after Coolidge delivered his State of the Union address, Castle met with Claudel. Claudel's task in this meeting was to derail the negotiations. His initial proposal was that the two countries turn their attention either to renewing or to replacing their bilateral arbitration treaty. This prompted Castle to ask "whether he was referring to the draft of a treaty outlawing war submitted through Mr. Herrick by M. Briand. . . . The Ambassador went on to say, however, that he thought the world was obviously not yet sufficiently advanced to make a treaty of this nature acceptable." Castle replied by expressing the view that the proposed treaty "might be of some use in its appeal to sentiment" but that "it could easily be of very real harm if it were a treaty concluded between the two countries only." Further, he told Claudel that he "could not see any particular harm in a treaty of this nature if it could be concluded between a great number of countries" even if "in the present stage of world sentiment, these treaties would hardly be more than words." Castle's diary entries and memoranda reveal him as something of a skeptic, who saw the primary virtue of the negotiations as an opportunity to paint the French into a diplomatic corner.

After Castle had directly raised the notion of a multilateral treaty with a French representative for the first time, Claudel sought to counter by raising the possibility that constitutional complications would prevent the United States from ratifying a strong treaty. Castle recalled Claudel arguing as follows: "after all, if we could have a really strong preamble we should have done what we can with words and satisfied public sentiment and that it would then do no harm to have what some people would call a 'weak treaty'" (quoted in Ferrell 1952, 132–33). Castle then solicited Claudel's suggestion for an arbitration treaty preamble renouncing war; Claudel complied, and "pointed out that the actual treaty might well be substantially the present arbitration treaty." Thus, by 10 December, France was aware that the Coolidge administration would call for a multilateral version of Briand's treaty, and responded by seeking a diplomatic re-treat. Claudel pursued this retreat by attempting to merge the war renunciation treaty with the renewal of the Franco-American arbitration treaty. Including the reference to war renunciation in the preamble of a bilateral treaty would both avoid a multilateral document and rob the language of its legal force. Further, he sought to entice the American government by offering the French retreat as a solution both to constitutional issues and to the very public pressure that Briand had created in the first place.

In fact, the bilateral arbitration treaty was renewed on 6 February 1928 (Ferrell 1952, 135); however, Kellogg and his associates would not let Briand off the hook so easily. At a closed hearing of the Senate Foreign Relations Committee on 22 December 1927, Borah joined the emerging consensus that the best response was to expand the original French proposal. He stated that "I think, Mr. Secretary, you may consider it the sense of the committee that you go ahead with the negotiation of a pact to include all countries" (Ferrell 1952, 139). Kellogg handed the French ambassador the first official reply to the French proposal on 28 December 1927, and it proposed just such a multilateral pact. Claudel's reply was "that he doubted if Briand would consider a multilateral treaty unless Kellogg could explain clearly why the United States could not conclude a bilateral treaty." In response, Kellogg observed that such a treaty between the United States and Germany would be sure to cause tension with France, and that American public opinion would conclude that any bilateral treaty "looked too much like an alliance and too short a step toward universal peace" (Ferrell 1952, 145).

The crucial point is that Claudel's response, to demand a justification for the American position, is entirely consistent with the argument of the book that actors pursue change in social rules by engaging in a rule-governed practice of rule-making. The same can be said of the justification Kellogg provided, which privileged the reaction not only of another great power but also that of American public opinion. Castle, in particular, was acutely aware of the awkward position that the United States had maneuvered France into; he wrote exultantly that Briand "has now got a bad case of cold feet. They will be positively frozen when we drive him out into the open and make him do something, or refuse to do something" (quoted in Ferrell 1952, 147).

The note delivered to Claudel deliberately conformed as closely as possible to the language employed in the original French draft. It cast the notion of a multilateral treaty as "a more signal contribution to world peace" than a bilateral version and suggested "a treaty among the principal Powers of the world, open to signature by all nations, condemning war and renouncing it as an instrument of national policy in favour of the pacific settlement of international disputes" (quoted in Wheeler-Bennett 1928, 75). Over the winter of 1928, several diplomatic notes were exchanged between France and the United States that comprise the heart of the negotiation over what would become the Kellogg-Briand Pact. It quickly became evident that debate would revolve around five interrelated issues: the specific signing procedure to be adopted for a multilateral pact, the precise language adopted in order to ban war, the compatibility of the proposed treaty with existing diplomatic arrangements (especially Locarno and the League of Nations), the status of the right to self-defense, and the consequences of a breach of the treaty.

Three days after Claudel received the American diplomatic note, Briand met Whitehouse in Paris. With the failure of his attempt to replace the war renunciation treaty with the preamble of the arbitration treaty, Briand now pursued a different tactic. He informed Whitehouse that France opposed a multilateral treaty and suggested instead that the countries create a diplomatic protocol to the same effect (Ferrell 1952, 147). This attempt to downgrade the legal status of any multilateral product is consistent with the attempt to restrict war renunciation language to a treaty preamble, and makes sense only if Briand believed the specific legal form of a treaty mattered—and that other states would also take this view. The suggestion was not accepted by the United States, and Briand set about crafting his official reply, dated 5 January 1928.

In his note, Briand acknowledged the potential for the American proposal to inspire other states to adhere to the treaty, and he attempted to create the impression of agreement. He wrote that:

> I am authorized to inform you that the Government of the Republic is disposed to join with the Government of the United States in proposing for agreement by all nations a treaty to be signed at the present time by France and the United States and under the terms of which the high contracting parties shall renounce all war of aggression, and shall declare that for the settlement of differences of whatever nature which may arise between them they will employ all pacific means (quoted in Wheeler-Bennett 1928, 77).

There were two material differences between Briand's note and Kellogg's. The first, that France and the United States should negotiate and sign the treaty before inviting other states to adhere, was designed to achieve the substance of a bilateral accord. The second dealt with the language creating the ban on war. Kellogg's proposal had self-consciously adopted Briand's language regarding the renunciation of war "as an instrument of national policy"; in contrast, Briand had seemingly narrowed the scope of the treaty to preclude only "war of aggression." The latter change, to French language from Briand's original proposal, was made "without comment or explanation"; David Hunter Miller, an American treaty expert, concluded that the French note "was not well framed and seems to have been written without much thought of American official or American popular sentiment" (Miller 1928, 20).

Regardless, Briand's changes were immediately noticed by the State Department. Castle wrote in his diary on 7 January: "We shall not sign anything with France unless we know very well that the other nations will sign it also and we shall not be willing to include the phrase 'aggressive war' because that immediately links the thing up with the League of Nations and makes a definition of aggression necessary" (quoted in Ferrell 1952, 150–51). In the meeting at which he delivered Briand's note, Claudel proposed yet another alternative that would prevent the creation of a multilateral treaty: a "declaration of principles" governing the Franco-American relationship. France clearly continued to cast about for alternatives sanctioned by relevant secondary rules, going to great lengths not to directly refuse the American proposal.

The American reply of 11 January 1928 directly raised the two changes Briand had sought to insert. With regard to the plan to sign a bilateral treaty that would be open for adherence, Kellogg argued that "this procedure would be open to the objection that a treaty, even though acceptable to France and the United States, might for some reason be unacceptable to one of the other great Powers." In contrast, if the negotiations were multilateral, "the views of the Governments concerned could be accommodated through informal preliminary discussions and a text devised which would be acceptable to them all" (quoted in Wheeler-Bennett 1928, 78–79). The rejection of Briand's proposal was articulated in terms of prudential considerations, but this concern was rooted in the secondary rules that provided states with the right to be bound only by the rules they had agreed to. Kellogg's reply also envisioned special consideration for the great powers in negotiating the treaty text.

On the matter of the language to be employed in banning war, Kellogg capitalized on the lack of explanation in order to deflect what Castle's diary indicated was seen as an attempt to ensnare the United States in the legal machinery of the League, which could potentially lead to unwanted security obligations in Europe. Kellogg wrote that he hoped the change in language did not indicate that France would decline to join him in proposing:

> that the original formula submitted by M. Briand, which envisaged the unqualified renunciation of all war as an instrument of national policy, be made the subject of preliminary discussions with the other great Powers for the purpose of reaching a tentative agreement as to the language to be used in the proposed treaty (quoted in Wheeler-Bennett 1928, 80).

Kellogg closed his note by suggesting that the official diplomatic correspondence to date be copied to the United Kingdom, Germany, Italy, and Japan.

The French reply, dated 21 January 1928, responded directly to Kellogg's criticisms. It asserted that the French suggestions were not substantive differences, but rather procedural conveniences. The plan for a bilateral treaty open to accession reflected "a desire more speedily and more surely to achieve the result which [France] seeks in common with the United States." Briand then conceded that France was "ready to concur in any method which may appear to be most practicable." The French note similarly offered a post hoc justification along with an effective concession on the matter of the draft language for the treaty. It claimed that the phrase "war of aggression" was "inspired by the formula which has already gained the unanimous adherence of all the States Members of the League of Nations, and for that reason might be adopted by them with regard to the United States, just as it has already been accepted among themselves." Thus, the language was merely intended to allow the treaty to include League members. Nevertheless, the note made clear that France would "very gladly welcome any suggestions offered by the American Government which would make it possible to reconcile an absolute condemnation of war with the engagements and obligations assumed by the several nations and the legitimate concern for their respective security." While conceding a return to what Kellogg had called Briand's "original formula," France insisted on alterations designed to ensure the continued legitimacy of self-defense and the protection of the vital security guarantees embodied in Locarno and the League of Nations (quoted in Wheeler-Bennett 1928, 82–84).

In his next note of 27 February, Kellogg attacked the French claim that qualification of the ban on war was necessary in order to allow France to sign a multilateral treaty without endangering its commitments under Locarno and to the League. He sought to make his point first on an abstract level, objecting that "it is hardly to be presumed that members of the League of Nations are in a position to do separately something they cannot do together." In a more practical vein, Kellogg pointed out "the recent adoption of a resolution by the Sixth International Conference of American States expressing . . . unqualified condemnation of war as an instrument of policy in their mutual relations." He emphasized that "of the twenty-one States represented at the Conference, seventeen are members of the League of Nations." His strategy was to point out that other League members interpreted their obligations such that they were consistent with exactly the type of war renunciation language Briand had initially proposed, to force France to abandon its objection or at least to provide further justification. He also sought, at a more general level, to create a compatibility of purpose between the League and the type of treaty he envisioned. He argued that a universal treaty "would be a most effective instrument for promoting the great ideal of peace which the League itself has so closely at heart" (quoted in Wheeler-Bennett 1928, 86–87).

Kellogg expanded his position with respect to the effect of his treaty proposals on the obligations of League members at a 15 March speech to the Council on Foreign Relations. The crucial issues at stake were the collective security provisions contained in Article 10 and Article 16 of the Covenant. Neither, he noted, contained a positive obligation for League members to go to war. To the contrary, the League's membership had consistently interpreted Article 10 to vest the decision whether or not a state would participate in collective security action with its constitutional authorities. This interpretation had been established, at least informally, by a Canadian resolution to the Fourth Assembly that had been blocked by only a single dissenting vote (Wheeler-Bennett 1928, 92–93).

By early March, there is evidence that Kellogg's pursuit of a strong treaty—initially a tactical position taken to embarrass Briand into abandoning his unwelcome attempt to create a de facto alliance—had become sincere. On 6 March, Castle's diary records his surprise at a change in Kellogg's attitude: "The funny thing is that [Assistant Secretary of State] Olds and the Secretary seem to take it all with profound seriousness" (quoted in Ferrell 1952, 165). Kellogg himself wrote, in a 21 July letter to journalist Walter Lippmann, that he saw the pact as a "valuable, practical and psychological enforcement of existing efforts to maintain world peace" (quoted in Cohrs 2006, 418). The sources of this personal change of heart are not vital to my argument; however, it does not seem unreasonable to conclude that it was at least related to the experience of negotiating the agreement over the course of a full year. In any event, Kellogg's sincere pursuit of a treaty took the same form as when it was a tactical gambit. This consistency is evidence of a settled social practice—regardless of his motives, Kellogg knew how to effectively pursue a multilateral treaty by legal and diplomatic argument, believed this was a legitimate response to the French proposal, and thought that other relevant actors would share this assessment of procedural legitimacy.

The next French diplomatic note, dated 26 March, was delivered by Claudel on 30 March. It again pressed the claim that a multilateral treaty could not employ the same language as a bilateral treaty between France and the United States:

> In order to pay due regard to the international obligations of the signatories, it was not possible, as soon as it became a question of a multi-lateral treaty, to impart thereto the unconditional character desired by Your Excellency without facing the necessity of obtaining the unanimous adherence of all the existing States, or at least of all the interested States, that is to say, those which by reason of their situation are exposed to the possibility of a conflict with any one of the contracting States (quoted in Wheeler-Bennett 1928, 96).

In addition to protecting the sanctity of the League Covenant and Locarno, the French reply was concerned with the case of a state being attacked by a nonparty. Accordingly, it contained two proposals. First, the treaty should "only come into force after having received universal acceptance, unless the Powers having signed this treaty or acceded thereto should agree upon its coming into force, despite certain abstentions." Second, that "if one of the signatory States should fail to keep its word, the other signatories should be released from their engagement with respect of the offending State." On this point, as well as the compatibility of the treaty with Locarno and the Covenant, Briand now felt comfortable declaring that "the French Government now believes itself fully in accord with the Government of the United States." In addition, the note stated that France "likewise gathers from the declarations which Your Excellency was good enough to make to me on March 1st last, the assurance that the renunciation of war, thus proclaimed, would not deprive the signatories of the right of legitimate defence" (quoted in Wheeler-Bennett 1928, 98).

Despite these signs of convergence in the French and American interpretations of the text's meaning, the French note made a point of disputing Kellogg's reference to the resolutions passed at the Havana conference of American states. It noted that the unconditional condemnation of war Kellogg had touted was contained in the preamble of a resolution that "in itself constituted only a kind of preliminary tending toward a treaty of arbitration to which numerous reservations were formulated." Further, it pointed out that the same conference had adopted a *second* resolution "limited to the very terms 'war of aggression' which the French Government felt compelled to use in characterizing the renunciation to which it was requested to bind itself by means of a multi-lateral treaty" (quoted in Wheeler-Bennett 1928, 96). France and the United States had begun the process of reconciling their interpretations, but important points of contention still remained, and questions of procedure were vital parts of an ongoing collective practice of rule-making and interpretation.

Kellogg had preferred a joint text be communicated to the other great powers; however, in light of the difficulty encountered in reaching final agreement, the United States circulated a draft to France, the United Kingdom, Germany, Italy, and Japan on 13 April 1928—with the understanding that France would provide an alternate text shortly thereafter. Rather than settling disputes about the treaty text bilaterally and transmitting a joint proposal, the negotiations would expand with the task of adjudicating between the French and American drafts unfinished. The American draft treaty of 13 April, like the proposal made to France on 28 December 1927, adopted the language of Briand's original proposal; the only changes were those required to create a multilateral rather than a bilateral instrument. The covering note explained that France would communicate its position separately, but that the United States "has not conceded that such considerations necessitate any modifications of its proposal for a multi-lateral treaty" and pointed out the fidelity of its draft to the original French proposal.[18]

In contrast to the spare three-article American draft, the French text contained six articles. The first specified the preservation of legitimate self-defense, as well as collective security actions pursuant to the League Covenant and Locarno agreements. The second article required signatories to employ

---

[18] The covering note is reproduced in Wheeler-Bennett (1928, 101–2).

peaceful means to settle disputes. The third article provided that parties would be released from their obligations under the treaty toward any state violating the ban on war. The fourth article stipulated that the treaty did not circumscribe the obligations created by prior international treaties. The fifth provided that the treaty would enter into force only with universal accession, unless the parties agreed otherwise. The final article dealt with the details for ratification (Ferrell 1952, 171–72).

The first reply to the American draft came in the form of an eager acceptance from the German government, delivered on 27 April 1928 (Wheeler-Bennett 1928, 110–13). This reaction was consistent with Schubert's goal to "devalue as far as possible the superior position of military power of states like France through legal commitments" (quoted in Cohrs 2006, 463). Before any other replies were made, however, Kellogg delivered a crucial speech before the American Society of International Law on 28 April. The address essentially made public an internal analysis of the French draft Kellogg had prepared for American ambassadors on 23 April to ensure a consistent American voice (Ferrell 1952, 175–76). Kellogg began by summarizing the six articles of the French draft before expressing his position that the French concerns had been met in the language of the American draft.

He asserted that the right of self-defense "is inherent in every sovereign State and is implicit in every treaty." He continued by taking the position that "no treaty provision can add to the natural right of self-defence" and that, therefore, "it is not in the interest of peace that a treaty should stipulate a juristic conception of self-defence, since it is far too easy for the unscrupulous to mould events to accord with an agreed definition" (quoted in Wheeler-Bennett 1928, 107). Here, Kellogg departed from the expectations of his European counterparts, who were consistently more eager to specify the rules of adjudication that would allow the parties to clearly interpret the proposed treaty and successfully apply its provisions to particular cases. While there was no substantive disagreement about the status of self-defense under the treaty, France and the United Kingdom would subsequently push Kellogg to agree to the inclusion of language designed to prevent future difficulties in arriving at shared conclusions about how the treaty would operate in practice. This type of dispute is emblematic of processes of global rule-making in that it deals with specifying how a proposed rule interacts with other existing rules as part of a larger rule system.

The second subject Kellogg dealt with was the compatibility of the American draft with the obligations entailed by the League Covenant and Locarno. He reiterated the position he had staked out in his 15 March address to the Council on Foreign Relations: that the League's own members had consistently upheld the right of states to decide for themselves whether or not to go to war in particular cases of collective action and that, similarly, any positive obligation to go to war under the provisions of Locarno "certainly would not attach until one of the parties has resorted to war in violation of its solemn pledges thereunder." These facts enabled Kellogg to advance a creative argument. If the members of the League and the parties to Locarno all adhered to the antiwar treaty, any situation requiring collective action would also entail a breach of the obligation not to employ war as an instrument of national policy. Accordingly, "the other parties to the anti-war treaty would thus, as a matter of law, be automatically released from their obligations thereunder and free to fulfil" their collective security commitments. It was Kellogg's attitude that "any express recognition of this principle of law is wholly unnecessary" (quoted in Wheeler-Bennett 1928, 108–9). Again, Kellogg made clear that the difference between the American and French drafts was not a difference in substance, but rather a procedural difference about the extent to which the text should explicitly specify the appropriate interpretation of the pact's meaning.

There was, however, one important substantive difference between the American and French drafts. The French text provided for the treaty to enter into force only when it had been universally ratified; in contrast, the American proposal was for entry into force upon the treaty's ratification by the six great powers—the United States, France, the United Kingdom, Germany, Italy, and Japan. Kellogg relied on a practical argument against the French position; namely, that the French formula would allow a "spoiler" to entirely defeat the treaty either by acceding to it and then refusing to officially ratify the accord or by simply refusing to sign. Further, he argued that "the coming into force among the above-named six Powers of an effective anti-war treaty and their observance thereof would be a practical guarantee against a second world war" (quoted in Wheeler-Bennett 1928, 110). Even if universal adherence could not be secured, a partial treaty among the great powers would still have considerable value.

From April 1928, negotiations broadened to include the other great powers, and eventually the British Dominions and India, as well as the remaining Locarno powers. Among this group of original signatories to the pact, Britain stands out in terms of its active role in negotiations. The British Foreign Office had been apprised of the substance of the American proposal as early as 27 February 1928 but was not publicly involved in the negotiations until after the circulation of Kellogg's April draft (Cohrs 2006, 456). In the meantime, legal expert Cecil Hurst had been tasked with examining the proposal. His analysis was optimistic about the compatibility of the antiwar treaty with British interests; however, by the end of March he had revised his position. Hurst had come to believe that the American draft could "bar Britain from defending key imperial interests, notably in Egypt." In addition, he was less sanguine about its impact on British obligations both under Locarno and pursuant to the League Covenant. Accordingly, he "advised Chamberlain to insist, first, on including all Locarno powers into it and, second, on incorporating a provision that released the other signatories from their obligations should one of them break the pact" (Cohrs 2006, 459, 467).

The legal character of the British response to the pact was consistent. Hurst's recommendations would form the core of the official British reply of 19 May, and Chamberlain also backed Briand's desire for an international conference of jurists that would further the negotiations by attempting to reconcile the two drafts. Kellogg opposed this latter proposal, insisting that he sought to address the issue from "a broad point of view, not a narrow legalistic one" (quoted in Cohrs 2006, 468). This reply is curious, given the clearly legalistic basis of Kellogg's diplomatic and public arguments blocking French proposals—and his consistent preference for a formal legal treaty rather than other modalities France had sought to employ. It seems likely that Kellogg reacted as he did out of a desire to avoid direct negotiation that gave equal consideration to the French and American drafts, and evaluated them on the basis of strictly legal criteria. In any event, while the European powers abandoned their attempt to hold a formal legal conference including the United States, the legal experts of the French, British, and German governments met informally in July 1928, before any of the three governments had officially accepted the treaty's final text. While Kellogg was able to prevent a formal conference, the practice of international legal consultation had become an important component of global rule-making processes among the European great powers.

As noted above, Hurst's legal analysis drove the official British reply. Pressed by David Lloyd George and Ramsay MacDonald in the House of Commons to accept the American draft, Chamberlain noted the twin difficulties of consulting the Dominions and of ensuring the protection of Britain's existing commitments under Locarno and the League Covenant (Ferrell 1952, 178–79). The eventual reply relied explicitly on Kellogg's speech to the American Society of International Law in interpreting his official note. On the basis of the two documents together, Chamberlain adopted the position that there was "no serious divergence between the effect" of the French and American drafts. He then proceeded to stake out a middle ground, siding with the American text on some issues and the French on others. He concurred with Kellogg that the war-renunciation language in the US draft would "exclude action which a State may be forced to take in self-defence." This expansive reading of an unenumerated provision for self-defense most likely stemmed from Hurst's concerns about the impact of the draft on imperial defense, an issue Chamberlain would return to later in his note.

Article 2 of the American and French drafts, Chamberlain concluded, contained "no appreciable difference" in their requirement that parties employ peaceful means of dispute resolution. Indeed, the universal acceptance of such language is a striking indication of the robust support for rule-based legal and quasi-legal mechanisms for dispute resolution. This bears emphasis. While the ban on resort to war was treated by the parties as deeply controversial, the accompanying obligation to employ only pacific means of dispute resolution was far less so. Given the strong logical relationship between the negative obligation not to go to war and the positive obligation to employ alternate legalistic dispute resolution mechanisms, this is surprising. The negative obligation was more specific, and thus may have been perceived as more constraining, but in fact the positive obligation to use nothing other than peaceful means of dispute resolution amounted to the same thing. The lack of controversy surrounding the positive obligation thus likely owes more to the deep legitimacy of such peaceful practices and their consistency with relevant secondary rules.

Chamberlain gave clear support to the language proposed by the third and fourth articles of the French draft, which respectively provided certainty that parties would be released from their obligations toward treaty violators and that the treaty would have no impact on preexisting treaties such as Locarno or the Covenant. Regarding the third French article, he stated that "His Majesty's Government are not satisfied that, if the treaty stood alone, the addition of some such provision would not be necessary." He then expressed his optimism that "means can no doubt be found without difficulty of placing this understanding on the record in some appropriate manner so that it may have equal value with the terms of the treaty itself." Chamberlain tied, as Kellogg had, the matter of a breach of the treaty to the obligations contained in Locarno and the Covenant. He noted that both agreements "go somewhat further" than the draft treaty banning war, "in that they provide certain sanctions" to prevent violations. He expressed concern that "a clash might thus conceivably arise between the existing treaties and the proposed pact unless it is understood that the obligations of the new engagement will cease to operate in respect of a party that breaks its pledge and adopts hostile measures against one of its co-contractants." The inclusion of the French draft's third article was, however, insufficient protection for the other European security arrangements. The note made clear that the Baldwin government "would for their part prefer to see some such provision as Article 4 of the French draft embodied in the text of the treaty." Chamberlain pressed this point by insisting, perhaps disingenuously, that "to this we understand there will be no problem," on the basis that Kellogg's speech to the ASIL had—on Britain's view—made clear the United States "had no intention by the terms of the new treaty of preventing the parties to the Covenant of the League or to the Locarno Treaty from fulfilling their obligations." This assertion placed Kellogg in the difficult position of dropping his objection to the French article or having his position that the proposed treaty was compatible with Locarno and the Covenant called into question.

The British note proceeded by briefly concurring that "it is not necessary to wait until all the nations of the world have signified their willingness to become parties" in order to allow the treaty to enter into force, thus accepting the American formula over the French. The final and most novel aspect of Chamberlain's note pertained to the matter of imperial defense. In order to preserve Britain's strategic freedom of action, Chamberlain insisted that "there are certain regions of the world the welfare and integrity of which constitute a special and vital interest for our peace and safety." He alluded to similar US interests, a transparent reference to the Monroe Doctrine, and also sought to buttress his argument by subsuming the matter under Kellogg's expansive treatment of self-defense. Indeed, Chamberlain went so far as to condition Britain's acceptance of the treaty "upon the distinct understanding that it does not prejudice their freedom of action in this respect." Chamberlain's final demand with respect to imperial defense was that India and the Dominions—Canada, the Irish Free State, Australia, New Zealand, and the Union of South Africa—be accepted as original signatories to the pact, thus extending its umbrella of protection.[19]

The other great power signatories sent much less extensive replies. Italy's reply, dated 5 May, expressed support for the proposal and articulated the view that the proposed conference of jurists "can only be effective if the participation of a legal expert of the Government of the United States is assured" (quoted in Wheeler-Bennett 1928, 114). The Japanese reply, dated 26 May, displays significantly more attention to legal detail. The note declared that the American draft "is understood to contain nothing that would refuse to independent States the right of self-defence, and nothing which is incompatible with the obligations of agreements guaranteeing the public peace, such as are embodied in the Covenant of the League of Nations and the Treaties of Locarno" (quoted in Wheeler-Bennett 1928, 120). Japan was a relative newcomer to the international system[20] and remained one of a small number of states that did not share in the Western liberal tradition of philosophy and law. As such, its adherence to secondary rules based on this system is striking and indicative of the extent to which these practices were considered "settled"; deeply contested practices are less likely to be adopted by new group members (Johnston 2001).

By mid-May, Kellogg had officially agreed to incorporate the Locarno parties as signatories to the antiwar treaty, as had been contemplated in his 28 April speech; shortly thereafter, he accepted the British request to include India and the Dominions (Ferrell 1952, 182). At Kellogg's request, A. B. Houghton, the American ambassador in London, addressed a letter to Chamberlain providing invitations to join the negotiations to Australia, New Zealand, South Africa, and

---

[19] The British note is reproduced in Wheeler-Bennett (1928, 115–19).
[20] On Japan's socialization into the international system, see Suzuki (2009).

India. Invitations to Canada and the Irish Free State were presented directly through American representatives in Ottawa and Dublin. The six replies arrived in relatively short order and were generally consistent both with each other and with the British note of 19 May.[21] This consistency is perhaps the most interesting thing about them. None of the Dominions objected to the idea, and none raised new hurdles that had not already been discussed.

Most important, all were essentially "fluent" in the relevant secondary rules and resulting social practices of rule-making and interpretation. The Irish note referred directly to Kellogg's landmark April address and concurred in its analysis; the responses of Australia, New Zealand, and India were all brief and positive. The two most substantial replies were written by the South African and Canadian governments. The South African note addressed the issues of self-defense, as well as the idea that signatories would be released from their obligations toward violators. It concluded by insisting that "it is not intended that the Union of South Africa, by becoming a party to the proposed treaty, would be precluded from fulfilling, as a member of the League of Nations, its obligations toward the other members thereof under the provisions of the Covenant of the League." Finally, the Canadian reply indicated that W. L. MacKenzie King's government was "convinced that there is no conflict either in the letter or in the spirit between the Covenant and the multilateral pact, or between the obligations assumed under each" and that "the proposed multi-lateral treaty does not impose any obligation upon a signatory in relation to a State which has not signed the treaty or has broken it." The common thread is the familiarity evident in the notes with the standards for argument over the contents of treaties. The replies exceeded simple utilitarian acceptances of the American invitation; they placed understandings and beliefs on the diplomatic record because such a procedure was understood to be important in safeguarding sovereign rights and prerogatives.

Perhaps seeking to capitalize on British support for the third and fourth articles of the French draft, Briand used the occasion of a visit by Chamberlain to Paris on 2 June to remark to the press that "the powers consulted since and Mr. Kellogg himself... have come to our point of view" (quoted in Ferrell 1952, 186). Four days later, in a meeting with American ambassador Myron Herrick, Briand remarked that the shared understanding evident after Kellogg's 28 April speech could be placed either in an altered preamble or an accompanying protocol interpreting the treaty. The French ambassador in London, Aimé de Fleuriau, asked Chamberlain for the assistance of the British ambassador to Washington in pursuing this plan. The French strategy remained one of employing procedural rules and diplomatic forms to insert their more specific understandings of

---

[21] The American note and the individual replies are reproduced in Wheeler-Bennett (1928, 122–34).

the text into Kellogg's sparse draft. The British embassy in Washington informed Kellogg of the French request on 18 June. Kellogg reacted by seeking to head off the French proposal; he immediately prepared and sent a revised draft of his treaty to the initial set of great powers, the Dominions, and India, as well as the remaining parties to the Locarno agreements.

The American draft of June 1928 would become the final text of the Kellogg-Briand Pact. Its accompanying diplomatic note insisted the United States "remains convinced that no modification of the text or its proposal for a multilateral treaty for the renunciation of war is necessary to safeguard the legitimate interests of any nation." While maintaining that self-defense and release in the event of violation were self-evidently correct interpretations of the treaty, and that the adherence of all Locarno parties obviated any possible fear of incompatibility, it announced that the United States was circulating a new draft. The rationale for this decision was laid out as follows: "it appears that, by modifying the draft in form though not in substance, the points raised by other Governments can be satisfactorily met and general agreement upon the text of the treaty to be signed promptly reached." The new draft was identical to that of 13 April, save for amendment of the list of signatories and a revised preamble. This new preamble gave "express recognition to the principle that, if a State resorts to war in violation of the treaty, the other contracting parties are released from their obligations under the treaty to that State."[22]

Kellogg had consented to an alteration in his text, to meet European concerns related precisely to issues of adjudication and interpretation. Though the great powers were in substantive agreement on these matters—reflecting underlying secondary rules that provided, inter alia, guidance on interpreting treaties—they had differed on the necessity and desirability of placing them on the official record, and again on the best among multiple legitimate means for doing so. This outcome, in which a compromise was attained, simultaneously highlights the limits of persuasion in practices of rule-making (especially where actors have partially divergent understandings of secondary rules, as the Republican Coolidge administration did) as well as the possibility of reaching agreement in the absence of persuasion. The rules of international law and diplomacy operative in this context allowed states to place conflicting viewpoints and interpretations on the record, and accorded to those claims and statements the presumption of equal authority even as supplementary rules of great power management facilitated an outcome that could avoid irreconcilable alienation of crucial players. It is important to note that nothing about the existence of such effective secondary rules was inevitable. They are, themselves, social

[22] The above passages are reproduced in Wheeler-Bennett (1928, 144–46).

constructions—albeit overlooked and often invisible ones, at least to the contemporary study of International Relations.

Kellogg's new draft generated a swift wave of positive replies, but only after an informal meeting of French, British, and German legal experts at the Berlin home of Friedrich Gaus. This unofficial location and the absence of American representation symbolized the divide between American and European approaches to practices of global rule-making. Ferrell reports that the three European leaders had agreed not to reply to Kellogg's note until after the meeting. Contemporary press accounts "asserted the three jurists had agreed that Kellogg's note of 23 June covered almost every possible eventuality"; this is confirmed by Miller, who reported that, on this basis, "the final decision was not to seek any further conventional paper" specifying the pact's meaning (Ferrell 1952, 188–89; Miller 1928, 99).

Even more than the replies to the April draft, the responses to the June 1928 draft display a remarkable consistency. All fourteen arrived over a ten-day period, from 11 to 20 July.[23] The one potential complication, British repetition of the imperial defense doctrine advanced in Chamberlain's 19 May note, was studiously ignored by both the United States and the other signatories.[24] Almost universally, the replies noted and concurred with American interpretations of the crucial issues, in most cases adopting strikingly similar language.

The pact was signed in Paris on 27 August, at a formal signing ceremony in the Quai d'Orsay. Briand summarized the effective change in the rules of international politics as follows: "Considered of yore as of divine right and having remained in international ethics as an attribute of sovereignty, that form of war becomes at last juridically devoid of what constituted its most serious danger: legitimacy" (quoted in Wheeler-Bennett 1928, 174). Perhaps the most interesting aspect of his speech was the inclusion of language explicitly intended to mollify the states not invited to become initial signatories to the treaty. Briand exhorted them to "realize, in this hour of complete union, our unanimous regret that for purely technical reasons it was found imperative to adopt the procedure best calculated to ensure and expedite, for the benefit of all, the success of the great undertaking." He then noted that the French Foreign Ministry had directed the flags of each of the world's states to be flown at the signing ceremony, rather than only those of the invited signatories (Wheeler-Bennett 1928, 176). The American note inviting other states to adhere to the treaty went even further; it noted that the inclusion of India and the Dominions was necessary to satisfy

---

[23] The replies are reproduced in Wheeler-Bennett (1928, 150–70).

[24] Cohrs argues, plausibly, that this lack of attention—at least on the part of the United States—became part of a "tacit agreement" between the United States and the United Kingdom that "each side's prerogatives were unaffected by the pact" (Cohrs 2006, 460).

Britain, and that the Locarno powers were included as a necessity to gain French adherence. The inclusion of some secondary states but not others was evidently a breach of protocol that required justification, though the inclusion of great powers did not. The American note further insisted that the signatory list "was based entirely upon practical considerations" intended to reach agreement on a treaty as quickly as possible and also that the United States believed "that if these Powers could agree upon a simple renunciation of war as an instrument of national policy there could be no doubt that most, if not all, of the other Powers of the world would find the formula equally acceptable" (quoted in Wheeler-Bennett 1928, 179).

Among the uninvited states, the only one to cause concern for the negotiating parties was the Soviet Union. Its very exclusion from the negotiations was an indication of the importance of secondary rules; Soviet hostility to the rules and practices of international politics—including diplomacy and international law—had resulted in its virtual exclusion from international society. In the weeks before the signing ceremony, statesmen feared that a Soviet delegation would attend uninvited, and that even a simple invitation to adhere to the treaty would be greeted in Moscow as an opportunity to engage in hostile rhetoric (Ferrell 1952, 202–3). Ultimately, an invitation to adhere was transmitted not by the United States but by France, which had maintained diplomatic relations. Unexpectedly, it received an affirmative—albeit critical—response. The Soviet note of 31 August 1928 began by summarizing the contents of the secondhand American note inviting its adherence.[25] It then sought to seize the moral high ground and establish Soviet bona fides on the subject of international security, noting the rejection of Soviet disarmament proposals as well as the omission of disarmament provisions from the Kellogg-Briand Pact. It went on to point out an earlier Soviet proposal for bilateral war renunciation pacts, and its actual conclusion of such agreements with Germany, Turkey, Afghanistan, Persia, and Lithuania. The note declared that "other States silently ignored the proposal, making the strange explanation that unconditional renunciation of aggression was incompatible with their obligations toward the League of Nations." This, of course, was a thinly veiled accusation of hypocrisy; the arguments used to reject the Soviet proposal had been discarded in considering a substantively similar proposal from France and the United States.

The note then changed direction, noting that its invitation to adhere "does not mention any conditions which would permit the Soviet Government to secure any modifications in the text." In response, it declared that "the Soviet Government postulates as an axiom that under no conditions can it consent to being deprived of that right which the other signatory Governments had or could

---

[25] The Soviet note is reproduced in Wheeler-Bennett (1928, 182–87).

have had, and on the basis of that axiom it must first make several reservations as to its attitude towards the Pact itself." This is plainly the assertion of a right grounded in sovereignty and the secondary rules relevant in international law and diplomacy; such an act is only possible if the speaker is aware of those rules and is only rational if he believes the audience will consider them—or at least be expected to consider them by important third parties. The note then specified and justified several key reservations to the treaty. The first dealt with a lack of "precision or clarity in the first clause as regards the very formula for the prohibition of wars, which permits various and arbitrary interpretations." The Soviet view was that "there must be a ban not only on war in its formal juridical sense (such as normally follows a declaration of war) but also such military actions as a blockade or the occupation of foreign territory, etc."

Second, the note objected to "the British reservation in paragraph 10 of its Note of May 19th of this year, whereby the British Government reserves its freedom of action as regards a series of regions not specifically mentioned." The Soviet analysis of this claim was that "if this reservation is meant to refer to regions already belonging to the British Empire or its Dominions, it is apparently superfluous, since they are already included in the Pact, and the possibility of their being attacked is provided for in it. If, however, some other regions are meant, the participants of the pact are entitled to know exactly where the freedom of action of the British Government begins and ends." It further criticized this right on the basis that it "might be an example for other nations to follow who by virtue of equality of status would take advantage of the same right." Finally, the Soviet note opposed the British doctrine with a procedural argument, asserting that it was not binding on the USSR because "the British Government's Note referred to has not been communicated to the Soviet Government as being an integral part of the Pact or its annexes."

This procedural argument was used again to warrant the Soviet Union's insistence that it "cannot consent to any other reservations which might be calculated to serve as justifications for war, particularly reservations made in the correspondence designed to exempt from the application of the Pact obligations ensuing from the Covenant of the League of Nations and the Locarno Agreement." Despite this refusal to accept a core aspect of the treaty, the Soviet government agreed to subscribe to it as the best available option for the maintenance of peace since it "objectively imposes certain obligations on the Powers before world opinion." While one incident is insufficient to support any general conclusion about the socialization of the Soviet regime to the rules and practices of international politics, its reaction to the Kellogg-Briand Pact clearly displays an awareness of the basic rules and procedures for global rule-making and an ability to engage in them. Given the revolutionary stance of the early Soviet Union, its participation is indicative of the underlying strength of secondary rules.

Reaction to the treaty at the League of Nations was more positive. Lithuanian representatives proposed the amendment of the Covenant in light of the Kellogg-Briand Pact at the Ninth Assembly in September 1928; however, "it was thought that any such action pending the coming into force of the Treaty would be premature" (Miller 1928, 5–6). Despite the initial failure of this attempt, it was renewed the next year at the Tenth Assembly, which adopted a resolution that asserted "it is desirable that the terms of the Covenant of the League of Nations should not any longer accord to Members of the League a right to have recourse to war in cases in which that right has been renounced by the provisions of the Pact of Paris." The Secretary-General was asked to disseminate British draft amendments to League members, and the Council was asked to create a committee to report on reconciling the Covenant with the Kellogg-Briand Pact. After prolonged debate, the matter was referred to the Disarmament Conference, where it ultimately failed to come to fruition (Rappard 1940, 173).

Despite the wider failure of League diplomacy and of disarmament discussions, the Kellogg-Briand Pact was taken seriously by actors, and treated as an important advance; this is reflected by its near-universal ratification. The US Senate approved the treaty on 15 January 1929, and President Coolidge signed the instrument of ratification on 17 January. After the American ratification, Poland, Belgium, and France quickly followed suit. The treaty would enter into force on 24 July 1929, when Japan provided the final great power ratification. The Japanese government had delayed acting due to confusion over language in the treaty declaring that the signatories adhered to it "in the names of their respective peoples"; the problem was that this language contravened the Japanese Constitution, under which the Emperor signed treaties on his own behalf. The controversy was resolved only after Kellogg personally assured the Japanese government that the troublesome language was synonymous with signing "on behalf of" the Japanese people and thus posed no constitutional danger to imperial authority (Ferrell 1952, 254–56). This incident indicates the gravity with which secondary rules, and issues of form and procedure (in this case relating to the authority to sign treaties), were treated, and also highlights the increasing relevance of domestic secondary rules to processes of rule-making at the international level. The relative novices in the Japanese government sought outside counsel and accepted Kellogg's assurance as authoritative. As Kellogg possessed no authority in interpreting the Japanese constitution, it is clear that the question was regarded within the Japanese government as possessing an international dimension. The treaty would be ratified by its initial fifteen signatories as well as forty-eight other states, culminating with Brazil's ratification on 10 May 1934. These states encompassed the vast majority of the contemporary international community and excluded no important state.[26]

Conclusion

The Kellogg-Briand Pact represents the apex of efforts to ban war in the interwar period, and yet it was also an initially unintended outcome shaped by the secondary rules that constituted contemporary practices for global rule-making and interpretation. Although my primary goal is to identify and illustrate this practice, and show its causal effectiveness in shaping outcomes, the question of the agreement's effectiveness looms large in this case. Two broad criticisms can be made of the Kellogg-Briand Pact. The first is that the agreement was meaningless because it lacked sanctions. While it is certainly true that the agreement did not contain either the guarantee of territorial integrity provided by Locarno or the provisions for collective action contained in the League Covenant, these omissions are far less important if the treaty is considered in wider context. This conclusion is shared by Miller, who argues persuasively that "in the matter of sanctions the Treaty is to a large extent implemented in advance by the Covenant" (Miller 1928, 137). In the event of a violation, the antiwar provisions ceased to apply to the violator; meanwhile, all of the other provisions of international law—including those for collective security—would remain in effect, allowing for remedial action. Just such an approach is evident in the handling of the Manchurian crisis. The League investigated and eventually called for Japanese withdrawal from Chinese territory along with affirmation of Chinese sovereignty over the region. Although League efforts were unsuccessful, the discursive response indicates the existence and perceived relevance of the Kellogg-Briand Pact, as does restoration of Manchukuo to China after 1945. American handling of the Manchurian crisis also indicates support for the Kellogg-Briand restrictions on the use of force. The Stimson Doctrine made clear that the United States would no longer recognize the legality of territorial acquisition by conquest. During the crisis, the United States also sought to quietly support League action. In particular, the Hoover administration arranged for an American representative to join League Council deliberations on the crisis, and also agreed to suspend American insistence on neutral rights with respect to freedom of the seas by pledging not to oppose a potential League blockade of Japan.[27]

The second criticism of Kellogg-Briand is that it was a hopelessly utopian project. As I have argued, however, this position does not account either for

---

[26] For a complete list of ratifications, see Ferrell (1952, 258).

[27] On the crisis, and on the American response, see O'Mahoney (2014).

important subsequent changes to state practice in the 1930s or for the reliance on the substance of the pact as a central pillar of the post-1945 order. In important respects, the Second World War was a case of norm violation and enforcement, rather than an instance of "business as usual." On this view, Allied condemnation of Axis aggression is crucial; Hitler's Germany was clearly seen and treated as a norm violator in initiating the war. This evaluation of German conduct is reflected in the inclusion of charges of aggression explicitly based on the Kellogg-Briand Pact in the Nuremberg trials. Equally important, the general norm has clearly *survived* the instance of norm violation. The preamble to the Charter of the United Nations enshrines as the organization's first purpose the task of saving "succeeding generations from the scourge of war," and Article 2.4 of the Charter specifically embodies the essence of the Kellogg-Briand Pact. It declares that "all Members shall refrain in their international relations from the threat of war or use of force against the territorial integrity or political independence of any state, or in any other manner inconsistent with the Purposes of the United Nations."[28] Finally, the norm against interstate warfare can be observed in operation. One useful example is the contrast between the Persian Gulf War (1990–1991) and the American invasion of Iraq in March 2003. In both instances, the United States sought to justify its action according to international rules and standards, and other states evaluated these claims. While international disapproval did not prevent the 2003 invasion, the fact that the coalition supporting American action was far less broad than in 1991 indicates that the George W. Bush administration's claims were widely rejected and that it paid a price. Similarly, the difference between the international reaction to post-9/11 American claims with regard to Afghanistan and Iraq indicates a process of evaluating claims according to shared rules and standards that deny the legality of acquiring territory by conquest (Byers 2005). Finally, ongoing controversy over the illegality of Russia's 2014 seizure of Crimea demonstrates that this rule of international law remains central to the global governance of warfare, and that the international community remains engaged in a shared process of interpreting and applying the rule to new cases.[29]

This process exists because of the rule outlawing warfare contained in the Kellogg-Briand Pact. That treaty, in turn, was the culmination of a series of proposals and negotiations during the 1920s that were shaped by (and that proceeded according to) relevant secondary rules. Beyond its importance in illustrating my argument about the dynamics of global rule-making, this finding is of value to International Relations scholars because it undermines realist claims that the interwar period was one of failed idealism. Given the foundational

---

[28] Charter of the United Nations (1945).
[29] On Russian action in Crimea, see Gardner (2016); Allison (2017).

importance of the interwar period to modern IR realism, a re-evaluation of this case further calls into question the value of realist theory for the development of knowledge about international relations.[30]

Finally, the case suggests two important points connected to the study of global rule-making. First, the creation of new rules does not guarantee actors will comply with them in particular cases. The outbreak of the Second World War—to say nothing of the various wars of the 1930s—clearly demonstrates that the rule against warfare was broken. If we take the counterfactual validity of norms and rules seriously, however, this is not a problem for the main argument in this book—especially if other actors respond by calling attention to, and criticizing, such violations. The Stimson Doctrine provides an example of just such a response by the United States, and the Second World War can also be seen as a response against Axis aggression in violation of Kellogg-Briand. Second, disagreement with regard to secondary rules significantly hampers efforts to conduct processes of rule-making. The absence of agreed-upon standards and procedures to make, interpret, and apply rules presents a significant challenge to the stability of a social system. While the differences with respect to secondary rules in this case were relatively minor, they complicated American participation in interwar processes of global rule-making. The problem is all the more pressing in the international system of the early twenty-first century, which has become massively more culturally diverse than the one that confronted Kellogg, Chamberlain, and Briand. This last point is central to the next case.

---

[30] A similar argument is made in Hathaway and Shapiro (2017).

CHAPTER 4

Social Practices of Rule-Making and the Global War on Terror

Terrorism has typically been understood in International Relations as a tactic whereby rational political actors pursue preferred policy outcomes by inflicting costs on opponents in the form of civilian casualties, and by undermining public confidence in security services (Kydd and Walter 2006).[1] While there are reasons to doubt whether rank-and-file members join or remain part of terrorist groups for reasons related to their ideological or political goals (Abrahms 2008), it is clear that terrorist groups' leaders are indeed pursuing political goals. Wahhabist groups like al-Qaeda and the Islamic State in Iraq and Syria (ISIS) can be narrowly portrayed as demanding withdrawal of American forces from the Middle East, to facilitate the overthrow of secular governments in the region in favor of more theocratic state forms. The primary difference between al-Qaeda and ISIS, on this view, is the latter's willingness to take, hold, and govern territory.

This view is limited in its ability to explain or account for an extensive history of public dialogue between al-Qaeda and the United States that took place in the early days of what has been called the "Global War on Terror" (from the 1996 "Declaration of Jihad" issued by al-Qaeda until the American invasion of Iraq in March 2003). This dialogue included clear and consistent efforts on both sides to speak about actual and preferred rules for the international system, and the way they should be applied. It also featured mutual criticism and justification on procedural grounds. The existence and apparent importance of these exchanges is puzzling from the perspective of rationalist IR theory. Both sides knew that conflict was overdetermined, and quickly realized that they also had deep disagreements about legitimate procedural rules for global rule-making. So why would they attempt a futile dialogue? This choice is particularly puzzling if

---

[1] Such accounts draw heavily on the rationalist literature on bargaining models of war (Wagner 2000; Powell 2002; Reiter 2003; Smith and Stam 2004).

one takes the common rationalist view that talk is cheap, since actors with such beliefs should not bother engaging in such pointless behavior.

One plausible explanation is that each side was in fact speaking primarily to a like-minded public audience that shared its views about the proper purpose of political life and about legitimate practices for rule-making and interpretation. This dynamic was certainly important. However, relatively esoteric appeals to issues of legitimate process for making and interpreting rules occupy a more prominent place in both sides' rhetorical choices than should be expected given the availability of other appeals more likely to motivate the general public, such as the deployment of American troops or the deaths of civilians in terrorist attacks. Further, the main actors invoked surprisingly emotional, heated language in their procedural criticisms of the other side. Such vivid language suggests that matters of procedural legitimacy were regarded not as minor technical issues, but as something more important.

The explanation advanced in this chapter is that each side had an internalized notion of legitimate practices of rule-making and interpretation, and that actors tied these procedural understandings to conceptions of the appropriate nature and ends of political community. Notably, al-Qaeda and the Bush administration each adopted conceptions of appropriate secondary rules that were highly controversial within their own political traditions, and did so to advance controversial political programs. Each faced considerable criticism for doing so from other actors within their own political traditions, including on the procedural grounds that my argument expects. This dimension of the case is not my primary focus, however, in large part because it is less surprising than the existence of sustained efforts at rule-making and interpretation that actors must have known would be futile. In addition to demonstrating that actors saw these practices as an important part of their conflict, and that they continued to engage in them despite negligible prospects of success, the evidence shows that both sides were constrained by their understandings of legitimate rule-making procedures, not only in dealing with the other, but also in interaction with other relevant audiences. Even where the primary parties lacked a common set of secondary rules, their understandings of legitimate procedures for rule-making and interpretation continued to shape outcomes.

The chapter proceeds in three parts. In the first, I review the primary rules of the international system, focusing on those that the parties sought to alter. In the second, I review the two sides' respective understandings of appropriate secondary rules. In the third, I show how these understandings of secondary rules structured the resulting attempts at rule-making and interpretation and shaped the success or failure of particular attempts to make, interpret, and apply rules. I conclude with some brief remarks on the implications of my findings for efforts to counter ISIS and other manifestations of radical Islamist views about the international system.

Primary Rules

In this section, I demonstrate that both al-Qaeda and the Bush administration saw the rules of the international system as relevant to the conflict between them. In doing so, I pay particular attention to the rules that each side sought to alter, beginning with al-Qaeda. Accordingly, I take the view that al-Qaeda does possess an affirmative political program (Phillips 2010, 270–71), while acknowledging that the content of this program has changed somewhat over time (Torres, Jordan, and Horsburgh 2006), and that there is variance and contestation among group members.

AL-QAEDA

Ultimately, whether al-Qaeda sought (and seeks) to change the rules of the international system is an empirical question. It is worth nothing, as a prima facie answer, that Osama bin Laden answered this question affirmatively on multiple occasions. In a January 2000 message issued to correspond with the Eid al-Fitr holiday that marks the end of Ramadan, bin Laden was reported to have said "we do not accept the world order of the United States"; instead, he asserted, he and his associates "believe only in the world order of Allah" (FBIS 2004, 136).[2] The salient point here is that bin Laden clearly articulated both a rejection of the current international system and an endorsement of a positive program rooted in Islamic ideas. In an interview given on 28 September 2001, bin Laden explicitly distinguished between opposition to the United States and opposition to the international system, claiming that "we are not hostile to the United States. We are against the system, which makes other nations slaves of the United States, or forces them to mortgage their political and economic freedom" (FBIS 2004, 181).[3] Asked on 21 October 2001 about al-Qaeda's strategy in the Arabic world, bin Laden replied that "our aim is to support our nation and remove the injustice, humiliation and submissiveness. Our aim is also to *remove the rules* [emphasis added] that the United States has imposed on its agents in the region [i.e.,

---

[2] Bakht Ullah Jan Hasrat, "Usama Bin Ladin Denounces US-Sponsored 'World Order'," 9 January 2000, translated and reproduced in "Compilation of Usama Bin Ladin Statements 1994–January 2004," 136.

[3] "Exclusive Interview with Usama Bin Ladin on 11 September Attacks in US," *Karachi Ummat*, 28 September 2001, translated and reproduced in FBIS (2004, 181).

secular Arab states]. We want this nation to be ruled according to the book of God, who created it" (FBIS 2004, 242).[4] Finally, in his "Letter to the American People" of 26 October 2002, bin Laden provided his most extensive statement to a Western audience on al-Qaeda's goals and demands. After detailing specific policy grievances, he made a more general statement of positive proposals. The first of these was that Americans should convert to Islam, and embrace "the love of Allah, complete submission to His orders, and the discarding of all the opinions, orders, theories and religions which contradict with Allah's orders." Bin Laden continued, clarifying the importance of altering Western rules: "you are the nation who, rather than ruling by the law of Allah, choose to implement your own inferior rules and regulations, thus following your own vain whims and desires." He then specified several subjects on which he believed Western rules to be illegitimate, encompassing the personal (alcohol, gambling, pornography) and the clearly international-political (use of nuclear weapons, climate change, human rights, etc.) (FBIS 2004, 217–19).[5]

Al-Qaeda criticisms of the international order can be grouped under three broad headings: (1) rejection of the special rights and responsibilities accorded (often implicitly) to great powers; (2) objections to central elements of the modern state system; and (3) dismissal of important human rights norms. In each of these areas, al-Qaeda seeks patterned changes in international practice. However, assembling an account of specific rule changes sought by al-Qaeda is complicated by two major factors. First, more than any actor in either previous case, al-Qaeda is an outsider to the international system, and particularly to accepted international practices of rule-making. This outsider status, combined with the existence of a robust alternative set of secondary rules rooted in a particular interpretation of Islamic jurisprudence, has given rise to a Tower of Babel situation. The result has been an instance of rule-making and interpretation in which the main parties speak less to each other than they do to a shifting, partially overlapping audience that includes states but is also directed at global public opinion. As a consequence, many of al-Qaeda's proposals are couched in terms alien to Western listeners and that often bear little direct resemblance to the current international system. In the relatively rare but significant cases where al-Qaeda leaders sought to speak to Western listeners (and, equally, when the Bush administration and other Western speakers have targeted Muslim audiences), statements and claims seem all the more tactical in their presentation—complicating efforts to assess their sincerity. One possible

---

[4] "Full text of Interview Held with Al-Qa'ida Leader Usama Bin Ladin on 21 October 2001," *Jihad Online News Network*, 21 January 2003, translated and reproduced in FBIS (2004, 242).

[5] "Letter from Usama Bin Ladin to the American People," www.waaqiah.com, 26 October 2002, reproduced in FBIS (2004, 217–19).

reading of al-Qaeda's proposals is a fundamentally conservative one: to maintain state sovereignty, while simply creating a large Muslim state loosely analogous to the European Union. This interpretation is unconvincing, I will argue, because al-Qaeda's positions rest on bases fundamentally dissimilar to those underlying the current international system, and because al-Qaeda has made explicit its own hostility to that system. Al-Qaeda does not understand itself as trying to preserve the international system; we should take their stated intentions seriously.[6]

Second, presenting a specific account of al-Qaeda's positive program—that is, of the rules it advocates—runs the risk of overstating the internal consistency and completeness of the group's beliefs. Al-Qaeda represents only a part of a broader network of individuals and groups committed to ideals rooted in radical Salafi—more particularly, Wahhabi—beliefs. This network, like Islam more broadly, is decentralized in its operation both as a practical matter in light of determined international opposition and as a matter of sincere belief about proper and legitimate social relations. Further, al-Qaeda and like-minded groups have generally become even more decentralized since the 9/11 attacks (Hoffman 2007; Lia 2008). Just as al-Qaeda's operational practices evolved, so did its criticisms of the extant international order and associated demands. Most notably, it widened its ambit of concern beyond bin Laden's initial demands for the removal of Western troops from Saudi Arabia and for the adoption by Muslim states of domestic policies consistent with Islamist demands. At their maximum, al-Qaeda statements advocated the establishment of a caliphate encompassing the territory of all Muslim states (FBIS 2004, 146–67, 242).[7] These maximalist claims for a caliphate were vague and inchoate; the term was used in multiple ways, referring variously to a post-Westphalian notion of governance, a Westphalian state with an Islamist government, and a vague post-millennialism. James Gelvin concluded that this vagueness "has more to do with the difficulty of coming up with an entirely original program for governance-cum-disciplinary mechanism from a vantage point located within the existing nation-state system than with maintaining a purposeful tactical ambiguity" (Gelvin 2008, 573–74; see also Phillips 2010, 277).

---

[6] There is similar debate over whether ISIS should be treated as a terrorist group, a state, or a "caliphate" distinct from a state (Cronin 2015; Hashim 2014; Walt 2015). I return to the question of ISIS in the conclusion of the chapter.

[7] For example: "Usama Bin Ladin's 'Letter' Calling for 'Global Islamic State'," *Rawalpindi Nawa-i-Waqt*, 7 January 2001, translated and reproduced in FBIS (2004, 146–47); "Full Text of Interview Held with Al-Qa'ida Leader Usama Bin Ladin on 21 October 2001," *Jihad Online News Network*, 21 January 2003, translated and reproduced in FBIS (2004, 242). These statements stand in contrast to the 1996 "Declaration of Jihad" as well as "Text of World Islamic Front's Statement Urging Jihad against Jews and Crusaders," *Al-Quds al-'Arabi*, 23 February 1998, translated and reproduced in FBIS (2004, 56–58). The latter statements do not mention the establishment of a caliphate.

Despite these complications, some meaningful conclusions can be reached regarding al-Qaeda's proposals for rule change in the international system. First, it aimed to eliminate the privileges and responsibilities accorded to great powers and to international organizations. In a December 1998 interview, bin Laden asserted that "what we want is the right of any living being. We want our land to be freed of the enemies; we want our land to be freed of the Americans" (FBIS 2004, 158).[8] The phrasing adopted indicates that bin Laden saw freedom from external influence as a general right—which would entail a corresponding duty (rule) to respect it. The specific reference to the United States indicated he regarded that right as enforceable regardless of power imbalances between specific actors. Later in the same interview, bin Laden also articulated the belief that United Nations resolutions are illegitimate. His reasoning is examined below; for now, the important point is that his opposition to external influence extended beyond direct military occupation to encompass even such diffuse interference as that created by international organizations.

The general theme of noninterference is ubiquitous in al-Qaeda rhetoric. In an interview on 28 September 2001, bin Laden linked ideas of non-interference, reciprocity, and friendship:

> The United States has no friends, nor it wants to keep one [*sic*] because the prerequisite of friendship is to come to the level of the friend or consider him at par with you. America does not want to see anyone equal to it. It expects slavery from others.... (FBIS 2004, 179)[9]

The cultural terms of reference here (friendship and slavery) demonstrate the chasm dividing bin Laden from modern state practices of international relations, but the substance of his claim can be broadly understood to require equitable relations and relations of friendship to be founded on the basis of mutual noninterference. This interpretation is buttressed by bin Laden's statements in his "Letter to the American People," dated 26 October 2002. In it, he criticized the United States for its "duality in both manners and law," and alleged that "your manners and policies have two categories: one for you and one for the others." He further insisted that the United States "deal with us [the Islamic world] and interact with us on the basis of mutual interests and benefits" (FBIS 2004, 219–20).[10] On its face, the al-Qaeda position closely resembles notions

---

[8] "Al-Jazirah TV Broadcasts Usama Bin Ladin's 1998 Interview," 20 September 2001, translated and reproduced in FBIS (2004, 158).

[9] "Exclusive Interview with Usama Bin Ladin on 11 September Attacks in US," *Karachi Ummat*, 28 September 2001, translated and reproduced in FBIS (2004, 179).

[10] "Letter from Usama Bin Ladin to the American People, www.waaqiah.com, 20 October 2002, reproduced in FBIS (2004, 219–20).

of sovereign equality familiar to students of International Relations; however, these doctrines have historically been qualified by recognition of legitimate—or at least acceptable—great power rights and responsibilities, typically defended on grounds of maintaining system stability.[11] These supplementary rules have also formed a good deal of the justificatory basis for the authority delegated to international organizations, as well as for the international legal doctrine that customary law is binding on all states independent on their consent. Al-Qaeda's position opposes each of these rules, and thus presents a significant challenge to the contemporary international system.

The second conclusion that can be drawn is that al-Qaeda seeks to alter many core features of the state system itself. Chief among these is the current system of generating state boundaries along ostensibly national lines. Phillips notes that "where the nation-state rests on mutually exclusive national jurisdiction, jihadists emphasise the artificiality of the nation-state, decrying it as a Western impo-sition designed to fragment the global community of believers (the *ummah*)" (Phillips 2010, 259).[12] Like their objections to the role of great powers, and of international law and organizations, jihadi opposition to the state system (or, at minimum, the inclusion of the Islamic world in that system) is essentially in-strumental to the deeper goal of re-establishing a caliphate and basing social re-lations within it on legitimate Islamic rules and institutions rather than imposed Western ones.[13] On this basis, they "call for the establishment of *sharia* law and the dissolution of nation-states in favour of an Islamic Caliphate as remedies to the spiritual and moral malaise they see gripping the Islamic world" (Phillips 2010, 271). These commitments are evident in the text of an al-Qaeda letter mailed to a Pakistani newspaper in January 2001. The letter asserted that "every member of the Muslim world agrees that all the Muslim countries of the world having boundaries on the basis of nationality, geography, religious discord, color and race, should be merged into one Muslim state, where men do not rule men." It went on to specify further proposals for the governance arrangements in this state: "There should be only one caliph for the whole state whose capital should be Mecca. There should be one currency and defense for this state and the Holy Koran should be its constitution" (FBIS 2004, 147).[14] Enclosed with the letter, according to the newspaper report, was a world map—with the territory of the proposed caliphate shaded green.

---

[11] See chapter 2, as well as Keene (2013).

[12] The conclusion that al-Qaeda fundamentally challenges the state system is also reached in Mendelsohn (2005, 45–68).

[13] Altering the domestic policies of Islamic states, especially Saudi Arabia, has been an important aspect of al-Qaeda's motivation since its founding (Orbach 2001).

[14] "Usama Bin Ladin 'Letter' Calling for 'Global Islamic State'," *Rawalpindi Nawa-i-Waqt*, 7 January 2001, translated and reproduced in FBIS (2004, 147).

It is unclear from al-Qaeda's statements whether this caliphate would co-exist either within or alongside the remnants of the state system. The more limited view, that the two could coexist, is consistent with statements insisting that al-Qaeda had no particular animosity toward the United States and that it simply wanted to be free from interference. On the other hand, there is significant support in al-Qaeda's statements for a more radical view—that establishment of the caliphate is seen as an interim step toward its eventual global expansion. This development, of course, would entail the destruction and replacement of the current state system. This view is suggested by bin Laden's calls for Americans to convert to Islam, and by his assertion that a "clash of civilizations" is inevitable (FBIS 2004, 242).[15] Further, on multiple occasions, bin Laden invoked a Koranic phrase that casts the conflict in Manichean terms: "and fight the pagans all together as they fight you all together . . . fight them until there is no more tumult or oppression, and there prevail justice and faith in God" (FBIS 2004, 58, 207).[16] Finally, bin Laden maintained in a video broadcast on 4 January 2004 that "the struggle between us and them, the confrontation, and clashing began centuries ago, and will continue because the ground rules regarding the fight between right and falsehood will remain valid until Judgment Day." The "ground rule" to which he refers is that "there can be no dialogue with occupiers except through arms" (FBIS 2004, 273).[17] Ultimately, both the limited and radical positions entails major changes in the rules governing the international system.

Al-Qaeda also sought change in global rules regarding human rights. Bin Laden articulated broad criticisms of various freedoms and practices accepted in the international community (FBIS 2004, 214–20).[18] While such rules are clearly of great importance to individuals' life chances, they are of less relevance to the operation of the international system. Indeed, the international system existed and operated long before any such rights or freedoms had been widely established. Therefore, I will not dwell on them, other than to note that they represent rules al-Qaeda sought to alter.

[15] "Full Text of Interview Held with Al-Qa'ida Leader Usama Bin Laden on 21 October 2001," *Jihad Online News Network*, 21 January 2003, translated and reproduced in FBIS (2004, 242).

[16] "Text of World Islamic Front's Statement Urging Jihad against Jews and Crusaders," *Al-Quds al-'Arabi*, 23 February 1998, translated and reproduced in FBIS (2004, 58). The verse is also quoted in "Al-Qa'ida Issues Statement under Bin Ladin's Name on Afghan War Anniversary," *Al-Qalah*, 14 October 2002, translated and reproduced in FBIS (2004, 207).

[17] "Bin Ladin Warns of 'Grand Plots' against Arabs, Criticizes Gulf Rulers," *Al-Jazirah TV*, 4 January 2004, translated and reproduced in FBIS (2004, 273).

[18] "Letter from Usama Bin Ladin to the American People," www.waaqiah.com, 26 October 2002, reproduced in FBIS (2004, 214–20).

THE UNITED STATES

Like al-Qaeda, the Bush administration sought to leverage the 9/11 attacks to alter the primary rules governing the international system. In contrast to the jihadis, however, the Bush administration's attempts are more easily recognizable and intelligible—precisely because they employed arguments and procedures more consistent with established secondary rules. American challenges to the rules of the international system can be grouped under three headings. First, the Bush administration sought to establish a positive obligation for states to disrupt and dismantle terrorist organizations operating within their borders. The second, directly related, proposal was an attempt to make preventive war legal in at least some circumstances—specifically where states failed to meet the obligation entailed in the first proposal. The third American challenge to existing international rules related to the rules of conduct in warfare, especially those concerned with the treatment of individuals detained in the course of a conflict.

The idea of a positive obligation on the part of states to prevent the operation of terrorist groups within their borders was articulated by President George W. Bush in his national address on 20 September 2001, in which he declared that "from this day forward, any nation that continues to harbor or support terrorism will be regarded by the United States as a hostile regime" (Bush 2001).[19] This position was reflected in American demands that the Taliban hand over senior al-Qaeda leaders for trial; refusal of this demand, on the basis of Pashtun codes specifying obligations of hosts to their guests,[20] was the proximate justification for the initiation of military operations in Afghanistan on 7 October 2001 (Byers 2005, 57–58). Michael Byers has noted that this American claim represented a deviation from the accepted practice in international law; "even when countries were directly implicated in acts of terrorism, acts of self-defence directed against them did not attract much international support—prior to 2001." The International Court of Justice (ICJ) ruling in the *Nicaragua Case* (1986) held that assisting rebels did not constitute an "armed attack"—and thus that UN Charter requirements for triggering self-defense rights had not been met (Byers 2005, 55–57).

Any possible doubt that the American position represented a proposal for a general rule governing the international system was removed in 2002. In his State of the Union address, President Bush made clear that he intended this requirement to apply to all states—and not simply to Afghanistan. He expressed his "hope . . . that all nations will heed our call and eliminate the terrorist parasites who threaten their countries and our own" before recognizing that

---

[19] George W. Bush, "Address to the Nation," speech given at Washington, DC, 20 September 2001.
[20] On Taliban diplomacy, see Sharp (2003).

"some governments will be timid in the face of terror." In those cases, he claimed, "make no mistake about it: if they do not act, America will." He then went on to specify three countries at risk of American action—the infamous "Axis of Evil," comprising North Korea, Iran, and Iraq (Bush 2002a).[21] The American proposal was further developed in the September 2002 National Security Strategy (NSS). Its introductory letter declared that "the United States is guided by the conviction that all nations have important responsibilities." The document then immediately specified several connected duties: "Nations that enjoy freedom must actively fight terror. Nations that depend on international stability must help prevent the spread of weapons of mass destruction. Nations that seek international aid must govern themselves wisely, so that aid is well spent. For freedom to thrive, accountability must be expected and required" (White House 2002).[22] The universalistic language and the invocation of concepts such as responsibility and accountability indicate that the intention was to generate a mandatory standard of behavior—in other words, a rule.

Alongside the attempt to establish a positive obligation for states to prevent the use of their territory for the conduct of terrorism, the United States also sought to alter international rules on the use of force such that they would permit preventive military action to deal with international terrorist networks. The language of a "war on terror" intended to go beyond the capture or elimination of al-Qaeda leaders was already in place by Bush's 20 September 2001 address.[23] In another major speech, at the West Point graduation on 1 June 2002, Bush sought to make a case that deterrence was insufficient to meet the threat posed by terrorist networks; instead, he claimed that "if we wait for threats to fully materialize, we will have waited too long" (Bush 2002b).[24] The commencement address stopped short of articulating the idea of justified intervention in cases where states failed to meet their obligation to combat terrorism. That task was again left to the 2002 NSS, which reiterated the putative inadequacies of deterrence, noting that "the United States has long maintained the option of preventive actions to counter a sufficient threat to our national security" and announcing that the United States was prepared to act with force in advance of an armed attack against it. The language in the report clearly reflects awareness on the part of its authors of its broader significance for the rules of the

---

[21] George W. Bush, "Address before a Joint Session of the Congress on the State of the Union," speech given at Washington, DC, 29 January 2002.

[22] The White House, "The National Security Strategy of the United States of America," Washington, DC: Government Printing Office, 2002.

[23] Bush stated that "Our war on terror begins with al-Qaeda, but it does not end there. It will not end until every terrorist group of global reach has been found, stopped and defeated" (Bush 2001).

[24] George W. Bush, "Commencement Address at the United States Military Academy at West Point," speech given at West Point, NY, 1 June 2002.

international system. It makes direct reference to established rules of international law authorizing preemptive self-defense, on the grounds that states "need not suffer an attack before they can lawfully take action against forces that present an imminent danger of attack." It continues by couching the American proposal as an attempt to "*adapt* [emphasis added] the concept of imminent threat," and therefore explicitly acknowledges that the American argument was an attempt to change the rules—or, at the very least, an attempt to reason about how to apply an existing rule to a novel case. Finally, the NSS took pains to prevent the use of the American proposal to authorize claims by other states in cases where the United States disagreed. It did so by qualifying resort to preemption in several ways.[25] That is, the document was part of a concerted effort to engage in rule-making and interpretation. This effort was pursued in ways that clearly demonstrate awareness of, and attempts to conform as much as possible with, established secondary rules. While clearly strategic in nature, this effort cannot be understood apart from these rules (Müller 2004), and the behavior itself was clearly rule-regarding even where procedural rules for rule-making and interpretation were not scrupulously observed.

The mechanics of these American proposals for rule change and their consistency with secondary rules will be examined in more detail in the third major section of this chapter; the point for now is that the administration's language in both cases indicates an attempt to create general rules of behavior for the international system. This point is worth dwelling on. In what appear on their face to be two of the strongest manifestations of American unilateralism, the Bush administration in fact engaged in a structured social practice aimed at establishing rules authorizing their unilateralist positions. From the standpoint of realist theory, this action presents a curiosity—if not an anomaly. In contrast, this behavior is completely consistent with the expectations of the argument advanced in this book.

Finally, the United States attempted to change the rules of the international system relating to the status and treatment of detainees. However, parallel to my decision not to focus on al-Qaeda's efforts to alter international human rights rules, I will not make the debate over detainees and torture a central concern in this case.[26] While these rules are of crucial importance, and while they demonstrate the operation of a social practice of rule-making and interpretation, they are not as central to the operation of the international system as the other rule changes pursued by the Bush administration.

---

[25] The White House, "The National Security Strategy of the United States of America," Washington, DC: Government Printing Office, 2002.

[26] On these questions, see Byers (2005) and Ralph (2009).

Secondary Rules

Both al-Qaeda and the United States sought to change the rules of the international system. Whether their attempts to do so are consistent with the argument I make in this book depends in the first instance on whether or not they employed methods consistent with accepted secondary rules (and, if not, whether they justified and were criticized for these deviations). Accordingly, this section examines these secondary rules. Whereas prior cases have occurred within sets of secondary rules broadly accepted by all parties, practices of rule-making and interpretation between al-Qaeda and the Bush administration after 9/11 were characterized by a split between actors reliant largely on the established secondary rules of the international system and actors reliant on secondary rules derived from particular traditions of Islamic jurisprudence.

SECONDARY RULES IN THE INTERNATIONAL SYSTEM

As with the primary rule changes sought after 9/11, the secondary rules employed by the United States—and the international community in general—are more readily intelligible to a Western observer. Indeed, the set of secondary rules employed in the international community has acquired a taken-for-granted quality both for many scholars and for practitioners of International Relations. The secondary rules that structure contemporary practices of global rule-making and interpretation are an extension of those identified in the prior two cases. My primary emphasis here will therefore be on trends and developments in secondary rules since the interwar period examined in the past chapter; two are of particular note.

First, as Christian Reus-Smit has argued, processes of modern rule-making are thoroughly multilateral in nature. While there is a deeper history of multilateral rule-making and interpretation (*avant la lettre*) in the process for the formation and evolution of customary international law,[27] and while precursors to multilateralism were readily identifiable in the Congress of Vienna and the negotiation of the Kellogg-Briand Pact, the norm of multilateralism has become more solidly entrenched and more extensively applied over the last several decades. This multilateralism is "thick" in nature, extending well beyond what John Ruggie helpfully referred to as a "nominal" multilateralism entailed by the mere participation of three or more parties. Rather, as Ruggie pointed out, modern multilateralism entails a "qualitative dimension" consisting of additional rules and norms designating how it is to be legitimately practiced (Ruggie

[27] I thank Nick Onuf for making this important point.

1992, 565–66). Just as this institutional form is used to reach trade agreements, it is also employed in processes of global rule-making that seek to change or contest the basic institutional architecture of the international system.

Second, the period since 1928 has seen several important attempts to codify secondary rules in international law. Whereas in 1815, secondary rules rested on informal agreements and understandings among European elites, the progressive democratization of politics at the state level and the global expansion of the European state system have spurred attempts to "shore up" the foundations of the international practice of rule-making. The most significant such achievements are the Statute of the International Court of Justice (1945), the Vienna Convention on Diplomatic Relations (1961), and the Vienna Convention on the Law of Treaties (1969).

As a result of these twin processes of multilateralization and codification, practices of global rule-making and interpretation have become more transparently specifiable. International agreements provide concrete directives to states on how to recognize a valid rule in the international system. Article 38 of the Statute of the International Court of Justice, for instance, specifies four sources of international law. Further, it differentiates among them by establishing the mutual priority of customary international law and international conventions, or treaties; in contrast, "judicial decisions and the teachings of the most highly qualified publicists of the various nations" are defined as "subsidiary means for the determination of rules of law."[28] Valid international legal rules, then, are rules created by states—primarily in the form either of international treaties or of rules of customary law. The Vienna Convention on the Law of Treaties (VLCT) and, to a lesser extent, the Vienna Convention on Diplomatic Relations (VCDR) provide a great deal of supplementary detail as to the mechanics for the creation and recognition of valid international legal rules. The VCLT includes specific provisions for how to deal with such questions as: how to determine who possesses legitimate authority to contract under international law on behalf of a state (Articles 6–8); how to authenticate a treaty text (Articles 9–10); how states should indicate their consent to be bound by a treaty (Articles 11–17); how to establish a valid rule in case of successive treaties dealing with the same subject (Article 30); and how states may register or respond to reservations that have the potential to exempt them from the application of particular treaty provisions (Articles 19–23).[29] The VCDR deals with, among other things, the means for establishing official and legitimate diplomatic relations between states, and the rights and immunities possessed by diplomats.[30] While rules of recognition

---

[28] Statute of the International Court of Justice (1945).
[29] Vienna Convention on the Law of Treaties (1969).
[30] Vienna Convention on Diplomatic Relations (1961).

with respect to international treaties are clear and relatively highly developed, the position with respect to customary international law is admittedly less so. However, legal scholars have established broad agreement that two components are necessary for the establishment of a rule of customary law. There must exist "a consistent and general international practice among states" and "the practice must be accepted as law by the international community." That is, states must perform the practice because they believe they are legally required to do so. This second component of determining customary law is referred to as *opinio juris* (Kindred et al. 2000, 129–30). While these requirements leave room for parties to reach different conclusions on the status of a putative rule, there are also basic standards for rule determination. These standards commit states to participation in a discursive practice of argumentation, and one which does not require consensus for rule creation.

Finally, the contemporary international system possesses detailed standards for interpreting rules, and for determining the applicability of general rules to particular cases. The Statute of the International Court of Justice deals with issues of interpretation in some depth, since this is the primary function of the court. However, the court's authority is explicitly recognized as deriving from that of states; indeed, the court exercises jurisdiction only where states refer cases to it or where states have previously indicated they accept the court's jurisdiction as compulsory.[31] The court's statute is remarkably thorough. It deals in detail with provisions for the selection of judges and the organization of the court (Articles 1–33). Further, the statute empowers the court to set its own procedural rules; Article 30 states that "the Court shall frame rules for carrying out its functions. In particular it shall lay down rules of procedure." Given the degree of specificity in the statute, this suggests that its drafters viewed procedural rules as relatively unproblematic. Rather than requiring precise elaboration by states, they could be left to the elected justices. The third major issue addressed in the statute is the proper form and practice for a judicial decision. Article 56 establishes that, in all cases, "the judgment shall state the reasons on which it is based" and Article 57 authorizes the familiar domestic legal practice of allowing dissents and minority opinions in cases where the justices do not unanimously agree on the entirety of the official decision. Finally, Article 60 states that "the judgment is final and without appeal," and that the court has sole authority to interpret its own decisions.

Despite the existence of the ICJ, international rules of adjudication also explicitly contemplate an adjudicative role for individual states. This identity of legislators, judges, and subjects of law is a defining characteristic of international law, and one that has caused a great deal of doubt about its "legal" status. What is

---

[31] Statute of the International Court of Justice (1945).

vital is that, though states are empowered—at least in many circumstances—to be judges in their own cases, they are not legitimately entitled to judge however they please. Article 31 of the VCLT establishes the "general rule of interpretation" for treaties. It states that "a treaty shall be interpreted in good faith in accordance with the ordinary meaning to be given to the terms of the treaty in their context and in the light of its object and purpose." The article further specifies that the "context" of a treaty refers to its text, preamble, annexes, as well as other relevant agreements reached by the parties. Further, it allows states to refer to "any subsequent agreement between the parties regarding the interpretation of the treaty or the application of its provisions" as well as to "any subsequent practice in the application of the treaty which establishes the agreement of the parties regarding its interpretation" and "any relevant rules of international law applicable in the relations between the parties." If these data points are insufficient, Article 32 establishes that "recourse may be had to supplementary means of interpretation, including the preparatory work of the treaty and the circumstances of its conclusion." Thus, secondary rules for interpreting and applying primary rules of behavior in given cases are highly specific. They require states to reason in particular ways, and to do so in a public manner subject to response and rebuttal by other states.

Though these examples are drawn from international treaties that establish fundamental rules of law (most notably treaty-making and international adjudication), it would be inappropriate and mistaken to draw the conclusion that practices of global rule-making and interpretation are coextensive with procedural rules of international law. After all, treaty-making is fundamentally as much a diplomatic practice as it is a legal one; and, as I have demonstrated in the previous two chapters, diplomats and public officials employ similar processes of reasoning in negotiations, even when they are not directly legal in character. Indeed, it is more accurate to say that *both* diplomacy and international law are—at least in part—instantiations of prior secondary rules. That is, they are institutions that perform the crucial function of stabilizing actor expectations about legitimate practices of rule creation, interpretation, and contestation in the international system—just as constitutional democracy and domestic legal systems perform these tasks at the state level.

AL-QAEDA AND SECONDARY RULES

It might be objected at this point that, even if the international community at large possesses a relatively stable, legitimate set of secondary rules, al-Qaeda and like-minded groups reject these rules. While this is true, al-Qaeda does not reject the *concept* of secondary rules; it merely rejects important elements of the secondary rule system on which global practices of rule-making are based. In the remainder of this section, I will demonstrate the existence of well-established Islamic secondary rules and practices for rule-making and interpretation.

Islamic practices of rule-making and interpretation proceed from a fundamentally different basis than do the contemporary international practices outlined above. Unlike the positive law foundation of international practices, Islamic practices begin from the presumed validity of particular religious texts; that is, from something akin to a natural law basis. First, "all Muslims agree on the importance of *al-sharia*—that is, they agree that there is a 'path' or way to live that accords with human nature, and is consistent with divine guidance." Second, "they further agree that the best way to discern the contours of that path involves reading and interpreting approved sources—the Qur'an and 'sound' reports of the Prophet's practice, understood as 'signs' that point to the approved way." Third, "Muslims agree that the proper way of interpreting these sources, in conversation with the consensual judgment of previous generations, is to find analogies between textual, historical precedents and the circumstances of contemporary believers" (Kelsay 2008, 601–2). The first agreement corresponds to a rule of recognition that legitimate rules are those provided for humanity by Allah. The second agreement establishes that these rules are recorded in the Koran and in the *sunna* and *hadith* (the customs and sayings of Mohammed and his companions).[32] The third agreement deals with proper procedures for interpreting and applying these source rules to particular cases. This final category, rules of adjudication, plays an especially prominent role in Islamic practices of rule-making and interpretation. Unlike a positive law framework, where all rules are susceptible to alteration by the parties with standing to participate in rule-making, natural law systems contain rules of superior status that are sheltered from human alteration. As a result, the "action" or dynamism in such systems rests disproportionately on the ability of agents to make socially compelling reinterpretations of existing rules and novel interpretations of what divinely mandated rules require in particular cases.

A brief historical sketch of the evolution of Islamic jurisprudence (*fiqh*) illustrates the relevance and accuracy of this analysis, and provides crucial context required to understand and explain the rhetorical choices made by al-Qaeda leaders. Reuben Levy argued that early Islamic officials and rulers were faced with high degrees of uncertainty about the dictates of their faith—both with respect to political and social affairs in the public realm and also to basic matters of faith. For instance, Levy notes that "for a century or more after the death of the Prophet it was not definitely known, or decided, actually how many periods of

---

[32] The concepts of *sunna* and *hadith* play a major role in Islamic jurisprudence, and will be discussed in greater detail below.

worship were laid down nor at what hours worship was to be performed." In addition, military conquests placed Muslims in positions of rule over non-Muslim populations, including former citizens and subjects of the Roman and Persian empires. These rulers struggled to reach decisions on public matters consistent with their faith: "Having in the Koran, even if they knew or studied it, no comprehensive guide either in political emergencies or when social or legal problems arose, the Muslim governors were driven to adopting local usage or else to applying their own reason or common sense as a way out of their difficulties" (Levy 1962, 155). In such an environment, secondary rules became a crucial matter of debate and contestation.

The relevance and legitimacy of the Koran, and the rules contained in it, has not been a serious point of contention. However, like any major religious text, attempts to interpret the Koran as a guide for human society have been more controversial. At base, this is in part true because the Koran (like any rule system) is both vague and internally inconsistent.[33] In fact, the Koran explicitly addresses problems of internal contradictions. Sura 2:100 states that "if we abrogate any verse, or cause it to pass into oblivion, we bring a better one than it, or as good." Sura 13:39 instructs that "what he pleases God will blot out or confirm; and with him is the 'Mother of the Book'" (quoted in Levy 1962, 163). The term "abrogation" (*naskh* in Arabic) is a technical one in Islamic jurisprudence. Levy quotes the thirteenth-century Persian commentator Baydawi as justifying *naskh* on the grounds that "laws are formulated and verses revealed as they are required to suit mankind" (quoted in Levy 1962, 163). Though the Koran thus provided for its own reinterpretation, the appropriate process for abrogation was not specified. Even absent internal contradictions in the Koran, early Muslims were faced with the problems of ambiguity and incompleteness in its prescriptions and directives. The initial strategy in resolving such problems was to refer to the *sunna* and *hadith*. While the two words are often used interchangeably, "the *hadith*, properly speaking, is the report of the Prophet's *sunna* or course of conduct, or of his doings and sayings, to any one of which a particular *hadith* may refer." Levy notes that "the *sunna* acquired an authority only a little less than that of the Koran itself" and that "in the later times of Islamic theology the *sunna* came to be held as of equal origin and equal validity with the Koran." Despite the importance of *hadith* to Islamic practices of rule-making, no universally accepted collection of them exists. The most that can be said is that *hadith* typically have two components: "the *isnad* or the chain of authorities who have transmitted the report" and "the *matn*, the text or substance of the report" (Levy 1962, 170). Further, despite the extensive proliferation of *hadith*, it would be extremely difficult to maintain either that the Koran and *hadith* adequately

---

[33] On incompleteness and inconsistency in rule systems, see Sandholtz (2008).

address every possible situation that may require the interpretation or application of Islamic rules, or that the relevance and meaning of particular verses is always self-evident. Indeed, early Muslims differed substantially on how to translate their faith into social and political rules. Between approximately 767 and 855 AD, a series of debates culminated in the emergence of four distinct schools of Sunni jurisprudence. All four continue to exist today.[34]

The Hanafi school dates approximately from the death of its founder (Abu Hanifa) in 767 AD. Hanifa and his followers accepted the legitimacy of using human reason and judgment in interpreting the primary sources of Islamic law—the Koran, *sunna*, and *hadith*. This use of reason (*ra'y*) offered flexibility in adapting rules to changing circumstance, but only at the potential cost of religious orthodoxy. Accordingly, Hanifa held that proper interpretation and application of rules must attempt "to penetrate behind the wording of the text to the *'illa*, or motive of the provisions made. In the new application of the text, or in the law derived from it, there must be the same *'illa* as in the Koranic revelation or traditional usage." This procedure came to be known as *qiyas*, or reasoning by deductive analogy. Hanafi scholars explicitly recognized the problem created by conflicting conclusions generated via *ra'y* and *qiyas*. Accordingly, they concluded that "in the last resort it was the consensus of the learned in any one period— what came to be known as *ijma*—which decided whether any law obtained by *qiyas* had valid force (Levy 1962, 166–67).

The Hanafi school originated in what is now Iraq. Its reason-based approach was rejected by scholars in Medina, who preferred to augment the loose and indeterminate set of social rules laid out in the Koran "by deliberately inventing *hadiths* of the prophet to justify their new regulations or fresh ways of applying Koranic laws." This group of scholars was led by Malik ibn Anas, founder of the Maliki school. Early Muslims were likely aware of the suspect provenance of many *hadith* but accepted many as legitimate on consequentialist grounds. For Malik, "it was tradition, either that of the Prophet or local custom, which had first claim to consideration after the Koran. If *hadiths* differed, he gave preference over them to local practice (*'amal*)." The infallible status attributed to Mohammed created an inevitable tension between entrenched local practice and Koranic orthodoxy. To resolve this, Maliki jurists developed the notion "that somewhere there existed another prophetic *hadith* abrogating the inconvenient one, and that upon it the *ijma* is based" (Levey 1962, 170–74).

The Shafi'i school expanded the concept of *ijma* "to include all the immense body of ideas and decisions which those competent to do so in Islam—apart,

---

[34] Because the radical jihadist networks carrying out attacks directed against the international system—as opposed to attacks directed against the state of Israel—are, to date, virtually entirely Sunni, I leave aside Shi'a approaches.

of course, from the Prophet Muhammad himself—had formulated and agreed upon." This expansive notion of *ijma* is in direct contrast to that of the Maliki school, which restricted standing to determine *ijma* to the scholars of Medina. Despite the inclusion of scholars from outside the Arabian Peninsula, the Shafi'i school differentiated between laypersons and accredited jurists (*faqihs*). Only the latter were empowered to determine *ijma*. Like the Hanafi jurists, Shafi'i scholars accepted the use of *qiyas* as a subsidiary means of determining the law (Levy 1962, 177–79).

The last of the four Sunni schools of jurisprudence is the Hanbali school, named for Ahmad ibn Hanbal, which emerged slowly after its founder's death in 855 AD. The Hanbali school is noted as "the most reactionary," primarily because it rejects "the unlawful 'innovation' (*bid'a*) of the *ijma*." Adherents of this school resolutely oppose the use of reason to interpret and extend the rules specified in the Koran, on the basis that the use of reason allows for subjective interpretations of law. While the Hanbali school claims the fewest adherents of the four major schools of *fiqh*, its importance is magnified by the fact that it is accepted by the Wahhabi sect of Islam, a variant of Salafist Islam that dominates both in Saudi Arabia and among radical Islamist groups (Levy 1962, 179–80).

The purpose and importance of this review is to establish key sites of agreement and contestation among Sunnis with respect to secondary rules. The four Sunni schools of jurisprudence agree on the core sources of Islamic law (the Koran, and the *sunna* as recorded in *hadith*), and on the necessity for supplementary means of determining how to apply rules to particular cases—that is, on the necessity of rules of adjudication in addition to rules of recognition. However, they disagree on precise methods to be used in interpreting and applying rules. Al-Qaeda's leaders adhere to a reactionary, minority position on secondary rules that remains deeply controversial among Muslims. Their Hanbali beliefs are the most literalist in applying the Koran and *hadith* to real-world situations; their version of secondary rules allows the smallest degree of freedom and adaptability. Further, Salafi radicals engage in the controversial practice of *takfir*— declaring other Muslims apostates and thus outside of the *Dar al-Islam*. Bin Laden's 1996 "Declaration of Jihad" claims that using "man-made law instead of the Sharia ... would strip a person of his Islamic status" (quoted in Orbach 2001, 59).[35]

---

[35] The Foreign Broadcast Information Service compilation of al-Qaeda statements translates this passage as "Upholding temporal laws and supporting heretics against Muslims are prohibited in Islam, as the ulema have ruled. God said 'whoever does not rule by God's law is a heretic,' and He said: "But no, by the Lord, they can have no (real) faith until they make thee judge in all disputes between them, and find in their souls no resistance against thy decisions, but accept them with the fullest conviction." See "Bin Ladin Declares Jihad on Americans," *Al-Islah*, 2 September 1996,

The lack of robust agreement among Muslims on procedures for creating, altering, interpreting, and applying social rules is evident in al-Qaeda's political rhetoric. Kelsay notes that al-Qaeda leaders "speak in ways that suggest a serious engagement with Muslim sources" and concludes that "in the end, jihadists are engaged in an argument with other Muslims regarding the nature of Islamic practice" (Kelsay 2008, 601). These intra-Islamic disputes are not my primary analytic focus, since they relate most directly to issues of domestic governance; however, they may have indirect relevance to rule-making at the system level insofar as they present opportunities for the consolidation of a modus vivendi on rule-making and interpretation that includes significant portions of the Muslim world.

The uncertainty and disagreement over legitimate Islamic practices of rule-making must also be viewed in light of the continuing legacy of colonialism in the Muslim world. Disruption of early Islamic practices for rule-making has destroyed significant social capacity, capacity that Muslim societies continue to struggle to rebuild. As Anver Emon points out, "in the premodern period, the existence of legal professionals, licensing procedures, curricula, and training centers made possible an Islamic rule of law system that ensured transparency, accountability, and expertise." Emon contrasts this situation with the modern, postcolonial world: "while a premodern *madrasa* student would have delved deeply into the study of the Qur'an, prophetic traditions, and related fields, the modern law student in the Muslim world works with codes of various sorts, many of which are drawn largely from European inspiration." Where *sharia* is applied in Muslim legal systems, Emon essentially argues that it is used mainly as a system of primary rules governing behavior, and that it has been displaced as a procedural system of jurisprudence by practices adopted from European legal systems (Emon 2009, 102–3). This shift has been largely consolidated at the state level, but has struggled to deeply penetrate many Islamic societies; traditional notions of Islamic law remain influential at the societal level, at the same time as social expertise in operating traditional systems of rule has eroded. Bin Laden and al-Qaeda are directly reflective of these shifts. On traditional understandings of Islamic practice, bin Laden's standing to participate in legal processes of rule-making is questionable. As Orbach notes, "it is a basic tenet of Islam that only trained clerics can issue *fatwas* (decrees), but bin Laden has not hesitated to do so" despite his lack of such training (Orbach 2001, 56).

The erosion of the distinction between rule-makers and the laity deserves special attention because it highlights an important corollary to my argument about the operation of settled social practices of rule-making. To the extent that

translated and reproduced in FBIS (2004, 18). The Salafi practice of *takfir* is also noted in Moghadam (2008/09, 62).

important actors are unwilling or unable to operate applicable practices of rule-making and interpretation, disputes about the contention, interpretation, and application of primary rules are more likely to be resolved violently.[36] This observation has particularly serious implications given the Trump administration's apparent rejection of the post-1945 global order and perhaps even of multilateralism and international organizations more generally.

The "amateur" status of key al-Qaeda figures—with respect to both Islamic and contemporary international practices—significantly complicated processes of rule-making and interpretation in this case. To a lesser extent, the neoconservative figures in the Bush administration shared this "outsider" status. The combination of two outsider groups in key positions played an important role in shaping the dynamics of rule-making and interpretation following the 9/11 attacks. Both groups were generally aware of the secondary rules relevant in their own immediate cultural contexts, to the extent that they could function as socially competent but not especially skillful participants; their social competence with each other's practices, however, was even more limited. To the extent al-Qaeda and the Bush administration attempted to engage the other side, these attempts generally took the form of appeals designed to play to narrow outlying segments of the opponent's audience—elements of Western public opinion in the case of al-Qaeda, and moderate or liberal Muslims in the case of the Bush administration. Such attempts are more appropriately characterized as bad-faith tactical efforts than as attempts to conduct genuine dialogue. Nevertheless, despite these limitations both sides generally attempted to adhere to their own understandings of legitimate procedures for rule-making and interpretation—even when these offered no realistic prospect of success in persuading the other side, and even where secondary rules imposed constraints. Further, both sides portrayed the other's practices of rule-making and interpretation as central to the conflict, and did so in unusually emotionally charged language.

Social Practices of Rule-Making in the Absence of Shared Secondary Rules

While complete agreement between parties on the content and proper interpretation of any complex rule set (including secondary rules) is highly unlikely, this case stands out for the parties' starkly different perspectives on legitimate

---

[36] Note that such cases are distinct from those in which secondary rules explicitly stipulate force as a means of dealing with conflicts over rules. Examples of the latter could include forms of ritual combat such as dueling, or potentially also Wendt's notion of Hobbesian cultures of anarchy (on the latter, see Wendt 1999, ch. 6).

rule-making procedures. The parties were aware of these differences, and portrayed them as an important issue in the conflict; but these differences did not lead the parties to abandon efforts to speak about issues of rule-making and interpretation. Rather, they continued to do so, relying on their own culturally relevant secondary rules and associated practices. The case therefore demonstrates the influence of secondary rules on outcomes even in the absence of shared secondary rules.

AL-QAEDA'S CASE FOR JIHAD

The 1996 "Declaration of Jihad" against the United States and the February 1998 *fatwa* calling on Muslims to kill Americans issued by the World Islamic Front establish a pre-9/11 context, and provide insight on al-Qaeda's initial goals, proposals, and justifications. The central point about these documents is that they are primarily concerned with crafting a convincing case for jihad rooted in Islamic practices of rule-making and interpretation, and are therefore directed primarily at an Islamic audience.

The ultimate target, especially in the 1996 declaration, is the Saudi government. Operations against the United States are portrayed as derivative of, and instrumental to, the goal of establishing a genuinely Islamic government in Saudi Arabia. Further, the document makes clear that the primary defects of the current Saudi government relate in large part to its alleged violation of Islamic rule-making practices. While the document criticizes the Saudi government for its decision to admit American troops during the Persian Gulf War, bin Laden goes to great lengths to make clear that violence against the Saudi regime is justified by its failure to respond appropriately to attempts at peaceful dialogue, and more broadly by "its suspension of the Islamic Shari'ah laws" in favor of "temporal laws." This issue of the proper basis for law is significant; it is essentially a charge of apostasy setting up the practice of *takfir*. Bin Laden argues that "upholding temporal laws and supporting heretics against Muslims are prohibited in Islam, as the ulema have ruled." Thus, al-Qaeda's conflict is, from the beginning, a conflict precisely over the terms of legitimate practices for rule-making. The document is also noteworthy in asserting a legitimate role for violent resistance in political life if parties are unwilling to employ proper practices for rule-making and interpretation. Finally, bin Laden grounds his position in the Islamic tradition by direct invocation not only of the authority of the *ulema*, but also of particular Koranic verses: "God said, 'whoever does not rule by God's law is a heretic', and He said: 'But no, by the Lord, they can have no (real) faith until they make thee judge in all disputes between them, and find in their souls no resistance against thy decisions, but accept them with the fullest convictions.'" On this view, accepting man-made law is inconsistent with making God "the judge of all disputes" (FBIS 2004, 16–18).[37]

The declaration claims that bin Laden and other like-minded individuals acted first according to "the gentle and lenient method of wisdom and good advice calling for reform and penance for the major wrongdoings and corruption that transgressed the categorical religious limits and the public's legitimate rights." In support of this contention he describes a pair of petitions presented to the Saudi king calling for domestic reforms and the expulsion of American forces. Because "the only response . . . was rejection, disregard, and ridicule," he argues, "silence was no longer appropriate and overlooking the facts was no longer acceptable" (FBIS 2004, 16).[38] He thus expresses the conviction that violence is legitimate only after the failure of peaceful attempts at dialogue. Whether this claim was genuine is, of course, open to serious question. The point, though, is that bin Laden apparently believed making this rhetorical move was at least potentially politically useful. Such a conclusion only makes sense if he was aware of expectations among at least part of his target audience that peaceful political means rooted in Islamic practice were the appropriate response to problematic government policies.

The notion that bin Laden was consciously engaged in a practice of political contestation of Saudi policy is bolstered by the fact that his letter directly engages with Saudi justifications of American presence. He dismisses "the claim that the crusaders' presence in the land of the two holy mosques is a necessity and a temporary matter aimed at defending this land" and asserts that "it is an old and obsolete story especially after the destruction of Iraq and its military and civilian infrastructures." He notes that "here we are approaching the seventh year since their arrival" and concludes that "the regime is unable to move them out. The regime does not want to admit to its people its inability to do so" (FBIS 2004, 21–22).[39] If the justification for the American presence was to defend the Saudi kingdom from Iraq, then removal of the threat should have led to the withdrawal of American forces.

Although Saudi apostasy and apostasy by other pro-Western Islamic governments are bin Laden's primary concerns, he concludes in this letter that rectifying the problem requires attacks against American targets. The connection between what are known to jihadis as the "near enemy" (pro-Western Islamic states) and the "far enemy" (primarily the United States, but in some

[37] "Bin Ladin Declares Jihad on Americans," *Al-Islah*, 2 September 1996, translated and reproduced in FBIS (2004, 16–18).

[38] "Bin Ladin Declares Jihad on Americans," *Al-Islah*, 2 September 1996, translated and reproduced in FBIS (2004, 16).

[39] "Bin Ladin Declares Jihad on Americans," *Al-Islah*, 2 September 1996, translated and reproduced in FBIS (2004, 21–22).

constructions more broadly the Western industrial democracies) (Gerges 2005) is evident in bin Laden's contention that "while we know that the regime is fully responsible for what has afflicted the country and the people, the main disease and the cause of the affliction is the occupying US enemy" (FBIS 2004, 23).[40] This is because, according to bin Laden, "whenever a reform movement appears in the Islamic states, that Jewish-crusade alliance pushes its agents in the region, the rulers, to exhaust and abort such a reform movement" (FBIS 2004, 19).[41] Securing an American withdrawal and altering the international system so as to prevent further external interference are thus vital steps toward achieving domestic political change.

This sense of external threat is crucial to the final noteworthy aspect of bin Laden's 1996 declaration: his call for Muslim unity in opposing the United States. This argument was carefully couched in terms of Islamic tradition. He drew on the writing of the thirteenth- and fourteenth-century Hanbali scholar Ibn Taymiyah, who he reports as having argued "that all Muslims should join hands in warding off the great heresy controlling the Islamic world." He then directly quoted Taymiyah's argument that "one of the principles of the Sunnah and the [Prophet's] group is to do conquest using every good as well as sinful person, for God supports this in the interest of the cause of religion" because it will ensure that "most of the rules of Islam are established, if not all." Bin Laden himself casts the matter as one of how to appropriately reconcile conflicting duties. He argues that "when duties are numerous the most important takes priority." On his view, this means that "warding off that American enemy is the top duty after faith, and nothing should take priority over it, as decreed by the ulema." Thus, "it is incumbent on every tribe in the Arabian Peninsula to fight for God's cause and purge their territory of these occupiers" (FBIS 2004, 19, 26).[42]

The initial call for Muslims in the Arabian Peninsula to use violence to prompt a US withdrawal was followed by a February 1998 statement purporting to be a *fatwa*, or religious ruling, signed by bin Laden, Ayman al-Zawahiri, and representatives of a handful of jihadi groups identifying themselves collectively as the World Islamic Front. The document explicitly presents itself as conforming with Islamic practices of rule-making and interpretation; its authors declare that "in compliance with God's order" they "issue the following fatwa to all Muslims." Despite the fact that the authors' standing to issue a *fatwa* was unclear, they maintained that "the ruling to kill Americans and their allies—civilian and

[40] "Bin Ladin Declares Jihad on Americans," *Al-Islah*, 2 September 1996, translated and reproduced in FBIS (2004, 23).

[41] "Bin Ladin Declares Jihad on Americans," *Al-Islah*, 2 September 1996, translated and reproduced in FBIS (2004, 19).

[42] "Bin Ladin Declares Jihad on Americans," *Al-Islah*, 2 September 1996, translated and reproduced in FBIS (2004, 19, 26).

military—is an individual duty for every Muslim who can do it in any country in which it is possible to do it, in order to liberate the al-Aqsa Mosque and the holy mosque [Mecca] from their grip, and in order for their armies to move out of all the lands of Islam, defeated and unable to threaten any Muslim." The letter seeks to establish the validity of its conclusion by citing two particular Koranic passages: "this is in accordance with the words of Almighty God, 'and fight the pagans all together as they fight you all together', and 'fight them until there is no more tumult or oppression, and there prevail justice and faith in God.'" In addition, it adopts a justificatory argument parallel to that of the 1996 declaration; it notes that "for over seven years the United States has been occupying the lands of Islam in the holiest of places, the Arabian Peninsula." Similarly, it maintains that the "best proof" of American hostility "is the American's continuing aggression against the Iraqi people using the Peninsula as a staging post." Finally, the 1998 *fatwa* draws on the authority of religious scholars (*ulema*) in justifying its position (FBIS 2004, 57–58).[43] The innovations in the 1998 document are its relatively greater degree of formalization, especially its direct claim that it constitutes a *fatwa*, and the postulation of an individual duty to violently oppose the United States applicable to all Muslims—rather than the more equivocal 1996 position, which called for Muslim unity but directed its call for action primarily at inhabitants of the Arabian Peninsula.

The 1998 *fatwa* was followed, roughly six months later, by the embassy bombings in Kenya and Tanzania. These attacks damaged relations between Western states and the Taliban. However, the *fatwa* and attacks were not bin Laden's only attempts to communicate with the United States in this period. As he gained notoriety, he gave two of his only interviews with Western media. The first, roughly two months before the embassy bombings, was conducted by John Miller for *Esquire*, who "told one of Bin Ladin's agents, 'we could frame his issues about America in such a way that people might find his arguments reasonable.'" The response was instructive: "The man smiled. 'It may be better if he does not appear to be too reasonable,' he said" (FBIS 2004, 89).[44] This exchange demonstrates that al-Qaeda figures are aware of the differences in standards for evaluating arguments between the West and the Islamic world, and that they believe there are political advantages in failing to conform, at least completely, with Western standards.

Finally, bin Laden reiterated the claim in his 1998 *fatwa* that al-Qaeda would target civilians in addition to military personnel. He stated that "we do

---

[43] "Text of World Islamic Front's Statement Urging Jihad against Jews and Crusaders," *Al-Quds al-'Arabi*, 23 February 1998, translated and reproduced in FBIS (2004, 57–58).

[44] "A Conversation with the Most Dangerous Man in the World," *Esquire*, February 1999, reproduced in FBIS (2004, 89).

not differentiate between those dressed in military uniform and civilians." He maintained that this was justified by American action: "American history does not distinguish between civilians and military, not even women and children. They are the ones who used bombs against Nagasaki. Can these bombs distinguish between infants and military?" (FBIS 2004, 99).[45] The political purpose here is likely twofold. For moderate Muslims and liberal-minded Western citizens, the statement attempts to establish a degree of moral equivalency between al-Qaeda and the United States. For most Western citizens, the purpose of the statement is to generate fear by demonstrating an absence of moral restraint.

The second interview bin Laden granted after the release of his 1998 *fatwa* came in late 1998, after the embassy bombings. In this interview, he sought to further justify his call for jihad against the United States. He sought to do so by comparing American policy to criminal behavior: "Any thief or criminal or robber who enters another country in order to steal should expect to be exposed to murder at any time." He also addressed the issue of nuclear proliferation, expressing his opinion that "it would be a sin for Muslims not to try to possess the weapons that would prevent the infidels from inflicting harm on Muslims." The most interesting aspect of the interview dealt with the relationship between al-Qaeda and their Taliban hosts. Asked what he would do if his hosts asked him to leave Afghanistan, bin Laden answered only "that is not something we foresee." The journalist wrote in the resulting article that after the embassy bombings, bin Laden "heeded the orders of his host, the Taliban militia" to avoid further attacks. The Taliban decision to make this request is attributed to a belief that "the Taliban's leaders evidently didn't want to complicate their budding relations with the outside world" (FBIS 2004, 83–85).[46]

THE TALIBAN'S COMPLEX ROLE

The relationship between al-Qaeda and the Taliban prior to 9/11 was complex. The Taliban was in some ways less committed to contesting the rules of the international system, and al-Qaeda was constrained by the social legitimacy of the Taliban movement. Like al-Qaeda, the Taliban is a Salafist jihad group with a lineage clearly traceable to the Soviet occupation of Afghanistan. Similarly, the Taliban employ propaganda and rhetorical arguments in attempting to generate and maintain political support (Rashid 2001). Both groups reject the notion that social rules can be legitimately made or altered by humans. The Taliban deputy

---

[45] "A Conversation with the Most Dangerous Man in the World," *Esquire*, February 1999, reproduced in FBIS (2004, 99).

[46] "Wrath of God: Usama bin Ladin Lashes Out against the West," *Time Asia*, 11 January 1999, reproduced in FBIS (2004, 83–85).

foreign minister reportedly defended implementation of *sharia* law to German diplomats in November 1996 on the grounds that "we have not introduced this law." Similarly, Mullah Omar responded to Amnesty International criticism of his regime's human rights record by asserting that "we are just applying the divine injunction." Jurgen Kleiner concludes that, for the Taliban, any constitution can be "only declaratory," and that "the divine injunctions are applied without being sanctioned by an act of law of men" (Kleiner 2000, 21–22). The Taliban also accept a similar set of procedures for interpreting and applying rules drawn from the Koran and *hadith*; they moved to establish religious courts, supplemented by *shuras*, or tribal councils. Ultimately, however, decision-making authority rested in the hands of Mullah Omar and his immediate circle of advisors. Taliban spokesman Mullah Wakil Ahmed Mutakil reportedly indicated that the Taliban "abide by the Amir's [Mullah Omar's] view even if he alone takes this view" (Kleiner 2000, 28).

Despite their mutual acceptance of similar practices of rule-making and interpretation, and the desirability of political governance rooted in fundamentalist interpretations of Islam, the Taliban and al-Qaeda did not always agree on policy or tactics. The most striking difference is found in their orientations toward the international system of sovereign states. While al-Qaeda sought to violently oppose and to undermine the American-led international system, the Taliban repeatedly sought to *join* it. William Maley describes securing recognition as the legitimate government of Afghanistan as the main objective of Taliban "foreign policy" in this period. He notes that "the Taliban, upon taking Kabul, immediately demanded recognition from other states as the government of Afghanistan, and Afghanistan's seat in the General Assembly." In order to press the latter claim, they reportedly participated in a crucial procedural practice of international law. UN General Assembly 396(V), adopted on 14 December 1950, provides that "wherever more than one authority claims to be the government entitled to represent a Member State in the United Nations and this question becomes the subject of controversy in the United Nations, the question should be considered in the light of the Purposes and Principles of the Charter and the circumstances of each case." The practical process for implementing this requirement is fulfilled by the Credentials Committee of the UN General Assembly, which voted annually from 1996 to 2000 not to recognize the Taliban as the legitimate occupant of the Afghan seat in the General Assembly (Maley 2000, 8–9). While the Taliban failed to secure UN membership, in pursuing UN and diplomatic recognition they were required to engage with modern international practices of rule-making. This may indicate potential for conscious efforts to forge broader consensus on legitimate procedural rules for global rule-making.

The Taliban effort to secure the Afghan UN seat was not the group's only effort to secure international recognition. Indeed, the Taliban succeeded in gaining formal diplomatic recognition from Pakistan, Saudi Arabia, and the United Arab Emirates (UAE). This foothold in international society provided the basis for a limited degree of learning and adaptation on the part of the Taliban, introducing them to rudimentary elements of international rule-making practices. While this encounter did not induce the Taliban to fundamentally alter either their values or domestic policies, or to hand over al-Qaeda leaders for criminal trial, relatively settled practices of rule-making have not eliminated violent conflict in the international system. The crucial point is that the case demonstrates the possibility that actors can be socialized to international practices of rule-making even if those practices are initially regarded with suspicion or hostility, and even if they are culturally alien to the new actor.[47]

The brief tenure of Mullah Zaeef as the Taliban ambassador to Pakistan (October 2000–November 2001) highlights both the potential to integrate actors with Wahhabist worldviews into the international system, and the challenges associated with bridging significant differences in understandings about legitimate practices of rule-making. Prior to being stripped of diplomatic status, deported to Afghanistan, and turned over to American custody, Zaeef performed an array of functions in a strikingly typical manner. In addition to the embassy in Islamabad, he oversaw consulates in Karachi, Quetta, and Peshawar, and reached bilateral agreements with Pakistan on dams, food aid, development assistance, treatment of prisoners, refugees, and other issues (Sharp 2003, 484). He also met repeatedly with Western diplomats, including American and British representatives, despite lacking formal recognition from any Western state. The fact of these meetings is significant; it demonstrates the potential to extend and strengthen practices of global rule-making across significant cultural divides—and specifically to extend those practices to include actors accustomed to Wahhabist rule-making practices. However, perhaps unsurprisingly, these meetings achieved little of substance. Sharp notes the crippling effect of the lack of agreement on secondary rules; the initial meeting "was not so much a negotiation . . . as an encounter between parties with little mutual understanding of what was supposed to be going on." While the Taliban had expected their capture of Taloqan,[48] the last major city outside Taliban control, to result in diplomatic recognition at the UN, Zaeef nevertheless continued to meet Western diplomats after the General Assembly's Credentials Committee denied the Taliban application for the fifth and final time (Sharp 2003, 485–87).

---

[47] Historical examples include the socialization of the Ottoman Empire, the Soviet Union, China, and Japan, as well as the experiences of postcolonial states.

[48] This expectation is evidence that the Taliban were aware of international criteria for recognition, and that they understood these criteria on at least a rudimentary level.

In addition to engaging with Western practices, Zaeef also sought to engage Western actors in discourse on the basis of Islamic secondary rules. In the course of his dealings with Western diplomats, Zaeef dealt with four primary issues: the possibility of oil and gas pipeline projects; human rights concerns, especially the treatment of women; disputes over the destruction of the Bamiyan statues, which the Taliban regarded as idolatrous and the international community regarded as an important cultural heritage site; and the question of Osama bin Laden and al-Qaeda. The question of pipeline construction is of minimal interest for my purposes here. On the remaining issues, Zaeef was engaged in clear efforts to interpret and apply rules across a significant cultural divide. Especially with respect to the Bamiyan statues and, surprisingly, the status of Osama bin Laden and al-Qaeda, he made at least sporadic attempts to "translate" Taliban understandings about legitimate practices of rule-making and interpretation for the international community. In contrast, on the question of women, he maintained that the Taliban had sought to protect Afghan women from abuses committed by warlords.

With respect to the Bamiyan statues, Zaeef typically contrasted international concern with statues with what he argued was a morally indefensible lack of concern with humanitarian conditions in Afghanistan. Despite this rhetorical ploy, he seems to have attempted to suggest a potential resolution to the impasse. On 6 March 2001, he suggested that "maybe if there is a message from religious scholars of the Arabic world this may help" and that "so far we have not received any message or proposal which is based on reasons of Sharia law." He further promised that "such a message . . . will be considered." The international community took up this opening. Two days later, the Egyptian foreign minister "announced that the Mufti of the Republic had decided that destroying the statues did not express the spirit of Islam." On 9 March, an Organization of the Islamic Conference (OIC) delegation arrived in Kandahar, accompanied by Zaeef. Zaeef pledged that "if both sides issue a unanimous fatwa (edict) saying the destruction of the statues is not proper, we will accept it." However, after the meeting, the Taliban maintained "that while the Kandahar Ulema had listened to its counterpart from the other Islamic countries respectfully and would do so in the future, it had heard no good reason for halting the destruction." In particular, the Kandahari scholars had concluded that "the ulema from abroad . . . had only acted under pressure from non-Islamic countries." The Taliban deliberately sought to alter the secondary rules being applied—to secure a discussion in terms of Islamic rather than Western rules (Sharp 2003, 489–90).

Whether this move is best explained by consequentialist logic or a logic of appropriateness, the result was that the Taliban were drawn into a discursive exchange. That the OIC delegation failed to secure a change in Taliban action is similarly beside the point. Social practices are rarely determinative—especially when the practice is explicitly deliberative in nature. Rules are rarely obeyed completely; often, the point is precisely that what rules require is contested, especially in situations with multiple, complex, and simultaneously valid sets of rules. There are three important points. First, as the argument in the book expects, the Taliban articulated a justification for their position—and, further, a justification rooted in procedural propriety. The Taliban claim was essentially that the OIC delegation had not fulfilled the requirement of conducting rule interpretation on genuinely Islamic grounds because the ultimate impetus for OIC action was Western pressure. Second, the Taliban explicitly reaffirmed the relevance and legitimacy of Islamic practices of rule-making and interpretation. While they maintained their freedom to destroy the statues, they publicly declared themselves bound to accept certain practices of rule-making that could, in other cases, require them to alter their behavior. Though actors can certainly bend and manipulate procedural rules to suit their interests and their preexisting goals, their ability to persuasively do so in a public fashion is not infinite. Third, following the episode with the OIC delegation, the Taliban continued to assert justifications directed at international audiences for their refusal to discuss the Bamiyan statues. Zaeef and his staff consistently maintained that the issue of the statues was less important than humanitarian needs, and that international insistence to the contrary was indicative of disregard for Afghans' basic rights. When it became apparent that changing the applicable secondary rules had not resolved the issue, at least to the satisfaction of the international community, the Taliban ambassador displayed a willingness and ability to engage with international diplomatic rules and practices by adopting a form of linkage politics.

The question of how to handle al-Qaeda arose on two separate occasions during Zaeef's tenure: the fall of 2000, in response to the attack on the USS *Cole*, and the fall of 2001, in response to the 9/11 attacks. As with the Bamiyan statues, in both cases the Taliban sought to ensure that questions related to al-Qaeda would be resolved according to Islamic rules and practices. The significance of this point deserves elaboration: the Taliban responded to Western demands by invoking what they understood to be legitimate standards—and what their supporters in Afghanistan and the broader Muslim world broadly understood to be legitimate standards—for determining whether the demand to hand over bin Laden and other senior al-Qaeda leaders was binding. Established practices for rule-making and interpretation were regarded as relevant and were actually employed. Further, Zaeef attempted to secure acceptance of these practices from the international community.

The basic Taliban position was that handing al-Qaeda leaders over for trial was prohibited both by Islamic rules and by a body of Pashtun tribal rules referred to as Pashtunwali.[49] However, they made two alternate proposals that

---

[49] On Pashtunwali, and the relationship between Pashtunwali and Sharia in Taliban thought, see Kleiner (2000, 25–26).

could potentially secure justice while remaining faithful to these rules. First, the United States could provide evidence to the (Taliban-appointed) Supreme Court of Afghanistan, "which would try him with the aid of religious scholars from Saudi Arabia and a third or fourth country and possibly with monitors from the Organization of the Islamic Conference (OIC)." Second, even if the United States refused to provide evidence leading to a mutually satisfactory trial, Sharp reports that the Taliban unilaterally pledged they "would '... contain and supervise...' Bin Laden to prevent him using Afghan territory as a base for operations against third countries." Zaeef also articulated a justification for the refusal to turn bin Laden over; to do so, Agence France Presse reported on 23 January 2003, would "amount to giving a kind of superiority to non-Islamic laws over Islamic laws" (Sharp 2003, 487). That is, it would violate legitimate practices for applying rules to particular cases.

Following 9/11, Zaeef declared the attacks inconsistent with Islam, but he also reportedly insisted they "were beyond the technical ability of Bin Laden, who was under surveillance and lacked trained pilots" and "reiterated the request for evidence if the US wanted Bin Laden tried." Shortly after making these statements, Zaeef accompanied a Pakistani delegation to Kandahar that was to present evidence in an effort to arrange extradition. The result of this mission was "a request from the Kandahar Council of Ulemas to Bin Laden that he should leave Afghanistan"; however, Zaeef "explained that the request was advisory and non-binding until Omar approved it." When Omar remained silent, "the delegation returned to Pakistan with a promise to meet again and a request for OIC and UN investigations of the bombings." The final noteworthy comment from Zaeef on the bin Laden question was his confirmation "that, Omar's silence notwithstanding, the Ulema's recommendation that he should leave had been given to Bin Laden, but that there had been '... no response'" (Sharp 2003, 487).

It is unclear whether the Taliban was sincere in its offer to arrange a trial of bin Laden and his associates. An Internet report on a Pakistani website on 3 April 2001, prior to the 9/11 attacks, quoted Mullah Omar as saying, "half of my country has been destroyed by two decades of war. If the remaining half is also destroyed in trying to protect Bin Ladin, I'm prepared for this sacrifice." Further, the report quoted a Taliban source as insisting that bin Laden "is not going to be handed over if there is any prospect that he will be convicted." These statements suggest that Zaeef's overtures to the international community were cynical in nature, or that Zaeef was operating without approval. Even if the proposal was cynical, it would demonstrate that the Taliban were willing and able to employ practices of rule-making and interpretation in a strategic manner. However, there is reason to suspect the Taliban regarded Islamic rules and practices as binding, or at least constraining. The same report indicating Taliban commitment to protecting al-Qaeda also reported tension between the two groups. It quoted a letter from bin Laden to Mullah Omar, in which bin Laden complained that "the United States is free to do whatever it feels like and I have been placed under restrictions" (FBIS 2004, 150–51).[50] This complaint suggests that the Taliban had followed through on their promise to "contain and supervise" al-Qaeda— at least to an extent. Further, bin Laden suggested elsewhere that al-Qaeda was constrained not primarily by Taliban might, but rather by the social legitimacy the Taliban enjoyed. In an Al Jazeera interview conducted in December 1998, he acknowledged that "we are in a state with an Emir of the Faithful." As a result, al-Qaeda was "legally bound to obey him in whatever that does not violate God's words" (FBIS 2004, 171).[51] This formulation establishes the centrality of established Islamic practices of rule-making and interpretation in determining the limits of Mullah Omar's authority over al-Qaeda. The crucial question would be whether Omar's directives violated the requirements of Islam.

These same social rules appear to have restricted al-Qaeda, both in its relations with the Taliban and with the outside world. Despite his complaints about Taliban restrictions, bin Laden had publicly expressed the understanding that he was legally bound to obey the Taliban as long as he resided in Afghanistan. More specifically, bin Laden seemed to accept the legitimacy of a trial under Islamic law. In the Al Jazeera interview, he indicated he was "ready at any time to appear before any religious court, in which both plaintiff and defendant stand." He added that "if the plaintiff is the United States, we will also sue it for many things and cardinal sins it committed in the land of Islam." This possibility seems to have been understood as something more than a rhetorical canard. Bin Laden revealed that the United States had asked the Taliban to hand him over before December 1998, presumably in response to the embassy bombings. He criticized this demand explicitly on the grounds that it failed to conform with what he understood to be legitimate procedures, noting that the US "refused to apply the shari'ah" in dealing with him, and connected this refusal to his common assertion of American "arrogance" (FBIS 2004, 164).[52]

The case thus involves three different actors—the US government, the Taliban, and al-Qaeda—playing by two distinct sets of secondary rules. These rules shaped the options available to the actors, enabling and constraining them in pursuit of their goals and in their responses to the others. Al-Qaeda publicly

[50] Ismail Khan, "Usama Regrets Curbs by Taliban," *Karachi Dawn*, 3 April 2001, reproduced in FBIS (2004, 150–51).

[51] "Al-Jazirah TV Broadcasts Usama Bin Ladin's 1998 Interview," 20 September 2001, translated and reproduced in FBIS (2004, 171).

[52] "Al-Jazirah TV Broadcasts Usama Bin Ladin's 1998 Interview," 20 September 2001, translated and reproduced in FBIS (2004, 164).

acknowledged Taliban authority, within the limits prescribed by secondary rules, and also accepted the prospect of participating in a trial—what would amount to an authoritative legal interpretation of the relative merits of contending positions on the rules of the international system—so long as the trial was conducted according to what it understood as legitimate procedural rules. The Taliban stands out for its attempt—albeit inconsistent and very likely tactically motivated—to bridge Islamic and international practices for making and interpreting rules. In fact, it is the only actor to have attempted such a fusion. This should not be understood as excusing Taliban behavior with respect to human rights; rather, it demonstrates the potential for expanding agreement on international practices for rule-making and interpretation in what is a fairly hard case—a radical Wahhabist militant group. Even where the chasm between Western and Islamic practices could not be bridged, or in domestic cases where international practices had little obvious relevance, the Taliban seems to have been influenced by Islamic practices of rule-making. The meetings with delegations of foreign Muslim scholars may not have stopped or altered Taliban policies, but they did commit the Taliban to an external process of review for their actions that in some ways extends beyond baseline international obligations in the context of state sovereignty. Further, the Taliban seem to have concluded that while rules of hospitality enjoined them from extraditing bin Laden, they also established positive obligations on the Taliban for the behavior of their guests. Finally, these same rules of hospitality led the Taliban to ask bin Laden to leave the country after 9/11, but still prohibited them from expelling him—even in the face of a virtually certain American reprisal that threatened the military gains they had made in consolidating their de facto hold on the Afghan state.

The United States, along with its allies, made slight deviations from established international practice to accommodate and potentially integrate the Taliban, effectively according them informal diplomatic status "as if" they constituted the formally recognized government of Afghanistan without ever extending official recognition. Further, it is likely that OIC and other Muslim efforts to engage the Taliban in reasoning on their own terms enjoyed at least the tacit acceptance of major powers. While it is impossible to say how these attempts to find a modus vivendi would have developed without the spectacular nature of the 9/11 attacks, it is noteworthy that integrative efforts were in many ways driven by major terror attacks—the embassy bombings and the attack on the USS *Cole*. Collectively, all of this suggests that there may have been developing (and ultimately missed) diplomatic opportunities prior to 9/11. While it is unlikely that a mutually satisfactory set of rules for a trial could have been created, rather, the point is a more general one—that conscious effort to broaden the legitimacy of global practices of rule-making may yield positive long-term results that reduce the appeal of extremist actors in the Muslim world and elsewhere.

SECONDARY RULES AS A MATTER OF JUSTICE

Regardless, the 9/11 attacks fundamentally altered the political dynamics of al-Qaeda's attempts to change the international system. Just as the attacks drew Western engagement with the Taliban to a close, they raised the curtain on a new act of political theater featuring the United States playing directly opposite bin Laden. In his televised address on 20 September 2001, American president George W. Bush referred to the attacks as an "act of war" and declared that "al-Qaeda is to terror what the mafia is to crime." Despite the mixed analogies, Bush was clear that al-Qaeda's "goal is remaking the world." He then noted that "the terrorists practice a fringe form of radical extremism that has been rejected by Muslim scholars and the vast majority of Muslim clerics—a fringe movement that perverts the peaceful teachings of Islam" (Bush 2001).

Bush was clearly aware that al-Qaeda sought changes to the international system, and his administration articulated a reply based in important part on an internal critique of al-Qaeda's positions as being inconsistent not only with international practice, but also with proper *Islamic* standards for rule-making and interpretation. He went on to declare that "the United States of America makes the following demands on the Taliban: Deliver to United States authorities all the leaders of al-Qaeda who hide in your land." Bush continued, insisting on release of and protection for all foreign journalists, diplomats, and aid workers, and that the Taliban act to "close immediately and permanently every terrorist training camp in Afghanistan, and hand over every terrorist, and every person in their support structure, to appropriate authorities." Bush insisted that these demands, along with provisions for the United States to verify Taliban compliance, were "not open to negotiation or discussion" (Bush 2001).

Procedurally, the American demands were noteworthy for two reasons. First, they were directed not to al-Qaeda but to the Taliban. This likely reflects both the international effort to engage the Taliban given its de facto control of Afghanistan, and a calculated move to deny standing in discussions over the rules of the international system to violent non-state actors. Second, the American demands were strikingly broad and invasive in their scope, penetrating deep inside Afghanistan's sovereign prerogatives—especially considering that international law did not clearly authorize states to hold other states directly responsible for the actions of terrorist groups operating both inside their borders and transnationally (Byers 2005, 55–57). The address articulated, in embryonic form, the core of what would become the "Bush Doctrine": that "any nation that continues to harbor or support terrorism will be regarded by the United States as a hostile regime." Perhaps as a result of the far-reaching nature of these positions and their significant implications for the functioning of the international system, the address concluded with a justification of the American position aimed at the international community. Bush argued that "this is the world's fight. This is civilization's fight. This is the fight of all who believe in progress and pluralism, tolerance and freedom." He also expressed the belief that members of "the civilized world . . . understand that if this terror goes unpunished, their own cities, their own citizens may be next. Terror, unanswered, can not only bring down buildings, it can threaten the stability of legitimate governments." The statement reflects the Bush administration's awareness that its proposals would face scrutiny from allied governments and world opinion, and that they therefore required justification in the context of existing international practices. Interestingly, the language employed in the address also evinces the belief that terrorism posed a potential threat to "the stability of legitimate governments" (Bush 2001). That is, in addition to destruction of property and loss of life, terrorism was a problem because it could undermine established practices of rule-making and interpretation.

Al-Qaeda had succeeded in changing the stakes of its dispute with the United States, which saw the conflict in a different light than it previously had. Both sides were clear that the nature of the international system was at stake, but they also retained sharply divergent and incompatible views not only of the *substance* of desirable alterations to that system, but also of the legitimate practices for creating such changes. Remarkably, these differing views did not cause either side to abandon what it regarded as legitimate practices of rule-making and interpretation. Instead, both continued to employ culturally relevant practices. As I will argue, this pattern is best explained by two factors. First, realization on the part of the Bush administration and al-Qaeda leadership that even if they did not mutually agree on practical means for rule creation and interpretation, that each also sought to convince third-party audiences with which they *did* agree broadly on such practices. Each side not only sought to convince audiences using arguments consistent with secondary rules—they also sought to leverage those secondary rules to undermine the legitimacy of the opposing side. Second, each side held sincere beliefs about the legitimacy of their preferred practices as instrumental to a particular notion of the proper nature and ends of political community. Key figures on both sides repeatedly invoked such imagery using vivid and emotional language. Further, the link to the good life helps explain the rigidity shown by both sides with respect to procedural matters—rules of procedure, on this view, are not goods susceptible to easy substitution. If employing improper procedures for rule-making can threaten the fundamental aims of human community, stakes are raised immeasurably. Actors pursuing conceptions of justice may be particularly resistant to compromise (Welch 1993; Albin 2001; Welch 2014). At least in this case, sincere belief coupled with instrumental links to a notion of the good life appear to have significantly reduced the willingness and ability of key decision makers to even imagine potential compromises and alternative procedures for rule-making and interpretation.

It is hard to imagine an alternate, intelligible explanation for the determined resort to preexisting practices of rule-making and interpretation on the part of both al-Qaeda and the Bush administration. Both articulated proposals about the creation and interpretation of rules in patterned ways that were intelligible as such to their listeners, to varying degrees. Further, they evaluated the proposals of other actors in a similarly patterned way, just as those audiences evaluated their own proposals. When presentation or evaluation of proposals broke from practices specified as legitimate, offending actors presented justifications and audience members engaged in critical responses. Finally, when terms of evaluation were seen as incompatible, actors treated each other as secondary rule violators even as they employed violence against each other—showing little willingness or ability to collaborate improvisationally to create shared practices of rule-making and interpretation. At most, they engaged in critical responses rooted in their own practices.

Available alternate explanations do a poor job accounting for this overall behavior. Realist theories cannot adequately account for instances in which actors passed up better material outcomes for procedural reasons. Perhaps the most striking example in this case is the Taliban decision in fall 2001 to request that al-Qaeda leave their country while simultaneously refusing to declare the organization persona non grata, even in the face of international military action. They also fall short more fundamentally in explaining why anyone would bother creating all this remarkably patterned "cheap talk." While neoliberal institutionalist theories offer some purchase on the stickiness of institutions, they are less helpful in explaining actions driven by logics of appropriateness or logics of practice, or in explaining the formation of interests in the first place— let alone the formation of values or identities. The argument offered here also builds on existing constructivist work. Most notably, it draws attention to the standards and criteria that actors employ in making and interpreting rules, and therefore to the relationship between rules and practices. It further helps to account for the answer to an important puzzle: how actors know *how* to contest rules. Finally, it offers additional analytical leverage on questions about the form, process, and timing of change in rules and their interpretation. In the remainder of this section, I demonstrate that secondary rules shaped the interaction between the Bush administration and al-Qaeda from the period following the 9/11 attacks to the eve of the American invasion of Iraq in March 2003.

President Bush's 20 September 2001 address sought to deny standing to al-Qaeda. From the perspective of international practice this was unsurprising: as al-Qaeda, unlike the Taliban, did not even make a claim to status as the government of a state, it was not a legitimate participant in global rule-making.

However, denying standing to al-Qaeda on procedural grounds did not necessarily require extending that status to the Taliban. While the Taliban had de facto
control of Afghanistan, as well as formal recognition from three states in the region and a brief history of quasi-diplomatic interaction with the United States,
it had been rebuffed five times in its efforts to secure UN membership and had
never been officially recognized by the United States. It may have been easier
for the Bush administration to secure authorization from officials in the former
Rabbani government, and to have intervened in Afghanistan on this basis. It
seems reasonable to conclude that the American decision may have been driven
at least in important part by a perceived need to secure legitimacy for military
action by first exhausting all potential peaceful means of conflict resolution with
the most state-like party available—the Taliban. Even if the underlying motivation to adopt this course of action was one of self-interest (for example, a need
to placate Pakistani officials given the close ties between the Taliban and the
Pakistani security establishment, or a desire to attract a broader international
coalition as a means to limit the financial and other costs of intervention), the
vital point is that the American decision to issue demands to the Taliban was not
the only (or even the most obvious) course of action available. It was, however, a
course of action consistent with a vital international rule requiring initial resort
to peaceful means of conflict resolution in advance of military action, even when
that military action could be convincingly portrayed both as self-defense and as
furthering international security.

As discussed above, the attempt to induce or compel the Taliban to hand
over al-Qaeda leaders ultimately failed, despite some indications that Taliban
leadership searched for an internationally acceptable compromise consistent
with their reading of what Islamic and Pashtun practices allowed. The failure
to reach agreement led the United States to pressure Pakistan into rescinding
the diplomatic status of Mullah Zaeef, who was deported to Afghanistan in late
2001 and subsequently taken into custody by the United States. Even before
the final breakdown in relations between the United States and the Taliban,
however, al-Qaeda had spoken out—following up its spectacular operational
success with a series of discursive interventions in an effort to shape international discussions.

These initial interventions illustrate clear constraints on al-Qaeda attributable to secondary rules. In a 28 September 2001 interview with *Karachi Ummat*,
bin Laden initially disavowed direct responsibility for the attacks, stating
that "I am not involved in the 11 September attacks in the United States." He
added: "Neither had I any knowledge of these acts nor I consider the killing of
innocent women, children, and other humans as an appreciable act." Finally, he
acknowledged that "Islam strictly forbids causing harm to innocent women,
children, and other people. Such a practice is forbidden even in the course of a

battle" (FBIS 2004, 179).[53] Bin Laden's denial of his greatest triumph is striking, and surprising. There are at least two potential explanations rooted in practices of rule-making and interpretation that render it intelligible. First, the denial of direct responsibility is actually the *norm* in al-Qaeda operations prior to 9/11 rather than the exception.[54] It is likely that this pattern of denying direct involvement while asserting a right to "rouse" attacks via *fatwas* and public statements reflects a carefully calculated effort to advance his political agenda without running afoul of Taliban restrictions on his activity that were the price for his protection against expulsion. In this way, Islamic and Pashtun practices meaningfully constrained bin Laden's attempts to capitalize politically not only on the 9/11 attacks but also on the embassy bombings. Second, as he directly admitted, bin Laden was aware that the 9/11 attacks would be seen by many Muslims as a violation of proper Islamic behavior. Thus, the denial of involvement was a means to shield himself against recrimination and criticism on Islamic grounds. In fact, as I will demonstrate, al-Qaeda would later go to considerable lengths to develop explicitly Islamic justifications for the 9/11 attacks to more effectively counter such charges. While it is somewhat surprising that such justifications had not been prepared in advance for immediate articulation after the attacks, the point for now is merely that bin Laden was apparently constrained in publicly taking credit for the 9/11 attacks in part because he was unable to justify them in terms consistent with the expectations of the Islamic world regarding legitimate means of social or political protest.

Indeed, bin Laden's 28 September 2001 interview was preoccupied with shoring up support in the Islamic world. He articulated a Salafist argument establishing jihad as a sixth primary duty ("pillar") of the Islamic faith, and he also addressed the opposition to his political program by major Muslim states, arguing that to "support the attack of the Christians and the Jews on a Muslim country like Afghanistan" was contrary to "the orders of Islamic Shariat." The interview is also important for an insight bin Laden provided on the importance he places on political discourse; he said that "today's world is of public opinion and the fates of nations are determined through its pressure." Bin Laden coupled this admission of his desire to be politically persuasive and assessment of the power of intersubjectivity with a warning to jihadists about the dangers of practices of global rule-making. He argued that "rejections, explanations or corrigendum only waste your time and through them, the enemy wants you to

---

[53] "Exclusive Interview with Usama Bin Ladin on 11 September Attacks in US," *Karachi Ummat*, 28 September 2001, translated and reproduced in FBIS (2004, 179).

[54] For instance, bin Laden denied responsibility for the 1998 embassy bombings in at least two interviews. See "Time Magazine Interview with Bin Ladin," *Time*, 11 January 1999, reproduced in FBIS (2004). See also "A Conversation with the Most Dangerous Man in the World," *Esquire*, February 1999, reproduced in FBIS (2004).

engage in things which are not of use to you" (FBIS 2004, 180–81).[55] This observation demonstrates a savvy political operator with a relatively sophisticated understanding of differing standards of argumentation employed in jihadi circles as compared to corresponding international practices, and the significant political consequences associated with the terms on which rule-making and interpretation are conducted.

In an interview dated 21 October 2001, bin Laden continued his intervention in debates surrounding the 9/11 attack and attempted to respond both to Islamic critics and to the Bush administration. Asked again if he was connected to the 9/11 attacks, bin Laden replied by rejecting "the description of these attacks as terrorism." Rather, he maintained, the hijackers "acted with God's grace in the way we understand and uphold it and in self-defense. It was in defense of their brothers and sisters in Palestine and the liberation of their holy places." The interview carried bin Laden's rejection of the "terrorist" label a step further, by directly invoking Bush's own words. He noted that "Bush has said that the world must make a choice between one of two parties; there is the party that supports him, and that any state that does not join the Bush government and the world Crusade will necessarily be considered with the terrorists." He then asked, rhetorically, "can there be a clearer terrorism than this one?" Finally, he asserted that "many states that do not control their own affairs had to go along with this powerful world terrorism" (FBIS 2004, 238).[56] While stopping short of directly claiming responsibility for the attacks, bin Laden defended them and articulated justifications for them. He also sought to make the case that the United States not only terrorized Muslims, but also employed terror as a means of persuading states to accept its condemnation of al-Qaeda. This last point is a procedural one; bin Laden accused the United States of corrupting processes of rule-making and interpretation with threats of force.

After noting bin Laden's 1998 *fatwa* and its finding that Muslims were under an individual duty to kill Americans, the interviewer observed that "other ulema issued different fatwas. Some have supported you, but others have criticized or opposed your fatwa. Some have asked: under what basis must we kill a Jew, or Crusader or a Christian simply because of his religion?" (FBIS 2004, 239).[57] In response, bin Laden directly invokes three specific *fatwas* that reached similar conclusions and particularly notes that one was issued in Pakistan and another in Saudi Arabia. These appeals to concurring authority clearly establish bin

[55] "Exclusive Interview with Usama Bin Ladin on 11 September Attacks in US," *Karachi Ummat*, 28 September 2001, translated and reproduced in FBIS (2004, 180–81).

[56] "Full Text of Interview Held with Al-Qa'ida Leader Usama Bin Ladin on 21 October 2001," *Jihad Online News Network*, 21 January 2003, translated and reproduced in FBIS (2004, 238).

[57] "Full Text of Interview Held with Al-Qa'ida Leader Usama Bin Ladin on 21 October 2001," *Jihad Online News Network*, 21 January 2003, translated and reproduced in FBIS (2004, 239).

Laden's awareness of key Islamic standards for making and interpreting rules, and further provide geographic indications about his core audience.

Asked next about the charge that terror attacks kill innocent civilians, bin Laden displays the evolution of al-Qaeda's justificatory response over a short period of under a month. First, bin Laden indicates his awareness of such charges both from "the United States and some intellectuals." He replies first to the international community by leveling a charge of hypocrisy. He asserts that "when we kill their civilians the whole world from East to West cries out" before claiming that the same standards are not applied to protect Muslims. In presenting this argument, bin Laden invoked two parables. First, he reported that "a tradition by the prophet [*hadith*] says: 'A woman was put in hell for tying up a cat, without feeding it or letting it feed itself.' This was just a cat. How about the millions of Muslims who are being killed?" He then invoked "Arab history" to make a point about the equal moral worth of human lives regardless of power or social station, relating a case in which "an Arab king once killed a man." While "people then were used to kings killing people," he noted that "the brother of the victim lurked for the king and killed him." According to bin Laden, the brother defended his conduct by arguing that "souls are equal." Leveraging this putatively analogical case, bin Laden asserted that he and his followers would "kill the kings of infidelity [Muslim rulers aligned with the West], the kings of the Crusaders [Western leaders], and the infidel civilians for killing our sons." He maintained that "this is permissible legally and logically"—essentially making a claim that justice entailed an eye for an eye. Not content to treat the response as a sufficiently convincing reply to potential critics, bin Laden also contended that, under Islamic practice, "the ban on killing innocent children is not absolute. There are provisions that restrict it." Reprising his prior arguments about reciprocity, he invoked Koranic authority by quoting the following passage: "God says: 'And if ye do catch them out, catch them out no worse than they catch you out.'" He then changed gears and asserted what amounts to an Islamic rule of "double effect": the 9/11 attacks were morally acceptable because the attackers "did not intend to kill children." Instead, they had attacked the Pentagon—a military target—and the World Trade Center, which was a target of strategic economic importance (FBIS 2004, 240–41).[58] Both these arguments represented significant steps toward the development of a justification for the 9/11 attacks explicitly intended to counter criticisms both from inside and outside the Islamic community that could damage public support for al-Qaeda and its positions. Both were also advanced in the context of Islamic practices for determining the

---

[58] "Full Text of Interview Held with Al-Qa'ida Leader Usama Bin Ladin on 21 October 2001," *Jihad Online News Network*, 21 January 2003, translated and reproduced in FBIS (2004, 240–41).

applicability of rules—in this case concerning the legality and morality of taking lives to further political goals—to particular, concrete cases.

Next, bin Laden again sought to fend off the pejorative label of "terrorism," though this time in a novel manner: by distinguishing "good" from "bad" terrorism. He sought to accomplish this by arguing that "not every kind of terrorism is censured. There is malignant terrorism and benign terrorism. The criminal thief is frightened of the police. Do you tell the police you are a terrorist because you frighten the thief? No, police terrorism of criminals is benign terrorism. The criminal's terrorism of innocent civilians is malignant terrorism." In its allegedly larcenous and murderous behavior toward the Islamic world, the United States represented the criminal committing malignant terrorism; in contras, jihadis, dispensing justice and acting to remedy injustice (understood as an individual obligation in Islamic theology and jurisprudence) conducted benign terrorism (FBIS 2004, 242).[59] This interpretation is decidedly outside the mainstream in Islamic society; bin Laden, who regularly engaged in theological criticism of Muslim societies, was presumably aware of this. The fact that he made such a marginal argument, in terms of likely audience reaction, is potentially indicative of concern that the "terrorist" label may have political power even within the Muslim community; the fact that he chose to reply by grounding his position in a problematic and somewhat tortured interpretation of Islam demonstrates the deep and consistent influence of Islamic practice on al-Qaeda's political speech.

The final noteworthy aspect of bin Laden's 21 October 2001 interview is his discussion of pro-Western Islamic governments. In many ways, this is the cornerstone of al-Qaeda's political program, the root grievance against the apostate "near enemy" that instrumentally justifies the conflict against the "far enemy." Bin Laden's discussion of the issue in this interview is a direct response to criticism from the Saudi interior minister over al-Qaeda's willingness to engage in the practice of *takfir*, or declaring other Muslims to be infidels or apostates. Bin Laden reported the charge directly: "He said we consider Muslims infidels, God forbid!" He then flatly denied it, maintaining "we believe Muslims are Muslims." However, bin Laden followed this denial with a curious qualification; he said "we do not consider any one of them infidel, unless he violated any of the known Islamic rules intentionally." Al-Qaeda's position thus clearly accepts the practice of *takfir*. Bin Laden's defense against Saudi criticism essentially amounted to an assertion that the apostate himself ends his Islamic status before he is recognized as an infidel by a Muslim observer. It is worth quoting bin Laden at length on this issue:

[59] "Full Text of Interview Held with Al-Qa'ida Leader Usama Bin Ladin on 21 October 2001," *Jihad Online News Network,* 21 January 2003, translated and reproduced in FBIS (2004, 242).

I swear to God anyone who follows Bush in his plan is a renegade from the creed of Muhammad. . . . This is one of the clearest rules in God's book and the traditions of the prophet. . . . The ulema have issued fatwas on this subject. And the proof is in the words of God when addressing the faithful: "O ye who believe take not the Jews and the Christians for your friends and protectors; they are but friends and protectors to each other. And he among you that turns to them (for friendship) is of them." (FBIS 2004, 243)[60]

Bin Laden had spoken publicly on the interpretation of this same passage in a December 1998 interview with Al Jazeera, insisting that the phrase "is of them" meant that "he becomes an infidel like them" (FBIS 2004, 175).[61] The crucial point to note is that bin Laden defends the practice of *takfir* by directly invoking key Islamic sources of authority. In addition to his direct quotation from the Koran, bin Laden asserts that his position is consistent with the traditions of the prophet, or the *hadith*, as well as with *fatwas* issued by Islamic *ulema*. Islamic secondary rules and practices of rule interpretation were therefore central to bin Laden's response to the Saudi interior minister's criticism of al-Qaeda's arguments about the apostasy of the Saudi government and other pro-Western governments in the Islamic world. Both sides clearly understood their dispute as susceptible to resolution according to particular practices and methods of interpretation. While broad agreement on standards for evaluating claims about appropriate rules did not result in resolution of this dispute about the legitimacy of *takfir* or the dispute over the Saudi relationship with the United States, both sides continued to employ relevant practices of rule-making and interpretation. Further, although al-Qaeda continued to advance its arguments, they remained controversial even within the Wahhabi community. Indeed, the entire strategy of attacking the "far enemy" was born of al-Qaeda's inability to achieve broad gains in establishing its position within the Islamic world.

Though bin Laden and his associates ascribed this failure publicly to material support from the United States for the apostate regimes, an alternate analysis might attribute the outcome in part to the poor fit between al-Qaeda's argument and relevant secondary rules. The historical rejection of *takfir* within the Islamic community, for example, stems from its role in early Islamic sectarian conflicts that threatened the political and social community of the *ummah*. The eventual resolution of this conflict was premised on a compromise banning judgments

---

[60] "Full Text of Interview Held with Al-Qa'ida Leader Usama Bin Ladin on 21 October 2001," *Jihad Online News Network*, 21 January 2003, translated and reproduced in FBIS (2004, 243).

[61] "Al-Jazirah TV Broadcasts Usama Bin Ladin's 1998 Interview," 20 September 2001, translated and reproduced in FBIS (2004, 175).

pertaining to the authenticity of another Muslim's beliefs.[62] Reopening this compromise thus represents a major breach of Islamic traditions and practices of rule-making and interpretation on the part of al-Qaeda; as the argument advanced in the book should expect, many in al-Qaeda's audience have rejected the conclusions flowing from this discursive move, and they have done so on the grounds that *takfir* is procedurally illegitimate.

In the period immediately following the 9/11 attacks, al-Qaeda was constrained in taking public credit for its act, and invested considerable energy in developing progressively more complex justifications for the attacks that were clearly informed by Islamic practices of rule-making. These statements replied directly to different lines of criticism both from the international community and especially from within the Islamic world. There were few efforts to speak directly to the target of the 9/11 attacks.

Primary concern with domestic, or in-group, audiences and determined adherence to existing practices of rule-making and interpretation also characterized American claims after 9/11. In his first State of the Union address following the attacks, on 29 January 2002, Bush spoke of American objectives in military terms. He pledged that the United States would "continue to be steadfast and patient and persistent in the pursuit of two great objectives. First, we will shut down terrorist camps, disrupt terrorist plans, and bring terrorists to justice. And second, we must prevent the terrorists and regimes who seek chemical, biological, or nuclear weapons from threatening the United States and the world" (Bush 2002a).[63] The speech was silent on al-Qaeda's grievances, and did not acknowledge the existence of an instance of rule-making and interpretation between the parties. Instead, it advanced propositions about rule changes in the international system that the Bush administration would pursue at least through its first term of office.[64] Bush insisted that if other states "do not act" to combat terrorism, "America will." This frank expression of American readiness to disregard procedural norms of multilateralism as well as UN restrictions on the use of force, and even basic norms of sovereignty, would later be asserted in the form of a Bush Doctrine[65] that justified these changes by drawing attention to Iranian and North Korean nuclear programs, before famously asserting that "states like these

[62] The emergence of this practice of tolerance is discussed by Levy (1962, 183–85); and van Ess (2001, 153–54).

[63] George W. Bush, "Address before a Joint Session of the Congress on the State of the Union," speech given at Washington, DC, 29 January 2002.

[64] Philip H. Gordon has argued persuasively that the Bush administration was essentially forced to abandon pursuit of the Bush Doctrine in its second term of office, primarily due to (material and social) resource constraints. Gordon (2006).

[65] The literature on the Bush Doctrine, and on Bush administration foreign policy more generally, is immense. See, for example, Gordon (2006); Dunn (2006); Lafeber (2002); Ralph (2009).

and their terrorist allies constitute an axis of evil, arming to threaten the peace of the world." Insisting that "rogue states" "pose a grave and growing danger" to the United States and its allies, he maintained that the price of indifference would be catastrophic" (Bush 2002a).[66] He sought to stigmatize certain actors (Adler-Nissen 2014) for violating key international rules, as well as to arrogate to the United States the right to identify and punish such violations.

In addition to these nascent arguments about necessary alterations to the rules of the international system, Bush made comments on the importance of differences in practices of rule-making, casting al-Qaeda's understandings as alien and illegitimate. He maintained that "no people on Earth yearn to be oppressed," and sought to exploit cleavages within the Muslim world by inviting "skeptics" to "look to Islam's own rich history, with its centuries of learning and tolerance and progress." He then declared that "America will lead by defending liberty and justice because they are right and true and unchanging for all people everywhere." While the practical implications of this statement can be called into doubt given the lack of agreement on the substantive content of liberty and justice even within the Western tradition, Bush clarified his position somewhat in enumerating "the non-negotiable demands of human dignity," which he specified as entailing "the rule of law; limits on the power of the state; respect for women; private property; free speech; equal justice; and religious tolerance" (Bush 2002a).[67] These criteria, while obviously of broad relevance to everyday life, also have clear significance for practices of rule-making far beyond the immediate issue of whether attacks by non-state groups on military and civilian targets are acceptable means of social protest. Bush's only reply to al-Qaeda was thus an indirect one—that al-Qaeda was an illegitimate participant to be denied standing in global rule-making because of its choice of tactics, but also because its preferred practices of rule-making were regarded by the United States as illegitimate even for use at the domestic level.

Bush would build on these themes in a major address at the United States Military Academy at West Point, New York, on 1 June 2002. He insisted that American views on combating terrorism were consistent with a desire to "preserve the peace by building good relations among the great powers." Further, he defended the idea of a grand strategy premised on preventive use of force by insisting that the prior strategy of deterrence had been rendered insufficient; "deterrence—the promise of massive retaliation against nations—means nothing against shadowy terrorist networks with no nation or citizens to

[66] George W. Bush, "Address before a Joint Session of the Congress on the State of the Union," speech given at Washington, DC, 29 January 2002.

[67] George W. Bush, "Address before a Joint Session of the Congress on the State of the Union," speech given at Washington, DC, 29 January 2002.

defend." Similarly, he claimed that "containment is not possible when unbalanced dictators with weapons of mass destruction can deliver those weapons on missiles or secretly provide them to terrorist allies" (Bush 2002b).[68] The unstated conclusion derived from these premises was that restrictions on the use of force had been rendered inapplicable by a change in circumstances. This amounted to a claim of *clausula rebus sic stantibus* under international law, an exception to the general rule *pacta sunt servanda* codified in Article 62 of the Vienna Convention on the Law of Treaties, which is entitled "Fundamental Change of Circumstance." The Vienna Convention stipulates that such claims are valid only in two specific cases: if the circumstances prior to the change were "an essential basis of the consent of the parties to be bound by the treaty" (1969 A.62.1.a), or if "the effect of the change is radically to transform the extent of the obligations still to be performed under the treaty" (1969 A.62.1.b).[69] The most obviously applicable general treaty restricting the use of force is the Charter of the United Nations. It is doubtful that the absence of terrorist groups was "an essential basis of the consent of the parties" to this treaty both because of the broad scope of the United Nations and the clear intent of the parties to establish an ongoing regime "to save succeeding generations from the scourge of war."[70] Further, an argument under A.62.1.a would likely be unpersuasive because terrorism predated the creation of the United Nations, thus undermining the factual basis of any truly changed circumstance. It is at least more plausible to present such a claim under A.62.1.b and argue that mass-casualty terrorist attacks present a fundamentally new problem. This line of argument, in fact, closely resembles the actual Bush administration position, suggesting that the language in the West Point speech (later elaborated in the 2002 National Security Strategy, discussed below) was crafted with knowledge of the relevant provisions of international law and also with the expectation that the administration's claims would be evaluated on these criteria. In fact, this process of evaluating American policy according to international legal criteria was already underway by June 2002, not only in foreign capitals but also within the American legal community.[71]

Finally, Bush's speech at West Point returned to his insistence that al-Qaeda's vision of "the good life" and of legitimate governance practices were fundamentally flawed. He went so far as to insist that "the 20th century ended with a single surviving model of human progress" and that this model was "based on the nonnegotiable demands of human dignity" he had enumerated in his State of the

---

[68] George W. Bush, "Commencement Address at the United States Military Academy at West Point," speech given at West Point, NY, 1 June 2002.

[69] Vienna Convention on the Law of Treaties, 1969.

[70] Charter of the United Nations, 1945.

[71] Major international law journals devoted considerable attention to these issues. See, for example, Koh (2002); Charney (2001); Franck (2001).

Union address, and which he subsequently reiterated (Bush 2002b).[72] The consistency of this message between two major addresses separated in time by more than five months suggests that the choice of words was deliberate and politically significant. The point was that secondary rules were both critically important in the eyes of the Bush administration and not subject to debate or revision.

While the State of the Union address and the West Point speech were important, public elaborations of American thought, the most detailed defense of administration policy is found in the September 2002 National Security Strategy (NSS). The document reviews American policy under several subheadings that constitute major planks essential to enhancing national security. Its purpose was, at least in part, to address actual and anticipated objections to American policy both from domestic and international critics. It is therefore intrinsically part of a broader social practice of rule-making and interpretation at both the domestic and international levels. The first substantive means of enhancing national security discussed in the memo is a commitment to "champion aspirations for human dignity"; the section commits the United States to working toward the global realization of the same list of "non-negotiable demands of human dignity" Bush articulated in his State of the Union and reiterated in his West Point address. Anticipating potential accusations of cultural insensitivity, the report allows that "these demands can be met in many ways." Most significant, in addition to advancing human rights and democracy, it pledges that "our principles will guide our government's decisions about international cooperation" and that "they will guide our actions and our words in international bodies." Thus, the advancement of human rights, the rule of law, and other core liberal values are portrayed both as means to enhance American security, and also as procedural commitments that the United States affirms are applicable in global rule-making processes (White House 2002, 3–4).[73]

The second substantive section of the NSS deals with alliances to combat terrorism. Here, again, the memo is clear on the procedural illegitimacy of al-Qaeda's tactics. While conceding that "grievances deserve to be, and must be, addressed within a political process," it insists that "no cause justifies terror." Accordingly, it declares that "the United States will make no concessions to terrorist demands and strike no deals with them," and that "we make no distinction between those who knowingly harbor or provide aid to them." Despite this ostensibly principled refusal to engage in rule-making and interpretation, the memo details several more proactive steps in furtherance of "a war of ideas to win the battle of

---

[72] George W. Bush, "Commencement Address at the United States Military Academy at West Point," speech given at West Point, NY, 1 June 2002.

[73] The White House, "The National Security Strategy of the United States of America," Washington, DC: Government Printing Office, 2002, 3–4.

ideas against international terrorism." The first is "using the full influence of the United States and working closely with allies and friends, to make clear that all acts of terrorism are illegitimate so that terrorism will be viewed in the same light as slavery, piracy or genocide: behavior that no respectable government can condone or support and all must oppose." Accomplishing this goal entails engaging in the kind of discursive criticisms that constitute practices of rule-making and interpretation. The same is true of the second strategy elaborated in the memo—"supporting moderate and modern government, especially in the Muslim world." Insofar as sustainably establishing such governments requires either genuine internalization of international norms or marginalization of fundamentalist interpretations of Islam in favor of reformist or liberal ones, this task requires employing means for creating and altering social rules. Finally, the strategy paper called for "using effective public diplomacy to promote the free flow of information and ideas to kindle the hopes and aspirations of freedom in societies ruled by the sponsors of global terrorism" (White House 2002, 5–6).[74] Despite the deliberately neutral language employed in this formulation, public diplomacy is (by its very nature) political speech designed to persuade or to otherwise achieve a purpose. Conducting public diplomacy amounts to engaging in the kinds of practices of rule-making and interpretation I refer to in this book.

The NSS provides one additional illustration of American attempts to engage in global rule-making. While there was significant international sympathy for American efforts to pursue al-Qaeda leaders, the assertion of a general doctrine supporting the preventive use of force was more controversial. The NSS took pains to address such concerns, tying the necessity of preventive intervention to changed circumstances created by the combination of "rogue states" pursuing weapons of mass destruction, and transnational terrorist networks. In addition to invoking the allegedly precarious status of deterrence, it directly addressed extant international rules for the use of force. It did so in a fashion that explicitly responded to potential objections to the American position. The memo asserted that "for centuries, international law recognized that nations need not suffer an attack before they can lawfully take action to defend against forces that present an imminent danger of attack." It continued, maintaining that "legal scholars and international jurists often conditioned the legitimacy of preemption on the existence of an imminent threat—most often a visible mobilization of armies, navies, and air forces preparing to attack." The memo concluded that the changed circumstances made evident by the 9/11 attacks meant that the

---

[74] The White House, "The National Security Strategy of the United States of America," Washington, DC: Government Printing Office, 2002, 5–6.

international community "must adapt the concept of imminent threat" to allow the preemptive use of force.[75]

This analysis was a socially competent and politically daring attempt to change a major rule of international law. It demonstrated awareness of the existing state of international law regarding the use of force, which is based on the *Caroline* case. However, as Michael Byers has argued, it studiously avoided reference to the UN Charter's more restrictive statutory expression of the customary legal standards developed in the *Caroline* case. This focus on the more permissive standards was a consistent part of the American response to 9/11, and had been evident as early as the Security Council resolutions of 12 and 28 September 2001, which "were carefully worded to affirm the right of self-defence in customary international law" at the expense of Charter authority (Byers 2005, 58). The American NSS also elided the concepts of preemption and prevention. International law typically distinguishes these precisely on the presence or absence of imminent threat (Byers 2005, 52), and even as the Bush administration argued for the expansion of preemption it studiously adopted forward-looking language that proactively applied its desired definition to its present behavior. In this respect, the NSS is a demonstration of the malleability embodied in practices of global rule-making. However, even if existing practices provided opportunities for the United States to make a self-serving and self-interested proposal, the fact remains that the world's sole remaining superpower participated in a practice of justifying a decision of core concern to its national security, and it did so in ways shaped by intersubjectively shared standards for rule-making and interpretation.

Further, the NSS also made a subsidiary argument that contemplated the *rejection* of its proposal for the expansion of the concept of imminent threat. Regardless of the status of its argument about the effect of changed circumstances and the alteration of standards of imminent threat, it asserted that "the United States has long maintained the option of preemptive actions to counter a sufficient threat to our national security." In effect, this claim amounts to a legal reservation, an accepted practice in international law providing for an "escape clause." Finally, the United States also took steps both to limit the scope of its own freedom under this reservation and, presumably, to limit the ability of other states to invoke the American claim as a basis for their own actions. The memo pledged that "the United States will not use force in all cases to preempt emerging threats" and insisted that states should not "use preemption as a pretext for aggression." It specified that, in conducting a "preemptive" intervention, "the purpose of our actions will always be to eliminate a specific threat to the United States or our allies and friends." Procedurally, it also pledged that "the reasons

---

[75] The White House, "The National Security Strategy of the United States of America," Washington, DC: Government Printing Office, 2002, 13–15.

for our actions will be clear, the force measured, and the cause just" (White House 2002, 15–16).[76] These self-imposed restrictions are intelligible only if the United States regarded them as a necessity for securing acquiescence to its reservation regarding the legitimacy of preventive action, or if it was worried about other states making parallel arguments to justify interventions of their own; this latter concern makes sense only if the United States either believed that such arguments would be legitimate or expected that other members of the international community would regard them as such. Thus, the episode illustrates the effects of secondary rules on American policy and diplomacy in an area intimately connected to the high politics of national security.

The relevance and importance of secondary rules are affirmed in two further passages of the NSS. The first, in the context of its discussion of great power relations, expresses the expectation that these leading states "can build fruitful habits of consultation, quiet argument, sober analysis, and common action." Further, it notes that "these are the practices that will sustain the supremacy of our common principles and keep open the path of progress." Finally, the document pledges that "in exercising our leadership, we will respect the values, judgment, and interests of our friends and partners" and that "when we disagree on particulars, we will explain forthrightly the grounds for our concerns and strive to forge viable alternatives" (White House 2002, 28–31).[77] The overall tone of these statements are at odds with the general tendencies and reputation of the Bush administration, and tempt the conclusion that they were simply meaningless platitudes distracting from a nakedly power-political, unilateralist foreign policy.

While it would be unconvincing to suggest either that the Bush administration lived up to the commitments made in the NSS, or perhaps even that they consistently made good-faith efforts to do so, these inconsistencies do not warrant the conclusion that secondary rules were ineffective or irrelevant, for two primary reasons. First, by virtue of its power (social as well as material), the United States is a clear outlier in the international community. It should not be surprising to expect that it may therefore enjoy a greater degree of freedom than a typical state, or that it would be inclined to make maximum possible use of that freedom after an unexpected, mass-casualty attack on its capital and its financial hub. Second, even in these extraordinary circumstances, a unilateralist administration behaved in a procedurally orthodox manner even as it sought to alter the rules of the international system. The more appropriate conclusion

---

[76] The White House, "The National Security Strategy of the United States of America," Washington, DC: Government Printing Office, 2002, 15–16.

[77] The White House, "The National Security Strategy of the United States of America," Washington, DC: Government Printing Office, 2002, 28–31.

is that contemporary international practices of rule-making and interpretation were remarkably robust in difficult circumstances—and that they are resistant to change even when willingness to construct mutually acceptable standards with a social outsider could pave the way for compromise or for peaceful conflict resolution.

In October 2002, taking advantage of the anniversary of the 9/11 attacks and the American intervention in Afghanistan, bin Laden made two efforts to speak directly to the United States. The first, reported by Al Jazeera on 6 October 2002, purported to deliver the following "message to the American people": "Peace be to those who follow the right path. I am an honest adviser to you. I urge you to seek the joy of life and the afterlife and to rid yourself of your dry, miserable, and spiritless materialistic life. I urge you to become Muslims, for Islam calls for the principle of 'there is no God but Allah,' and for justice and forbids injustice and criminality. I also call on you to understand the lesson of the New York and Washington raids, which came in response to some of your previous crimes. The aggressor deserves punishment." This relatively brief statement deserves comment for two reasons. The call for Americans to adopt Islam provides a direct parallel to the Bush administration's assertions of the superiority of its value system—including its practices of rule-making and interpretation. The statement also articulates bin Laden's fundamental claim that American policy has unjustly harmed Muslims, and that the 9/11 attacks were therefore justifiable as punishment. This statement makes clear the political content of those attacks, and their relation to al-Qaeda's broader political program including its desire to alter the international system. Bin Laden concluded the message by communicating the potential for a reduction in hostilities, contingent on American reaction, stating that "whether America escalates or de-escalates this conflict, we will reply to it in kind, God willing" (FBIS 2004, 205).[78]

Bin Laden's second attempt to speak to the American audience took the form of an open letter posted in English on a jihadist website on 26 October 2002. The letter is much more detailed than the earlier message broadcast on Al Jazeera, and is more sophisticated in its performance of practices of rule-making and interpretation. It begins by placing itself in the proper context:

> Some American writers have published articles attempting to explain
> the motivation behind our fight against the United States of America
> and others who have the blood of Muslims on their hands. These ar-
> ticles have generated a number of replies from a spectrum of people,

---

[78] "Bin Ladin Threatens Attacks on 'Key Sectors' of US Economy," 6 October 2002, translated and reproduced in FBIS (2004, 205).

with a variety of sources from which they quote. Some explanations have been made based on Islamic Law, yet some quite clearly have not.

Bin Laden demonstrates his awareness of debate over al-Qaeda's motivations and demands, and makes clear that he regards Islamic law as the proper background for understanding them. He then announced that the remainder of the letter will "outline our reply to two questions addressing the Americans"; namely, (1) "why are we waging jihad against you?" and (2) "what advice do we have for you and what do we want from you?" He then insisted that "the answer to the first question is very simple: because you attacked us and continue to attack us. He enumerates the places in which the United States has attacked Muslims, mentioning Somalia as well as purported American support (and therefore responsibility) for Russian conduct in Chechnya, Indian conduct in Kashmir, and Israeli conduct in Lebanon. However, the most significant justifications for hostility to the United States focus on the status of Palestine and on American support for secular Muslim regimes. Bin Laden discusses both topics in some detail, providing justifications for his positions clearly rooted in Islamic practices.

With respect to Palestine, bin Laden describes American support for Israeli statehood as based on "your fabricated lies saying that the Jews have a historical right to live in Palestine as it was promised to them in the Torah." He then seeks to refute this position not by focusing on questions of international law, or claims about the illegitimacy of the international action involved in establishing the modern Israeli state, but rather by delving into the proper interpretation of the Old Testament. He argued that "the Arabs of Palestine are pure Arabs and are the real Sams (from the prophet Sam). Muslims are all followers of Musa [Moses] (peace be upon him) and it is the Muslims who have inherited the real Torah that has not been changed." On the basis of this lineage, he asks: "when those who say that the Torah mentions that the followers of Musa should live in Palestine, do they not also see that the Muslims are best suited for this position?" (FBIS 2004, 214).[79] Bin Laden's argument is that the international community has used illegitimate man-made rules to determine the status of contending claims to Palestine. The proper procedure, on his view, is instead based on the interpretation of divinely provided texts.

The grievance stemming from American support for secular Muslim states is justified in slightly different terms. Bin Laden explains that "the policies employed in these countries stop our nation from establishing the Islamic Shariah, thereby causing great harm to this Ummah." Further, the American client states structure their economies "so that a few of the elite may indulge themselves

---

[79] "Letter from Usama Bin Ladin to the American People," www.waaqiah.com, 26 October 2002, reproduced in FBIS (2004, 214).

whilst the general population starves to death." According to bin Laden, "the removal of these policies is an individual obligation" for Muslims "so as to make the Shariah the supreme law and to regain Palestine." Because Americans "are the chief designers and sponsors for these policies," it follows that "our fight against these policies is the same as fighting against you." In addition to articulating his justifications for al-Qaeda's opposition to American policy, bin Laden dealt with the legitimacy of al-Qaeda's tactics. He wrote that the articulation of arguments criticizing al-Qaeda for targeting civilians "contradicts your claim that America is the land of freedom and democracy, where every American . . . has a vote." He maintained that "it is a fundamental principle of democracy that the people choose their leaders, and as such, approve and are party to the actions of their elected leaders." In support of this position, he noted that "time and time again, polls show that the American people support the policies of the elected Government." This argument is a different one from what bin Laden had employed in justifying the 9/11 attacks to a Muslim audience, illustrating the al-Qaeda leader's expectation that the two audiences would respond to different rationales. Despite this effort to frame his arguments in a manner consistent with Western practices and standards for rule-making, however, bin Laden seems to recognize the underlying difficulty. He concludes his explanation of his hostility to the United States by informing his audience that "in our religion, Allah, the Lord of the Worlds, gave us the permission and the option to take revenge and return to you what you gave us." The determination to employ this reciprocal resort to force is warranted by the alleged "fact" that "since its inception, America has illustrated that it does not understand the language of love and manners." Because of these persistent differences in standards for conduct (including for making, interpreting and applying rules), he and his followers "are using the language [violence] they understand" (FBIS 2004, 215–17).[80] Where shared secondary rules do not exist, the legitimate response entails strict reciprocity—up to and including the use of violence.

Next, bin Laden turned to the question of al-Qaeda's demands and its "advice" to the United States. He began by reiterating that "the first thing we are inviting you to is Islam, the religion of Tawheed and to association with Allah." This would entail "the discarding of the opinions, orders, theories and religions which contradict with Allah's orders." This demand, however unrealistic, is essentially an attempt to secure the adherence of Americans to Islamic practices for making and interpreting rules, as bin Laden makes clear when he criticizes Americans as "the nation who, rather than ruling by the Law of Allah, choose to implement your own inferior rules and regulations, thus following your

---

[80] "Letter from Usama Bin Ladin to the American People," www.waaqiah.com, 26 October 2002, reproduced in FBIS (2004, 215–17).

own vain whims and desires" and failing to realize the proper form and ends of human community (FBIS 2004, 217).[81] This passage highlights, again, the importance placed by leaders from both sides on the fact that the parties held starkly different conceptions of legitimate secondary rules. While it is certainly possible that these moves were at least partially tactical attempts to rally third parties or simply to ensure any potential agreements were reached on favorable procedural terms, the consistency with which such arguments were made, the pride of place accorded to them relative to other arguments, and the emotional language employed in making them at least suggest that the arguments were genuinely regarded as important. Further, the mere fact of a relatively consistent emphasis on the importance of procedural rules by actors with clearly divergent understandings of the *substance* of these rules requires explanation. This overall pattern is intelligible only if both sides have a conception of a generic practice of rule-making and interpretation—regardless of whether they employ it cynically or in good faith.

After making his general argument for the United States to embrace Islam, bin Laden connected American reliance on its man-made "inferior rules and regulations" to various failings in American foreign and domestic policy, including compound interest, the consumption of alcohol, the spread of HIV/AIDS, refusing to sign the Kyoto Protocol, and the use of nuclear weapons in 1945. He also criticized what he called a "major characteristic" of American policy—a "duality in both manners and law" entailing differential treatment of Americans and non-Americans in such areas as democracy and respect for election outcomes, the legitimacy of various governments possessing weapons of mass destruction, respect for UN resolutions, war crimes prosecutions, and human rights. The letter concludes with a list of specific demands for American policy; the most notable of these are demands that the United States withdraw its forces and personnel from Muslim countries, end its support for Israel and other states involved in conflicts against Muslims, and end its support for pro-Western governments in the Islamic world (FBIS 2004, 219–30).[82]

The most interesting aspect of these demands, collectively, is that they are couched specifically in terms of American foreign policy rather than in the systemic terms bin Laden adopted in other documents examined in this study. I cannot definitively explain this choice. It may be a difference in audience—he may have believed that the American public is more inclined to think in terms of parochial foreign policy rather than in systemic terms. Regardless, his demands

---

[81] "Letter from Usama Bin Ladin to the American People," www.waaqiah.com, 26 October 2002, reproduced in FBIS (2004, 217).

[82] "Letter from Usama Bin Ladin to the American People," www.waaqiah.com, 26 October 2002, reproduced in FBIS (2004, 219–30).

can be relatively easily translated from one vocabulary to the other; for instance, the insistence that the United States leave Muslim states and cease interference in the domestic politics of Muslim states would likely have applied equally in bin Laden's view to China or Russia. Further, the fact that the diagnosed cause of illegitimate American policy (reliance on illegitimate secondary rules and practices of rule-making) is structural in nature suggests—as demonstrated in his other writings and statements—that bin Laden understood his cause in systemic terms. On this basis, it is appropriate to understand this letter to the American people as part of an attempt to alter the international system, in part by articulating and justifying demands. Though the lack of mutually agreeable secondary rules complicated these efforts, and bin Laden's interpretation of Islamic rule-making practice justified the use of violence against civilians as a means of pursuing such chances, bin Laden still attempted at least sporadic communication of his demands and their justifications, though he did so with frequent reference to Islamic practices and with limited ability or willingness to articulate demands in a fashion consistent with contemporary international expectations.

RESPONSES AND JUSTIFICATIONS TO IN-GROUP CRITICS

While al-Qaeda and the Bush administration portrayed themselves as the champions of starkly different political and cultural traditions, both were criticized by members of their respective in-groups. Many, though by no means all, of these criticisms pertained to issues of proper rule-making and interpretation. Both al-Qaeda and the Bush administration attempted to answer their critics, and to justify their positions. Although this dimension of the case is not my primary focus, I address it briefly before concluding.

Bin Laden's efforts to engage the American audience in October 2002 took place alongside continuing efforts to conduct parallel practices of rule-making and interpretation within the Muslim world. A statement signed by bin Laden dated 12 October 2002 was posted in Arabic on a jihadist website two days later. The statement began by noting "the passage of one year since the start of the Crusade against Afghanistan" and American preparation "for a new round in its crusade against the Muslim world" expected to take place in Iraq. It then presented a harshly critical appraisal of American operations, alleging failure to destroy al-Qaeda or the Taliban, failure to create a strong government in Kabul, the commission of major human rights violations and the infliction of civilian casualties, as well as failure to rebuild the country. He then alleged that the United States was "seeking to cover up its failure in Afghanistan . . . by beating the drums of war on Iraq." Despite the American failures, bin Laden insisted on several necessary steps "if we want Allah to assign victory to us and achieve for us this triumph in this confrontation." According to bin Laden, "the first thing we should do is to turn to Allah with sincere repentance . . . by letting shari'ah rule all aspects of our work and dealings, of every minor and major detail of our lives" (FBIS 2004, 206–08).[83] The point of reference for this demand is the governance arrangements employed in Islamic states and communities.

Second, bin Laden argued for Muslim unity, quoting a Koranic passage that exhorts believers to "hold fast all together to the rope of Allah." Bin Laden justified this demand by arguing that "if it is axiomatic that dispute and difference are one of the most significant causes of the failure and loss of power from which our nation is suffering today, then it is also axiomatic that unity, consensus, and holding fast to the rope of Allah is the key to victory and triumph and the door to sovereignty and leadership." Anticipating objections that many differences among Muslims have their roots in differing religious doctrines and interpretations, bin Laden wrote that his position "does not necessarily need putting an end to disputes over all small questions and minor issues." Rather, he was concerned with "the unity of the constants of the creed, the dogmatism of the religion, and the schools of shari'ah." This second demand, taken together with the first, represents a call—justified with appeals to Islamic authority—for acceptance of al-Qaeda's resistance to the United States, and its interpretation of the Muslim faith.

The third proposal in bin Laden's message, pertaining to "mobilizing and unleashing the nation's resources," focused on the particular social roles of various groups in accomplishing al-Qaeda's political program. Bin Laden praised Muslim youths, referring to them as "the knights of the fight and the heroes of the battle." He exhorted them to live up to Koranic passages drawn, respectively, from Surah al-Tawbah and Surah al-Anfal: "fight and slay the pagans wherever ye find them, and seize them, beleaguer them, and lie in wait for them in every stratagem (of war)," and "fight them until there is no more tumult or oppression." However, the document is more interesting for its discussion of the role of scholars, who are given pride of place in bin Laden's discussion of groups vital to achieving his aims. He writes that scholars "are the prophet's heirs and the bearers of the trust of learning, the duty of propagation, and the upholding of the rules that this entails." In particular, he wrote that their "first duty is to tell the truth to the nation and to declare it in the face of darkness without equivocation or fear," and he justified this claim by invoking a passage stating that "Allah took a covenant from the People of the Book, to make it known and clear to mankind, and not to hide it." The political significance of these comments is made clear by bin Laden's own words, telling scholars "the importance of your

[83] "Al-Qa'ida Issues Statement under Bin Ladin's Name on Afghan War Anniversary," *Al-Qal'ah*, 14 October 2002, translated and reproduced in FBIS (2004, 206–8).

task stems from the dangerous act of deception and misguidance practiced by the authority's scholars and the rulers' clerics who are trading with religion, who were put in charge of it before the nation, and who have sold their soul for temporal gain" (FBIS 2004, 208–9).[84] The document, taken together, reads as a criticism of moderate Muslim scholars as corrupt traitors who have violated the trust placed in them to deliver corrupt religious rulings that are not based on proper interpretive practices.

Despite these harsh criticisms, bin Laden extends an olive branch by allowing that "there are some differences in interpretations between those working for Islam that can be ignored"; however, despite the possibility of such good faith differences, he argues that "it is neither acceptable nor reasonable for us to remain the prisoners of some dispute over small questions and minor issues, thus disrupting action in accordance with the rules of religion and the schools of shari'ah at such a critical time in the nation's history" (FBIS 2004, 209–10).[85] The argument is that the conflict against the United States takes precedence over intra-Islamic conflicts because the defeat of the "far enemy" is a condition of possibility for the realization of the properly-ordered *ummah*, regardless of the particular account of what that entails.

These arguments were controversial, and al-Qaeda was placed on the defensive. On 19 January 2003, the Saudi-backed website *Al-Shara Al-Awsat* published an article reporting on "a new message prepared by the 'Islamic Studies and Research Center' in Pakistan, the main mouthpiece for the Al-Qa'ida organization." The Saudi website reported that bin Laden wrote a foreword presenting this message as part of "the commendable efforts that are closing an important gap" between Muslims regarding differing religious positions on al-Qaeda's causes. Bin Laden is reported to have described the message's method as setting out "the most important evidence from the Holy Book, the Sunnah, and the sayings of the nation's ulema concerning the need for unity and consensus and renunciation of disunity and differences." The website reported that the substantive purpose of the message was to assert "the need for adhering to the course followed by the people of the Sunna and for a set of shari'ah rules that govern the relationship between Muslims and those working for Islam so as to protect their Islamic brotherhood even if they hold different scholastic views and practical interpretations." The al-Qaeda message also reportedly addresses "mistakes" made by jihadist leaders and scholars. It is quoted as arguing that "rules ought to be laid down that protect their dignity from being destroyed and their status

---

[84] "Al-Qa'ida Issues Statement under Bin Ladin's Name on Afghan War Anniversary," *Al-Qal'ah*, 14 October 2002, translated and reproduced in FBIS (2004, 208–9).

[85] "Al-Qa'ida Issues Statement under Bin Ladin's Name on Afghan War Anniversary," *Al-Qal'ah*, 14 October 2002, translated and reproduced in FBIS (2004, 209–10).

from being wrecked for some mistakes they made." The al-Qaeda message demonstrates an ongoing conflict over proper interpretation of the Islamic faith and what it requires in terms of opposition to American policy and general orientation toward the West. Even the defensive stance taken in this message proved controversial; *Al-Shara Al-Awsat* concluded that "there is contradiction in the message that ignores the mistakes of Al-Qa'ida leaders and demands that rules be laid down to protect its ulema's dignity while at the same time not ignoring the mistakes of" *ulema* that disagree with its positions (FBIS 2004, 231–34).[86] The crucial point is that the dispute is centrally concerned with rules for resolving disputes between religious scholars over the political implications of the Islamic faith for contemporary politics. As such, it is part of an ongoing practice of rule-making and interpretation. As the argument advanced in the book expects, the various parties to this practice were actively engaged in evaluating and criticizing proposals and arguments according to their consistency or inconsistency with relevant procedural rules.

Bush's 2003 State of the Union address likewise provides a picture of an actor concerned primarily with justifying a controversial position to a skeptical audience with which it agreed broadly on legitimate practices for rule-making and interpretation; in this case, Bush sought to address domestic and international criticism of his plan to invade Iraq. He relied heavily on his argument from 2002, linking rogue states and weapons of mass destruction. He declared that "the gravest danger in the war on terror, the gravest danger facing America and the world is outlaw regimes that seek and possess nuclear, chemical, and biological weapons." He also alluded to the alleged inadequacy of deterrence in a manner that portrayed his speech as the continuation of an ongoing debate, noting that "some have said we must not act until the threat is imminent" before asking rhetorically, "since when have terrorists and tyrants announced their intentions, politely putting us on notice before they strike?" Bush's answer to his rhetorical question was consistent with that advanced by the 2002 NSS; he argued that "if this threat is permitted to fully and suddenly emerge, all actions, all words, and all recriminations would come too late." These justifications, like those articulated in 2002, are properly understood in relation to rules drawn from customary international law and from the UN Charter pertaining to restrictions on the legitimate use of force, and in the context of the general procedural rules of international law and diplomacy. However, the 2003 State of the Union address also sought to justify the American position on Iraq as consistent with preexisting UN Security Council resolutions and as a matter of enforcing existing

---

[86] "Bin Ladin Message Urges Islamic Factions to Unite, Fight 'External' Enemy," *Al-Shara Al-Awsat*, 19 January 2003, translated and reproduced in FBIS (2004, 231–34).

rulings—rather than merely an attempt to assert a somewhat controversial claim of self-defense (Bush 2003).[87]

The president first pursued this line of argument when he stated that the United States had "called on the United Nations to fulfill its charter and stand by its demands that Iraq disarm." This construction presents a demand to the United Nations and, indirectly, to its member states, calling on them not to acquiesce to an American claim of self-defense, but instead to enforce prior Security Council resolutions. In support of this demand, Bush noted that "almost 3 months ago, the United Nations Security Council gave Saddam Hussein his final chance to disarm" and alleged that his failure to meet those demands ("to show exactly where it is hiding its banned weapons, lay those weapons out for the world to see, and destroy them as directed") amounted to "utter contempt for the United Nations and for the opinion of the world." Accordingly, he declared that "the United States will ask the U.N. Security Council to convene on February the 5th to consider the facts of Iraq's ongoing defiance of the world." While he promised that "we will consult," he also insisted that "if Saddam Hussein does not fully disarm, for the safety of our people and for the peace of the world, we will lead a coalition to disarm him." The complex politics, foreign and domestic, of the Iraq war have been extensively debated and are in any case beyond the scope of this book.[88] My purpose here is merely to illustrate the ongoing and thorough engagement of the Bush administration with established global practices of publicly arguing about the status and interpretation of social rules. Rather than a sporadic, epiphenomenal distraction from the true "stuff" of international relations, such practices are at the heart of relations between political communities. Further, the deployment by the Bush administration of multiple independent (and often false) rationales for its position suggests that attention was paid to multiple audiences that may react differently. This pattern also suggests that decision makers sought to avoid rejection of their proposals.

The Iraq war, which began on 19 March 2003, altered the political dynamics of this instance of rule-making and interpretation to the extent that it can more accurately be treated as a distinct case. Whereas Afghanistan and its environs, as well as al-Qaeda itself, are predominantly Sunni, Iraq's population consists of a Shi'a majority. Further, the Iraq war introduced a host of new tribal and ethnic players. Also, whereas American operations against al-Qaeda enjoyed a strong presumption of international legitimacy as a result of their reactive nature, the invasion of Iraq was rooted in controversial post-9/11 claims about a broader right of preventive self-defense that were not broadly accepted by the international

---

[87] George W. Bush, "Address before a Joint Session of the Congress on the State of the Union," speech given at Washington, DC, 28 January 2003.

[88] For an excellent history of the war, see Ricks (2006).

community, and that remained controversial within the United States. Finally, missteps in planning and executing the war rendered it a topic of debate in its own right, and thus distracted from debate about al-Qaeda. Given al-Qaeda's lack of an institutional platform to articulate its message (Phillips 2010), as well as the determined efforts of the international community to deny it standing and voice (and to defeat it militarily), its inability to sustain its challenge to the international system is perhaps unsurprising; however, al-Qaeda and its affiliates still exist, and its mantle was taken up by its most prominent offshoot, the Islamic State. I address the contemporary relevance and lessons of this case in the conclusion of this chapter.

Conclusion

There are four central findings that can be drawn from this case. First, both al-Qaeda and the Bush administration consistently engaged in practices of rule-making and interpretation, despite lacking mutually legitimate secondary rules. Second, in the absence of such rules, each party made use (with mixed skill and success) of practices of rule-making and interpretation drawn from its own cultural and political traditions. Third, each party was constrained by these secondary rules and practices of rule-making not only in dealing with the other, but also in its interactions with other relevant audiences—namely, broader Islamic public opinion in the case of al-Qaeda and domestic and international opinion in the case of the Bush administration. Fourth, each party regarded the other's use of different practices of rule-making and interpretation as an issue of primary concern and as an important reason for their inability to peacefully resolve their differences.

As a result, the case provides evidence supporting the overall argument of the book that secondary rules and associated practices of rule-making shape international political outcomes. The case is particularly notable because it demonstrates that secondary rules influence such outcomes even in cases where the primary players do not agree on the substance of these rules. It also highlights that, in such cases, secondary rules themselves can become an important part of the stakes in the conflict and that actors connect these procedural rules to highly value-laden referent objects such as the appropriate form and substance for political community. In so doing, disputes about secondary rules may render underlying conflicts less susceptible to peaceful resolution precisely because secondary rules and questions of procedural justice are understood to be threatened by the other party.

The role of the Taliban deserves further comment. Its inconsistent and limited efforts to bridge the gap between Wahhabist practices for rule-making and interpretation on the one hand, and contemporary international practices on the other hand, met with a degree of initial success. This demonstrates that disagreements on secondary rules can be bridged—even when those differences are a product of fundamentally distinctive underlying cultural and political traditions. It also serves as a reminder that neither the Western nor the Islamic traditions are monolithic or unchanging. However, the tension between a natural law tradition and a positive law tradition may not be fully resolvable, in that the former holds at least some rules to be exogenously given and therefore not legitimately subject to human alteration or reinterpretation. Natural law traditions may also be less flexible about permitting standing to participate in processes of rule-making and interpretation to outsiders. Both problems are evident in this case. Further, the case shows that resolving differences in secondary rules in parallel with disputes about primary rules is likely to be especially difficult. This is likely to be particularly the case where the dispute about primary rules involves highly important issues such as security or justice. Where possible, such issues should be decomposed and dealt with separately.

The Islamic State, like al-Qaeda, sought to realize a fundamental transformation of the Middle East, and the international system more broadly.[89] Also like its estranged parent organization, it has been subjected to a sustained international military effort to decapitate its leadership structure and degrade its capabilities. Regardless of the eventual fate of the Islamic State, the broader political, social, and economic challenges facing the Middle East in the aftermath of the Arab Spring defy any single ameliorative effort. Solutions to these challenges, in the Middle East and elsewhere, ultimately will require local agency and cannot be externally imposed. However, the defeat of particular networks and organizations is unlikely to prevent other groups from coalescing around these ideas in the future (Owen 2010). To the extent that grievances held by individuals sympathetic to such groups are rooted in part in beliefs that core global practices of rule-making are fundamentally illegitimate, diminishing the appeal of radical Islamist groups and ideas is likely to require an explicit, conscious effort both to make the case for existing practices that are socially intelligible to Muslims, and to undertake renovation of existing practices to enhance confidence in them in the Islamic world while maintaining or augmenting their legitimacy in the eyes of Western public opinion. It is not immediately obvious whether there are modalities for practices of rule-making and interpretation that can satisfy these conditions, especially in light of increased populism in many Western democracies; however, the lack of certain prospects for success should not prevent the effort from being made.

---

[89] For a review of scholarship on the Islamic state, see Byman (2016).

The broader context of this breakdown in consensus on legitimate practices of global rule-making and interpretation is the increasing cultural diversity in the international system, as a result of decolonization and the increasing political and economic importance of communities with little cultural or historical connection to the Western legacy practices employed in the international system. The dispute between the United States and a small yet highly committed group of jihadists may be a "canary in the coal mine"—a harbinger of more, and more intractable, disputes over the creation and interpretation of rules in the years and decades to come. Given the importance of the rule-based global order to human welfare and international security, it is difficult to escape the conclusion that a broad-based global effort to renovate and publicly reaffirm the legitimacy of secondary rules and related practices of rule-making and interpretation is a fundamental, yet overlooked, diplomatic interest. The complexity of such a task suggests the need for an extended diplomatic effort, with broad global participation and leadership from major powers—a parallel in spirit, though not in form, to the creation of the United Nations.

CHAPTER 5

Rules for State Conduct in the Cyber Domain

Efforts to govern the effects of information and communication technologies (ICTs) for international security date to at least 1998, when the Russian Federation introduced a draft resolution at the United Nations entitled "Developments in the Field of Information and Telecommunications in the Context of International Security" (Maurer 2011; Tikk-Ringas 2012). This draft became the basis for a concerted diplomatic effort in the First Committee of the United Nations General Assembly, later joined by a significant number of other states, to create a new legal instrument governing state use of ICTs for military purposes. The work process in the First Committee has centered on several iterations of an expert working group, the Group of Governmental Experts on Developments in the Field of Information and Telecommunications in the Context of International Security (hereinafter, the GGE). The third GGE report, issued in 2013, contained an important advance in state thinking about these issues. It asserted that "international law, and in particular the Charter of the United Nations, is applicable and is essential to maintaining peace and stability and promoting an open, secure, peaceful and accessible ICT environment." Beyond the UN Charter, it specifically enumerated state sovereignty, human rights, and the law of state responsibility as among the applicable bodies of international law governing state use of ICTs (UNGA 2013a, A/68/98, 8). The 2015 GGE report indicated further progress. It contained an explicit discussion of the applicability of international law in this area, explicitly building on the 2013 report by invoking core legal obligations including the settlement of disputes by peaceful means, the obligation to refrain from the use and the threat of force against the territorial integrity or political independence of states, and even the obligation of nonintervention in the internal affairs of other states. Finally, the document "notes the established legal principles, including, where applicable, the principles of humanity, necessity, proportionality and distinction" (UNGA 2015b,

A/70/174, 12–13). While this language may be interpreted as falling just short of clearly affirming the applicability of the law of armed conflict in the cyber domain, and is in any event not legally binding, it is clear that the GGE has made considerable progress in a relatively short period of time.

Remarkably, this rapid progress on the emergence of potential norms for state conduct in the cyber domain came amid developments hostile to such an outcome: (1) a precipitous decline in diplomatic relations between the Russian Federation and most advanced industrial democracies, largely over Russia's behavior in Ukraine; and (2) increased contention over Internet governance and cybersecurity issues at the global level (Bradshaw et al. 2015). Accordingly, I seek to explain a puzzling but welcome shift toward agreement on cyber norms for the state use of ICTs. While revelations about Russian interference in democratic elections make this case all the more timely, these events come mainly after the period under examination and are therefore addressed primarily in the conclusion.

The central argument in the chapter is that state representatives to the GGE engaged in a rule-governed social practice of applying old rules to new cases. They drew on existing procedural rules of diplomacy and international law to advance their positions on the most desirable and appropriate rules to govern state use of ICTs. These secondary rules simultaneously empowered and constrained state representatives in advancing their positions and in evaluating proposals made by their counterparts. They can therefore be understood as partial explanations for the outcome.

Social practices of rule-making, structured by procedural rules, are a necessary part of a satisfactory explanation for an important and puzzling outcome— relatively rapid progress on developing potential norms for state use of ICTs at a time when conditions should not lead us to expect this result. The available evidence, drawn largely from analysis of UN documents, is often suggestive of ways that these procedural rules shaped individual state decisions, especially about the form and manner in which they articulated their positions and reacted to positions articulated by other states. The evidence also indicates that states with greater procedural competence were more able to secure their preferred outcomes. The empirical analysis identifies these indications of ways that procedural rules and social practices of rule-making shaped specific state choices and helped account for the ability of states to secure outcomes consistent with their preferences; however, the recency and relative opacity of the process entail limitations on the available evidence that preclude strong causal claims about specific actor choices. Accordingly, my focus is on accounting more broadly for an important part of the larger outcome—a shift from stalemate to international agreement on a set of candidate norms addressing major questions about the legality of state military use of ICTs, in conditions that should lead us to believe such an outcome would be unlikely. This outcome cannot be explained without accounting for the ways that procedural rules and social practices of rule-making prefigured the ongoing social process in which states sought to deal with questions about the legality of state military use of ICTs.

At present, this ongoing social process has resulted in provisional agreement by a group of significant states (including the permanent members of the United Nations Security Council): (1) that the state use of ICTs is governed by existing bodies of international law that impose substantial restrictions on the military use of ICTs, and (2) that the proposal for a multilateral treaty should be eschewed in favor of continued efforts to govern resulting disputes about state use of ICTs by means of the decentralized legal processes fundamental to the contemporary international system—most notably including the provisions of the UN Charter, the law of armed conflict, and the customary law of state responsibility. The rejection of a Russian proposal for a new international treaty in favor of this alternative approach is the result of a concerted effort (led by the United States under the Obama administration) to apply old rules to a new case. The relatively rapid embrace of this position by a diverse group of countries with divergent positions on Internet governance issues as well as different interests and capabilities in the cyber domain, during a period in which cyber issues have become increasingly contentious, indicates that relevant secondary rules have relatively strong effects on state behavior. That the reports essentially endorsing the American position were issued on a consensus basis by a group including many of the states contesting the issue (including Russia and China) is a further indicator of the strength of these procedural rules.

These outcomes depended in a deep way on the particular set of procedural rules accepted by the actors. If the procedural rules had differed, it is unlikely that states would have made the same choices about how to address concerns pertaining to state military use of ICTs. For example, without procedural rules about both the modalities for negotiating multilateral treaties and the appropriateness of doing so on issues of international security, it is unlikely that Russia would have raised the issue in the First Committee, or that states such as Spain and Japan would have expressed openness to these ideas in spite of opposition from close allies. Similarly, without informal rules about the appropriateness of relying on expert advice, states might well have chosen a means of negotiation other than the creation of the GGE. Without established professional communities of diplomats and international lawyers accustomed to interpreting and applying bodies of existing international law to novel cases, both in international courts and in advisory settings such as the International Law Commission, it is unlikely that GGE participants could have agreed that existing international law applies online despite evident and abiding disagreements over a range of substantive issues pertaining to Internet governance and digital policy issues in general and the state military use of ICTs in particular. At one level, this argument is simply an acknowledgment that path dependence matters in international politics (March and Olsen 1998) and that processes of international law (Brunnée and Toope 2010; Diehl and Ku 2010) and international organization (Johnson 2014) can take on a life of their own. However, it makes an important contribution in demonstrating the relevance of procedural rules for rule-making, interpretation, and application to producing these path-dependent effects of specific international legal and institutional settings.

Even more fundamentally, the outcome depended on the existence of *agreement* among the parties on appropriate procedural rules, independent of their substantive positions. Put another way, if parties had disagreed about procedural rules, it is extremely unlikely that the GGE would have been created, or that it could have issued either its 2013 or 2015 report. The documentary record is remarkable in part for the absence of disagreement about procedural issues, in sharp contrast to other comparable international processes dealing with Internet-related issues (Bradshaw et al. 2015; Hill 2015; Hill 2016). The 2012 attempt to update the International Telecommunication Regulations ended in a split outcome that resulted in fragmentation of the regime into two operative treaties with different sets of parties, and the 2016 IANA transition process resulted in a new arrangement for governing Internet naming and addressing functions, but one that left many parties dissatisfied. In both cases, disagreement about procedural rules complicated attempts to reach agreement (Bradshaw et al. 2015; Raymond and DeNardis 2015) in a manner similar to that evident in the post-9/11 case in this book.

In highlighting the role of procedural rules for rule-making, interpretation, and application in explaining the apparent failure of Russian attempts to secure a multilateral treaty governing state use of ICTs for military purposes and the success of American efforts to extend existing rules of international law to this new domain, the chapter connects these rule systems to the outcome of a high-profile, contested case in the realm of international security. The efficacy of these rules in shaping state behavior (including that of the great powers), and helping to account for the eventual outcome, in what should be a hard case for constructivist arguments sheds light on the nature and potency of established international rule-making practices. The evidence suggests that, even in the realm of high politics and considerable uncertainty about the implications of a disruptive new technology, state representatives understand themselves as engaged in established and ongoing practices of rule-making and interpretation. This finding extends and builds on recent constructivist work re-examining the importance of diplomacy (and diplomatic practices) to IR theory (Neumann 2002; Sharp 2003; Sharp 2009; Adler-Nissen 2009; Neumann 2012; Pouliot 2016). It does so in part by demonstrating the utility of a focus on procedural rules in realizing potential gains from practice-turn constructivism.[1]

The chapter departs somewhat from the format used in the other case chapters. Since the fundamental question was whether there *were* existing rules governing state use of ICTs, explication of the parties' attitudes and positions with respect to primary rules can be accomplished relatively quickly. Further, since the discussion took place within a long-standing institutional forum (the UNGA First Committee), the parties had clear and generally settled views with respect to legitimate secondary rules. Finally, these secondary rules have been discussed at length in previous chapters. Additional comment and elaboration will be provided where relevant to the analysis, in lieu of a dedicated section discussing the secondary rules relevant to the case. The chapter, therefore, has two major sections. The first discusses the background to the case and briefly explicates the empirical puzzle introduced above. The second part presents a case study of the attempt to establish cyber norms in the First Committee of the United Nations General Assembly. The chapter concludes by discussing the findings of the case, and its contemporary relevance in light of Russian interference in democratic elections and other relevant cybersecurity issues.

The Evolving Status of International Law in the Cyber Domain

The 2013 GGE report represents an important milestone in clarifying the rules of the road for state behavior in the cyber domain. The group was reasonably representative: it included all permanent members of the United Nations Security Council, as well as major emerging markets such as India and Indonesia, and middle powers Australia and Canada. It was also selected according to UN practices for ensuring regional balance. The group made important substantive progress, reaching the first multilateral consensus report declaring the official view of a group of major states that international law is applicable in its entirety to the cyber domain. Notably, this consensus represents a departure from longstanding efforts initiated by Russia (and later co-sponsored by China and other states) in pursuit of a formal multilateral treaty governing state use of ICTs. Perhaps most important, the GGE continued its work by issuing another consensus report in 2015 that built upon its 2013 discussion of international law and by agreeing to recommend yet another iteration of the process in 2016–2017.

---

[1] On the relationship between the practice turn and constructivism, see McCourt (2016).

While the 2017 GGE did not reach consensus on a report, this outcome did not invalidate or even criticize the results of the 2013 or 2015 processes.

Agreement that existing international law applies to state use of ICTs was facilitated by a realization over time on the part of authoritarian states that UN Charter protections for sovereignty ensured rather than threatened their preferences for domestic Internet regulation and control. In this manner, an American-led effort to both maintain a key military advantage and protect a free and open Internet contributed to an outcome more in line with what Demchak and Dombrowski have described as a "cyber Westphalia" (Demchak and Dombrowski 2011). While the process of rule-making and interpretation in the First Committee did not transform Russian and Chinese preferences in the sense of making them compatible with Western views, these states and their like-minded counterparts were both constrained by procedural rules and also enabled by them to creatively advance their own values and interests in ways that their interlocutors appear not to have fully appreciated in advance, and certainly did not intend. There are indications, however, that Western states are utilizing the GGE reports to hold Russia accountable for its apparent interference in democratic elections. Such efforts demonstrate ongoing processes of rule-making and interpretation, and suggest that these processes have begun to shape state behavior and discourse in ways that may contribute to international security.

Beyond the general reluctance of some IR scholars to accept the causal relevance of norms, rules, and institutions (especially in security cases),[2] there are two more specific reasons that the agreement and its timing might be regarded as puzzling. First, this progress has come rather suddenly despite a substantial worsening of diplomatic relations between two of the major players, Russia and the United States. Russia's claim to annexation of Crimea, its involvement in the Syrian conflict, and its recent efforts to interfere in democratic elections have caused deep disagreements with the United States and its allies, as well as the imposition of economic sanctions; yet, despite these differences, work on cyber norms has yielded some important successes since 2013. While it is true that Russia and the United States were also able to work together on negotiations pertaining to the Iranian nuclear program in this time period, that case is less puzzling given the great powers' long-standing agreement on maintaining their nuclear oligopoly to the extent possible. The Iranian case also involves a structured diplomatic and legal framework that draws on many of the same procedural

---

[2] Mearsheimer (1994/95). Constructivists have sometimes also accepted the claim that security cases are "hard cases" for their theories, though this is to some extent a tactical move driven by a desire to gain acceptance from non-constructivists. See, for example, Wendt (1995, 77).

rules that proved effective in the case examined here. It is possible that cooperation in these two cases is partially explained by this common factor.

Second, agreement on norms of responsible state behavior for the use of ICTs is puzzling because it has come alongside continuing contention over closely related issues of global Internet governance (DeNardis 2014; Bradshaw et al. 2015). If anything, IR theory suggests that agreement on security norms should have been more difficult than agreement on "low politics" issues pertaining to the institutional modalities for governing Internet naming and numbering, as well as the development of Internet technical protocols. These problems mainly involve coordination rather than cooperation problems, and while important distributional consequences flow from the selection of particular equilibria rather than others, these kinds of problems are generally thought to be less problematic for international cooperation (Martin and Simmons 1998; Koremenos, Lipson, and Snidal 2001). Yet the evidence shows precisely the opposite pattern. Russia and the United States have agreed that international law applies to the use of ICTs while continuing to advance starkly different proposals for the future of Internet governance despite the recent transition of oversight for the Internet Assigned Numbers Authority (IANA) functions away from the American government. This is partly because Internet governance has been politicized in a manner that invokes issues of procedural legitimacy in addition to issues of substantive fairness associated with distributional questions (DeNardis 2014; Raymond and DeNardis 2015). In contrast, discussions of cybersecurity in the UN General Assembly's First Committee have been notable for the absence of procedural conflict, reflecting the presence of a greater degree of agreement among the parties on the relevant procedural rules.

In the remainder of this chapter, I present an explanation of the puzzling rapid emergence of agreement on the applicability of international law to the state use of ICTs. In doing so, I make two major claims. First, that actors in the international system are, inter alia, engaged in a rule-governed social practice of making, interpreting, and applying social rules. Second, that these procedural rules partially determine important outcomes in the international system.

Applying Old Rules to New Cases

Existing studies have documented the work of the General Assembly's First Committee on cyber issues from the initial discussions in 1998 through the 2010 GGE process (Maurer 2011; Tikk-Ringas 2012). From 1998 to 2004, the Russian resolution on ICTs in the context of international security was adopted in the First Committee without a vote. However, this did not indicate complete agreement among the parties on the substantive issues. From the outset, states in the First Committee were involved in a structured practice of rule-making and interpretation. The core of the Russian position was a call for a multilateral treaty. Russia sought to initiate a rule-making process on the grounds that "contemporary international law has virtually no means of regulating the development and application" of a cyber-weapon (UNGA 1999, A/54/213, 8). The United States initially maintained that "it would be premature to formulate overarching principles pertaining to information security in all its aspects" and that "the international community needs to do a substantial amount of systematic thinking before going further" (UNGA 1999, A/54/213, 13). The American position likely reflected a Bush administration preference to preserve a strategic advantage; however, the crucial point is that rather than simply refuse to engage the Russian proposal or plainly indicate a preference based on a perceived national interest, the United States chose to proceed by interpreting the Russian proposal in light of procedural rules of great power diplomacy and international law. In particular, the American response relies on procedural rules about the need to engage rule-making proposals advanced by other great powers in good faith to preserve common practices of managing the international system, and about the value of prudence and patience in altering international rules and institutions.

By 2004, the United States had concluded that "an international convention is completely unnecessary." Its rationale was that "the law of armed conflict and its principles of necessity, proportionality and limitation of collateral damage already govern the use of such technologies" (UNGA 2004, A/59/116/Add.1, 4). Thus, the United States now replied to the Russian proposal for a new treaty by arguing that new rules were not needed because existing rules already covered this novel case. This is a clear example of interpreting and applying rules, and of employing the broader procedural frameworks of diplomacy and international law to evaluate (and in this case to oppose) a rule-making proposal by another actor. Specifically, the amended American argument had moved in a more legal vein, relying on established rules and practices for interpreting existing treaties such as the UN Charter and the Geneva Convention, as well as for applying rules of customary international law such as the law of armed conflict and the law of state responsibility. The argument was effectively that these bodies of law were technologically neutral, and thus governed all state military conduct whether accomplished by means of ICTs or not.

This dispute over how to correctly interpret and apply existing rules of international law to a novel, complex, and important case ultimately prevented the first iteration of the GGE from issuing a consensus report. Crucially, this view has been expressed publicly by some of the participants. The chair, Russian diplomat A. V. Krustkikh, explicitly attributed this failure in part to "differing interpretations of current international law in the area of international information security" (quoted in Tikk-Ringas 2012, 7). Another member of the Russian delegation, A. A. Streltsov, called this issue "the main stumbling block" (quoted in Maurer 2011, 33). From 2005 to 2008, the United States voted against the Russian resolution. It was the only state to do so. By 2008, Russia had attracted thirty co-sponsors for its resolution in favor of a multilateral cyber arms control treaty (Tikk-Ringas 2012, 7). Over its first decade, the Russian effort to promote new rules for state use of ICTs thus appeared to have gained greater traction among the members of the UN than the competing interpretation proposed by the United States.

A complete explanation of the apparent reversal in state positions by 2013 would include a number of factors. These include reputation damage suffered by Russia as a result of its alleged orchestration of cyberattacks against Estonia in 2007 and Georgia in 2008 (Tikk-Ringas 2012, 7); change in composition of the GGE membership; and state learning about ICTs and their policy implications, in light of continued rapid technological evolution and diffusion over the period 2008–2013. Ebert and Maurer (2013) suggest that regime type is an important intervening variable affecting state positions on cyber issues. They make a convincing case that regime type is important in accounting for intra-BRICS differences on cyber issues, but I would add two points to their analysis. First, this effect unfolded over time, as states learned about the technology and received input from civil society stakeholders. Second, democracies have nevertheless proven quite willing to contemplate extensive cyber monitoring programs that might be regarded as inconsistent with democratic values and also with human rights. My argument here does not discount any of these factors in explaining the emergence of a consensus that international law applies in its entirety in cyberspace. Rather, I argue that these other factors do not account either for the actual social process of rule-making that took place in the First Committee or for the way in which procedural rules of diplomacy and international law differentially empowered states in making and evaluating specific proposals, or the two overarching positions—that new rules were needed and that existing global rules already governed state use of ICTs.

Accordingly, I focus on the period covering the 2013 and 2015 GGE reports. Participants in these processes and the UN General Assembly's First Committee were engaged in a rule-governed social practice of making, interpreting, and applying rules—in this case for state conduct in the cyber domain. In doing so, they explicitly drew on agreed-upon procedural rules both in presenting their arguments and in evaluating those made by other participants. There was clear variation in actors' competence in performing this social practice. This competence is essentially a function of actors' expertise in employing the procedural rules that structure it. These rules exerted sufficient influence on the outcome to create consensus on the American proposal despite countervailing conditions that seem clearly to work against the emergence of such an agreement. Note that this argument allows for the possibility of state action on the basis of logics of appropriateness but does not require it. At least some of the states pursuing a multilateral treaty-based regime for Internet issues do not seem to have abandoned their position; available evidence does not suggest that they have internalized the American position. However, in endorsing the reports by allowing them to be issued on a consensus basis, they have nevertheless conceded important ground that will structure the playing field in future iterations of this game of global cyber rule-making. Likewise, the United States has also ceded ground in ways that American participants seem not to have fully appreciated. The applicability of international law in the cyber domain provides authoritarian regimes with important support for their preferred doctrines of cyber sovereignty.

THE 2013 GROUP OF GOVERNMENTAL EXPERTS

The third iteration of the GGE process met in three sessions from August 2012 through June 2013. Its consensus report was issued on 24 June 2013.[3] The report couched its conclusions as extensions of the previous GGE process, noting that the 2010 report had "recommended further dialogue among States on norms pertaining to State use of ICTs" (UNGA 2013a, A/68/98, 6). It broke new ground in affirming that "the application of norms derived from existing international law relevant to the use of ICTs by States is an essential measure to reduce risks to international peace, security and stability" (UNGA 2013a, A/68/98, 8). This is a direct affirmation by the GGE members that they understood themselves to be involved in a collective process of applying legal rules to a novel case. However, the 2013 report also noted that the application of such norms could not be settled in a single interpretive act. It acknowledged that "common understandings on how such norms shall apply to State behaviour and the use of ICTs by States requires further study" (UNGA 2013a, A/68/98, 8).

The 2013 GGE report makes clear that the member states had already begun this interpretive process. It made the explicit claim that "international law, and in particular the Charter of the United Nations, is applicable and is essential to maintaining peace and stability and promoting an open, secure, peaceful and accessible ICT environment." In itself, this is a clear shift toward the American position that existing international legal rules already governed state use of ICTs, especially as the 2013 GGE included both Russia and China. By allowing the production of a consensus report (in contrast to the first iteration of the GGE),

---

[3] The report also made important progress on applying confidence-building measures in the cyber domain and on justifying the importance of international assistance for capacity-building. While both are important to global cybersecurity governance, they are beyond the scope of my concern here.

these states were now on the record in supporting the American position. The report also made further progress in identifying important bodies of international law of particular relevance to the state use of ICTs. It indicated the view of the GGE that "state sovereignty and international norms and principles that flow from sovereignty apply to State conduct of ICT-related activities, and to their jurisdiction over ICT infrastructure within their territory." Further, it found that "State efforts to address the security of ICTs must go hand-in-hand with respect for human rights and fundamental freedoms set forth in the Universal Declaration of Human Rights and other international instruments." Finally, it concluded that "States must meet their international obligations regarding internationally wrongful acts." This last finding connects the state use of ICTs specifically to the law of state responsibility, which governs the limits on self-help in the event a state is injured by another state's breach of an international legal obligation. In particular, the GGE identified two potential circumstances in which the law of state responsibility might be applicable. The report asserted that "States must not use proxies to commit internationally wrongful acts" and that "States should seek to ensure that their territories are not used by non-State actors for unlawful use of ICTs" (UNGA 2013a, A/68/98, 8).

As part of the First Committee's ongoing work on cyber issues, the UN secretary-general receives national submissions on an ongoing basis. These submissions provide information about state positions on relevant issues, the development of national cybersecurity efforts, and "possible measures that could be taken by the international community to strengthen information security at the global level" (UNGA 2013b, A/68/156, 1). State submissions are voluntary but include entries from a variety of states—including members of the GGE as well as nonmembers, states at a variety of levels of development, and states with a variety of political regime types. Despite this variety, the data are too partial to create generalizations about variables that explain specific state positions. In any event, the approach taken in this book emphasizes that state positions are at least partly endogenous to the social process of rule-making and interpretation undertaken in the First Committee. Accordingly, it is impossible either to explain or predict outcomes simply by examining state characteristics.

Instead, the national submissions are useful as evidence of state positions on the interpretive work being undertaken by the GGE and in the First Committee, which constituted the immediate audience for the GGE report. The submissions included in the 2013 report by the secretary-general range from May through September 2013. All were therefore made after the GGE had begun its work, and the majority were made prior to the production of the consensus report.

The United States did not make a submission to the UN secretary-general; however, several of its close allies did. These submissions generally adopted positions similar to the previously expressed American view that international law already governed state use of ICTs. Britain, in a submission made in May 2013 (prior to the GGE report), indicated its view that the "paramount concept" applicable to improving international security in the cyber domain was "that of the application of international law and the existing norms of behaviour that govern relations between and among states." It asserted that "the United Kingdom firmly believes that these principles apply with equal force to cyberspace and an unambiguous affirmation by States that their activities in cyberspace will be governed by these laws and norms would lay the foundations for a more peaceful, predictable and secure cyberspace." Britain also explicitly addressed the question of the appropriateness of an international treaty. It made clear that "the United Kingdom does not believe that attempts to conclude comprehensive multilateral treaties, codes of conduct or similar instruments would make a positive contribution to enhanced cybersecurity for the foreseeable future." Its rationale was that "the complex and comprehensive nature of any binding agreement across the entirety of a cyberspace that is evolving at 'net speed' means that it could not be effective or command widespread support without many years, possibly decades, of painstaking work on norms of behaviour and confidence-building measures to build up the necessary understanding and trust among signatories and to ensure that they can be reliably held to account for their adherence to their commitments." The pragmatic nature of this rationale was reinforced by the claim that "experience in these agreements on other subjects shows that they can be meaningful and effective only as the culmination of diplomatic attempts to develop shared understandings and approaches, not as their starting point" (UNGA 2013b, A/68/156, 18–19).

The British position entailed two central claims. The first is that existing international law already applies to state use of ICTs and thus to state conduct in the cyber domain. The second is that a multilateral treaty is unworkable and undesirable. With respect to the first claim, the British position draws on existing secondary rules that empower states to determine individually whether other states have breached international legal obligations owed to them. This kind of decentralized adjudication is essential to the customary law on state responsibility (International Law Commission 2001) and also to international legal doctrines on self-defense. The argument on this ground is therefore that the cyber domain presents a straightforward example of applying existing rules to a novel case, in a way that states are explicitly authorized to do by the procedural rules of international law, subject to limits set out mainly in the law of self-defense and the law of state responsibility. Like the earlier American response to the Russian proposal for a multilateral treaty, this position likely reflects Britain's substantive preferences, but the British government made the argument with reference to specific, identifiable standards for interpreting and applying existing international law.

With respect to the second claim, the British submission adopts a much more pragmatic tone that relies on diplomatic experience rather than international legal rules. This is likely because the position adopted by the United States, the United Kingdom, and other states was on weaker legal ground in opposing the idea of a multilateral arms control treaty in the cyber domain. After all, the Russian position could be grounded in prior state practice erecting arms control regimes for both nuclear and conventional weapons. It would be hard to sustain the argument that such a decision would be procedurally inappropriate, and even if existing rules of international law applied online, this would not procedurally preclude a multilateral treaty codifying or extending existing legal rules. This basic consistency of the Russian position with past state practice, and with accepted procedures for governing security problems arising from new technologies, likely helps to explain the willingness of many states to co-sponsor the Russian resolution and to endorse the more concrete notion of a multilateral treaty on cybersecurity.

However, the British submission also rejected the terminology of "information security" employed by the Russian government and others sympathetic to it. It indicated that "the United Kingdom does not recognize the validity of the term 'information security' when it is used in this context, since it could be employed in attempts to legitimize further controls on freedom of expression beyond those agreed to in the Universal Declaration of Human Rights and the International Covenant on Civil and Political Rights" (UNGA 2013b, A/68/156, 15). Thus, the British submission also argued against the appropriateness of the specific kind of cybersecurity treaty preferred by Russia and other like-minded governments, on the grounds that such a treaty would be inconsistent with other international legal obligations. This kind of critical evaluation of another actor's rule-making proposal is consistent with the argument advanced in this book that states engage in a rule-governed practice of making, interpreting, and applying international rules. The British objection was clearly based in a substantive preference that reflected support for the protection of civil and political rights, but was expressed in terms of procedural rules that require consideration of the effect of proposed rules on states' existing international legal obligations. It demonstrates that, when evaluating proposed global rules, states explicitly consider the compatibility of multiple simultaneously valid rule sets, and that they are aware of secondary rules governing the interaction of these sets.

In enumerating threats to international peace and security emanating from cyberspace, the German submission (lodged the day after the GGE report) noted that "prevailing ambiguity about what norms apply in cyberspace creates additional unpredictability" (UNGA 2013c, A/68/156/Add.1, 5). Accordingly, the submission noted that "Germany advocates developing broad, non-contentious, politically binding norms of State behaviour in cyberspace." It expressed the view that such norms "should be acceptable to a large part of the international community and should include measures to build trust and increase security." The submission therefore spoke directly to issues of procedures for agreement on rules and rule interpretations. The framing of the submission in terms of "politically binding norms" rather than binding international legal obligations is somewhat puzzling. It may reflect a desire to avoid giving the appearance of endorsing a multilateral treaty-based approach, in light of the long-standing Russian diplomatic effort for such a legal instrument. However, the German reply provided a clear endorsement of the GGE report. It indicated that Germany "strongly welcome[s] the commendations of the Experts on norms, rules or principles of responsible behaviour of States." The German submission also affirms the relevance of many of the same bodies of international law deemed relevant by the GGE report. For example, it notes "the necessity to start a debate on international cooperation in the framework of attribution of cyber attacks. . . . State responsibility for cyber attacks launched from their territory when States do nothing to end such attacks, despite being informed about them, and the responsibility of States not to facilitate areas of lawlessness in cyberspace, for example, by knowingly tolerating the storage of illegally collected personal data on their territory" (UNGA 2013c, A/68/156/Add.1, 8–9). These observations make clear that Germany endorsed the application of the Charter provisions on sovereignty, the law of armed conflict, the law of state responsibility, and international human rights law in the cyber domain. Just as the United States and Britain had done, Germany expressed its preferences in a manner simultaneously enabled and constrained by procedural rules for interpreting and applying existing rules of international law. It accepted the argument that existing bodies of international law were applicable, and also indicated that this finding required an ongoing process of interpretation to clarify how these rules applied in this substantive domain.

Like Germany, Canada and the Netherlands made national submissions after the production of the GGE report. The Canadian submission was less detailed in addressing questions of international law than those made by Britain and Germany. Nevertheless, it clearly endorses the GGE report's conclusion. Canada asserted that "existing treaty and customary law is applicable to the use of information and communications technologies by States, and is essential to maintaining peace and stability, and promoting an open, secure, peaceful and accessible information and communications technology environment." Like the German submission, the Canadian response specifically enumerates the UN Charter, as well as international human rights law and international humanitarian law as bodies of international law relevant to the state use of ICTs (UNGA 2013c, A/68/156/Add.1, 8–9). The Dutch response indicated that "the Netherlands is of the opinion that the development of norms for State conduct does not require a reinvention of international law, but rather needs to ensure consistency in the application of existing international legal frameworks." It therefore engaged the question of the appropriateness of a multilateral treaty, and concluded that such an instrument was unnecessary (UNGA 2013c, A/68/156/Add.1, 4).

The similarity evident in the positions articulated by these NATO allies likely reflects their similar substantive preferences. But these similar substantive preferences cannot fully explain the similarities in the *form* these states adopted in articulating their positions, which also reflect highly specialized legalized diplomatic discourses directly concerned with the resolution of tensions among rules in complex and overlapping rule sets (Sandholtz 2008) characteristic of the social practice of international legality (Brunnée and Toope 2010). Similarity in substantive preferences also cannot explain either the positions articulated by states with different stated preferences, or the existence of different procedural interpretations advanced by other NATO members or close allies that expressed support for a free and open Internet, most notably including Spain and Japan.

Armenia and Turkey provided national submissions that did not address the question of the applicability of existing international law to cyberspace or the question of the appropriateness of a multilateral treaty. Each of these replies focused more on elucidating their national cybersecurity efforts (UNGA 2013c, A/68/156/Add.1, 2–3, 21–24). It is possible that this lacuna indicates a relative lack of competence in applying international legal rules to this novel and complex technological domain, but it is impossible to rule out (on the basis of available data) explanations based in domestic politics or in conceptions of national interest, though it is hard to imagine why a state might conclude that it lacks a national interest in participating in global rule-making, especially in a case where all permanent Security Council members endorsed the report.

Oman's submission, filed two days after the GGE report, proposed "regulating e-transactions and information and interstate cybersecurity by establishing an international organization under the auspices of the United Nations." Given that international organizations are typically constituted by a multilateral treaty, this position can be read as supporting the Russian proposal for such a legal instrument. However, the Omani submission illustrates the potential for broad state agreement on the applicability of international law to the cyber domain. It endorsed a clear sovereigntist position asserting state authority over nonstate actors, in asserting that "stakeholders must comply with the particular values and principles that each country seeks to uphold." Oman also articulated a variation of the Russian justification for an international instrument, in asserting that "States must join forces and cooperate to combat information security threats" (UNGA 2013c, A/68/156/Add.1, 19–20). Adoption of this terminology indicates a particular interpretation of state authority vis-à-vis societal actors, and of the appropriate way to handle violations of human rights law in light of state sovereignty. But it is notable that these preferences were articulated in international legal terms that displayed awareness of international legal rules of sovereignty having to do not only with the state's substantive rights to autonomy, but also with its superior position relative to nonstate actors in questions of rule-making, interpretation, and application, as well as its equal position with respect to other states in these matters.

Ukraine, under the pro-Russian Yanukovych government, likewise expressed support for the Russian position. Its national submission defined information security as "the degree to which national interests in the field of information are shielded from external and domestic threats" and explicitly indicated that this definition included the "use of information infrastructure to disseminate information that incited animosity and hatred, in general or in a specific country" as well as the "use of cyberspace to destabilize society and undermine the economic, political and social system of another State or to spread misinformation designed to distort cultural, ethical and aesthetic values" (UNGA 2013b, A/68/156, 9–10). In service of these interests in maintaining regime stability, the Ukrainian submission expressed the view that "it may be time to draft a set of international principles to strengthen information and telecommunications network security and international security policy overall." According to the Yanukovych government, "an important aspect of this would be to determine the international legal status of cyberspace and to enshrine, in regulatory and legal instruments, States' jurisdictions with regard to the national components of this space (comparable to States' air space and territorial waters) and the further regulation of issues related to cyberwar, cyberaggression, and so on" (UNGA 2013b, A/68/156, 14). Like Oman, Ukraine was able to express its support for Russian positions on information security and a multilateral treaty in a manner consistent with existing procedural rules, and evidently saw value in doing so.

Thus far, national submissions have generally accorded with regime type: democracies (UK, Germany, Canada, the Netherlands) oppose a multilateral treaty and accept the argument that existing international law is applicable to cyberspace, while more authoritarian regimes (Oman, Ukraine) support a multilateral treaty to deal with perceived gaps in the applicability of international law in this domain. The irony of authoritarian regimes promoting a multilateral legal instrument is indicative of the broad legitimacy of the procedural rules of the contemporary international system. This point is worth emphasizing. Despite illiberal preferences inconsistent with prevailing notions of thick multilateralism (Ruggie 1992; Reus-Smit 1999), authoritarian states have regularly and consistently adopted the vernacular of multilateralism and of contractual international law to advance their agendas. Far from making the claim that participation in the post-1945 rule-based global order (Ikenberry 2001) has transformed the identity of these states or that these states have internalized the norms and rules underpinning that order, I am arguing instead that to varying degrees, these rules: (1) constrain illiberal states, requiring them to take pains to express their positions in terms at least ostensibly consistent with those rules; and/or (2) enable them to advance such interpretations, albeit in ways that are subject to limits and constraints. Three national submissions are noteworthy in illustrating how procedural rules and the social practices they constitute can sometimes create strange bedfellows.

Unlike the United States, and its other allies, Japan was skeptical about the applicability of existing international law to the cyber domain. Its national submission, made after the 2013 GGE report, expressed the view that "we must with urgency start developing realistic and feasible norms of behaviour to address current issues in a non-legally binding form." The Japanese government based this proposal on its conclusion that "there are no international norms that regulate cyber attacks or cyber espionage in security, economic and social arenas. In addition, the validity of legally binding norms in cyberspace remains unclear at this stage" (UNGA 2013c, A/68/156/Add.1, 14–15). That Japan would express this view despite being a member of the GGE (and thus having endorsed its consensus report) is unusual. The expressed desire for norms rather than legally binding rules may reflect opposition to a multilateral treaty specific to cybersecurity issues, but this reading still places the Japanese position at odds with the conclusion of the GGE as a whole that the broader corpus of international law (treaty and custom) was already applicable. The internal inconsistency in the Japanese endorsement of the 2013 GGE report and its submission of a national position contradicting that report highlights the importance of distinguishing between applicable procedural rules for global rule-making and specific performances of that practice, which may be more or less socially competent. Japan effectively made contradictory assessments about whether there were rules or norms applicable to cyberspace without seeming to notice or justify this inconsistency, indicating a less skillful performance of the social practice of global rule-making. Skillful performances should generally be internally consistent, and should also anticipate and preempt such obvious potential criticisms. Nevertheless, the Japanese submission also demonstrates both the plasticity of procedural rules for international rule-making as well as the apparent consistency of the Russian position with at least some applicable procedural rules for evaluating the applicability of international law to the cyber domain, even in the eyes of an established democracy.

It its May 2013 submission, lodged prior to the GGE report, Spain similarly asserted that "the protection of an international legal framework to meet cybersecurity threats is lacking." It concluded that "there is a need for multilateral cooperation agreements in this area (analogous or similar to the International

Convention for the Safety of Life at Sea (SOLAS)) whereby States would undertake to harmonize their legislation with a view to the prosecution of Internet crimes while attempting to ensure, to the extent possible, that anonymity, the absence of legislation and economic interests do not make the Internet the ideal breeding ground for crime and terrorism." The submission also endorsed the view that "the international community should adopt whatever protection measures are deemed necessary, basing its action on an integrated global vision and, if possible, creating a single authority to lay down rules and standards common to all countries" (UNGA 2013b, A/68/156, 8–9). The Spanish position is clear about the appropriateness of governing the issue according to international law and potentially also through an international intergovernmental organization; however, it does not display an appreciation of the implications of the Russian proposal for international human rights law, nor does it address the crucial question of whether existing international law applies in cyberspace. Indeed, in calling for the creation of a rule-making authority, the Spanish position appears to contradict fundamental principles of international law that arrogate rule-making functions to states collectively on a decentralized and formally equal basis. This may simply reflect Spanish belief in the appropriateness of a multilateral approach to cyber governance and a desire to pursue a substantively different version of such an approach than that advocated by Russia and its like-minded group, but the omission of analysis addressing the core question of the applicability of existing international law, including human rights law, is notable.

Finally, Iran made a creative national submission indicative of its efforts to employ international legal rules to meet its policy objectives. Its submission emphasized access to ICTs in the developing world, opposing "the adoption of any measure to deny or restrict the transfer for advanced information and telecommunications know-how, technologies and means, as well as the provision of information and telecommunications services, to developing countries." It seems likely this line of argumentation was intended as an attempt to delegitimize sanctions in this industrial sector by invoking accepted rules from other domains of international law establishing the appropriateness of flexibility and differential treatment for postcolonial, low-income states. This move leverages informal analogues to legal precedent in the international system that grant ideas accepted in other issue-areas a prima facie claim to acceptance, in this context to oppose the legal and political legitimacy of sanctions and export controls. While unlikely to sway industrial democracies, it is likely that this kind of claim would be well-received by members of the G77.

The Iranian submission also expressed its "view that the most appropriate international mechanism for consideration of the developments in the field of information and telecommunications in the context of international security is to launch a process within the United Nations with the equal participation of all States." This procedural argument effectively endorses a formal multilateral conference on the basis that it is consistent with the fundamental rule of juridical equality among states. In so doing, Iran explicitly tied the argument for a multilateral process to fundamental rules of international law holding that states are formally equal in establishing international legal obligations. The submission went on to suggest that "the main purpose of that process should be to develop a common understanding between States about the importance of enhancing security of information and telecommunications." It further recommended that this process be conducted "in the format of international conferences every five years to produce political outcomes ranging from declarations to codes of conduct" with "the ultimate goal" of "the progressive development of solid international legal foundations for strengthening and ensuring the security of global information and telecommunications." Here, Iran called for the utilization of commonly accepted procedures of periodic review, adopting a procedural form used in the Non-Proliferation Treaty and other arms control agreements, as well as in other high-profile areas like climate governance and ICT-related processes such as the International Telecommunication Regulations and the World Summit on the Information Society. Further, in referring to the progressive development of legal foundations, Iran referred explicitly to the mandate of the International Law Commission. This reference indicates awareness, and signals acceptance, of prevailing procedural rules for clarifying international legal disputes.

Despite its support for a diplomatic process leading to a multilateral treaty, Iran also acknowledged that "as a general principle, international law is applicable and therefore should be applied to the use of information and telecommunications technologies and means by States." It went on to indicate its interpretation of this claim as entailing states' legal obligations to respect UN Charter provisions in the cyber domain. In this respect, Iran specifically enumerated Article 2 obligations (paras. 3–4) to settle disputes by peaceful means and to refrain from the threat or use of force (UNGA 2013c, A/68/156/Add.1, 11–13). This latter interpretive argument is perhaps unsurprising given the injury suffered by the Iranian government as a result of Stuxnet, but it demonstrates that at least some authoritarian regimes were able to employ the accepted interpretive rules of international law and diplomacy to advance their values and interests in light of the American response to the Russian proposal for a multilateral treaty.

This conclusion clearly reflected Iran's recognition that the Charter accorded it valuable entitlements both to set its internal policies on Internet-related matters, and also to object to American violations of its sovereignty. But it is equally noteworthy that Iran understood the importance of registering these claims in the GGE process even as it still sought to advance a multilateral (as opposed to multistakeholder) process for creating, interpreting, and applying such rules in the future. Iran thus sought to recast the American position that existing international law applied in cyberspace as consistent with the Russian proposal for a multilateral treaty. This interpretation had been available since the 2004 American claim that existing international law applied online. It is not clear why the gap had not been bridged prior to 2013, but it does appear that this emerging understanding—arrived at via an international process of interpreting and applying rules—at least partially explains the puzzling outcome of agreement in the 2013 GGE despite inhospitable conditions.

The 2013 GGE report and the related national submissions demonstrate the continued existence of a diversity of state positions on the appropriateness of a multilateral cyber treaty. But, more fundamentally, they demonstrate virtually universal agreement on the legitimacy of the basic procedural frameworks of international law and diplomacy for dealing with these issues. Even the United Kingdom, a staunch supporter of the multistakeholder model of Internet governance, expressed the view that "it is for Governments to lead international efforts to improve understandings over acceptable State behaviour and in tackling cybercrime" (UNGA 2013b, A/68/156, 16). Similarly, states adopting revisionist positions sought to do so by virtue of a multilateral treaty and a new international organization within the broader UN system. States as diverse as Germany and Iran with respect to both their basic attitudes toward the international system, and toward Internet freedom and the state military use of ICTs, nevertheless agreed on the applicability of the UN Charter and other fundamental provisions of international law. No doubt this agreement on relevant rules was a product, in part, of increasing realization by authoritarian regimes that the American interpretation provided discursive resources for them to advance their Internet policy agendas both at the domestic and international levels, as reflected in the Iranian submission. Likewise, the near-unanimous expression of support for further interpretive work shows simultaneously that states regarded this rule-governed social practice as legitimate, that they regarded its implications for policy as unclear (to varying extents), and that they saw it as a way to advance their values and interests.

THE 2015 GROUP OF GOVERNMENTAL EXPERTS

The fourth iteration of the GGE began work in July 2014. In total, it met four times prior to issuing its June 2015 report. The group was enlarged, growing from fifteen states in its previous iteration to twenty states. It also became more culturally diverse in composition; Argentina, Australia, Canada, and India did not participate in the fourth GGE while Brazil, Colombia, Ghana, Israel, Kenya,

Malaysia, Pakistan, and the Republic of Korea were added. Despite its larger, more diverse membership, the GGE continued to make important gains in interpreting and applying existing rules of international law to the cyber domain. Its success was also achieved in spite of considerable international controversy over electronic espionage practices and over institutional modalities for governance of core Internet technical functions (DeNardis 2014; Bradshaw et al. 2015).

With respect to the application of existing international law to the cyber domain, the GGE endorsed the view that "the adherence by States to international law, in particular their Charter obligations, is an essential framework for their actions in their use of ICTs" and that "these obligations are central to the examination of the application of international law to the use of ICTs by States." Beyond a broad endorsement of the UN Charter, the GGE also enumerated several other core principles: "sovereign equality; the settlement of international disputes by peaceful means in such a manner that international peace and security and justice are not endangered; refraining in their international relations from the threat or use of force against the territorial integrity or political independence of any State, or in any other manner inconsistent with the purposes of the United Nations; respect for human rights and fundamental freedoms; and non-intervention in the internal affairs of other states" (UNGA 2015b, A/70/174, 12).

The report also provided consensus views on several other critical matters in applying international law to the cyber domain. First, it states clearly that "States have jurisdiction over the ICT infrastructure located within their territory." Questions pertaining to jurisdiction are of critical importance to resolving a variety of international legal disputes over cyber issues, including potential trade disputes and law enforcement cooperation on criminal matters. Second, the report "notes the established legal principles, including, where applicable, the principles of humanity, necessity, proportionality and distinction." These principles are central to the law of armed conflict, in particular to *jus in bello* law governing state conduct in armed conflict. While the GGE did not reach consensus on inclusion of the law of armed conflict as a cognate body of law clearly applicable in the cyber domain, the inclusion of its central principles in a consensus report encompassing the entirety of the permanent membership of the Security Council is an important progressive step in the development of international law. Finally, the GGE indicated its understanding with respect to some important implications of the application of the law of state responsibility to the cyber domain. It affirmed that "States must not use proxies to commit international wrongful acts using ICTs, and should seek to ensure that their territory is not used by non-State actors to commit such acts" (UNGA 2015b, A/70/174, 12–13). This conclusion is important to dealing effectively with cybercrime and also to ensuring that states do not exploit attribution difficulties in the cyber realm[4] in order to circumvent their legal obligations under the Charter. Finally, while affirming that "States must meet their international obligations regarding internationally wrongful acts attributable to them under international law," the GGE noted that "the indication that an ICT activity was launched or otherwise originates from the territory or the ICT infrastructure of a State may be insufficient in itself to attribute the activity to that State" (UNGA 2015b, A/70/174, 13). This is important both because prevailing interpretations of customary international law apply a high standard to the attribution of an activity to a state (International Law Commission 2001), and also because of the possibility that various kinds of parties (including increasingly sophisticated nonstate actors) may attempt to conceal their involvement in a cyberattack by launching it from a third-party state or by employing technical measures to make it appear that they have done so.

In addition to its interpretive work on applying existing international law to the cyber domain, the GGE also proposed several candidate norms for responsible state conduct. While it presented these as "voluntary, non-binding norms of responsible State behaviour" and commended them as useful ways to "reduce risks to international peace, security and stability," many of the candidate norms are themselves closely related to the interpretations of existing international law promoted by the GGE. In framing the proposed candidate norms, the GGE gave a definition of norms that very closely approximates constructivist scholarship. It declared that "norms reflect the expectations of the international community, set standards for responsible State behaviour and allow the international community to assess the activities and intentions of States." The GGE also affirmed its own status as a norm entrepreneur, in claiming that "the task before the present Group was to continue to study, with a view to promoting common understandings, norms of responsible State behaviour, determine where existing norms may be formulated for application to the ICT environment, encourage great acceptance of norms and identify where additional norms that take into account the complexity and unique attributes of ICTs may need to be developed" (UNGA 2015b, A/70/174, 7). The GGE thus clearly understood its work as entailing a structured, rule-governed process of rule interpretation and application.

These norms include the obligation to cooperate in improving cybersecurity and in preventing harmful ICT practices capable of undermining international security. They also include a cautionary norm for state conduct in responding to cyberattacks. This candidate norm calls on states to "consider all relevant information, including the larger context of the event, the challenges of attribution

[4] See Nye (2011); Bradshaw, Shull, and Raymond (2015).

in the ICT environment and the nature and extent of the consequences" before engaging in self-help measures (UNGA 2015b, A/70/174, 7). This norm explicitly contemplates, and specifies appropriate procedures for, ongoing attempts to apply existing rules to novel cases. These procedures closely resemble the provisions of the Vienna Convention on the Law of Treaties pertaining to treaty interpretation. This demonstrates that the GGE, as state representatives, saw secondary rules and resulting practices of global rule-making and interpretation as essential to international security.

A number of the proposed norms can be grouped under the heading of requiring states to govern their own territories in a responsible manner—that is, to carry out their international duties qua states.[5] These norms include: the obligation of states to police their own territory and to ensure it is not employed to carry out attacks on other states; an obligation to consider effective practices for law enforcement cooperation; and an obligation to respect human rights in the digital realm. These norms also address the state's role in the ICT market. In this regard, they assign states the responsibility to try to ensure supply chain integrity in hardware and software and the obligation to encourage reporting of ICT vulnerabilities. Finally, the norms proposed by the GGE deal with state obligations to assist other states requesting assistance with ICT attacks, and with state obligations to refrain from interference with or exploitation of computer emergency response teams (CERTs). In this manner, the proposed norm confers a "first responder" status on these groups akin to the protections afforded to the Red Cross and other similar humanitarian groups (UNGA 2015b, A/70/174, 7–8). Like past GGE reports, the report also consolidated global progress on confidence-building and capacity-building measures pertinent to international security (UNGA 2015b, A/70/174, 9–12).

As in the 2013 GGE process, the United States, China, and Russia all refrained from making public submissions of their national views to the UN secretary-general. However, the United States opted to publish its private submission to the GGE process in a State Department legal digest. The position paper supports the view that the United States understood itself as engaged in an ongoing process of interpreting and applying international legal rules to particular cases. Writing about the 2013 GGE, the paper noted the consensus regarding the applicability of existing international law to the cyber domain, and reminded the participants that "the Experts also noted the need to further study *how* international law applies, and recommended that States should further consider how best to cooperate in implementing norms and principles of responsible behavior in the ICT environment" (de Guymon, ed. 2014, 733).

---

[5] On this area of international law, see the Montevideo Convention on the Rights and Duties of States (1933).

The American contribution to the 2015 GGE also addressed the procedural challenges inherent in applying existing international law to a fast-moving technological environment. It pointed out that this kind of challenge is "not unusual" and that "similar challenges have been confronted when applying existing international law to other new technologies and situations." As a result, it concluded that "this UNGGE need not reach consensus on exactly how existing principles of international law apply to all conceivable cyber situations." This argument amounted to a recognition of the problem of the incompleteness of rule systems (Sandholtz 2008)—that rule sets can never specify ex ante every possible future situation. Rather, "it would suffice to identify the basic legal principles that apply and then reach a consensus on some of the relevant considerations States should take into account when they confront real-world situations." It reminded GGE members that "we need not spell out how international law applies to all hypothetical scenarios" and that states "have not done so with respect to other types of operations, and in any case there will undoubtedly be situations that arise that we are unable to predict given the speed of change in ICTs." Adopting a framework for modalities of interpretation "will assist all States in meeting the challenge of applying, and abiding by, existing international law when real-world situations involving the use of ICTs present themselves (de Guymon, ed. 2014, 733–34). The submission thus recognized the existence of rules providing for the decentralized, ongoing practice of interpreting how international law applies in cyberspace, and indicated the American government's willingness to participate in such a practice alongside its fellow states.

The American submission focused on principles pertaining to the law of armed conflict and its application in the cyber domain. In doing so, it advanced claims about how to apply existing rules of international law, albeit claims rooted in American interpretations of those rules. It asserted that "cyber activities may in certain circumstances constitute uses of force within the meaning of Article 2(4) of the UN Charter and customary international law." Accordingly, it concluded that "a State's inherent right of self-defense . . . may in certain circumstances be triggered by cyber activities that amount to an actual or imminent armed attack." It asserted that "this inherent right of self-defense . . . applies whether the attacker is a State actor or a non-State actor." This claim was accompanied by interpretive guidance that emphasized considerations of the nature and extent of the attack (e.g., whether it caused injury or loss of life, or the physical destruction of property), the nature of the attacker, the nature of the target, "and the intent of the actor" (de Guymon, ed. 2014, 734).

The American submission also advanced the argument that states may, at least in some circumstances, use cyber means to respond to kinetic attacks and vice versa. This argument amounts to the normalization of cyber weapons as a military means under international law, in direct response to earlier Russian attempts to regulate or perhaps even prohibit them. In its accompanying interpretive guidance, the submission indicated that "a State facing an imminent or actual armed attack by a non-State actor in or through cyberspace generally must make a reasonable, good faith effort to seek the territorial State's consent before using force on its territory against the non-State actor to prevent or end the armed attack." It further suggested that "the requesting State should give the territorial State a reasonable opportunity to respond, recognizing that the reasonableness of a timeframe in a particular context may be determined in relation to the nature of the actual or imminent armed attack." Notwithstanding this general obligation to seek consent, the submission is clear in expressing the American view that "a State may act without consent . . . if the territorial State is unwilling or unable to stop or prevent the actual or imminent armed attack launched in or through cyberspace." However, if it does so, it "must take reasonable measures to ensure that its defensive actions are directed exclusively at the non-State actors when the territorial State is not also responsible for the armed attack" (de Guymon, ed. 2014, 735).

These arguments represent far-reaching interpretations of the applicability of the law of armed conflict to the cyber domain that potentially enable states to undertake cyberattacks in a wide range of circumstances. The wisdom of these interpretations, and whether they are genuinely consistent with American national interests given the potential of such a regime to destabilize the Internet, are beyond the scope of my analysis here. The key point is that the American government clearly engaged in a process of applying existing legal rules to a novel case. It did not do so in a random fashion, but rather in a way shaped by procedural rules governing how to legitimately interpret and apply international law. The section of the submission dealing with the application of retorsion and other non-forcible countermeasures (de Guymon, ed. 2014, 738–39) was clearly shaped, for example, by deep understanding of the customary international law pertaining to state responsibility. At the same time, it clearly exercised discretion and judgment in these interpretive activities, conducting them in a way designed to shape prevailing international interpretations of international law in a manner consistent with official perceptions of American values and interests. The segments of the submission dealing with sovereignty and jurisdiction, for example, noted that "the exercise of jurisdiction by the territorial State, however, is not unlimited; it must be consistent with applicable international law, including human rights obligations" that protect freedom of speech independent of the medium and without regard to national frontiers (de Guymon, ed. 2014, 737–38). Similarly, the submission's approach to *jus ad bellum* issues, discussed above, seems clearly intended to exploit continuing American military dominance in the cyber domain as a means to project force at low cost should the need arise. The key point is that just as these interpretations reflected official understandings of American interests, they were also both enabled and constrained by American understandings of the appropriate ways to interpret and apply existing international law.

Russian efforts in conjunction with China and other members of the Shanghai Cooperation Organization (SCO) also evince clear efforts to construct persuasive interpretations of how international law should be applied in the cyber domain. In this regard, the most notable development was the presentation of an updated version of the proposed International Code of Conduct for Information Security. Originally advanced in 2011, the code of conduct prioritized state sovereignty and appeared to give lip service to human rights obligations while emphasizing the rights of states to control dissemination of information within and across their borders (Ebert and Maurer 2013, 1067). These proposals were consistent with long-standing Russian efforts to create a multilateral cyber treaty. However, the shift from a formal treaty to a soft law code of conduct reflects an increasingly sophisticated understanding on the part of these governments about the increasing reliance of the contemporary system of global governance on a variety of soft law mechanisms,[6] as well as of the opportunities to assert sovereignty afforded by acceptance of the idea that international law applied to state use of ICTs. This evolving understanding of contemporary procedural rules pertaining to the use of soft law instruments is thus a contributing factor in the willingness of Russia and its like-minded states to accept the applicability of existing international law.

In January 2015, an updated version of the code of conduct was submitted to the General Assembly by the governments of China, Kazakhstan, Kyrgyzstan, Russia, Tajikistan, and Uzbekistan (UNGA 2015c, A/69/723). An analysis of the differences between the 2011 and 2015 versions conducted by Henry Rõigas found that the 2015 version had been altered with a view to broadening its international support. For example, a reference in the earlier version to an international norm against using "information weapons" had been dropped, presumably out of recognition that many states were concerned about the effect of this language on international human rights.[7] In another attempt to make the code of conduct palatable to states emphasizing online rights, the 2015 code of conduct explicitly endorsed the notion of parity for human rights regardless of medium. However, as Rõigas noted, the section also prominently included the

---

[6] See Abbott and Snidal (2000) on soft law; Büthe and Mattli (2011) on the role of private standard-setting; Betts and Orchard, eds. (2014) on norm implementation; Mattli and Dietz, eds. (2014) on arbitration; and Abbott, Genschel, Snidal, and Zangl, eds. (2015) on the role of international organizations as orchestrators.

[7] It is impossible on available data to rule on the possibility that it may also have been dropped in part in preparation for the use of such tools to interfere in Western elections.

exceptions to the right of freedom of expression enumerated in Article 19 of the International Covenant on Civil and Political Rights.

Beyond these efforts to make the code of conduct compliant with the letter (if not the spirit) of international human rights law, the updated version contained two notable changes. First, it added a norm calling on states to refrain from acting "to take advantage" of a "dominant position in the sphere of information technology." While Rõigas concluded that this language was intended to blunt Western dominance, it might also be read as an attempt to reassure developing states that China would act with restraint in exerting its own technological influence. Second, the updated version addressed institutional modalities for Internet governance. In this regard, it asserted that "all States must play the same role in, and carry equal responsibility for, international governance of the Internet" (Rõigas 2015). This phrase was likely intended to capitalize on support for multilateral institutions and suspicion of multistakeholder processes throughout much of the developing world that are based in part on these states' relatively greater familiarity with the (and acceptance of) the procedural rules of multilateralism than multistakeholderism, and also to further undermine the legitimacy of the contractual relationship between the US Department of Commerce and the Internet Corporation for Assigned Names and Numbers for oversight of the so-called IANA functions critical to the technical operation of the Internet.

Increased sophistication on the part of Russia and its like-minded allies indicates that, despite the apparent success of the American interpretation that existing international law applies to cyberspace and the shift in SCO strategy toward a soft law code of conduct (at least as an initial step), the process of interpreting and applying international law in the cyber domain will continue. Available procedural rules conditioned the choices of all of these states, including permanent Security Council members, about the nature of their proposals and the ways in which they presented them, but they have not yet fundamentally altered the identity or preferences of Russian or Chinese policymakers. They should not be expected to do so in the near future.

As in the 2013 GGE process, procedural rules for making, interpreting, and applying international rules also shaped the efforts of other states to evaluate the proposals advanced by leading states (UNGA 2014a, A/69/112; UNGA 2014b A/69/112/Add.1; UNGA 2015a, A/70/172). Several submissions are worth noting. Even prior to the first meeting of the 2015 GGE, Australia (which would not continue its participation in the GGE itself) provided a national submission indicating its recognition "That the elaboration of how international law applies to States' use of cyberspace is a long-term task" (UNGA 2014a, A/69/112, 3). Colombia, a first-time participant in the upcoming GGE, also provided an early national submission to the secretary-general, which noted its accession to the European Convention on Cybercrime and called for states to take action aimed at "bringing domestic legal frameworks into line with existing international instruments in the area of cyber security" (UNGA 2014a, A/69/112, 4), thereby displaying a sophisticated understanding of the need in many cases for norm implementation at the domestic level (Betts and Orchard 2014, 11). The Colombian submission also noted that it would be especially desirable to have "clear rules on jurisdiction and entitlement to prosecute" (UNGA 2014a, A/69/112, 7).

Cuba, like Iran, had been an early adopter of the idea that accepting the American position on the applicability of international law to cyberspace would enable it to make legal claims against the United States. That interpretation was likewise advanced clearly in its submissions to the secretary-general in 2014 and 2015. However, Cuba also incorporated references to declarations adopted by the Community of Latin American and Caribbean States (CELAC) emphasizing the applicability of the UN Charter and of international law more broadly (UNGA 2014a, A/69/112, 7–9; UNGA 2015a, A/70/172, 45). These claims demonstrate Cuban facility with the rule-governed practice of interpreting and applying international rules, as well as the increasingly broad global reach and persuasiveness of the work conducted by the GGE. Again, while Cuba clearly drew on procedural rules in attempts to pursue its interests as well as its values, the key point is that it did so with reference to what it determined were other relevant rules of international law, and thus in ways enabled and constrained by accepted procedures for interpreting and applying these rules.

France noted its efforts "to establish an international normative framework based on current international law, as well as confidence-building measures and specific standards of conduct in cyberspace" (UNGA 2014b, A/69/112/Add.1, 3–4). It thus signaled its acceptance of the American interpretation of the applicability of existing international law to cyberspace. The Republic of Korea, another first-time participant in the GGE, expressed its view that "agreeing on a set of international norms and confidence-building measures, building the capacity of developing countries and promoting cooperation among computer emergency response teams are key areas for international cooperation." Filed on 30 June 2014, prior to the initial meeting of the GGE, this declaration serves as another indication that a novice participant was prepared to engage in the work of the GGE, and understood both the substantive nature of its work as well as the relevant process for participating in a socially competent manner.

Spain's submissions to the secretary-general during the 2015 GGE process are especially noteworthy, as they illustrate the clearest evolution of a national position in response to the social practice of rule-making and interpretation. In its 2013 submission, discussed above, Spain had expressed interest in "multilateral cooperation agreements" and the creation of "a single authority to lay down rules and standards common to all countries" (UNGA 2013b, A/68/156, 8–9). In contrast, by 30 June 2014 (prior to the first meeting of the 2015 GGE), Spain had altered its position. While it made clear its view that "the United Nations has a very important role to play in building international consensus in this area" and its support for "the holding of institutional dialogue within the framework of the United Nations in order to guarantee peaceful and secure use of information technologies," the Spanish government now also indicated that it "supports the recommendations of the 2013 report of the United Nations Group of Governmental Experts" (UNGA 2014b, A/69/112/Add.1, 5). The submission omitted any reference to the creation of multilateral treaty instruments or to the creation of a global authority to make rules pertaining to cybersecurity. Its 2015 submission evinces further movement in the Spanish position. Specifically, Spain now committed to the notion that "States should continue reflecting on how the principles and norms of international law should be interpreted and applied in cyberspace; especially those relating to the threat or use of force, to humanitarian law and to the protection of the fundamental rights and freedoms of the individual" (UNGA 2015a, A/70/172, 13). This position is couched explicitly in terms of a decentralized, informal social process of interpreting and applying specific bodies of existing international law, in line with those enumerated by the GGE in its work.

Participation in a rule-governed process of deliberation about how to interpret and apply existing rules of international law to state military use of ICTs thus coincides with a clear change in the Spanish position on the applicability of existing international law. That position converged with those of other states participating in the 2015 GGE. While available evidence does not permit strong causal claims about the effect of procedural rules relative to other factors in explaining the change in Spain's position, it is notable that there was no identifiable change over this same period in Spain's broader Internet policy, and thus no reason to expect Spanish interests explain the change of position. It is also notable that the Spanish position converged with those of the other GGE participants—despite the continued existence of varying preferences among those states on a range of crucial questions pertaining to Internet governance, digital human rights, and cybersecurity.

National submissions to the secretary-general pertaining to the 2015 GGE were not unanimous in their endorsement of the American approach. The Qatari submission, in particular, was clear in its preference for the multilateral approach. The 24 June 2015 submission indicated that "the State of Qatar believes that information security is crucial for national and global security." It thus endorsed the SCO terminology explicitly meant to communicate a concern with societal and regime stability. It further noted that "the State of Qatar believes that the international community can contribute to information security by continuing to work towards a binding international instrument to safeguard information security" (UNGA 2015a, A/70/172, 11–12). Furthermore, none of the states presenting the updated version of the code of conduct for information security provided national submissions to the secretary-general. Though Russia and China endorsed the consensus report of the 2015 GGE, they opted not to provide further interpretive clarification, at least through this mechanism, on their formal positions. Their modification of the proposed international code of conduct indicates growing familiarity with soft law mechanisms for making and applying international rules but does not likely signal a shift in their underlying preferences for cyber governance modalities.

Conclusion

Participants in the work of the First Committee and the GGE shared understandings about the nature of their common efforts. In particular, they understood themselves to be engaged in a common rule-making effort that required the interpretation and application of general rules in the context not only of particular cases but also of adjacent rule sets, such as the law of armed conflict and the law of state responsibility, as well as human rights law. Procedural rules shaped the proposals and the evaluative acts of all the participants in the work of the First Committee and the GGE. These rules, for example, shaped the terms in which the United States presented its opposition to the initial Russian proposal for a multilateral treaty. Rather than offering an outright rejection of the idea in order to preserve a then-dominant military position in the cyber domain, the United States claimed that existing international law applied—not only constraining its military use of ICTs, but also creating an opportunity for authoritarian states to avail themselves of legal protections afforded by sovereignty.[8] Procedural rules also shaped the American national submission to the 2015 GGE, which explicitly presented the GGE's work in terms of rule application, and which also engaged in detailed interpretive discussion of various bodies of international law and their application to the cyber domain.

Similarly, procedural rules shaped Russian actions. The initial Russian decision to pursue the question of information security via the First Committee of the General Assembly itself reflected a core degree of procedural competence. This competence is no doubt partially responsible for the initial success enjoyed by the resolution; it was regarded as procedurally competent by other states in that it was presented in a legitimate forum for discussion of these issues and in

---

[8] The American position therefore led in an indirect and unintended manner toward what Demchak and Dombrowski (2011) have provocatively termed a cyber Westphalia.

a manner consistent with past practice in handling new technologies with potentially disruptive effects on international security. However, in response to the interpretations of other states, Russia also showed the ability to update its procedural knowledge and substantive proposals. After gaining experience and comfort with soft law instruments, and realizing the potential advantages to be found in sovereignty claims over the cyber domain, Russia (joined by China and other states) shifted toward pursuit of an international code of conduct rather than—or at least as prelude to—a multilateral treaty. They further updated this proposed code of conduct in 2015 in an attempt to address the interpretive objections lodged by other states about the implications of their positions for adjacent bodies of international law, especially human rights law. These choices demonstrate that even as Russia pursued its interests, it did so in ways shaped by procedural rules for making, interpreting, and applying global rules; it also demonstrated over time that it was responsive to the interpretive evaluations of its proposals made by other states.

It is also noteworthy that after the 2013 GGE report, there was almost no contestation of the idea that existing international law applies in cyberspace. Instead, states went to work determining which specific bodies of international law were relevant and the ways in which they applied to the cyber domain. This work continued in yet another iteration of the GGE during 2016 and 2017. Clearly, states still have different ideas about the appropriate way to apply international law to cyberspace; American negotiator Michele Markoff noted that the 2015 GGE fell short of what the United States had hoped to achieve because "more robust statements on how international law applies were contested by a few key States" (Markoff 2015), particularly with respect to the law of armed conflict. The 2017 iteration of the GGE concluded without agreeing on a consensus report, likely in large part due to revelations about Russian interference in elections and worsening geopolitical tensions. But, crucially, the lack of a 2017 report does not negatively affect the validity of the 2013 and 2015 reports, and no state has thus far rejected or disavowed the substance of their findings. Cyber norms processes should not be expected to generate consistent progress (Finnemore and Hollis 2016), and norm violations remain likely despite such processes—as in every other domain of human activity. Criticism of state use of ICTs by Russia, China, the United States, and other countries is widespread, and has been lodged by states, international organizations, firms, technical experts' groups, and civil society actors. These criticisms demonstrate that a range of actors clearly have a variety of expectations about appropriate state use of ICTs, and thus that the problem is certainly not the absence of norms, but rather disagreement about the content of applicable norms and how to interpret them in light of other valid rule sets and apply them to concrete cases.

The influence of procedural rules can also be identified in the national submissions made to the secretary-general. These submissions collectively demonstrate first that participating states had a baseline understanding of appropriate procedures. This is an important point, and one easily overlooked. Despite their considerable substantive differences on various areas of cyber policy, states (including Cuba and Iran) were not at all confused about the appropriate venue and most of the appropriate procedures via which to proceed.

Nevertheless, the national submissions establish significant variance among states in terms of their social competence in performing specialized tasks for interpreting and applying rules. The most procedurally competent proposals were generally made by large, wealthy states that tended to accept the applicability of existing international law, and that tended to oppose the creation of a multilateral cybersecurity treaty. In particular, this group of states is distinguished by its greater propensity to accept the legitimacy of soft law modalities for global governance. At least some states that gave procedurally less competent performances in early phases of the interpretive process also showed improvement over time, adopting substantive positions and procedural understandings consistent with those adopted by the most competent performers. While it is difficult to separate the relative effects of procedural rules from the effects of common interests and values in explaining these patterns, it seems reasonable to conclude (at minimum) that the procedural rules served as a focal point for reducing transaction costs—a long-accepted mechanism for explaining cooperation in IR theory (Keohane 1984; Oye 1986). Shared ideas about appropriate procedures do make reaching agreement easier; they condition the nature of the agreements that states reach, and states with greater procedural competence are more likely to realize their preferred outcomes in rule-making processes.

Most fundamentally, agreement among states on legitimate rules for making, interpreting, and applying rules can help to account for the emergence of an agreement that existing international law applies in the cyber domain at a time when relations between the United States and Russia were deteriorating, and when cyber issues had become more contentious at the global level. Surprisingly, agreement on legitimate rules and norms for state military use of ICTs was less controversial than parallel rule-making processes pertaining to Internet governance, which had previously been conducted in a technocratic and relatively apolitical manner. Part of the explanation for this difference seems to be relatively greater agreement among states in the First Committee on legitimate procedural rules, as compared with the diverse array of state and nonstate actors involved in legacy mechanisms for Internet governance that adhere at least nominally to a more inchoate model of multistakeholder governance (Raymond and DeNardis 2015).

Agreement that existing international law applied to state use of ICTs was almost certainly dependent in part on realizations by authoritarian states that sovereignty would provide an effective justification for valued domestic attempts to curtail access to information in the pursuit of regime stability. Such concerns were central to the initial Russian proposal for a multilateral treaty, and are reflected in national submissions by Cuba, Iran, Oman, Qatar, and other states that have been supportive of Russian proposals. However, these realizations were not exogenous to the practice of rule-making and interpretation ongoing in the First Committee, but rather in significant part emerged *from* that process. This outcome was not intended by the United States when it made the initial claim that existing international law obviated the need for a multilateral cyber arms control treaty. This highlights the indeterminate nature of practices of rule-making and interpretation, and the very real possibility of unintended effects.

While the most recent iteration of the GGE concluded without agreeing on a consensus report, there are tentative signs that the conclusion that international law applies to state use of ICTs has already begun to affect state conduct and discourse on cybersecurity. On 30 June 2017, researchers affiliated with the NATO Cooperative Cyber Defence Centre of Excellence (CCDCOE) indicated publicly that apparent Russian efforts to interfere in democratic elections and other cyberattacks targeting government computer systems "could count as a violation of sovereignty" in violation of the UN Charter. They further indicated that such efforts "could be an internationally wrongful act, which might give the targeted states several options to respond with countermeasures" (CCDCOE 2017). Although such analysis does not carry the full force of a statement by a government or an international organization in its official capacity, the nature of the CCDCOE as an organ of the Western military alliance makes the statement noteworthy. This is especially the case since the analysis offered clearly relies on the substantive interpretive positions endorsed by the GGE in its 2013 and 2015 reports regarding the applicability of the UN Charter and the customary international law of state responsibility. Even though the GGE reports have not prevented relevant behavior in clear violation of international law, they provide important resources to participants that are being actively employed both to continue engaging in practices of rule-making and interpretation, and to criticize rule violations by other actors.

Conclusion

In this book, I have examined four distinct and important cases of rule-making and interpretation on international security issues, spanning just over two hundred years. What united these cases, as well as many others, is that participants engaged—often quite deliberately and knowingly—in collective processes of making and interpreting rules about international politics. Participants in each case presented and evaluated proposals for making, interpreting, and applying rules. They did not do so randomly; rather, they acted on the basis of relatively clear (and generally shared) expectations about how they were legitimately entitled to perform such activities. These shared expectations can be understood as procedural rules for rule-making and interpretation, or secondary rules.

These procedural rules constitute and govern distinctive, contextually specific social practices of rule-making. In doing so, they provide actors with instruction manuals that explain how actors know how to attempt to change the rules of the game, and also how they know how to respond to such attempts made by others. Further, these procedural rules are vital to understanding the form, timing, and process of changes in the rules and institutions that structure international politics. Whether actors are pursuing their interests, their values, or both, they do so in a manner that reflects what they understand to be legitimate procedures for making, interpreting, and applying rules. This may be because they have internalized those rules as standards of appropriate behavior, or simply because they believe complying with such rules will make their arguments more persuasive to relevant audiences. Finally, to the extent that audiences employ procedural rules for rule-making to evaluate potential interpretations and applications of existing rules and new rule candidates, these procedural rules are important components of any satisfactory explanation of the success or failure of individual attempts to create or change rules. Since the institutions that structure the international system are composed of sets of rules and associated practices, social practices of rule-making and the procedural rules that constitute and govern them are essential, overlooked explanatory factors in the study of the dynamics and morphology of the international system.

In this concluding chapter, I review and discuss the empirical findings from the individual cases and assess them in light of the overarching theoretical argument advanced in the book. Next, I discuss the book's major contributions to the constructivist International Relations literature. Finally, I discuss the importance of social practices of rule-making for the study of global governance and the study of the international system and rule-based global order. Specifically, I argue that the existence of a class of social practices of rule-making that are centrally connected to the dynamics and morphology of the institutions that structure international systems means that processes of global governance are essential to the study of the international system. Connecting these largely disparate parts of the IR literature offers payoffs in terms of the contemporary study of the future of rule-based global order. Even more fundamentally, I argue that recognizing the effects of social practices of rule-making and associated global governance processes on the social structure of the international system lends support to the idea that the assumption of anarchy as the defining characteristic of the international system is fundamentally mistaken.

Empirical Findings

Throughout the cases, actors generally conformed with relevant procedural rules for rule-making, interpretation, and application even in cases where issues of international security were at stake. They also continued to utilize what they understood as legitimate processes of rule-making and interpretation even when they were aware that not all participants shared the same understandings about proper rule-making practices. Even clear novices were often able to give socially competent performances of these practices, as is particularly evident in the Kellogg-Briand case. These findings highlight the existence and robustness of social practices of rule-making across a considerable temporal span, in distinctive issue-areas relating to international security, and among a varied set of participants—not all of whom shared the same cultural background.

In the current international system, practices of rule-making and interpretation are relatively but not completely decentralized. States are often entitled to decide such questions on their own, but the book clearly shows that they are not entitled to judge completely as they choose. They are constrained by established practices and rules of diplomacy and international law. The book also shows, albeit mainly in passing, that these secondary rules in the international system have evolved over time. Perhaps the greatest single change in the two centuries covered here has been the increasing codification of these rules in international law, in instruments like the Vienna Conventions on Diplomatic Relations and on the Law of Treaties, as well as in the ILC Draft Articles on state responsibility. Associated diplomatic norms have tended to remain relatively more informal. In noting the partial formalization of these rules, the book confirms and extends the findings of IR literature dealing with the legalization of world politics (Abbott et al. 2000). In particular, it builds on and extends the work of constructivist scholars examining the nexus of international law and international relations (Onuf 1994; Finnemore and Toope 2001; Brunnée and Toope 2010; Diehl and Ku 2010). It does so by directing analytical attention to a specific corpus of what might be called procedural international law, and by arguing that these explicitly legal procedural rules are most productively understood in tandem with more informal diplomatic rules of procedure for making and interpreting rules.

These secondary rules will continue to evolve. One way in which they may be evolving is in according greater rights and powers to nonstate actors, at least in some domains. Evidence suggests that in some economic and technical domains, states have increasingly ceded authority to private actors (Strange 1996; Büthe and Mattli 2011). In other domains, states govern alongside various private and voluntary-sector actors in what has sometimes been called multistakeholder governance (Raymond and DeNardis 2015). These trends are important, and deserve further study, but they are somewhat outside the scope of this book, which looks at the ways procedural rules shape outcomes in the international system. The inclusion of nonstate actors in the management of the international system is also, at least thus far, less advanced in security cases than in other issue-specific domains.[1]

The findings in the cases collectively make clear that actors participate in social practices of rule-making with varying, and often mixed, motives.[2] However, even in cases where actors are purely strategic, rules (including secondary rules) are still analytically relevant (Müller 2004). The cases contain no shortage of examples where actors made strategic and self-serving use of procedural rules to try to secure a preferred outcome. In doing so, they often made use of the inherent indeterminacy and ambiguity in rule systems (Sandholtz 2008). Ironically, this kind of strategy may become easier as rule systems become more complex, as actors can appeal to multiple simultaneously valid rule sets. They can often do so in situations where there are no clear precedents or established patterns of interpretation. The cases also show clearly that actors were constrained by procedural rules, in some cases because they had internalized them and in others at least in part on consequentialist grounds. Actors sometimes ruled out beneficial options

---

[1] Though see Krahmann (2008) on the increasing commodification of security, and some potential implications of this trend.

[2] For a treatment showing how rule compliance can stem from various motives, see Hurd (1999).

on grounds of procedural inappropriateness, and even where actors sought to press procedurally dubious claims, secondary rules functioned as constraints by providing resources that other actors regularly employed as the basis for criticism and to reject these claims.

The cases also provide reasons to believe that secondary rules are more than simply tools or constraints. Especially where actors were aware of stark differences about legitimate procedures for rule-making and interpretation, they were prone to connecting these rules to highly valued referent objects, and to speaking about procedural matters in unusually emotional language. Such patterns suggest that procedural legitimacy is connected in actors' understandings to group identity and ontological security (Mitzen 2006; Steele 2008), and to fundamental issues of justice (Reus-Smit 1999; Welch 2014). This kind of dynamic is most clearly evident in the al-Qaeda case, but is also present in Metternich's invocation of illness and disease in referring to constitutionalist movements, which must be seen in context of a larger contest about ideology and regime type (Owen 2010) that also had implications for rule-making at the international level.

These varied, complex motives suggest that it is rarely possible in practice to attribute social behavior to a single logic, and that multiple behavioral logics can operate simultaneously. Additional research on mixed motives in world politics would therefore be a valuable next step in the IR literature on behavioral logics (March and Olsen 1998; Ruggie 1998; Hopf 2010; Adler and Pouliot 2011), advancing the discussion beyond alternatives to consequentialist accounts of actor choice.

The cases demonstrate that secondary rules, and the practices of rule-making they constitute, are vital to understanding the causal mechanisms and processes associated with both the reproduction and transformation of social institutions. In doing so, the book contributes to understanding change in international norms and rules, which has focused primarily on the substantive content of the norms or rules in question, or on their "fit" with existing substantive norms. Though both of these factors are relevant in explaining the success or failure of particular candidate rules, neither is sufficient, if only because both presume some process by which actors come to shared determinations about such questions. Building on existing constructivist work, this book therefore contributes by identifying an overlooked factor in explaining the success or failure of particular rules and norms, and shows empirically that these processes of collective rule determination and interpretation do in fact shape outcomes in the international system.

Skill with procedural rules and associated practices of rule-making and interpretation is therefore an important source of power. Metternich exploited his advantages in deploying these rules to outperform leaders of great powers that enjoyed significant military and economic advantages over the Austrian Empire. Both al-Qaeda and the Bush administration, in contrast, struggled to convince like-minded audiences with whom they shared broad views about legitimate practices of rule-making about the appropriateness of their respective preferences for alterations in the substantive rules of the international system. While the general point that rules are power-laden is well known in the constructivist literature (Onuf 1989; Barnett and Duvall 2005), the book contributes by showing empirically that the subset of procedural rules for processes of global rule-making is deserving of sustained analytical attention from IR scholars concerned with sources and forms of power in world politics.

Further, the cases show that procedural rules can—at least in some cases—play a sufficiently important causal role that they generate outcomes the principal actors involved did not envision or intend at the outset of collective rule-making and interpretation. This was most evident in the Kellogg-Briand case, where a French effort to engineer a bilateral treaty that would ensure the United States would not enter a European war against France was transformed into a near-universal multilateral agreement renouncing war except in cases of self-defense or collective security. Far from being a result of harmonious discussion, this outcome was instead the product of strategic efforts by both parties to employ procedural rules to force the other to accept responsibility for the failure of negotiations. While both sides experienced frustration with the process, these procedural rules also prevented either side from walking away. In less than two years, Kellogg and Briand came to embrace the treaty, which was ultimately accepted even by the Soviet Union.

Finally, the cases include multiple instances in which procedural rules provide compelling explanations for otherwise puzzling outcomes. For example, Talleyrand exploited procedural rules to induce the other great powers to readmit France to processes of great power management of the international system on a nominally equal footing very shortly after Napoleon's defeat, allowing it to play a prominent role in the European Concert intended in significant part to prevent a renewed French bid for hegemony. Secondary rules and associated practices of global rule-making also play an important role in explaining the 2013 agreement in the UN General Assembly's First Committee that existing international law applies to state military use of information technology. The timing of this agreement is especially noteworthy, given deteriorating diplomatic relations between Russia and NATO, and increasing political controversy over cybersecurity and Internet governance. State representatives engaged in an explicit process of collective rule-making and interpretation and opted by consensus against an initial Russian proposal for a multilateral treaty in favor of the American position that existing international law applies to state use of ICTs. Participants undoubtedly gave careful consideration to their interests, though it is doubtful they fully appreciated the implications of this interpretation at the time. Nevertheless, the deliberation clearly demonstrated agreement among the parties on relevant procedures and evaluative criteria, despite diversity in interests and values. While the agreement has not halted problematic state conduct in the cyber domain, it has provided new discursive options to criticize such conduct as states continue to engage in rule-making on cyber issues both at the UN and in other venues.

Taken together, the cases provide strong support for the book's central claims about the existence of social practices of rule-making, and about the role of procedural rules about rule-making in constituting and governing those practices. Such rules and practices are never determinative of outcomes; however, they are clearly relevant even where some actors disregard or break the rules, and even where actors disagree about relevant secondary rules. It is especially noteworthy that secondary rules and social practices of rule-making are able in at least some cases to provide explanations of otherwise puzzling, and even clearly unintended, outcomes. Such outcomes show that these rules are more than simple constraints, and that they play important enabling or empowering functions; and also that they are not simply reducible to tools or power resources that actors use to accomplish their goals, but that they can also have generative properties. Having identified the most important patterns and themes that emerge from the empirical cases examined in the book, I next discuss the book's contributions to the constructivist IR literature before outlining its broader implications for the study of the international system.

Contributions to the Constructivist Literature

The proliferation of mechanisms and processes associated with the social construction of intersubjective knowledge in the constructivist literature reflects the period of theoretical innovation associated with the emergence of a major alternative to rationalist approaches to the study of world politics, as well as the diversity of influences and traditions that inform the broad family of constructivist work. This innovative, diverse character is a substantial strength of the constructivist IR literature; but the large number of mechanisms may also hinder the development of the constructivist research program if left unaddressed. It may fragment constructivists, for example into conventional versus critical groups; or into rule-oriented, linguistic, and practice-turn camps. Short of that kind of unfortunate (and hopefully unlikely) constructivist civil war, continued uncertainty about the relationships between strategic social construction, socialization, persuasion, norm localization, and other similar concepts may result in missed opportunities to compare, contrast, and aggregate findings. It is impossible to tell in advance what may come from any such effort, but my sense is that the effort is very much worth making.

To date, I am unaware of any such systematic effort, and it is not a project I undertake here. Such an effort would ideally be collaborative, involving a diverse group of scholars representing the variety of constructivist traditions and approaches. It also should not seek to fully synthesize all of these various mechanisms, or to engage in explicitly exclusionary boundary-setting. However, I am convinced that the central argument advanced in this book points toward one potentially fruitful path in thinking about this problem.

The book shows that actors know how and when to engage in particular ways of making and interpreting rules (and, more broadly, of creating or transforming intersubjective agreements) because there are procedural rules for how to do so in specific social settings. To be clear, it does not necessarily follow that this is true for all of the mechanisms identified for the social construction of all kinds of intersubjective knowledge. For example, some learning may occur via processes of emulation that do not rely on rules in any immediately obvious way. Similarly, it is also possible that some socialization, employing back-patting and opprobrium (Johnston 2001), does not rely even on informal rules about how or when to include or exclude a potential in-group member. However, at least in the contemporary international system this seems unlikely. Stigmatization is deliberately practiced (Adler-Nissen 2014) and is typically employed as a response to persistent rule violators. Doing so requires a collective determination that the conduct in question violates valid rules, which is fundamentally a task of interpreting and applying rules. These processes manifest in sanctions resolutions passed by the UN and other international organizations, and in official speech acts such as declaring another state a "rogue state."

At least for many of the mechanisms proposed in the constructivist literature, my hunch is that there are relevant context-specific procedural rules that can help us determine how actors know how and when to engage in them, and that would be enormously useful in thinking more clearly about whether all of these mechanisms are truly distinctive, as well as about scope conditions and the potential to aggregate (or at least systematically compare) findings. My focus on social practices of rule-making as a distinct class governed and constituted by procedural rules therefore provides a basis both to synthesize and to differentiate among the causal mechanisms identified in the constructivist literature on an empirical basis.

The book also contributes to the constructivist literature by identifying an important complementarity between rule-oriented and practice-turn constructivism, and by extending the range of applications of practice-turn constructivism to rule-making itself. Rule-making is a highly consequential practice endemic to virtually every social setting of any scale, but that has largely escaped explicit study in the context of the international system.

With respect to the relationship between rules and practices, the key point is that any practice, to exist as such, must have a basic set of procedural rules enabling certain actors to perform the practice by doing (or not doing) certain things. Without such shared understandings, there is no way for the practice to be mutually intelligible for the participants, or for them to judge the relevant social competence of various performances in a reasonably consistent manner. This is not to say that participants will always agree completely on the rules for the practice. Especially to the extent that these procedural rules for the practice are informal or unwritten, or the participants come from distinct cultural backgrounds with dissimilar versions of the practice, such disagreements are in fact quite likely. These disagreements are likely to be a source of conflict and may even destabilize the practice; but these are important questions that can only be asked if we start from the understanding that procedural rules play an important part in constituting, regulating, reproducing, and transforming social practices. Practice-turn constructivism has largely depended on the formulation of "background knowledge" to account for the existence and form of particular practices. The more concrete and specified formulation provided by procedural rules is helpful in that it focuses analytical attention on a key site where the most relevant background knowledge to answering such questions can be located.

The class of practices this book identifies is unusual in that it often involves a high degree of intentionality and reflexivity. Rule-making and interpretation are activities that actors typically do knowingly, and this tendency is evident in the cases. Given its emphasis on the everyday and habitual, the concept of practice might seem like a strange choice for this book. However, I believe the book offers two contributions to practice-turn constructivism with respect to the relationship between practice, habit, and conscious reflection.[3]

First, it shows that many of the procedural elements of rule-making in world politics remain relatively informal and have much in common with the routine and habitual dimensions of social practice. With the exceptions of the Vienna Conventions, parts of the UN Charter, and the procedural rules for international courts, the procedural components of international law remain relatively underdeveloped. The law of state responsibility, which deals extensively with the means of determining and responding to the existence of breaches of international legal obligations, has not been codified in treaty form. Efforts by the ILC to develop draft articles on this topic took several decades, and while they have been endorsed multiple times by the General Assembly, have thus far not been codified in treaty form. Similarly, the process and criteria for state recognition are outlined in the Montevideo Convention; but this artifact of the interwar period has only 16 parties out of more than 190 states in the contemporary

---

[3] I draw here on a recent article by Hopf (2017).

international system. Its influence emanates instead from the fact that it is widely regarded to express preexisting rules of customary international law. Further, the formalized rules of procedure in international law represent only a small portion of the knowledge needed to engage in the social practice of international legality (Brunnée and Toope 2010). The situation with respect to rules of diplomatic practice is even less formal, at least at the international level. To the extent these rules are formalized, they are expressed primarily in a decentralized fashion, in documents and training programs created and maintained by foreign ministries. Like procedural rules in international law, formalized diplomatic procedural rules are highly incomplete. Empirical studies (Pouliot 2016) have shown that even experienced diplomats take substantial amounts of time to learn the specific nuances of diplomacy in settings like NATO and the United Nations.

In the cases examined in this book, participants drew extensively on shared legal and diplomatic knowledge, or rules, about how to legitimately make, interpret, and apply rules. While some such rules were explicitly codified, many were not. Despite this, participants typically had little difficulty in determining appropriate procedural modalities, except in cases where they were operating with incompatible understandings of valid procedural rules. In such situations, actors often connected procedural disputes to issues of justice and standards of civilization. These patterns suggest that the procedural rules underlying social practices of rule-making are relatively stable and regarded as important by actors even in the absence of codification and formalization, and that even practices typically associated with high levels of conscious reflection in fact depend in important part on deeply internalized and routinized rules that have not been formally codified.

Second, the book contributes to more fully understanding the relationship between practices, reflection, and social change. In the first chapter, I argued that attention to procedural rules for rule-making builds on existing constructivist arguments about the role of the substantive content of a candidate rule and the "fit" of the candidate rule with other existing rules in explaining the success or failure of particular proposals for rule change. Ted Hopf has argued (2017) that practice-turn IR suggests a two-stage model of social change whereby practice leads to endogenous incremental change, except under certain scope conditions that make conscious, reflective change more likely. These scope conditions include exposure to difference and novelty, exposure to liminal cases, less socialized or institutionalized contexts, institutionalized difference or novelty, discursively resonant challenges to the status quo, the existence of intelligible or plausible alternatives to the status quo, and productive crises (Hopf 2017, 15). Hopf is undoubtedly correct that conscious, reflective change remains important even if we take the importance of routinized habit and practice seriously, and I do not take issue with his analysis of the way these various scope conditions can make actors more open to reconsidering taken-for-granted ways of doing things. However, I argue that the cases in this book demonstrate an additional pathway to social change enabled by a very particular kind of socialization and institutionalization that is not captured in Hopf's model. Hopf expects that conscious, reflective change is most likely when actors are in less institutionalized social contexts or when they are not fully socialized (2017, 11–12). My work, in contrast, shows that relatively conscious, reflective change has been institutionalized in the contemporary international system in the form of social practices of rule-making and interpretation. These social practices are, in effect, going on in tandem alongside the more incremental kinds of change that Hopf details in his model. The routinized and often taken-for-granted nature of the procedural rules constituting and governing these social practices of rule-making facilitates and enables actors to creatively formulate, interpret, apply, and evaluate existing and potential rules in much the same way that Hopf envisions.

One possibility is that this particular pathway, by which social practices of rule-making can lead to change in other institutions and practices, is a special case that applies only to relatively organized domains of human endeavor like politics. Even if this is the case, such fields of human social life are certainly important enough to warrant special attention. However, I think there are good reasons to expect that these social practices of rule-making are more endemic than that, and that they likely operate in tandem with more visible social practices in most social settings. This is because if, as Hopf suggests, actors are more likely to engage in conscious, reflective change in their social practices when they find themselves in unfamiliar settings or settings that involve marginal and liminal cases, they must do so in a collective manner. Without some kind of preexisting, mutually intelligible process for engaging in these kinds of exercises for rule-making, interpretation, and application, we are left with the puzzle that I noted earlier in the book. How do actors know *how* to collectively engage in such processes? The existence of a class of social practices of rule-making answers this question. Actors know how to engage in these processes because there are formal and informal rules that tell them how to do so, and because these rules collectively constitute and govern social practices of rule-making.

For these reasons, I believe that the argument advanced in this book makes an important contribution to the suite of constructivist tools for explaining and understanding social change, especially with respect to identifying, understanding, and explaining change in the rules and the institutions of the international system. Since the dynamics and morphology of the international system are issues of general interest to IR scholars, I conclude the book by detailing what I take to be the implications of my argument for the field more broadly.

Social Practices of Rule-Making, Global Governance, and the International System

Scholars of global governance have made important contributions to the study of International Relations, and to efforts to deal with a range of pressing global public policy challenges. These approaches have necessarily focused on studying global rules and institutions, as well as global deliberative and political processes. As such, global governance is inextricably bound up with the kinds of ongoing practices of making, interpreting, and applying rules that are the central concern of this book. The broad set of institutions, processes, and practices that comprise contemporary global governance do not simply provide means of addressing global challenges like biodiversity (Raustiala and Victor 2004), climate governance (Keohane and Victor 2011), energy (Colgan, Keohane, and Van de Graaf 2012), and Internet governance (Nye 2014; Raustiala 2016), as important as these challenges are. More broadly, this system of global governance provides the means for making, interpreting, and applying an increasingly dense, complex, and overlapping set of global rules. It should therefore be of central importance to debates about the study of the international system and of the rule-based global order. To date, however, the question of what the existence and nature of these practices means for the study of the international system more generally has been underexamined.

Recent efforts to evaluate the state of the art in global governance as a field of study have sought to historicize global governance (Weiss and Wilkinson 2014; Murphy 2014), to consolidate existing knowledge about it (Finnemore 2014), and to enumerate key themes and important questions (Weiss and Wilkinson 2014; Pegram and Acuto 2015; Paris 2015). In doing so, these interventions have advanced knowledge *about* global governance but have not dealt in depth with the ways that this literature can inform study of the international system and of International Relations more generally.

Similarly, scholars explicitly concerned with the study of the international system have often neglected the insights of constructivists, and of scholars of global governance. This literature tends to focus on great power transition in a straightforwardly realist manner (Brooks and Wohlforth 2015/16; Glaser 2015; Liff and Ikenberry 2014), treating the question of American versus Chinese global leadership as a question of military power and assuming that change in institutions will more or less automatically follow. To the extent that these literatures have been placed in conversation, recent scholarship has suggested that global governance scholars should accord more explanatory weight to considerations of material power and interest (Paris 2015).

The case studies in this book lead me to precisely the opposite conclusion. They show that robust practices of global rule-making and interpretation have been central to the evolution of the international system, including to the evolution of its core rules and institutions for governing security matters, for at least the last two centuries. A growing literature on historical international relations (among many others, see Watson 1992; Hobson and Sharman 2005; Keene 2007; Nexon 2009; Phillips 2010; Keene 2013; Phillips and Sharman 2015), including the history of global governance, demonstrates convincingly that rules and institutions for management of common problems among political communities are in fact much older. This extensive history of creating and using rules and institutions to manage politics among political communities suggests strongly, in turn, that historical analogues to contemporary practices of global rule-making can be found, and that these practices were structured by secondary rules. Accordingly, there seems to me to be no good reason to expect that these practices will cease to be vital parts of the operation of the international system in the near future. To the contrary, as the final case examined in the book demonstrates, states continue to employ collective practices of rule-making and interpretation to handle pressing problems of international security.

There is no guarantee, of course, that such efforts will be successful, or even that failures in collective rule-making will not become the catalysts for armed conflict. The point is simply that to overlook the importance of these processes is to overlook a fundamentally important part of the action in the international system, even if the concern is simply to understand contemporary great power politics. The stakes of great power competition are in significant part precisely the rules and institutions of the international system, and these rules and institutions are shaped primarily by practices of rule-making and interpretation rather than by military acquisitions and deployments. Both constructivists and scholars of global governance are better positioned to provide analysis of such dynamics than realists, since they acknowledge the importance of rules and institutions, and since they allow for endogenous effects of rule-making practices of the kind identified in this book.

Further, the disconnect between the study of global governance and the study of the international system risks blinding the field to other structural changes apart from those associated with great power competition. One important set of examples involves the emergence of private governance (Büthe and Mattli 2011) and multistakeholder governance (Raymond and DeNardis 2015). Both require changes in secondary rules that permit non-state actors such as firms and civil society groups to participate in social practices of rule-making at the global level. While the increasing importance of private actors, in particular, has been recognized for some time, this increased influence has more often been treated as a product of relative power and/or changing beliefs about the appropriate role of the state in relation to the market (Strange 1996). The argument I have advanced in this book suggests that these factors only partially capture the kinds of structural changes in the international system associated with the increasing acceptance of private and multistakeholder governance arrangements, and that fully explaining such changes and appreciating their nature and significance requires recognition of the role of the procedural rules that constitute and govern social practices of rule-making.

SOCIAL PRACTICES OF RULE-MAKING AND AUTHORITY IN THE INTERNATIONAL SYSTEM

More fundamentally, the argument advanced in this book suggests that the field's organizing assumption—that states coexist in an anarchic international system characterized by the absence of authority—is fundamentally mistaken. Discomfort with anarchy as an organizing assumption for IR theory is not new.[4] In addition, a rapidly increasing number of studies either question or reject the axiomatic status of anarchy as the singular organizing principle of the international system. This literature suggests, at minimum, that anarchy (typically expressed in institutional terms as emanating from sovereignty) exists alongside other institutions that also comprise parts of the structure of the international system (Reus-Smit 1999; Holsti 2004; Donnelly 2012). Some authors make stronger claims to the effect that the system has in fact been characterized by actual examples of hierarchy (Lake 2007; Hobson and Sharman 2005; Sharman 2013; Keene 2007; Keene 2013; Donnelly 2006; Pouliot 2016).

The literature on hierarchy in the international system generally treats authority as a property of an actor or of a relationship between actors. While I do not deny that it is sensible and appropriate to speak of authoritative actors and of authority relations, it is also true that this focus has tended to obscure the fact that both authoritative actors and authority relations acquire their authoritative status from (often unwritten) rules; and that rules can themselves be authority-bearing objects. When a rule is regarded as authoritative, it "takes on the quality of being authoritative over the actor." It follows from this that "the rule is then in some sense hierarchically superior to the actor, and partly determinative of the actor's behavior, by virtue of contributing to the actor's definition of its own interests" (Hurd 1999, 400). This point suggests that it is possible for authority to exist in the absence either of an authoritative actor or even of social relations of super- and subordination. Rules can empower (or, better, authorize) actors to perform certain tasks or to make particular decisions under specific circumstances. That is, they create "authority to"; traditional understandings of

---

[4] Early criticisms include Ruggie (1983), Onuf (1989), and Milner (1991).

authority in International Relations are limited to "authority over." While the distinction between "power over" and "power to" has been recognized (Barnett and Duvall 2005), the same has not been true for the concept of authority. Authorizing rules can instantiate hierarchical authority relations, but they can also distribute authority among several actors, a condition that Robert Dahl (1956, 1971) called polyarchy. Authoritative rules in the international system are ongoing accomplishments not only of the very social practices that they constitute and govern, but also of meta-practices of rule-making, interpretation, and application that unfold in tandem with these substantive practices.

There are several benefits to adopting this view of the relationship between rules and authority, and of the relationship between authoritative rules and social practices of rule-making. First, it provides leverage on how to determine actors' standards for what is authoritative. These determinations, like other determinations about rules, depend in important part on procedural rules for rule-making, interpretation, and application. Therefore, we should expect that relevant secondary rules will play a large role in determining the kinds of authoritative rules and institutions that actors create, and thus also the kinds of authoritative actors and authority relations evident in particular social settings.

Second, this approach to authority in the international system facilitates a nonexclusive understanding of authority relations that allows for the possibility that actors simultaneously accept multiple rule sets and institutions as authoritative. It thus paints a more complex and variegated picture of authority in social life. While this kind of complex web of authority relations has been portrayed as post-Westphalian and even neo-medieval (Ruggie 1993), the approach I take here suggests instead that overlapping, complex conditions of authority are endemic in social life. This position accords more easily with the empirical reality that even Westphalian states have owed obligations simultaneously to their citizens, to each other qua states (e.g., nonintervention), and to each other on the basis of more specific agreements. When these obligations clash, leaders are in the position of deciding how to reconcile conflicting authority claims. Further, it better accounts for post–Cold War efforts by a variety of nonstate actors to expand their role in global rule-making. They have done so in part by securing (still-contested) changes in secondary rules that authorize them to participate more fully and directly in global social practices of rule-making.

Fully detailing the implications of my argument about social practices of rule-making and the influence of procedural rules on international outcomes for understandings of authority in world politics and the viability of the anarchy assumption is beyond the scope of this book. My aim here is merely to introduce these claims, and to suggest that my argument builds on the hierarchy literature by showing that one valuable avenue in developing a post-anarchy understanding of the international system involves further investigation of secondary rules and associated practices of rule-making and interpretation. Such research should entail efforts to inventory collective practices of rule-making and interpretation across a variety of historical international systems, to compare the effects of different rule-making practices on the nature of the resulting rules and institutions (that is, on analogues to contemporary global governance), and on the incidence and severity of political violence, and other salient features of international systems. Further research should also investigate the origins and determinants of secondary rules themselves, which may be linked to broader cosmological worldviews (Allan 2018). Such research would deepen understanding of the contemporary international system and its origins, and would also place it in broader comparative context that will shed light on its potential future trajectories.

REFERENCES

Abbott, Kenneth W., Philipp Genschel, Duncan Snidal, and Bernhard Zangl, eds. *Orchestration: Global Governance through Intermediaries*. Cambridge: Cambridge University Press, 2015.

Abbott, Kenneth W., Jessica F. Green, and Robert O. Keohane. "Organizational Ecology and Institutional Change in Global Governance." *International Organization* 70, no. 2 (2016): 247–77.

Abbott, Kenneth W., Robert O. Keohane, Andrew Moravcsik, Anne-Marie Slaughter, and Duncan Snidal. "The Concept of Legalization." *International Organization* 54, no. 3 (2000): 401–19.

Abbott, Kenneth W., and Duncan Snidal. "Hard and Soft Law in International Governance." *International Organization* 54, no. 3 (2000): 421–56.

Abrahms, Max. "What Terrorists Really Want." *International Security* 32, no. 4 (2008): 78–105.

Acharya, Amitav. "How Ideas Spread: Whose Norms Matter? Norm Localization and Institutional Change in Asian Regionalism." *International Organization* 58, no. 2 (2004): 239–75.

Adler, Emanuel. "Seizing the Middle Ground: Constructivism in International Relations." *European Journal of International Relations* 3, no. 3 (1997): 319–63.

———. *Communitarian International Relations: The Epistemic Foundations of International Relations*. New York: Routledge, 2005.

Adler, Emanuel, and Patricia Greve. "When Security Community Meets Balance of Power: Overlapping Regional Mechanisms of Security Governance." *Review of International Studies* 35, no. S1 (2009): 59–84.

Adler, Emanuel, and Vincent Pouliot. "International Practices." *International Theory* 3, no. 1 (2011): 1–36.

Adler-Nissen, Rebecca. "Late Sovereign Diplomacy." *Hague Journal of Diplomacy* 4, no. 2 (2009): 121–41.

Adler-Nissen, Rebecca. "Stigma Management in International Relations: Transgressive Identities, Norms, and Order in International Society." *International Organization* 68, no. 1 (2014): 143–76.

Adler-Nissen, Rebecca, and Vincent Pouliot. "Power in Practice: Negotiating the International Intervention in Libya." *European Journal of International Relations* 20, no. 4 (2014): 889–911.

Albin, Cecilia. *Justice and Fairness in International Negotiation*. Cambridge: Cambridge University Press, 2001.

Albrecht-Carrié, Rene. *The Concert of Europe*. New York: Walker and Company, 1968.

———. *A Diplomatic History of Europe*. Rev. ed. New York: Harper & Row, 1973.

Allan, Bentley B. *Scientific Cosmology and International Orders*. Cambridge: Cambridge University Press, 2018.

Allison, Roy. "Russia and the Post-2014 International Legal Order: Revisionism and *Realpolitik*." *International Affairs* 93, no. 3 (2017): 519–43.

Banerjee, Sanjoy. "Rules, Agency, and International Structuration." *International Studies Review* 17, no. 2 (2015): 274–97.

Barnett, Michael, and Raymond Duvall. "Power in International Politics." *International Organization* 59, no. 1 (2005): 39–75.

Barnett, Michael N., and Martha Finnemore. "The Politics, Power, and Pathologies of International Organizations." *International Organization* 53, no. 4 (1999): 699–732.

———. *Rules for the World: International Organizations in World Politics*. Ithaca, NY: Cornell University Press, 2004.

Bartlett, C. J. *Castlereagh*. London: Macmillan, 1966.

Bernstein, Steven. "Legitimacy in Intergovernmental and Non-State Global Governance." *Review of International Political Economy* 18, no. 1 (2011): 17–51.

Betts, Alexander. "The Refugee Regime Complex." *Refugee Survey Quarterly* 29, no. 1 (2010): 12–37.

Betts, Alexander, and Phil Orchard, eds. *Implementation & World Politics*. Oxford: Oxford University Press, 2014.

Bially Mattern, Janice. *Ordering International Politics: Identity, Crisis, and Representational Force*. New York: Routledge, 2004.

Bially Mattern, Janice, and Ayşe Zarakol. "Hierarchies in World Politics." *International Organization* 70, no. 3 (2016): 623–54.

Bjola, Corneliu, and Markus Kornprobst. *Understanding International Diplomacy: Theory, Practice, and Ethics*. New York: Routledge, 2013.

Boyle, Francis Anthony. *Foundations of World Order: The Legalist Approach to International Relations, 1898–1922*. Durham, NC: Duke University Press, 1999.

Bradshaw, Samantha, Laura DeNardis, Fen Osler Hampson, Eric Jardine, and Mark Raymond. "The Emergence of Contention in Global Internet Governance." Global Commission on Internet Governance Paper Series, No. 17. Waterloo: Centre for International Governance Innovation, 2015.

Bradshaw, Samantha, Mark Raymond, and Aaron Shull. "Rulemaking for State Conduct in the Attribution of Cyber-Attacks." In *Mutual Security in the Asia Pacific: Roles for Australia, Canada, and South Korea*, edited by Kang Choi, Simon Palamar, and James Manicom, 125–43. Waterloo: Centre for International Governance Innovation, 2015.

Brooks, Stephen G., and William C. Wohlforth. "The Rise and Fall of the Great Powers in the Twenty-first Century: China's Rise and the Fate of America's Global Position." *International Security* 40, no. 3 (2015/16): 7–53.

Brunnée, Jutta, and Stephen J. Toope. *Legitimacy and Legality in International Law: An Interactional Account*. Cambridge: Cambridge University Press, 2010.

———. "Interactional International Law and the Practice of Legality." In *International Practices*, edited by Emanuel Adler and Vincent Pouliot, 108–35. Cambridge: Cambridge University Press, 2011.

Bukovansky, Mlada. *Legitimacy and Power Politics: The American and French Revolutions in International Political Culture*. Princeton, NJ: Princeton University Press, 2002.

Bull, Hedley. *The Anarchical Society: A Study of Order in World Politics*. 3rd ed. New York: Columbia University Press, 2002.

Bush, George W. "Address to the Nation." Speech given at Washington, DC, 20 September 2001. Accessed at www.presidentialrhetoric.com.

———. "Address before a Joint Session of the Congress on the State of the Union." Speech given at Washington, DC, 29 January 2002a. Accessed at www.gpoaccess.gov/sou/index.html.

———. "Commencement Address at the United States Military Academy at West Point." Speech given at West Point, NY, 1 June 2002b. Accessed at www.presidentialrhetoric.com.

———. "Address before a Joint Session of the Congress on the State of the Union." Speech given at Washington, DC, 28 January 2003. Accessed at www.gpoaccess.gov/sou/index.html.

Büthe, Tim, and Walter Mattli. *The New Global Rulers: The Privatization of Regulation in the World Economy*. Princeton: Princeton University Press, 2011.

Buzan, Barry, and George Lawson. *The Global Transformation: History, Modernity, and the Making of International Relations*. Cambridge: Cambridge University Press, 2015.

Byers, Michael. "Not Yet Havoc: Geopolitical Change and the International Rules on Military Force." *Review of International Studies* 31, no. 1 (2005): 51–70.

Byman, Daniel. "Understanding the Islamic State: A Review Essay." *International Security* 40, no. 4 (2016): 127–65.

Carr, Edward Hallett. *The Twenty Years' Crisis*. 3rd ed. New York: Palgrave, 2001.

Carr, Madeline. "Power Plays in Global Internet Governance." *Millennium: Journal of International Studies* 43, no. 2 (2015): 640–59.

Charney, Jonathan I. "The Use of Force against Terrorism and International Law." *American Journal of International Law* 95, no. 4 (2001): 835–39.

Charter of the United Nations (1945). Accessed at http://www.un.org/en/documents/charter/.

Checkel, Jeffrey T. "Why Comply? Social Learning and European Identity Change." *International Organization* 55, no. 3 (2001): 553–88.

Cohrs, Patrick O. *The Unfinished Peace after World War I: America, Britain, and the Stabilisation of Europe, 1919–1932*. Cambridge: Cambridge University Press, 2006.

Colgan, Jeff D., Robert O. Keohane, and Thijs Van de Graaf. "Punctuated Equilibrium in the Energy Regime Complex." *Review of International Organization* 7, no. 2 (2012): 117–43.

Cooperative Cyber Defence Centre of Excellence. "NotPetya and WannaCry Call for a Joint Response from International Community." *INCYDER News*, 30 June 2017. Accessed at https://ccdcoe.org/notpetya-and-wannacry-call-joint-response-international-community.html.

The Covenant of the League of Nations (1919). Accessed at http://avalon.law.yale.edu/20th_century/leagcov.asp.

Craig, Gordon A., and Alexander L. George. *Force and Statecraft: Diplomatic Problems of Our Time*. 3rd ed. Oxford: Oxford University Press, 1995.

Crawford, Neta C. *Argument and Change in World Politics: Ethics, Decolonization, and Humanitarian Intervention*. Cambridge: Cambridge University Press, 2002.

Cronin, Audrey Kurth. "Why Counterterrorism Won't Stop the Latest Jihadist Threat." *Foreign Affairs* 94, no. 2 (2015): 87–98.

Dahl, Robert A. *A Preface to Democratic Theory*. Chicago: University of Chicago Press, 1956.

———. *Polyarchy: Participation and Opposition* New Haven: Yale University Press, 1971.

de Bertier de Sauvigny, G. *Metternich and His Times*. Trans. Peter Ryde. London: Darton, Longman, and Todd, 1962.

de Guymon, CarrieLyn, ed. *Digest of United States Practice in International Law 2014*. Washington: Office of the Legal Adviser, United States Department of State, 2014. Accessed at https://www.state.gov/documents/organization/244504.pdf.

Demchak, Chris C., and Peter Dombrowski. "Rise of a Cybered Westphalian Age." *Strategic Studies Quarterly* 5, no. 1 (2011): 32–61.

DeNardis, Laura. *The Global War for Internet Governance*. New Haven: Yale University Press, 2014.

Derry, John W. *Castlereagh*. London: Allen Lane, 1976.

Diehl, David, and Charlotte Ku. *The Dynamics of International Law*. Cambridge: Cambridge University Press, 2010.

Diehl, David, Charlotte Ku, and Daniel Zamora. "The Dynamics of International Law: The Interaction of Normative and Operating Systems." *International Organization* 57, no. 1 (2003): 421–56.

Donnelly, Jack. "Sovereign Inequalities and Hierarchy in Anarchy: American Power and International Society." *European Journal of International Relations* 12, no. 2 (2006): 139–70.

———. "The Elements of the Structures of International Systems." *International Organization* 66, no. 4 (2012): 609–43.

Duffy, Gavan, and Brian Frederking. "Changing the Rules: A Speech Act Analysis of the End of the Cold War." *International Studies Quarterly* 53, no. 2 (2009): 325–47.

Dunn, David Hastings. "A Doctrine Worthy of the Name? George W. Bush and the Limits of Pre-Emption, Pre-Eminence, and Unilateralism." *Diplomacy and Statecraft* 17, no. 1 (2006): 1–29.

Dunne, Tim, Lene Hansen, and Colin Wight. "The End of International Relations Theory?" *European Journal of International Relations* 19, no. 3 (2013): 405–25.

Ebert, Hannes, and Tim Maurer. "Contested Cyberspace and Rising Powers." *Third World Quarterly* 34, no. 6 (2013): 1054–74.

Emon, Anver. "Techniques and Limits of Legal Reasoning in Shari'a Today." *Berkeley Journal of Middle Eastern and Islamic Law* 2, no. 1 (2009): 101–24.

Ferrell, Robert H. *Peace in Their Time: The Origins of the Kellogg-Briand Pact.* New Haven: Yale University Press, 1952.

Finnemore, Martha. "Fights about Rules: The Role of Efficacy and Power in Changing Multilateralism." *Review of International Studies* 31, S1 (2005): 187–206.

———. "Dynamics of Global Governance: Building on What We Know." *International Studies Quarterly* 58, no. 1 (2014): 221–24.

Finnemore, Martha, and Duncan B. Hollis. "Constructing Norms for Global Cybersecurity." *American Journal of International Law* 110, no. 3 (July 2016): 425–79.

Finnemore, Martha, and Kathryn Sikkink. "International Norm Dynamics and Political Change." *International Organization* 52, no. 4 (1998): 887–917.

———. "Taking Stock: The Constructivist Research Program in International Relations and Comparative Politics." *Annual Review of Political Science* 4, no. 3 (2001): 391–416.

Finnemore, Martha, and Stephen J. Toope. "Alternatives to 'Legalization': Richer Views of Law and Politics." *International Organization* 55, no. 3 (2001): 743–58.

Foreign Broadcast Information Service. "Compilation of Usama Bin Ladin Statements 1994–January 2004." Reston, VA: Foreign Broadcast Information Service, 2004. Accessed at https://fas.org/irp/world/para/ubl-fbis.pdf.

Franck, Thomas M. "Terrorism and the Right of Self-Defense." *American Journal of International Law* 95, no. 4 (2001): 839–43.

Gardner, Hall. "The Russian Annexation of Crimea: Regional and Global Ramifications." *European Politics and Society* 17, no. 4 (2016): 490–505.

Gelvin, James L. "Al-Qaeda and Anarchism: A Historian's Reply to Terrorology." *Terrorism and Political Violence* 20, no. 4 (2008): 563–81.

George, Alexander L., and Andrew Bennett. *Case Studies and Theory Development in the Social Sciences.* Cambridge, MA: MIT Press, 2005.

Gerges, Fawaz. *The Far Enemy: Why Jihad Went Global.* Cambridge: Cambridge University Press, 2005.

Gilpin, Robert G. *War and Change in World Politics.* Cambridge: Cambridge University Press, 1981.

Glaser, Charles L. "A U.S.-China Grand Bargain? The Hard Choice between Military Competition and Accommodation." *International Security* 39, no. 4 (2015): 49–90.

Gong, Gerrit W. *The Standard of Civilization in International Society.* London: Clarendon, 1984.

Gordon, Philip H. "The End of the Bush Revolution." *Foreign Affairs* 85, no. 4 (2006): 75–86.

Hart, H. L. A. *The Concept of Law.* Oxford: Clarendon Press, 1994.

Hashim, Ahmed S. "The Islamic State: From Al-Qaeda Affiliate to Caliphate." *Middle East Policy* 21, no. 4 (2014): 69–83.

Hathway, Oona A., and Scott J. Shapiro. *The Internationalists: How a Radical Plan to Outlaw War Remade the World.* New York: Simon and Schuster, 2017.

Hawkins, Darren G., David A. Lake, Daniel L. Nielsen, and Michael J. Tierney, eds. *Delegation and Agency in International Organizations.* Cambridge: Cambridge University Press, 2006.

Hayes, Jarrod. *Constructing National Security: U.S. Relations with India and China.* Cambridge: Cambridge University Press, 2013.

Helleiner, Eric. *The Status Quo Crisis: Global Financial Governance after the 2008 Meltdown.* Oxford: Oxford University Press, 2014.

Helleiner, Eric, and Stefano Pagliari. "The End of an Era in International Financial Regulation? A Postcrisis Research Agenda." *International Organization* 65, no. 1 (2011): 169–200.

Hill, Richard. "Dealing with Cyber Security Threats: International Cooperation, ITU, and WCIT," in *7th International Conference on Cyber Conflict: Architectures in Cyberspace*, edited by M. Maybaum, A.-M. Osula, and L. Lindstrom, 119–34. Tallinn, Estonia: NATO CCD COE Publications, 2015.

———. "Internet Governance, Multi-stakeholder Models, and the IANA Transition." *Journal of Cyber Policy* 1, no. 2 (2016): 176–97.

Hinde, Wendy. *Castlereagh*. London: Collins, 1981.

Hobson, John M., and J. C. Sharman. "The Enduring Place of Hierarchy in World Politics: Tracing the Social Logics of Hierarchy and Political Change." *European Journal of International Relations* 11, no. 1 (2005): 63–98.

Hoffman, Bruce. "The Global Terrorist Threat: Is Al-Qaeda on the Run or on the March?" *Middle East Policy* 14, no. 2 (2007): 44–58.

Holsti, Kalevi J. *Peace and War: Armed Conflicts and International Order 1648–1989*. Cambridge: Cambridge University Press, 1991.

———. *Taming the Sovereigns: Institutional Change in International Politics*. Cambridge: Cambridge University Press, 2004.

Hopf, Ted. "The Promise of Constructivism in International Relations Theory." *International Security* 23, no. 1 (1998): 171–200.

———. "The Logic of Habit in International Relations." *European Journal of International Relations* 16, no. 4 (2010): 539–61.

———. "Change in International Practices." *European Journal of International Relations*. OnlineFirst (2 August 2017). doi/10.1177/1354066117718041.

Hurd, Ian. "Legitimacy and Authority in International Politics." *International Organization* 53, no. 2 (1999): 379–408.

Ikenberry, G. John. *After Victory: Institutions, Strategic Restraint, and the Rebuilding of Order after Major Wars*. Princeton, NJ: Princeton University Press, 2001.

International Law Commission. "Draft Articles on Responsibility of States for Internationally Wrongful Acts, with Commentaries." 2001. Accessed at http://legal.un.org/ilc/texts/instruments/english/commentaries/9_6_2001.pdf.

Jacobson, Jon. *Locarno Diplomacy: Germany and the West, 1925–1929*. Princeton, NJ: Princeton University Press, 1972.

Jervis, Robert. "From Balance to Concert: A Study of International Security Cooperation." *World Politics* 38, no. 1 (1985): 58–79.

Johnson, Tana. *Organizational Progeny: Why Governments Are Losing Control over the Proliferating Structures of Global Governance*. Oxford: Oxford University Press, 2014.

Johnston, Alastair Iain. "Treating International Institutions as Social Environments." *International Studies Quarterly* 45, no. 4 (2001): 487–516.

Keck, Margaret E., and Kathryn Sikkink. *Activists beyond Borders*. Ithaca, NY: Cornell University Press, 1998.

Keene, Edward. "A Case Study of the Construction of International Hierarchy: British Treaty-Making against the Slave Trade in the Early Nineteenth Century." *International Organization* 61, no. 2 (2007): 311–39.

———. "International Hierarchy and the Origins of the Modern Practice of Intervention." *Review of International Studies* 39, no. 5 (2013): 1077–90.

Kellogg-Briand Pact (1928). Accessed at http://avalon.law.yale.edu/20th_century/kbpact.asp.

Kelsay, John. "Al-Qaida as a Muslim (Religio-Political) Movement: Remarks on James L. Gelvin's 'Al Qaeda and Anarchism: A Historian's Reply to Terrorology.'" *Terrorism and Political Violence* 20, no. 4 (2008): 601–5.

Keohane, Robert O. *After Hegemony*. Princeton, NJ: Princeton University Press, 1984.

———. "Multilateralism: An Agenda for Research." *International Journal* 45, no. 4 (1990): 731–64.

Keohane, Robert O., and David G. Victor. "The Regime Complex for Climate Change." *Perspectives on Politics* 9, no. 1 (2011): 7–23.

Kindred, Hugh M., Karin Mickelson, Rene Provost, Linda C. Reif, Ted L. McDorman, Armand L.C. deMestral, and Sharon A. Williams. *International Law: Chiefly as Interpreted and Applied in Canada.* 6th ed. Toronto: Emond Montgomery, 2000.

Kissinger, Henry A. *A World Restored: Metternich, Castlereagh, and the Problems of Peace, 1812–1822.* 2nd ed. London: Phoenix Press, 2000.

Kleiner, Jurgen. "The Taliban and Islam." *Diplomacy and Statecraft* 11, no. 1 (2000): 19–32.

Klotz, Audie. "Transnational Activism and Global Transformations: The Anti-Apartheid and Abolitionist Experiences." *European Journal of International Relations* 8, no. 1 (2002): 49–76.

Klotz, Audie, and Cecilia Lynch. *Strategies for Research in Constructivist International Relations.* Armonk, NY: M. E. Sharpe, 2007.

Koh, Harold Hongju. "The Spirit of the Laws." *Harvard International Law Journal* 43, no. 1 (2002): 23–39.

Koremenos, Barbara, Charles Lipson, and Duncan Snidal. "The Rational Design of International Institutions." *International Organization* 55, no. 4 (2001): 761–99.

Krahmann, Elke. "Security: Collective Good or Commodity?" *European Journal of International Relations* 14, no. 3 (2008): 379–404.

Krasner, Stephen D. "Structural Causes and Regime Consequences: Regimes as Intervening Variables." *International Organization* 36, no. 2 (1982): 185–205.

Kratochwil, Friedrich V. *Rules, Norms, and Decisions: On the Conditions of Practical and Legal Reasoning in International Relations and Domestic Affairs.* Cambridge: Cambridge University Press, 1989.

———. "Making Sense of 'International Practices.'" In *International Practices*, edited by Emanuel Adler and Vincent Pouliot, 36–60. Cambridge: Cambridge University Press, 2011.

Krebs, Ronald R. *Narrative and the Making of US National Security.* Cambridge: Cambridge University Press, 2015.

Krebs, Ronald R., and Patrick Thaddeus Jackson. "Twisting Tongues and Twisting Arms: The Power of Political Rhetoric." *European Journal of International Relations* 13, no. 1 (2007): 35–66.

Kustermans, Jorg. "Parsing the Practice Turn: Practice, Practical Knowledge, Practices." *Millennium: Journal of International Studies* 44, no. 2 (2016): 175–96.

Kydd, Andrew H., and Barbara F. Walter. "The Strategies of Terrorism." *International Security* 31, no. 1 (2006): 49–79.

Lafeber, Walter. "The Bush Doctrine." *Diplomatic History* 26, no. 4 (2002): 543–58.

Lake, David A. "Escape from the State of Nature: Authority and Hierarchy in World Politics." *International Security* 32, no. 1 (2007): 47–79.

Lebow, Richard Ned. *A Cultural Theory of International Relations.* Cambridge: Cambridge University Press, 2008.

Levine, Daniel J., and Alexander D. Barder. "The Closing of the American Mind: 'American School' International Relations and the State of Grand Theory." *European Journal of International Relations* 20, no. 4 (2014): 863–88.

Levy, Reuben. *The Social Structure of Islam.* Cambridge: Cambridge University Press, 1962.

Lia, Brynjar. "Doctrines for Jihadi Terrorist Training." *Terrorism and Political Violence* 20, no. 4 (2008): 518–42.

Liff, Adam P., and G. John Ikenberry. "Racing toward Tragedy? China's Rise, Military Competition in the Asia Pacific, and the Security Dilemma." *International Security* 39, no. 2 (2014): 52–91.

MacMillan, Margaret. *Paris 1919: Six Months That Changed the World.* New York: Random House, 2003.

Maley, William. "The Foreign Policy of the Taliban." New York: Council on Foreign Relations, 2000.

March, James G., and Johan P. Olsen. "The Institutional Dynamics of International Political Orders." *International Organization* 54, no. 4 (1998): 943–69.

Markoff, Michele. "Advancing Norms of Responsible State Behavior in Cyberspace." United States Department of State blog, 9 July 2015. Accessed at https://votesmart.org/

public-statement/992662/blog-advancing-norms-of-responsible-state-behavior-in-cyberspace#.WWU3cYjyuUk.

Martin, Lisa L., and Beth A. Simmons. "Theories and Empirical Studies of International Institutions." *International Organization* 52, no. 4 (1998): 729–57.

Mattli, Walter, and Thomas Dietz, eds. *International Arbitration and Global Governance: Contending Theories and Evidence.* New York: Oxford University Press, 2014.

Maurer, Tim. "Cyber Norm Emergence at the United Nations: An Analysis of the UN's Activities Regarding Cyber-security." Discussion Paper 2011-11. Cambridge, MA: Belfer Center for Science and International Affairs, Harvard Kennedy School, 2011.

McCourt, David M. "Practice Theory and Relationalism as the New Constructivism." *International Studies Quarterly* 60, no. 3 (2016): 475–85.

Mearsheimer, John J. "The False Promise of International Institutions." *International Security* 19, no. 3 (1994/95): 5–49.

———. *The Tragedy of Great Power Politics.* New York: W. W. Norton, 2001.

Mearsheimer, John J., and Stephen M. Walt. "Leaving Theory Behind: Why Simplistic Hypothesis Testing Is Bad for International Relations." *European Journal of International Relations* 19, no. 3 (2013): 427–57.

Mendelsohn, Barak. "Sovereignty under Attack: The International Society Meets the Al Qaeda Network." *Review of International Studies* 31, no. 1 (2005): 45–68.

Metternich, Richard, ed. *Memoirs of Prince Metternich.* Translated by A. Napier. Vol. 3. New York: Howard Fertig, 1970.

Miller, David Hunter. *The Peace Pact of Paris: A Study of the Briand-Kellogg Treaty.* New York: Knickerbocker Press, 1928.

Milner, Helen V. "The Assumption of Anarchy in International Relations Theory: A Critique." *Review of International Studies* 17, no. 1 (1991): 67–85.

Mitzen, Jennifer. "Ontological Security in World Politics: State Identity and the Security Dilemma." *European Journal of International Relations* 12, no. 3 (2006): 341–70.

———. *Power in Concert: The Nineteenth-Century Origins of Global Governance.* Chicago: University of Chicago Press, 2013.

Moghadam, Assaf. "Motives for Martyrdom: Al-Qaida, Salafi Jihad, and the Spread of Suicide Attacks." *International Security* 33, no. 3 (2008/09): 46–78.

Morgan, Patrick M. "The Practice of Deterrence." In *International Practices,* edited by Emanuel Adler and Vincent Pouliot, 139–73. Cambridge: Cambridge University Press, 2011.

Müller, Harald. "Arguing, Bargaining, and All That: Communicative Action, Rationalist Theory, and the Logic of Appropriateness in International Relations." *European Journal of International Relations* 10, no. 3 (2004): 395–435.

Murphy, Craig N. "Global Governance over the Long Haul." *International Studies Quarterly* 58, no. 1 (2014): 216–18.

Navari, Cornelia. "The Concept of Practice in the English School." *European Journal of International Relations* 17, no. 4 (2011): 611–30.

Neumann, Iver B. "Returning Practice to the Linguistic Turn: The Case of Diplomacy." *Millennium: Journal of International Studies* 31, no. 3 (2002): 627–51.

———. "Euro-centric Diplomacy: Challenging but Manageable." *European Journal of International Relations* 18, no. 2 (2012): 299–321.

Nexon, Daniel H. *The Struggle for Power in Early Modern Europe: Religious Conflict, Dynastic Empires, and International Change.* Princeton, NJ: Princeton University Press, 2009.

Nicolson, Sir Harold George. *The Congress of Vienna: A Study in Allied Unity, 1812–1822.* London: Constable & Co., 1946.

Nissel, Tzvika Alan. "A History of State Responsibility: The Struggle for International Standards (1870–1960)." Ph.D. dissertation, University of Helsinki, 2016.

Nye, Joseph S., Jr. "Nuclear Lessons for Cyber Security?" *Strategic Studies Quarterly* 5, no. 4 (2011): 18–38.

Nye, Joseph S., Jr. "The Regime Complex for Managing Global Cyber Activities." Global Commission on Internet Governance Paper Series, No. 1. Waterloo: Centre for International Governance Innovation, 2014.

O'Mahoney, Joseph. "Rule Tensions and the Dynamics of Institutional Change: From 'to the Victor Go the Spoils' to the Stimson Doctrine." *European Journal of International Relations* 20, no. 3 (2014): 834–57.

Onuf, Nicholas Greenwood. *World of Our Making: Rules and Rule in International Relations.* Columbia: University of South Carolina Press, 1989.

———. "The Constitution of International Society." *European Journal of International Law* 5, no. 1 (1994): 1–19.

———. *Making Sense, Making Worlds: Constructivism in Social Theory and International Relations.* New York: Routledge, 2013.

———. "Constructivism at the Crossroads; or, the Problem of Moderate-Sized Dry Goods." *International Political Sociology* 10, no. 2 (2016): 115–32.

Orbach, Benjamin. "Usama Bin Ladin and Al-Qa'ida: Origins and Doctrines." *Middle East Review of International Affairs* 5, no. 4 (2001): 54–68.

Orsini, Amandine, Jean-Frédéric Morin, and Oran Young. "Regime Complexes: A Buzz, a Boom, or a Boost for Global Governance?" *Global Governance* 19, no. 1 (2013): 27–39.

Ostrom, Elinor. "A Long Polycentric Journey." *Annual Review of Political Science* 13 (2010): 1–23.

Owen, John M. *The Clash of Ideas in World Politics: Transnational Networks, States, and Regime Change, 1510–2010.* Princeton, NJ: Princeton University Press, 2010.

Oye, Kenneth A. *Cooperation under Anarchy.* Princeton, NJ: Princeton University Press, 1986.

Panke, Diana, and Ulrich Petersohn. "Why International Norms Disappear Sometimes." *European Journal of International Relations* 18, no. 4 (2012): 719–42.

Paris, Roland. "Global Governance and Power Politics: Back to Basics." *Ethics & International Affairs* 29, no. 4 (2015): 407–18.

Payne, Roger A. "Persuasion, Frames, and Norm Construction." *European Journal of International Relations* 7, no. 1 (2001): 37–61.

Pegram, Tom, and Michele Acuto. "Introduction: Global Governance in the Interregnum." *Millennium: Journal of International Studies* 43, no. 2 (2015): 584–97.

Phillips, Andrew. "The Protestant Ethic and the Spirit of Jihadism: Transnational Religious Insurgencies and the Transformation of International Orders." *Review of International Studies* 36, no. 2 (2010): 257–80.

———. *War, Religion, and Empire: The Transformation of International Orders.* Cambridge: Cambridge University Press, 2011.

Phillips, Andrew, and J. C. Sharman. *International Order in Diversity: War, Trade, and Rule in the Indian Ocean.* Cambridge: Cambridge University Press, 2015.

Pouliot, Vincent. "'Sobjectivism': Toward a Constructivist Methodology." *International Studies Quarterly* 51, no. 2 (2007): 359–84.

———. *International Security in Practice: The Politics of NATO-Russia Diplomacy.* Cambridge: Cambridge University Press, 2010.

———. "Hierarchy in Practice: Multilateral Diplomacy and the Governance of International Security." *European Journal of International Security* 1, no. 1 (2016): 5–26.

Pouliot, Vincent, and Jérémie Cornut. "Practice Theory and the Study of Diplomacy: A Research Agenda." *Cooperation and Conflict* 50, no. 3 (2015): 297–315.

Powell, Robert. "Bargaining Theory and International Conflict." *Annual Review of Political Science* 5 (2002): 1–30.

Putnam, Robert D. "Diplomacy and Domestic Politics: The Logic of Two-Level Games." *International Organization* 42, no. 3 (1988): 427–60.

Ralph, Jason. "The Laws of War and the State of the American Exception." *Review of International Studies* 35, no. 3 (2009): 631–49.

Rappard, William E. *The Quest for Peace since the World War.* Cambridge, MA: Harvard University Press, 1940.

Rashid, Ahmed. *Taliban: Militant Islam, Oil, and Fundamentalism in Central Asia*. New Haven: Yale University Press, 2001.

Raustiala, Kal. "Governing the Internet." *American Journal of International Law* 110, no. 3 (2016): 491–503.

Raustiala, Kal, and David G. Victor. "The Regime Complex for Plant Genetic Resources." *International Organization* 58, no. 2 (2004): 277–309.

Raymond, Mark. "Renovating the Procedural Architecture of International Law." *Canadian Foreign Policy Journal* 19, no. 3 (2013): 268–87.

Raymond, Mark, and Laura DeNardis. "Multistakeholderism: Anatomy of an Inchoate Global Institution." *International Theory* 7, no. 3 (2015): 572–616.

Reiter, Dan. "Exploring the Bargaining Model of War." *Perspectives on Politics* 1, no. 1 (2003): 27–43.

Reus-Smit, Christian. *The Moral Purpose of the State: Culture, Social Identity, and Institutional Rationality in International Relations*. Princeton, NJ: Princeton University Press, 1999.

Ricks, Thomas E. *Fiasco: The American Military Adventure in Iraq*. New York: Penguin, 2006.

Ripsman, Norrin M. "Domestic Practices and Balancing: Integrating Practice into Neoclassical Realism." In *International Practices*, edited by Emanuel Adler and Vincent Pouliot, 200–28. Cambridge: Cambridge University Press, 2011.

Risse, Thomas. "'Let's Argue!': Communicative Action in World Politics." *International Organization* 54, no. 1 (2000): 1–39.

Rõigas, Henry. "An Updated Draft of the Code of Conduct Distributed in the United Nations— What's New?" *INCYDER News*, 10 February 2015. Accessed at https://ccdcoe.org/updated-draft-code-conduct-distributed-united-nations-whats-new.html.

Ruggie, John Gerard. "International Regimes, Transactions, and Change: Embedded Liberalism in the Postwar Economic Order." *International Organization* 36, no. 2 (1982): 379–415.

———. "Continuity and Transformation in the World Polity: Toward a Neorealist Synthesis." *World Politics* 35, no. 2 (1983): 261–85.

———. "Multilateralism: The Anatomy of an Institution." *International Organization* 46, no. 3 (1992): 561–98.

———. "Territoriality and Beyond: Problematizing Modernity in International Relations." *International Organization* 47, no. 1 (1993): 139–74.

———. "Political Structure and Dynamic Density." In *Constructing the World Polity: Essays on International Institutionalization*, 137–54. New York: Routledge, 1998.

———. "What Makes the World Hang Together? Neo-Utilitarianism and the Social Constructivist Challenge." Introduction to *Constructing the World Polity: Essays on International Institutionalization*, 85–101. New York: Routledge, 1998.

Ruggie, John Gerard, and Friedrich V. Kratochwil. "Epistemology, Ontology, and the Study of International Regimes." In *Constructing the World Polity: Essays on International Institutionalization*. New York: Routledge, 1998.

Sandholtz, Wayne. "Dynamics of International Norm Change: Rules against Wartime Plunder." *European Journal of International Relations* 14, no. 1 (2008): 101–31.

Schroeder, Paul W. *The Transformation of European Politics, 1763–1848*. Oxford: Oxford University Press, 1994.

Sharman, J. C. "International Hierarchies and Contemporary Imperial Governance: A Tale of Three Kingdoms." *European Journal of International Relations* 19, no. 2 (2013): 189–207.

Sharp, Paul. "Mullah Zaeef and Taliban Diplomacy: An English School Approach." *Review of International Studies* 29, no. 4 (2003): 481–98.

———. *Diplomatic Theory of International Relations*. Cambridge: Cambridge University Press, 2009.

Smith, Alastair, and Allan C. Stam. "Bargaining and the Nature of War." *Journal of Conflict Resolution* 48, no. 6 (2004): 783–813.

Spruyt, Hendrik. *The Sovereign State and Its Competitors*. Princeton, NJ: Princeton University Press, 1994.

Statute of the International Court of Justice (1945). Accessed at http://www.icj-cij.org/documents/index.php?p1=4&p2=2&p3=0.

Steele, Brent J. *Ontological Security in International Relations: Self-Identity and the IR State.* New York: Routledge, 2008.

Stimson, Henry L. "The Nuremberg Trial: Landmark in Law." *Foreign Affairs* 25, no. 2 (1947): 179–89.

Strange, Susan. *The Retreat of the State: The Diffusion of Power in the World Economy.* Cambridge: Cambridge University Press, 1996.

Suzuki, Shogo. *Civilization and Empire: China and Japan's Encounter with European International Society.* New York: Routledge, 2009.

Tikk-Ringas, Eneken. "Developments in the Field of Information and Telecommunication in the Context of International Security: Work of the UN First Committee 1998–2012. Geneva: ICT4Peace Publishing, 2012.

Torres, Manuel R., Javier Jordan, and Nicola Horsburgh. "Analysis and Evolution of the Global Jihadist Movement Propaganda." *Terrorism and Political Violence* 18, no. 3 (2006): 399–421.

Treaty of Mutual Guarantee between Germany, Belgium, France, Great Britain, and Italy (1925). Accessed at http://avalon.law.yale.edu/20th_century/locarno_001.asp.

United Nations General Assembly. "Developments in the Field of Information and Telecommunications in the Context of International Security: Report of the Secretary-General." A/54/213. 10 August 1999.

———. "Developments in the Field of Information and Telecommunications in the Context of International Security: Report of the Secretary-General (Addendum)." A/59/116/Add.1. 28 December 2004.

———. "Group of Governmental Experts on Developments in the Field of Information and Telecommunications in the Context of International Security." A/68/98. 24 June 2013a.

———. "Developments in the Field of Information and Telecommunications in the Context of International Security: Report of the Secretary-General." 16 July 2013b.

———. "Developments in the Field of Information and Telecommunications in the Context of International Security: Report of the Secretary-General (Addendum)." A/68/156/Add. 19 September 2013c.

———. "Developments in the Field of Information and Telecommunications in the Context of International Security: Report of the Secretary-General." A/69/112. 30 June 2014a.

———. "Developments in the Field of Information and Telecommunications in the Context of International Security: Report of the Secretary-General (Addendum)." A/69/112/Add.1. 18 September 2014b.

———. "Developments in the Field of Information and Telecommunications in the Context of International Security: Report of the Secretary-General." A/70/172. 22 July 2015a.

———. "Group of Governmental Experts on Developments in the Field of Information and Telecommunications in the Context of International Security." A/70/174. 22 July 2015b.

———. "Letter dated 9 January 2015 from the Permanent Representatives of China, Kazakhstan, Kyrgyzstan, the Russian Federation, Tajikistan, and Uzbekistan to the United Nations Addressed to the Secretary-General." A/69/723. 13 January 2015c.

van Ess, Josef. "Political Ideas in Early Islamic Religious Thought." *British Journal of Middle Eastern Studies* 28, no. 2 (2001): 151–64.

Vienna Convention on Diplomatic Relations (1961). Accessed at http://untreaty.un.org/ilc/texts/instruments/english/conventions/9_1_1961.pdf.

Vienna Convention on the Law of Treaties (1969). Accessed at http://untreaty.un.org/ilc/texts/instruments/english/conventions/1_1_1969.pdf.

Wagner, R. Harrison. "Bargaining and War." *American Journal of Political Science* 44, no. 3 (2000): 469–84.

Walt, Stephen M. "ISIS as Revolutionary State: New Twist on an Old Story." *Foreign Affairs* 94, no. 6 (2015): 42–51.

Waltz, Kenneth N. *Theory of International Politics.* Boston: McGraw-Hill, 1979.

Watson, Adam. *The Evolution of International Society: A Comparative Historical Perspective*. London: Routledge, 1992.

Weiss, Thomas G., and Rorden Wilkinson. "Rethinking Global Governance? Complexity, Authority, Power, Change." *International Studies Quarterly* 58, no. 1 (2014): 207–15.

Welch, David A. *Justice and the Genesis of War*. Cambridge: Cambridge University Press, 1993.

———. "The Justice Motive in International Relations: Past, Present, and Future." *International Negotiation* 19, no. 3 (2014): 410–25.

Wendt, Alexander. "Anarchy Is What States Make of It: The Social Construction of Power Politics." *International Organization* 46, no. 2 (1992): 391–425.

———. "Constructing International Politics." *International Security* 20, no. 1 (1995): 71–81.

———. "On Constitution and Causation in International Relations." *Review of International Studies* 24, no. 5 (1998): 101–18.

———. *Social Theory of International Politics*. Cambridge: Cambridge University Press, 1999.

———. "Driving with the Rearview Mirror: On the Rational Science of Institutional Design." *International Organization* 55, no. 4 (2001): 1019–49.

Wheeler-Bennett, J. W. *Information on the Renunciation of War, 1927–1928*. London: George Allen & Unwin Ltd., 1928.

White House. "The National Security Strategy of the United States of America." Washington, DC: Government Printing Office, 2002.

Wiener, Antje. "Contested Compliance: Interventions on the Normative Structure of World Politics." *European Journal of International Relations* 10, no. 2 (2004): 189–234.

Wilkinson, Rorden. *Multilateralism and the World Trade Organization: The Architecture and Extension of International Trade Regulation*. New York: Routledge, 2006.

INDEX

Page numbers followed by *f* and *t* indicate figures and tables, respectively.

Printed in the USA/Agawam, MA
July 9, 2020

757887.010